法大诉讼法学博士文库

总主编　卞建林

无罪推定研究

徐　灿　著

中国人民公安大学出版社

·北　京·

图书在版编目（CIP）数据

无罪推定研究／徐灿著．—北京：中国人民公安大学出版社，2019.4

（法大诉讼法学博士文库／卞建林主编）

ISBN 978-7-5653-3554-9

Ⅰ.①无…　Ⅱ.①徐…　Ⅲ.①无罪推定—研究　Ⅳ.①D915.180.4

中国版本图书馆 CIP 数据核字（2019）第 071804 号

无罪推定研究

徐　灿　著

出版发行：中国人民公安大学出版社
地　　址：北京市西城区木樨地南里
邮政编码：100038
经　　销：新华书店
印　　刷：北京市泰锐印刷有限责任公司

版　　次：2019 年 4 月第 1 版
印　　次：2019 年 4 月第 1 次
印　　张：9.875
开　　本：880 毫米×1230 毫米　1/32
字　　数：266 千字

书　　号：ISBN 978-7-5653-3554-9
定　　价：35.00 元

网　　址：www.cppsup.com.cn　www.porclub.com.cn
电子邮箱：zbs@cppsup.com　zbs@cppsu.edu.cn

营销中心电话：010-83903254
读者服务部电话（门市）：010-83903257
警官读者俱乐部电话（网购、邮购）：010-83903253
法律图书分社电话：010-83905745

总　　序

21世纪的中国诉讼法学将向何处去？这是每一位诉讼法学者都应当关心的重要问题。历史是昭示未来的一面镜子。我们不妨先从历史的角度来考察一下我国诉讼法学发展的轨迹和趋势。

我国近代诉讼法学肇始于一百多年前的清末修律。1906年，清政府创办了京师法律学堂，由沈家本亲自制定的法律学堂章程将刑事诉讼法与民事诉讼法均列为主要课程，这标志着诉讼法学作为一门新兴的学科开始独立存在。之后，夏勤、陈瑾昆、蔡枢衡、熊元襄、石志泉、邵勋、邵锋等学者在翻译和介绍日本、德国等国诉讼法律与诉讼理论方面都作出了杰出贡献，并在此基础上对诉讼法学基本原理进行了可贵的探索。至20世纪40年代，旧中国的诉讼法学理论体系得以初步形成。

新中国成立以后，随着旧中国的“六法全书”被废除，原有的诉讼法学理论体系和研究成果也被抛弃。受当时的政治环境影响，中国的法学理论工作者开始将目光转向苏联。在20世纪50年代，伴随着苏联法学教授来华授课，一批苏联的诉讼法学著作被翻译推介到我国。我国学者开始在学习苏联诉讼法律制度与法学理论的同时，结合中国无产阶级专政的实际经验与需要，尝试创建我国的诉讼法学理论体系。然而，不久后的“反右”运动和“文化大革命”动乱，法律虚无主义甚嚣尘上，诉讼法学研究长期陷入停滞。这种状况一直持续到20世纪70年代末期。

1978年改革开放以来，我国诉讼法学得以恢复并迅速发展。

随着1979年中国第一部刑事诉讼法的颁布实施，我国诉讼法学开始全面“复苏”。在“解放思想、实事求是”方针的指引下，诉讼法学的学术研究变得活跃起来，关于刑事诉讼、民事诉讼、证据理论、司法制度方面的多本专著先后问世。特别是20世纪80年代初、中期，国家统一组织编写刑事诉讼法学、民事诉讼法学、证据法学教材。这些统编教材，发行量大，适用面广，读者群众，影响力巨，基本确立了诉讼法学与证据学的理论框架与教学体系。诚然，此时的诉讼法学仍不够成熟，大多停留在注释法学的阶段，教学和研究的目的主要是解释法律、宣讲法律，先进的诉讼理念尚未确立。至20世纪90年代，此种状况得到很大改善。“刑事诉讼法学的研究登上了一个新的台阶……在理论方面，对刑事诉讼基础理论的研究开始起步并初有成就。”① 其标志性成果是一系列有关诉讼目的、诉讼构造、起诉制度、审判原理等基本理论问题的学术专著陆续出版。随着我国政治、经济、社会、文化等各个方面日新月异的发展与进步，随着“依法治国，建立社会主义法治国家”基本治国方略的确立与实施，我国社会主义民主与法治建设取得巨大成就。在此大背景下诉讼立法进程加快，诉讼制度日臻完善，诉讼法学理论研究也在不断深入。“程序正义”、“人权保障”等先进的诉讼价值观念得到大力弘扬和广泛传播，公平、正义、人权、自由、秩序、效率等价值观不仅是诉讼理论界热衷探讨的命题，并逐步得到立法和司法实务部门的理解和认同，甚至成为普通百姓耳熟能详的大众话语。进入21世纪以来，诉讼法学研究方面最显著的进展莫过于研究方法的转型。不仅实证研究方法受到重视，多元化、跨学科的研究方法也得到了提倡，哲学、社会学、逻辑学、经济学等多学科的研究方法被广泛地应用于诉讼法学和证据法学研究。甚至文理汇聚、社会科学与自然科学交融的现象也已出现，国

① 陈光中、卞建林：《刑事诉讼法学研究现状与发展趋势》，载《法学家》1996年第2期。

家自然科学实验基地中国政法大学证据科学研究院的成立就是明证。通过研究方法上跨学科、多学科的融通交汇，我国诉讼法学研究的广度和深度得到进一步拓展。

不同于单纯的理论法学研究，诉讼法学研究还具有时代性和实践性的鲜明特点，在研究基础理论的同时，应当及时反映司法现实、回应社会关切。随着“全面建成小康社会、全面深化改革、全面依法治国、全面从严治党”战略布局的提出与落实，政治、经济、社会、文化、军事等各个领域的全面改革成为我国现代化进程中的主旋律。司法体制改革是全面深化改革的重要一环，是全面推进依法治国的主要抓手。一系列司法改革重大举措的制定并落地，推进中国特色社会主义诉讼制度和司法体系日趋成熟完善。在此背景下，我国诉讼法学研究也愈加关注司法体制改革与社会现实问题，探求司法规律，彰显中国特色，研究成果更加务实、更加中肯、更具实际参考和应用转化价值。

回顾历史，笔者在为我国诉讼法学发展历程的艰难曲折而感叹的同时，也为当前诉讼法学研究所取得的巨大成就感到欢欣鼓舞。然而，值得注意的是，从历史上看，我国诉讼法学的成长始终伴随着对外来法律文化的学习：从萌芽与初创阶段对日、德等国诉讼理论的借鉴，到重建与停滞阶段对苏联诉讼理论的模仿，再到恢复与提升阶段对美、英等国诉讼理论的引入。达马斯卡曾经告诫我们：“与私法领域相比，程序法的意义和效果更加依赖于外部环境——尤其是直接依赖于所在国家司法制度运行的制度背景。”① 诉讼法对其制度背景的依赖使得这门学科较之其他学科具有更强的地域性特征。所以，我们需要思考的一个问题是：我们仿效外国经验而建构起来的理论，我们从西方国家那里所引入的理念以及我们参考国外做法而采用的研究方法，是否真的适合于我国？即使这些理论、

① ［美］米尔吉安·R. 达马斯卡著：《比较法视野中的证据制度》，吴宏耀等译，中国人民公安大学出版社 2006 年版，第 231~232 页。

理念和方法能够适合于我国，中国学者对人类法治文明的独特贡献又何在？

笔者认为，21世纪的中国诉讼法学应当以创建中国特色、中国风格的诉讼法学理论体系为努力方向。回首过去的一个多世纪，中国诉讼法学在对国外诉讼理论持续不断的“效仿”过程中渐渐迷失了自我，始终未能确立起自身的独立品格。因此，我国学者应当从中国实际出发，在了解和借鉴他国诉讼理论的同时，着力构建具有中国特色、中国风格的诉讼法学理论。这是一项艰巨而长期的历史任务。其艰巨性在于，曾经在世界法制发展史上占有一席之地的中华法系早已风光不再，一百多年来我国所进行的各项法制改革大多是跟在西方国家后面亦步亦趋，我国法学理论缺乏自主发展的传统。其长期性在于，我国民众存在着根深蒂固的“重实体、轻程序”观念，而观念的转变绝非一朝一夕可以实现的。昂格尔就曾经针对我国古代法律评论道，与其他非欧洲的法相比较，中国法是离“法治”（rule of law）理念最为遥远的一极。① 当然，伴随着我国全面推进依法治国和大力深化司法体制改革，我国诉讼法学研究已经开始摆脱西方话语体系、西方逻辑的研究“窠臼”，逐步走向自醒自觉，探索建立符合中国国情和司法规律二元目标的社会主义诉讼法学理论体系已经起步。同时也要认识到，建成体现中国特色、中国风格的具有独立思维和独立话语体系的社会主义诉讼法学理论体系非一时之功，可能需要几代学人的共同努力。

历史的经验告诉我们，对于任何事业来讲，人才都是关键。从我国京师法律学堂的创办与诉讼法学的诞生可以看出，诉讼法学学科的发展与诉讼法学人才的培养是分不开的。因此，针对我国诉讼法学研究任务的艰巨性和长期性，我们应当进一步加大对青年诉讼法学高级人才，尤其是对诉讼法学博士生的培养力度。法学博士生

① ［日］滋贺秀三：《中国法文化的考察——以诉讼的形态为素材》，载《明清时期的民事审判与民间契约》，王亚新等编译，法律出版社1998年版，第3页。

群体是一支重要的科研力量。博士生们大多风华正茂，正处于人生创造力最为旺盛的时期，有可能提出富有原创性的学术观点；博士生们思维活跃，较少受到成见的束缚，有利于发掘新思维、新视角，不断推陈出新；博士生们拥有最有利的学习环境和条件，有足够的时间和精力就某些专门问题深入钻研。也正是基于这些原因，有人认为，博士学位论文常常能够代表学者一生的最高学术成就。

中国政法大学是全国最早获得诉讼法学博士学位授予资格的高等学府，由于师资队伍、培养模式、图书资料、学术交流等诸多方面的优势，法大培养的诉讼法学博士人数众多，质量上乘，为我国诉讼法学的学科发展作出过重要贡献。早在20世纪80年代末期，中国政法大学前校长、诉讼法学学科带头人陈光中先生就呼吁学界进一步加强对刑事诉讼法学基本理论的研究和创新，并引进自然科学和其他社会科学中的相关学科的成果，开拓刑事诉讼法学研究的新领域。① 在法大导师们的指引下，一批优秀的法大诉讼法学博士生开始对诉讼法学基础理论进行了大胆探索，取得了很多填补空白的开拓性研究成果。我国诉讼法学界在20世纪90年代出版的具有代表性的基础理论著作大多是在他们的博士学位论文基础上完成的。曾经取得的辉煌成就使中国政法大学的诉讼法学学科在全国享有盛誉。1999年，中国政法大学诉讼法学研究中心（2006年更名为中国政法大学诉讼法学研究院）成立，这是诉讼法学专业唯一入选全国普通高等学校人文社会科学百所重点研究基地的研究实体。2013年，由中国政法大学牵头，以中国政法大学诉讼法学研究院和证据科学研究院为科研依托平台，联合吉林大学理论法学研究中心（教育部人文社会科学重点研究基地）和武汉大学环境法研究所（教育部人文社会科学重点研究基地）申报的司法文明协同创新中心顺利通过教育部和财政部的认定，成为全国首批14家“2011计划”协同创新中心之一。自此，中国政法大学在诉讼法学

① 陈光中：《中国刑事诉讼法学四十年（下）》，载《政法论坛》1989年第5期。

学科建设和人才培养方面掀开了新的一页。

“法大诉讼法学博士文库”是中国政法大学诉讼法学研究院主持编选并组织出版中国政法大学诉讼法学专业（含刑事诉讼法学、民事诉讼法学、行政诉讼法学、证据法学）博士学位论文的系列丛书。这套丛书旨在搭建学术平台，推出诉讼法学新人新作，营造百家争鸣的学术氛围。此外，由于博士学位论文不仅能够反映博士生个人的勤奋和智慧，还常常凝聚了博士生导师们的辛劳和心血。因此，这套丛书的出版也是对法大诉讼法学教学成果的集中展示。我们希望能够通过丛书的出版，进一步培养和造就高素质的诉讼法学博士生，推动诉讼法学年轻学者之间的互动和交流，促进我国诉讼法学的繁荣和发展。

中国政法大学诉讼法学研究院院长　卞建林

2016 年 11 月 16 日于北京

序

徐灿博士的学术专著《无罪推定研究》入选“法大诉讼法学博士文库”，即将由中国人民公安大学出版社出版，这是一件令人欣喜的事情。

无罪推定是现代法治国家的一项重要刑事司法原则，被称为刑事法治领域的一颗王冠明珠。无罪推定原则要求受刑事指控者在被证实有罪之前应被推定为无罪，证明责任由控方承担，证明应达到排除合理怀疑的证明标准，存疑案件的处理应有利于被指控人。在实践中，无罪推定的重要要求之一就是疑罪从无，不仅要求在有罪无罪存疑时按无罪处理，而且要求在罪重罪轻存疑时按罪轻处理。无罪推定还是行使辩护权的基础。实践中存在对于辩护权的抵触情绪在很大程度上是因为对无罪推定的精神不认同。我国现行刑事诉讼法虽然吸收了无罪推定原则的基本精神，在审查起诉和有罪判决的标准上体现了疑罪从无的要求，但对无罪推定原则没有明确加以规定。自 20 世纪 50 年代起，我就无罪推定问题先后发表过数篇论文，最近的一篇是发表于《法学杂志》2013 年第 10 期的《论无罪推定原则及其在中国的适用》，主张将无罪推定原则明确写入刑事诉讼法典，采取国际通行之无罪推定原则的表述；把排除合理怀疑与结论唯一结合适用；完善并坚决贯彻“存疑有利于被指控人”规则。对于无罪推定原则，无论是理论上还是实践中都存在较多争议，有待深入研究。在我国现行刑事诉讼法及相关司法解释中，无罪推定精神虽然在逐步展现和加强，但仍未真正到位，有待进一步完善。无罪推定问题关系到人权保障和司法文明进步，为社会所普遍关注。徐灿博士撰写并出版其学术专著《无罪推定研究》真可谓适逢其时，其试图探讨刑事诉讼法学发展的前沿问题，对无罪推定问题进行深入系统的研究，回应理论界的争议和实务界的困惑，这无疑具有重大的理论价值和实践意义。

这部专著是徐灿在其博士学位论文的基础上修改而成的。2016年，徐灿的博士学位论文就因为选题重大、观点独到、论证充分、具有开拓意义而被评为中国政法大学博士学位论文资助项目。一部优秀的学术专著并不是下笔一挥而就的。徐灿为这部专著的写作付出了不少心血。2014 年至 2015 年，徐灿被国家公派到美国斯坦福大学法学院进行博士联合培养。在斯坦福大学 1 年多的学习时间里，他大量收集、刻苦钻研了新鲜、翔实的第一手外文资料，进行了创造性的思考和探索，完成并发表了几篇相关论文，回国后潜心写作，最后写就了该博士学位论文。博士毕业后，他继续钻研无罪推定问题，追踪无罪推定在实践中的贯彻情况，并对专著进行了修改，使得这部专著既有全球视野又注重立足中国实际。

这部专著是国内第一部系统全面研究无罪推定的专著，是刑事诉讼法学中的基础性理论研究。它梳理了无罪推定的源流，深入探讨了无罪推定的内涵和适用范围，从多视角探寻了无罪推定的根据和正当性，系统阐述了无罪推定与沉默权、反对强迫自证其罪、正当法律程序和证据裁判原则等刑事诉讼相关范畴之间的关系，考察了无罪推定在中国的发展现状并分析了其中存在的问题，最后针对在中国进一步彰显无罪推定精神等问题，提出了诸多创新性观点和建议，建立了比较系统的无罪推定理论体系，填补了国内在这方面的空白。其中有的问题写前人所未写，引人思考，弥足珍贵，如从哲学、政治学、法学、伦理学、心理学和决策理论等视角对无罪推定的根据和正当性进行了深入多维的探讨，系统论述无罪推定的根据和正当性，这在国内应属首创，具有较大的开拓意义。

这部专著结构严谨，体系完整，内容丰富，略带文采，确实是一部颇有分量、值得一读的作品。

徐灿是我的学生，作为他的导师，看到他在学术方面能够脚踏实地取得初步成就，我由衷地感到高兴。我期望他以此专著为起点，在学术的道路上能够越走越远，越走越广，不断取得新成绩。

是为序。

中国政法大学终身教授

陈光中

2018年8月18日

目　　录

引 言

无罪推定是现代刑事司法制度的精髓，是现代司法文明的象征。从有罪推定，到疑罪从轻，再到无罪推定，这是人类刑事司法文明发展的普遍规律。[①] 当前，世界各国和地区都普遍在其刑事诉讼法或者宪法性文件中规定了无罪推定原则，许多国际人权公约也对此予以规定，如《欧洲人权公约》、联合国《公民权利和政治权利国际公约》等。[②]

中国还未在法律上正式规定无罪推定原则，也未明确规定适用联合国国际刑事司法准则中的无罪推定。我国刑事诉讼法第 12 条规定："未经人民法院依法判决，对任何人都不得确定有罪。"但其含义与联合国刑事司法准则中的无罪推定含义有明显区别。该条规定尽管体现了无罪推定原则的基本精神，但并非国际惯用的无罪推定原则的规范表述。从国际惯用之无罪推定原则的表述来看，强调的是被指控人在刑事诉讼过程中所处于的被推定为无罪的地位，因此无罪推定原则要求在刑事诉讼中赋予被指控人推定无罪所应享有的诉讼权利；而我国刑事诉讼法第 12 条之规定所强调的是人民法院的定罪权，即强调只有法院有权对被告人进行定罪，侧重点并不在于强调被指控人在刑事诉讼中的境遇问题。这种侧重点的差异

① 参见沈德咏：《论疑罪从无》，载《中国法学》2013 年第 5 期，第 5 页。

② 根据 M. 谢里夫 · 巴西奥尼（M. Cherif Bassiouni）的考证，截至 1993 年，已有至少 5 个国际公约和 67 个宪法性文件规定了无罪推定原则。See M. Cherif Bassiouni, Human Rights in the Context of Criminal Justice: Identifying International Procedural Protections and Equivalent Protections in National Constitutions, 3 *Duke Journal of Comparative and International Law* 235, 266-267 (1993).

表明了中国只是吸收了无罪推定的核心内容，并未完全确立无罪推定原则，也反映了中国立法在被追诉人的人权保障问题上仍然有待完善和发展。此外，中国的“存疑有利于被指控人”原则贯彻得并不彻底。这种不彻底性的主要表现之一就是“证据不足”的“疑案”无罪判决是“有所保留”的结果。根据无罪推定原则的要求，当证据不足不能认定被告人有罪的，所作出的无罪判决与证明达到清白程度的同等看待。但是，根据我国刑事诉讼法要求作出的却是另眼看待的判决。我国刑事诉讼法第200条规定：“……（二）依据法律认定被告人无罪的，应当作出无罪判决；（三）证据不足，不能认定被告人有罪的，应当作出证据不足、指控的犯罪不能成立的无罪判决。”此条第（三）项规定的判决就是中国实务部门通称的“存疑无罪判决”。[①] 最后，中国也没有规定可以适用联合国国际刑事司法准则中的无罪推定。因此，对于被告人无罪推定权利的保障不够彻底。中国学术界在努力推动无罪推定在中国法律制度中的完全建立，一些实务部门对此也表示赞成。

在中国的司法实践中，无罪推定原则也没有得到很好的贯彻。事实上，对于有罪无罪存疑的案件，司法实践中往往采取“疑罪从轻”的做法，对于重罪案件更是如此。在一些死刑案件中，如果出现有罪无罪存疑时，司法机关有时会放弃“疑罪从无”原则，仍然判决被告人有罪，但又不判死刑，而是留有余地地判处死缓、无期或有期徒刑。正是由于这种“疑罪从轻”、“留有余地”的做法导致了冤案错案的发生，佘祥林案、赵作海案、张氏叔侄案、萧山冤案等就是这种做法所形成的典型冤案。[②] 党的十八大以来，以习近平同志为总书记的党中央高度重视司法体制改革，将依法治国提到了一个新的高度。中共十八届四中全会发布的《中共中央关

① 参见陈光中、张佳华、肖沛权：《论无罪推定原则及其在中国的适用》，载《法学杂志》2013年第10期，第6-7页。

② 参见陈光中、张佳华、肖沛权：《论无罪推定原则及其在中国的适用》，载《法学杂志》2013年第10期，第8页。

于全面推进依法治国若干重大问题的决定》中明确提出要“加强人权司法保障”，“健全落实疑罪从无、非法证据排除等法律原则的法律制度。完善对限制人身自由司法措施和侦查手段的司法监督，加强对刑讯逼供和非法取证的源头预防，健全冤假错案有效防范、及时纠正机制”。党的十八大后纠正了大批冤假错案，[①] 纠正的模式也由以前过于依赖当事人申诉的被动模式逐渐转变为相对主动的纠正模式。

无罪推定关系到正义的价值，对于民主、自由和人权的保障具有重大意义，是建立实质法治国的要求，并已被世界上众多国家刑事诉讼和刑事证据立法采用，其科学性和可行性也经受住了许多国家司法实践的检验。尽管如此，中国的刑事诉讼法仍然没有完全确立，其中，除了中国刑事司法资源等客观条件限制之外，法律观念滞后是一个主要原因。特别是截至目前，虽然关于无罪推定的论文可谓汗牛充栋，但是，对于无罪推定根据的系统理论分析却寥寥无几，以致人们无法从心底认清和认同为什么要实行无罪推定，其根据或者理由到底是什么。这不仅不利于无罪推定精神在中国的进一步彰显，也不利于无罪推定原则在中国刑事诉讼法和宪法中的适当确立。因此，对这一问题进行深入系统研究具有重大的理论和现实意义，有利于改进中国民众对于这一问题的理解和促进中国的法律改革。

要探寻无罪推定的根据，仅仅从法学的视角出发是远远不够的，还必须深刻而广泛地探寻其与哲学、政治学、伦理学等其他学科之间的内在关联。作为一个法学概念，无罪推定的根据或者说终极缘由并不能从法学本身找寻到答案，或者说不能完全从法学本身

① 《十八大后纠正 23 起冤假错案 疑罪从无不再停留纸面》，http://www.chinanews.com/gn/2014/12-17/6883197.shtml，最后访问时间：2014 年 12 月 16 日。《最高法院发布司法改革白皮书：十八大以来纠正重大刑事冤假错案 34 起》，http://www.legaldaily.com.cn/zfzz/content/2017-02/28/content_7031724.htm? node=81122，最后访问时间：2017 年 11 月 13 日。

找寻到答案，而必须从更加广阔的领域去找寻其存在的根据和正当性。虽然从权利等特定视角去认识无罪推定具有一系列积极的意义，但是，毕竟无罪推定不仅仅是一项权利，还是一种理念、制度、原则。单纯或者过于强调从某一视角去研究无罪推定不利于对这一问题的全面准确认识，从在终极意义上贯彻无罪推定的角度看，容易失之偏颇，是有害的。单纯或者过于强调从权利的角度研究无罪推定者大都以“权利本位”为根据，并声称“现代社会是一个‘权利本位’的社会”[①]。然而，实际上，权利本位观体现的是人本主义的思潮，是人本主义思想观念在权利义务关系问题上的反映。而近代人本主义肇始于欧洲文艺复兴时期的思想启蒙运动，肇始于启蒙运动中对“人”的发现，从而使“人”从基督教“神本”的束缚中解放出来，是近代资产阶级革命的理论基础。然而，自那以后的资产阶级革命实践表明，人本主义虽然有利于解放个人、充分张扬个性，但也可能因此而忽视对社会和自然给予应有的尊重。为了追逐利润而疯狂破坏自然环境，过度鼓励和纵容享乐主义文化造成社会道德滑坡甚至崩溃，一些人为了满足极端变态的心理而残杀动物，甚至剥夺他人生命，过度以自我为中心而导致的极端个人主义，以至对他人生命和尊严的漠视，及其极端表现——第二次世界大战中德国、日本等纳粹法西斯和军国主义势力对人类尊严的无情践踏等都是这种不受约束的人本主义恣意发展走向极端和反面的恶果。因此，我们既要继承和保留人本主义尊重人、珍视人类自身价值的合理成分，又要将其控制在合理的范围内，不能因为坚持人本主义而忽视对于自然和社会给予应有的尊重，而要将人与自然、人与社会、人的主观世界和客观世界协调起来，努力实现人与自然、人与社会、人的主观世界和客观世界的和谐和科学发展。对于权利本位，我们既要继承和保留其合理因素，充分保障所有人的合法和正当权益，又要防止走向极端，片面强调和重视权利本位

① 张小海：《无罪推定权利论》，中国民主法制出版社 2015 年版，第 3 页。

而忽视对社会和自然给予应有的尊重，忽视对于他人、社会和自然应尽的义务；否则，人与自然、人与社会、人的主观世界和客观世界的关系也将失之于无序和混乱，最终也不利于人类的自身发展。因此，从权利的角度探索无罪推定具有其积极意义，但是，单纯或者过于强调从权利的角度探索无罪推定则具有一定的片面性和局限性，从长远和终极的观点看，还具有一定的危害性。

本书以社会主义价值观从哲学、政治学、法学和伦理学等视角对无罪推定进行重新诠释，通过对无罪推定的根据进行探索，努力填补我国学术界在这一令人熟知的刑事司法理念中的理论空白，试图以无罪推定这一中华文明古已有之的思想为抓手，倡导中华文明的伟大复兴。

第一章　无罪推定源流之考察

第一节　无罪推定的起源

一、作为思想的起源

无罪推定的思想广泛存在于世界各法律制度中——除了最原始的之外。即便在最原始的法律制度中也可能存在无罪推定的思想，只是没有法学家对其进行表述。①

中国很早就产生了无罪推定思想的萌芽。根据《左传·襄公二十六年》的引述，《尚书·夏书》中有“与其杀不辜，宁失不经”的记载。② 由于《夏书》记载这段话的部分属《尚书》佚文，其前后文已不得而知，因此无法从《夏书》原文的前后文判断这段话的准确含义。然而，引述这段话的《左传》作者肯定见过《夏书》原文，因此，他对这段话的理解应当是可靠的。③《左传·襄公二十六年》原文为“归生闻之：‘善为国者，赏不僭而刑不滥。’赏僭，则惧及淫人；刑滥，则惧及善人。若不幸而过，宁僭无滥。与其失善，宁利其淫。……故《夏书》曰：‘与其杀不辜，

① Kenneth Pennington, *Innocent until Proven Guilty*: *The Origins of a Legal Maxim*, 63 Jurist 106, 107 (2003). “... the general notion of a presumption or assumption of innocence... is remarkably widespread in every legal system that I' ve looked at-except the most primitive. It may even be there too, but there were no jurists to express the idea.”

② 左丘明：《左传》，蒋冀骋点校，岳麓书社2006年版，第207页。

③ 蒋铁初：《中国古代的罪疑惟轻》，载《法学研究》2010年第2期，第200页。

宁失不经。’惧失善也。”① 这段文字表明“与其杀不辜，宁失不经”的目的是避免刑滥而导致的失善，即无辜者受罚。为达此目的，即使致犯罪人逃脱处罚也是可以容忍的。这样看来，“宁失不经”就应理解为对疑罪被告人免予处罚，而不是从轻处罚。因为从轻处罚也是一种处罚，如果被告人确属无罪，从轻处罚依然可能导致失善。② 由此，这段话的含义应理解为当被告人是否有罪存疑时，应对疑罪被告人免予处罚。这明显体现了无罪推定思想。据此可知，我国可能早在夏朝时就已出现无罪推定思想的萌芽。

此外，《尚书·虞书·大禹谟》中有关于上古时期皋陶与帝舜之间对话内容的一段记载：“皋陶曰：‘帝德罔愆，临下以简，御众以宽；罚弗及嗣，赏延于世。宥过无大，刑故无小；罪疑惟轻，功疑惟重；与其杀不辜，宁失不经；好生之德，洽于民心，兹用不犯于有司。’”③ 然而，《尚书》有今文《尚书》和古文《尚书》之分，且古文《尚书》的真伪存有争议，而《大禹谟》仅存于古文《尚书》却未见于今文《尚书》。④ 因此，若古文《尚书》为真，则我国可能早在4000多年前的上古时期⑤就已出现无罪推定思想，而皋陶所提出的“罪疑惟轻”和“与其杀不辜，宁失不经”的思想也可能是世界上最早的无罪推定思想。

由于《尚书》所载内容可能并非都是其所标系时代的成品，

---

① 左丘明：《左传》，蒋冀骋点校，岳麓书社2006年版，第206-207页。

② 蒋铁初：《中国古代的罪疑惟轻》，载《法学研究》2010年第2期，第200页。

③《尚书·虞书·大禹谟》，http://so.gushiwen.org/guwen/bookv_3083.aspx，最后访问时间：2015年6月21日。

④ 参见胡治洪：《〈尚书〉真伪问题之由来与重辨》，载《江苏师范大学学报》（哲学社会科学版）2014年第1期。

⑤ 帝舜和皋陶都是中国上古时期的人物，生活在距今4000多年前的原始社会末期和奴隶社会初期（http://baike.baidu.com/link?url=qvbz1efniu2j8yejcbo5dm7dnruja0ga4gel8kf5ulbulnvoffakn0inhuwianyniusqgeh84mc6uc683nq9fcvlz8o0ae2tep8hg5xwljg，最后访问时间：2015年6月21日；http://www.linfen.gov.cn/Article_Show.asp?ArticleID=486，最后访问时间：2015年6月21日；http://baike.baidu.com/view/50374.htm#reference-[1]-50374-wrap，最后访问时间：2015年6月21日）。

其中《虞书》、《夏书》等部分可能是西周至春秋早期的文化精英们根据传述或书写的上古史料编成的经典，[①] 因此，其上述相关记载不一定真实和准确。然而，即便关于上述相关史实的记述失真，我国无罪推定思想的萌芽也至少可以追溯到《尚书》的成书时间。而作为中国现存最早的历史文献汇编，《尚书》早在先秦时期就已存在。[②] 因此，我国无罪推定思想的萌芽至少可以追溯到先秦时期。

综上，中国很早就产生了无罪推定思想的萌芽。中国无罪推定思想的萌芽至少可以追溯到先秦时期，甚至可以追溯到4000多年前的上古时期。皋陶所提出的“罪疑惟轻”和“与其杀不辜，宁失不经”的思想可能是世界上最早的无罪推定思想。

中国的经籍引起西方人士的重视和深刻的研究，可以追溯到16世纪。经籍的西译，传入欧洲则始于16世纪末。《尚书》的拉丁文译本于1626年刊印于世。此后，时历两三个世纪，又有法文、英文、德文诸译本陆续出现。中国台湾地区学者李学灯在考察中国古代无罪推定思想时指出，中国古代无罪推定思想在《尚书》等

① 参见胡治洪：《〈尚书〉真伪问题之由来与重辨》，载《江苏师范大学学报》（哲学社会科学版）2014年第1期，第121-122页。

② 参见胡治洪：《〈尚书〉真伪问题之由来与重辨》，载《江苏师范大学学报》（哲学社会科学版）2014年第1期，第113页。“无论先儒的说法有多少推想成分或传说因素，先秦时期实有《尚书》却是毫无疑问的，这是西汉以降所有《尚书》学者的共识，这种共识的根据就在于先秦诸多典籍曾频繁引述《尚书》。笔者曾从《论语》、《左传》、《礼记》、《孟子》、《墨子》、《荀子》、《吕氏春秋》等典籍中钩稽引《书》文句凡80余条，涉及《虞书》之《尧典》、《舜典》、《大禹谟》、《益稷》，《夏书》之《甘誓》、《五子之歌》、《胤征》，《商书》之《仲虺之诰》、《汤诰》、《伊训》、《太甲上》、《太甲中》、《咸有一德》、《盘庚上》、《盘庚中》、《说命上》、《说命中》、《说命下》，《周书》之《泰誓上》、《泰誓中》、《泰誓下》、《牧誓》、《武成》、《洪范》、《康诰》、《洛诰》、《无逸》、《君奭》、《蔡仲之命》、《君陈》、《君牙》、《吕刑》、《秦誓》诸篇，文繁不录。”

中国古籍译成西文后，对西方产生影响。[①] 需要指出的是，此处的影响，笔者认为应当是一种加强和直接指导式的影响，而非原始启发式的影响，因为西方在《尚书》等中国古籍译成西文之前就早已产生了无罪推定思想的萌芽（西方产生无罪推定思想萌芽的时间详见下文）。

古代西亚地区很早也产生了无罪推定思想的萌芽。迄今为止，世界上完整保存下来的最早的一部成文法典——古巴比伦国王汉谟拉比（约公元前1792—前1750年在位）颁布的《汉谟拉比法典》

---

① 参见李学灯：《证据法比较研究》，台北五南图书出版公司1992年版，第663-666页。李学灯先生指出，“中国的经籍，引起西方人士的重视和深刻的研究，可以远溯于十六世纪。经籍的西译，传入欧洲，则始于十六世纪之末。尚书为五经之一，于一六二六年译为拉丁文，刊印于世。自是以后，时历两三个世纪，又有法文、英文、德文诸译本，屡见迭出。关于尚书部分，在十七八世纪，传教士译著之较早者，据学者考证，康熙年间，有刘应（VisdeLou）之译本，现藏于梵蒂冈图书馆。康熙末年，又有马若瑟节译书经。雍正十三年（1735），法教士马多明（Parrenin）有六经注释。乾隆时，蒋友仁（Benoit）译书经，曾寄莫斯科。乾隆四年（1739），宋君荣有书经译本，寄往欧洲。法国当时的汉学德经，对此‘备极称誉，’‘推为宋氏译著中最佳者。’‘其书卷首有宋氏自序，述书经之历史，并附伏生及孔安国之今古文；’于宋氏殁十二年（1770）刊于巴黎。至于十九世纪，理雅各所译中国经籍，第三卷尚书，（其余为第一卷论语、大学、中庸，第二卷孟子，第四卷诗经，第五卷春秋左传），更为一般人所习见。由上述概略，中国经籍的大量西译，对于当时思想界必有重要影响。其中尚书经多次翻译，传布甚广。其中极为重要的思想，如前述重大的原则，应有深远的影响，可以想见。前面说过这些思想和原则，当然涉及一种政策上的主张，也当然涉及多方面的考虑。亦如以后西方学者所提及应予慎重考虑的理由。罪名不应轻加于人，否则会有不良影响延及于社会的后果。所以前述中国法官的名言，和以后在西方文献里表示这些思想所用的词句，不但在意义上出于同源，并且有些在文字上几于完全相类似”。“至于重视‘罪疑’的原则，逐渐演成合理怀疑的用语，在英国法上可以追溯至十八世纪的初期。最初系用于死罪的案件，此与中国尚书所谓与其杀不辜，特别提到杀字的用意相同。”“用疑字做标准，逐渐用‘无合理之怀疑’这几个字在一起，形成一个标准的用语。辩护人用为辩护意旨，请求考虑成为一个法则，经学者考证，似系迟至一七九八年，始于都柏林（Dublin）所审理谋逆的案件。其时距前述宋君荣所译尚书的出版，亦已远在二十八年之后。”另参见赵晓阳：《传教士与中国国学的翻译——以〈四书〉〈五经〉为中心》，载《近代中国研究》，2005年，http://jds.cass.cn/Item/433.aspx，最后访问时间：2016年1月2日。

就将证明被告人有罪的责任原则性地分配给控告方。[①] 该法典第 3 条规定："提起刑事控告的人须证明被告人有罪，如果不能证明所控告之罪且所控告之罪为死罪，则提起刑事控告的人应被处死。"根据该法典第 9 条至第 11 条之规定，若原告宣称被告人持有原告被偷窃的财产，则原告应提供证人证明该财产属于原告所有，否则，原告应被处死。[②] 虽然从这些法条字面本身只能得出不能证明所控告之罪对提起刑事控告之人所产生的后果，不能得出不能证明所控告之罪对被控告人所产生的影响（即是否对被控告人进行无罪处理），但是，考虑到该法典残忍和苛刻的特点以及其没有明确在这种情况下应当对被控告人进行有罪处理，通过体系解释和历史解释，还是能够得出不能证明有罪则被控告人应被视为无罪的结论。

古希腊和古埃及也产生了无罪推定思想的萌芽。公元前 352 年，古希腊雄辩家德摩斯梯尼就提出：不能仅因一个谋杀的指控就说一个人为凶手，"因为在宣判之前不应以凶手称呼任何人"[③]。同样，只有在被告人经适当的审判被定罪之后才能对其进行惩罚，

① 百度百科"汉谟拉比法典"词条，http://baike.baidu.com/link?url=bozlpinrr-ryksnr58kvdo6-saex5vwycqwic6zqptoqjq9s8azl5psjqwizbu12swrjpuzgdmlnm2mbqdlszjk，最后访问时间：2016 年 1 月 8 日。Allen H. Godbey, *The Place of the Code of Hammurabi*, 15 THE MONIST 199, 210 (1905) ("It is a fundamental principle of the code of Hammurabi that the presumption is always in favor of the innocence of the accused: the burden of proof is thrown upon the accuser").

② See "The Code of Hammurabi", available at http://www.sacred-texts.com/ane/ham/ham05.htm, last visited on June 23, 2015. Evan Andrews, "8 Things You May Not Know About Hammurabi's Code", December 17, 2013, available at http://www.history.com/news/history-lists/8-things-you-may-not-know-about-hammurabis-code, last visited on June 23, 2015. "Code of Hammurabi", available at http://en.wikipedia.org/wiki/Code_of_Hammurabi, last visited on June 23, 2015.

③ Demosthenes, Against Meidias, Androtion, Aristocrates, Timocrates, Aristogeiton 231 (J. H. Vince trans., Harvard University Press 1935).

"因为只有到那时良心才允许我们根据所知进行惩罚"[①]。拒绝给予被告人控诉和定罪之间的"中间程序"（审判）[②] 违反司法的基本原则。古埃及国王托勒密八世于公元前118年颁布了一条法令，禁止政府官员"因为私债、犯罪或者由于私人争端"[③] 而逮捕和关押任何人，并要求他们将嫌疑人带到"各省任命的地方法官面前"[④]"根据法令和规定"[⑤]进行处理。[⑥]

古罗马产生了相对完善的无罪推定思想的萌芽。古罗马无罪推定思想的萌芽包括证据规则和防范过早惩罚两个方面。

从证据规则的角度讲，在罗马法中，原告负有举证责任（actori incumbit probatio）。[⑦] 公元212年，古罗马皇帝安东尼纳斯

---

① Demosthenes, Against Meidias, Androtion, Aristocrates, Timocrates, Aristogeiton 229 (J. H. Vince trans., Harvard University Press 1935).

② Demosthenes, Against Meidias, Androtion, Aristocrates, Timocrates, Aristogeiton 235 (J. H. Vince trans., Harvard University Press 1935).

③④⑤ 参见古埃及国王托勒密八世于公元前118年4月28日颁布的法令，http://www.app.cc.columbia.edu/ldpd/app/apis/item?mode=item&key=berkeley.apis.263. 这份由20世纪末在古埃及特布突尼斯城（Tebtunis）遗址发现的七张纸莎草纸古文稿构成的文档现存于加州大学伯克利分校班克罗夫特图书馆（The Bancroft Library at the University of California, Berkeley）。

⑥ Francois Quintard-Morénas, *The Presumption of Innocence in the French and Anglo-American Legal Traditions*, 58Am. J. Comp. L. 107, 112 (2010).

⑦ William L. Burdick, The Principles of Roman Law and Their Relation to Modern Law 693 (1938). See also Samuel P. Scott, The Civil Law, including the Twelve Tables, the Institutes of Gaius, the Rules of Ulpian, the Opinions of Paulus, the Enactments of Justinian, and the Constitutions of Leo: Translated from the Original Latin, Edited, and Compared with All Accessible Systems of Jurisprudence Ancient and Modern 47-8 (Cincinnati, Vol. 13, 1932) ("The *onus probandi* rested on the plaintiff, who was obliged to establish his claim by affirmative evidence, as prescribed by the rule, '*Ei incumbit probatio qui dicit, non qui negat*,' a doctrine which has been adopted by all modern systems of jurisprudence").

颁布诏令宣布："想要提出指控的人必须有证据。"[①] 原告不能证实案情，被告人将被无罪释放（actore non probante，reus absolvitur），即便被告人没有提供证据[②]或者否认指控的事实，因为举证责任在主张者而不在否认者。[③④]

在刑事案件中，对证明的要求相当高，特别是在与被告人性命

① Code Just. 2. 1. 4 (Antonin 212). "4. The Emperor Antoninus to Epaphroditus. Persons who wish to bring an accusation must have the evidence, for neither law nor equity permits that power be granted to inspect the documents of the other side. Therefore, if the plaintiff does not prove his allegations, the defendant shall be discharged, even if he himself furnishes no evidence. Given on the fifth of the Ides of March, during the Consulate of the two Aspers, 223. "available athttp://www. constitution. org/sps/sps12. htm, last visited on June 29, 2015.

② Code Just. 2. 1. 4 (Antonin 212). "4. The Emperor Antoninus to Epaphroditus. Persons who wish to bring an accusation must have the evidence, for neither law nor equity permits that power be granted to inspect the documents of the other side. Therefore, if the plaintiff does not prove his allegations, the defendant shall be discharged, even if he himself furnishes no evidence. Given on the fifth of the Ides of March, during the Consulate of the two Aspers, 223. "available athttp://www. constitution. org/sps/sps12. htm, last visited on June 29, 2015.

③ Code Just. 4. 19. 23 (Diocletian & Maximian 304). "23. The Same, and the Csesars, to Menelaus. A plaintiff who alleges that he cannot establish his claim does not compel the defendant to prove the contrary; for, in accordance with the nature of things, the denial of a fact is no evidence. Given on the eighth of the Kalends of January, during the Consulate of the Csesars, 304." Available athttp: //www. constitution. org/sps/sps13. htm, last visited on June 29, 2015. DIG. 22. 3. 2 (Paul, Ad Edictum 69). "2. Paulus, On the Edict, Book LXIX. Proof is incumbent upon the party who affirms a fact, not upon him who denies it." Available at http: //www. constitution. org/sps/sps05. htm, last visited on June 29, 2015.

④ Francois Quintard-Morénas, *The Presumption of Innocence in the French and Anglo-American Legal Traditions*, 58Am. J. Comp. L. 107, 111 (2010).

攸关的案件中。[①]提起对“他人荣誉、财产以至身份和生命”[②] 的指控但没有证据予以证明是一项严重的罪行。[③] 并且，罗马人也许已经有了一项比排除合理怀疑甚至更高的刑事证明标准。[④] 格拉提安皇帝、瓦伦提尼安皇帝和狄奥多西皇帝于公元 382 年颁布的诏令要求所有的指控者提出的刑事指控必须有可靠的证人、最具说服力

---

① Francois Quintard-Morénas, *The Presumption of Innocence in the French and Anglo-American Legal Traditions*, 58Am. J. Comp. L. 107, 111 (2010) .

② Code Theod. 9. 1. 11. “11. The same Augustuses to Count Florianus. (After other matters.) According to the prescription of law, no person may prosecute a criminal action which he has proposed to institute unless he undergoes the bond of an inscription. For a person who has called into court the reputation, the fortunes, and finally the status and the life of another must know that a suitable penalty threatens him if he should not prove what he charged. (Etc.) Given on the fifth day before the ides of November at Constantinople in the year of the consulship of Valentinian Augustus and the fourth consulship of Valens Augustus. —November 9, 373; 368. INTERPRETATION: No person shall be accused or produced in court unless an inscription has been executed, because, just as a penalty constrains the convicted person, so also it constrains the accuser if he should not prove what he charged.” See Clyde Pharr, The Theodosian Code And Novels, And The Sirmondian Constitutions: A Translation With Commentary, Glossary, And Bibliography 225 (Princeton: Princeton University Press 1952) .

③ Code Theod. 9. 1. 11. “11. The same Augustuses to Count Florianus. (After other matters.) According to the prescription of law, no person may prosecute a criminal action which he has proposed to institute unless he undergoes the bond of an inscription. For a person who has called into court the reputation, the fortunes, and finally the status and the life of another must know that a suitable penalty threatens him if he should not prove what he charged. (Etc.) Given on the fifth day before the ides of November at Constantinople in the year of the consulship of Valentinian Augustus and the fourth consulship of Valens Augustus. —November 9, 373; 368. INTERPRETATION: No person shall be accused or produced in court unless an inscription has been executed, because, just as a penalty constrains the convicted person, so also it constrains the accuser if he should not prove what he charged.” See Clyde Pharr, The Theodosian Code and Novels, And The Sirmondian Constitutions: A Translation with Commentary, Glossary, and Bibliography 225 (Princeton: Princeton University Press 1952).

④ Tom P. Conom, *Bulwarks of Liberty: Presumption of Innocence and Reasonable Doubt*, 45 Wash. St. B. News 38 (1991) . William L. Burdick, The Principles of Roman Law and Their Relation to Modern Law 694 (1938) .

的书证或者比阳光还要清楚无疑的事实支持。①

此外，如果证明不完整或者不能得出确定性的结论，则要按照有利于被告人的方法处理，即存疑有利于被告人原则（in dubio pro reo）。罗马法中有条格言：当出现证据冲突时，应当采取对被告人最有利的解释。盖尤斯、保罗和马塞勒斯主张存疑时遵循对被告人更有利的（善意的）解释总是更加安全和公正的。② 根据《查士丁尼学说汇纂》，"任何人不得因怀疑而被定罪"，因为罗马皇帝图拉真（52—117 年在位）宣布："准许一个罪人的罪行逃脱惩罚好过判处一个无辜之人。"（satiusenim esse impunitum relinquifacinus no-

① Code Just. 4. 19. 25 (Gratian, Valentinian & Theodose 382). "25. The Emperors Gratian, Valentinian, and Theodosius to Florus, Prsstorian Prefect. All accusers are hereby notified that they cannot bring a criminal charge for anything which has [not] been established by reliable witnesses; or clearly proved by documentary evidence; or shown to be true by undoubted testimony clearer than light." Available at http: //www. constitution. org/sps/sps13. htm, last visited on June 29, 2015.

② Francois Quintard-Morénas, *The Presumption of Innocence in the French and Anglo-American Legal Traditions*, 58Am. J. Comp. L. 107, 112 (2010). Tom P. Conom, *Bulwarks of Liberty: Presumption of Innocence and Reasonable Doubt*, 45 Wash. St. B. News 38 (1991). William L. Burdick, The Principles of Roman Law and Their Relation to Modern Law 692-3 (1938). DIG. 50. 17. 56; "56. The Same, On Legacies Relating to the Urban Edict, Book III. In questions which are doubtful, the more benevolent opinion should always obtain the preference." DIG. 50. 17. 125 (Gaius, Ad edictum provinciale 5). "125. Gaius, On the Provincial Edict, Book V. Defendants are regarded with greater favor than plaintiffs." 50. 17. 155. 2; "155. Paulus, On the Edict, Book LXV. ... (2) In penal cases, the most benevolent construction should be adopted." 50. 17. 192. 1. "192. Marcellus, Digest, Book XXIX. ... (1) In matters which are ambiguous, it is not less just than safe to adopt the more benevolent interpretation." Available at http: //www. constitution. org/sps/sps11. htm, last visited on June 29, 2015.

centis quam innocentem damnari)[①] 根据美国最高法院首席大法官怀特（White）在科芬诉美国（Coffin v. United States[②]）一案中所言，无罪推定在古代适用的一个经典例证被发现于尤里安皇帝（331—363 年在位）的一则关于审理一个叫作努梅里乌斯（Numerius）的省长的轶事中。[③] 法院引用尤里安皇帝的轶事如下[④]："皇帝审理的刑事案件中有一个被告人是位省长。该案没有充分的证据给否认自己罪行的被告人定罪。看到指控的失败不可避免，控诉方无法自控

---

① DIG. 48. 19. 5（Ulpian, De Officio Proconsulis 7）. "5. Ulpianus, On the Duties of Proconsul, Book VII. The Divine Trajan stated in a Rescript addressed to Julius Fron-tonus that anyone who is absent should not be convicted of crime. Likewise, no one should be convicted on suspicion; for the Divine Trajan stated in a Rescript to Assiduus Severus: 'It is better to permit the crime of a guilty person to go unpunished than to condemn one who is innocent.' Persons, however, who are contumacious and do not obey either the notices or the edicts of Governors, can, even though absent, be sentenced, as is customary in private offences. Anyone can safely maintain that these things are not contradictory. What, then, should be done? With reference to parties who are absent it is better to decide that pecuniary penalties, or those which affect the reputation, even to the extent of relegation, can be imposed if they, having been frequently notified, do not appear through obstinacy; but if any more serious punishment should be inflicted, as, for instance, hard labor in the mines, or death, it cannot be imposed upon the parties while they are absent.（1）It must be said that where an accuser is absent, heavier penalties are sometimes imposed than that prescribed by the Turpillian Decree of the Senate.（2）A distinction must be made in more serious crimes, that is whether they have been committed intentionally, or accidentally. And, indeed, in all offences, this distinction should either induce a penalty to be inflicted in strict compliance with the law, or admit of moderation in this respect." Available at http://www.constitution.org/sps/sps11.htm, last visited on June 29, 2015. Cf. Demosthenes, Against Meidias, Androtion, Aristocrates, Timocrates, Aristogeiton 269（J. H. Vince trans., Harvard University Press 1935）（observing that it is "equally irreligious to let slip the guilty, and to cast out the innocent before trial"）.

② 156 U. S. 432, 455.

③ Tom P. Conom, *Bulwarks of Liberty*: *Presumption of Innocence and Reasonable Doubt*, 45 Wash. St. B. News 38（1991）.

④ Reported in Rerum Gestarum, L. 18, c. 1.

地喊道：'哦，杰出的凯撒！如果这足以否认其罪的话，今后有罪之人的结果将会如何？'对此，尤里安回答道：'如果这足以定罪的话，无辜之人的结果将会如何？'"①

从防范过早惩罚的角度讲，罗马法禁止未经审判而对犯罪嫌疑人或者被告人进行惩罚。罗马人认为在任何情况下"像野蛮人或无所顾忌的暴君那样，不经审理而处罚某人的做法，都不应在和平时期采纳，这样将会成为可怕的先例"②。马切尔在《论公诉》第2卷中提到，罗马有一个关于判决前被追诉人法律地位的元老院决议，其内容是："在罗马作出判决并宣告之前，任何人都不得被认为被判罪。"③ 霍诺留斯皇帝和狄奥多西皇帝于公元423年颁布诏令提醒律师、执政官、元老院议员和护民官被指控死罪的被告人不应当仅仅因为其被指控而立即被视为有罪，以免无辜之人遭受不公

① William L. Burdick, The Principles of Roman Law and Their Relation to Modern Law 693 (1938).

② [爱尔兰] J. M. 凯利：《西方法律思想简史》，王笑红译，法律出版社2002年版，第73页。

③ 《学说汇纂》(第48卷·罗马刑事法)，薛军译，中国政法大学出版社2005年版，第353页。

正的对待。① 如果指控不等于定罪并且只有定罪才导致惩罚，那么

① Code Theod. 9. 1. 19. "19. Emperors Honorius and Theodosius Augustuses to the Consuls, Praettors, Tribunes of the People, and their own Senate, Greetings. We order that the procedure formerly instituted by law for making accusations shall be maintained; that a person who is summoned to undergo the risk of a capital penaly shall not be considered immediately a defendant who could be accused formally, lest We make innocence subject to harm. But whoever it may be that brings a criminal charge, he shall come into court, incdicate the name of the accused, undertake the bond of inscription, and submit to a custody similar to that of the accused, with due consideration, however, of his rank; and he shall know that the wantonness of a false accusation will not go unpunished, since by similarity of penalty vengeance is exacted of false accusers. I. No person, however, who has confessed his own guilt under torture shall flatter himself that, by accusing another of any crime whatever, he may hope for pardon on account of the wrongs of his accomplice, or that he may expect to be associated with a personage of higher rank by reason of mutual participation in the crime, or that by the punishment of a personal enemy he may share with him the lot of his last moments, or that he may trust that he can be saved by the efforts or privilege of a person named by him, since the authority of the ancient law does not permit those persons who have confessed their own guilt even to be questioned about the guilty knowledge of others. Therefore, when a person confesses his own crime, no one shall interrogate him about another's guilty knowledge. No one shall believe a person who is trying to escape punishment when he willingly contrives the punishment of another. We absolutely refuse credence to letters of instruction that have been secretly entrusted. (Etc.) Given on the eighth day before the ides of August at Ravenna in the year of the consulship of Asclepiodotus and Marinianus. —August 6, 423. interpretation: Before the execution of an inscription, no person is considered criminal; for when an inscription has been made in due order, the accused shall be received by the judge and delivered into custody along with his accuser, in such a manner, however, that the rank of the accused as well as that of the accuser shall be considered; and the judge shall cause each one to be guarded before the trial according as his hereditary status and rank permit. If those persons, however, who have confessed their own guilt under torture wish to speak about others, the judge shall not believe them, because it has been established by the law and statutes that an accused person cannot bring charges against another merely by a spontaneous declaration, and when a person has confessed that he is a criminal, his testimony shall not be credited with regard to another." See Clyde Pharr, The Theodosian Code and Novels, and The Sirmondian Constitutions: A Translation with Commentary, Glossary, and Bibliography 227 (Princeton: Princeton University Press 1952).

这将意味着嫌疑人必须受到与其地位相符的对待。除了叛国罪之外，[①] 罗马法允许被告人管理其财产、[②] 立遗嘱、[③] 捐赠、[④] 还债[⑤] 或者从其债务人处接收钱款以便其不被剥夺自我辩护的手段。[⑥] 在上诉期间，犯罪嫌疑人保留其完全公民权。除非最终判决作出对其

① DIG. 48. 20. 11. 1 (Marcian, De Publicis Iudicis) . "11. The Same, Book. When anyone who has been convicted appeals, and dies while the appeal is pending, his property is not confiscated; for even a second will, if he should make one, will be valid. The same must be said even if the appeal is rejected. (1) A defendant, except when accused of high treason, can administer his own property, pay his debts, and receive what is due to him, if it is paid in good faith; but every alienation which he has made for the purpose of defrauding the Treasury after his conviction can be set aside." Available at http: //www. constitution. org/sps/sps11. htm, last visited on July 1, 2015.

② DIG. 49. 14. 46. 6 (Hermogenian, Iuris Epitomaruin 6) . "46. Hermogenicmus, Epitomes of Law, Book VI. (6) He who has been accused of an offence can administer his property, and his debtor can pay him in good faith." Available at http: //www. constitution. org/sps/sps11. htm, last visited on July 1, 2015.

③ DIG. 28. 1. 9 (Ulpian, Ad Edictum 45) . "9. Ulpianus, On the Edict, Book XLV. If anyone accused of crime should die in prison before being convicted, his testament will be valid." Available at http: //www. constitution. org/sps/sps06. htm, last visited on July 1, 2015.

④ DIG. 39. 5. 15 (Marcian, Institutionum 3) . "15. Marcianus, Institutes, Book III. According to a Constitution of the Divine Severus and Antoninus, donations made after the accusation of a capital crime are valid, unless the defendant is convicted." Available at http: //www. constitution. org/sps/sps09. htm, last visited on July 1, 2015.

⑤ DIG. 46. 3. 42 (Paul, De Adulteriis 3) . "42. Paulus, On Adultery, Book HI. Nor is it held to be forbidden for payment to be made by the accused party to his creditor." Available at http: //www. constitution. org/sps/sps10. htm, last visited on July 1, 2015.

⑥ DIG. 46. 3. 41 (Papinian, De Adulteriis 1) . "41. Papinianus, On Adultery, Book I. Where a creditor is accused of a crime, there is nothing to prevent the payment of money by his debtors; otherwise, many innocent persons would be deprived of the necessary means of defence." Available at http: //www. constitution. org/sps/sps10. htm, last visited on July 1, 2015.

不利的宣告，否则，其不承受不名誉。① 至于被指控的官员，可以保留其官衔；② 其仅被禁止寻求新的尊荣③或者利用其职能的特权

---

① DIG. 3. 2. 6. 1 (Ulpian, Ad Edictum 6) . "(1) Where a party who has been convicted of theft, or any other infamous offence, appeals, he is not to be included among infamous persons while the case is pending, but where the time fixed for the appeal has elapsed, he is considered infamous from the date of his conviction; although if his appeal appears to be ill founded, I am of the opinion that he should be branded from that day, and not from the time of the judgment." Available at http: //www. constitution. org/sps/sps03_ j2-03. htm, last visited on July 1, 2015.

② DIG. 50. 1. 17. 12 (Papinian, Responsorum 1). "17. Papinianus, Opinions, Book I. (12) Where accusations of a capital crime are brought against persons nominated for office, they cannot be admitted to any new employments before their cases have been disposed of, but, in the meantime, they will retain their former rank." Available at http://www.constitution.org/sps/sps11.htm, last visited on July 1, 2015.

③ Code Just. 10. 60. 1 (Alexander Severus). "1. The Emperors Severus and Antoninus. It is a perfectly clear rule of law that a father is not responsible for his emancipated son, even if he has given his consent for him to be made a decurion, for where he has agreed to this, he will only be liable if his son is under his control. He, however, is considered to have consented, if he did not show any opposition to his appointment." Available at http://www. constitution. org/sps/sps15. htm, last visited on July 1, 2015. See also DIG. 50. 4. 7 (Marcian, Publicorum 2). "7. Marcianus, Public Prosecutions, Book II. A person who has been accused of crime is forbidden by the Imperial Constitutions to aspire to municipal honors before his case has been decided. It makes no difference whether he is a plebeian or a decurion. He cannot, however, be prevented from accepting such an office after a year has elapsed from the time when he was accused, unless he is to blame for the case not having been heard during the year. The Divine Severus stated in a Rescript that when a man is elected a magistrate, and his opponent appeals, and while the appeal is pending he takes possession of the office, he should be punished. Therefore, if anyone who is prevented by a decision from obtaining municipal honors takes an appeal, he should, in the meantime, refrain from demanding the office." Available at http://www. constitution. org/sps/sps11. htm, last visited on July 1, 2015.

来逃避惩罚。①被指控犯罪的罗马公民可以提交保释金以获得保释，除非指控罪名严重确需审前羁押。②对于被监禁的人，罗马法

① Code Just. 9. 22. 21. 1 (Constantine 316). "21. The Emperor Constantine to Mechilius Hilariamis. If a decurion should write a will, a codicil, or any other instrument for. the disposition of the property of a person who is dying, or should officially draw up any public or private documents, and then be prosecuted for forgery, he shall be deprived of his office, and subjected to torture if the case requires it. He, however, who is accused of an act of this kind, does not immediately cease to be a decurion, for he will remain such so far as his municipal functions are concerned; but he cannot avail himself of the privileges of the decurionate with reference to the matter in controversy, the truth of which is to be ascertained. Nor can he who was formerly a notary, and afterwards became a decurion, plead the privileges of this office for the purpose of escaping torture on account of documents which he formerly drew up, as their genuineness must be proved by the author himself if circumstances demand it. Given on the third of the Kalends of February, during the Consulate of Sabinus and Rufinus, 316." Available at http://www.constitution.org/sps/sps15.htm, last visited on July 1, 2015.

② DIG. 48. 3. 1 (Ulpian, De Officio Proconsulis 2). "1. Ulpianus, On the Duties of Proconsul, Book II. When accused persons are to be placed in custody, the Proconsul should determine whether they should be sent to prison, delivered to a soldier, or committed to the care of their sureties, or to that of themselves. This is usually done after taking into consideration the nature of the crime of which the defendant is accused, or his distinguished rank, or his great wealth, or his presumed innocence, or his reputation." Available at http://www.constitution.org/sps/sps11.htm, last visited on July 1, 2015.

禁止任何严厉的对待,[①] 并规劝法官尽快开始审理以便惩罚有罪之

① Code Just. 9. 4. 1 (Constantine 353) . "1. The Emperor Constantius to Florentinus. As soon as the defendant is produced in any case, whether an accuser is responsible for his appearance, or whether a public official has caused his arrest, his trial must at once proceed, so that if he is guilty, he may be punished, and if he is innocent, he may be discharged. When the accuser is absent, or the presence of the accomplices of the accused is considered necessary, they should be found as soon as possible. In the meantime, however, handcuffs should not be placed on the defendant, which bind him closely, but he should be placed in longer chains (if the nature of the offence demands the harshness of chains); so that he may not be subjected to suffering, but still remain in safe custody. He should not, however, be confined in a dark dungeon, but where he can be reached by light, and enjoy it; and, as night demands double vigilance, he ought to be lodged in the vestibule of a prison, or some other healthy place, and, when day returns, he should immediately be brought out into the light, as soon as the sun rises, in order that he may not die through imprisonment, which is considered unfortunate in the case of innocent persons, but not sufficiently severe so far as those who are guilty are concerned. The following rule must also be observed, namely, that it shall not be lawful for those who perform the duties of jailers, or their attendants, to sell their cruelty to accusers, by destroying innocent persons through confinement in narrow dungeons, or, by delaying the hearing of their cases, cause them to waste away with disease; for a judge is not only liable to loss of reputation, but he will also incur serious risk if he does not punish with the penalty of death any jailer or his attendants, who, through negligence, or for any other reason whatever, permit anyone to remain in prison a longer time than he should, or to punish by starvation. Given on the day before the Kalends of July, during the Consulate of Constantine, Consul for the sixth time, and the Caesar Constantius, 353." Available at http: //www. constitution. org/sps/sps14. htm, last visited on July 1, 2015. But see Yann Riviere, Detention preventive, in Carcer: Prison et Privation de Libertg dans l'Antiquitg Classique 72 (1999) (cautioning against interpreting literally provisions reflecting imperial propaganda rather than a true commitment to justice) .

人,[①] 释放无辜之人，拘留的目的是安保而非惩罚。[②]假若被告人在定罪或者上诉期间死亡，那么其财产依法不得被充公,[③] 并且其继承人可以接收该遗产。[④]

8世纪末期，法兰克王国国王查理曼大帝将“并非起诉本身，而是有罪判决使之成为真正的罪犯”（non statim qui accusatur reus est, sed qui convincitur criminosus）[⑤] 这条体现无罪推定思想的格言

---

① Code Just. 9.4.1（Constantine 353）.

② DIG. 48.19.8.9（Ulpian, De Officio Proconsulis 9）. “8. Ulpianus, On the Duties of Proconsul, Book IX. Or condemnation with infamy, or degradation from rank, or the prohibition of some act.（9）Governors usually sentence criminals to be confined in prison, or to be kept in chains; but they should not do this, for penalties of this kind are forbidden, as a prison should be used for the safe-keeping of men, and not for their punishment.” Available at http://www.constitution.org/sps/sps11.htm, last visited on July 1, 2015. See also Demosthenes, Against Meidias, Androtion, Aristocrates, Timocrates, Aristogeiton 269（J. H. Vince trans., Harvard University Press 1935),（“When under arrest he will suffer no injury in gaol until after his trial”）.

③ DIG. 48.21.3.7（Marcian, De Delatoribus）. “3. Marcianus, On Informers.（7）It is, however, provided by the Imperial Mandates that the property of those who die either while in confinement or at liberty under bond shall not be confiscated, as long as the result of their cases is uncertain.” Available at http://www.constitution.org/sps/sps11.htm, last visited on July 1, 2015.

④ DIG. 49.14.45.1（Paul, Sententiarum 5）; Code Just. 7.66.2（Alexander Severus 222）. “45. The Same, Sentences, Book V.（1）The estates of those who expire in prison, in chains, or in shackles, whether they die testate or intestate, are not taken away from their heirs.” Available at http://www.constitution.org/sps/sps11.htm, last visited on July 1, 2015.

⑤ On the origins of this maxim, see Richard M. Fraher, *'Ut nullus describatur reus prius quam convincatur': Presumption of innocence in medieval Canon law?*, Proceedings of the Sixth International Congress of Medieval Canon Law, Berkeley, California, 28 July-2 August 1980, at 493（1985）（cited in Randy Martin Johannessen, Cardinal Jean Lemoine: Curial Politics and Papal Power 216 n.6（1990）（unpublished Ph. D. dissertation, University of California, Los Angeles））.

纳入他的法令集之中，从而使该格言成为法兰克法律的一部分。① 这条格言在整个中世纪被教会法学者用作一条法律规定以说明“在被定罪之前，被告人不应当被视为有罪”的思想。②

英国也产生了无罪推定思想的萌芽。在英国，存在这样一种思想：被告人必须被视为无罪直至其在法庭上被确定性地证明有罪，由此可以得出，如果被逮捕之人未被依正当法律程序迅速进行审判，那么，被视为无罪之人便不应受到不当监禁之惩罚。这一思想的存在可以追溯到公元 10 世纪的西撒克逊王国时期。③ 克莱门蒂（Clementi）主张被称为埃塞尔雷德二世（II Ethelred）的法典第 8

---

① 1 Capitularia regum Francorum 1079（Paris，1780）（cited in Louis Charondas le Caron，Memorables，ov observations dv droict Francois rapporte av romain civil et canonic 166（Paris，1601））.

② Francois Quintard-Morénas，*The Presumption of Innocence in the French and Anglo-American Legal Traditions*，58Am. J. Comp. L. 107，113-4（2010）.

③ D. Clementi，*The Anglo - Saxon Origins of the Principle “Innocent until Proven Guilty”*，Herrschaftsvertrge，Wahlkapitulationen，Fundamentalgesetze 68-76 at 69，70（Gottingen：1977）.

条和第 9 条①为这一思想的存在提供了证据。该法典第 9 条规定“否认总是强于指控”。埃塞尔雷德二世是西撒克逊王国的国王。

① F. Liebermann, Die Gesetze der Angelsachsen. Berlin 1903, 1 224-227. A. J. Robertson, The Laws of the Kings of England. Cambridge 1925 pp. 60-63. In A. J. Robertson's translation, the clauses in question run as follows: "8. If anyone attaches what he has lost, the man in whose possession it is attached shall declare how it came to him. He shall give pledges and furnish surety that he will produce his warrantor, when the case shall be brought into court. 8. 1 If he vouches a living person to warranty and the man whom he vouches is in another county, he shall be granted as long adjournment as is necessary for the purpose. He shall lay it to the charge of the man who sold it to him, and request him to justify the transaction, if he can. 8. 2 If the latter accepts the charge, he [thereby] clears the man in whose possession it has been attached. He himself shall afterwards declare how it came to him. 8. 3 If he can specify the county in which the man whom he vouches to warranty lives, he shall have a week's adjournment; if he can locate him within two counties, he shall have two weeks; if within three, he shall have three weeks—the number of weeks' adjournment granted him shall correspond to the number of counties which he names. 8. 4 And vouching to warranty shall always take place where the property has been first attached. 9. Formerly it was the rule that vouching to warranty for the first three times should take place where the goods were first attached, and afterwards the process should be transferred to the locality indicated (by the evidence of the third man) (Liebermann: ' der (ziehende) Mann erklarte'.) Then the authorities (The Anglo-Saxon text and Liebermann's translation "witan", Quadripartitus: sapientes.) decided that it would be better for the vouching to warranty always to take place where the property was first attached, until it should appear where the process would end (Cf. II Ethelred 9. 4.) lest a man of small means should be burdened by long and distant journeys in order to recover his property. The burden should rather be borne by him who has in his possession (Anglo-Saxon text and Liebermann's translation: "who has in his hands".) property to which he is not entitled, than by him who is putting forward a just claim to it. 9. 1 Likewise, he who attaches his goods shall see to it that he has trustworthy security in every case of vouching to warranty, and shall beware of attaching wrongly, lest the burden he had thought should be borne by the other man should be laid on him. 9. 2 If anyone vouches a dead person to warranty—unless he have an heir who can answer the charge—he who vouches him to warranty shall show by means of witness, if he can, that he is acting justly, and by means of them shall clear himself. Then the dead man will be held guilty, unless he have friends who will clear him according to the law, as he himself would have been obliged to do, had he been able or had he been alive. 9. 3 If, however, he has friends who are prepared to do so, the vouching to warranty shall fail as completely as if he had himself been alive and had proved his denial. Then he in whose possession (Anglo-Saxon: "se de hit on handa haefd"; Liebermann: "wer das (im Anfang Eingeklagte) in Besitz hat".) the goods are, will be held guilty of theft, because denial is always stronger than accusation. 9. 4. Further, in the course of vouching to warranty, if anyone accepts and does not carry the process any farther but desires to declare himself, the owner [of the goods], no-one can deny his claim, if trustworthy witnesses establish his ownership of the goods, for a priori the actual possessor must be regarded as having more right than the claimant."

其在位时间为公元978年至1016年。埃塞尔雷德二世法典并非一部纯粹的盎格鲁—撒克逊法典，因为其包含着国王埃塞尔雷德二世于991年借以收买成功的维京人入侵者奥拉夫·特吕格瓦松的条约中的条款。[①] 然而，这一条约与附加其后的第8条和第9条之间没有明显的关联，以致利伯曼（Liebermann）被迫根据这两条自身包含的证据来追溯其具体的年代。利伯曼感到第8条和第9条的时间段在很大可能上可以被缩小到950年至1000年的50年间。他的这一观点基于以下几个理由：第一，当地政府制度的发展阶段，因为这两条表明郡（the shires）已经完全形成；第二，其包含的与财产销售有关的规定所表明的法律演进中的关键点标示了埃塞尔雷德一世法典之前的日期。鉴于此，由于在944年至955年埃德雷德王（King Edred）好战的统治期间或者其继任者殉教者爱德华（Edward the Martyr）的短暂统治期间，我们没有发现立法记录，因此，将这两条出现的时间归属到埃塞尔雷德统治早期显然很可能是正确的。确实，这两条只提到国王贤人会议而没有提到国王的事实也指向埃塞尔雷德王的短期统治期间。此外，利伯曼非常明确地表达了这样的观点，即如果他发现了非附属的条款，他会将其编入"Bruchstucken von Gesetzen ohne Konigsnamen hinter Forfang"这一他认为应当追溯到公元1000年之前的片段集。第三，他发现语言学证据也指向埃塞尔雷德的早年统治时期，并且他进一步作出了一个有趣的评论，大意是这两条所使用的词汇排除了丹麦语影响的可能性，因为完全不存在北方的外来词。因此，克莱门蒂作出以下结论："从埃塞尔雷德二世法典第8条和第9条所包含的证据，可以稳妥地假定，远在公元1000年以前，在盎格鲁—撒克逊英格兰就已存在一项构成审判法律基础的原则，这一原则赋予被告人由法庭假定其无罪直到其被证明有罪的优势。而且，由于这两个条款没有包含北方的外来词，因此，很可能这一新的法律思想来自西撒克

① F. M. Stenton, Anglo-Saxon England 371 f (Oxford 1947).

逊。”然而，正如肯尼斯·彭宁顿（Kenneth Pennington）在其《被证明有罪之前即无罪——一条法律格言的起源》① 一文中所言，克莱门蒂提出了无罪推定的优点，但是，“被证明有罪之前即无罪”这一格言在克莱门蒂所解释说明的文本中完全不存在；“‘被证明有罪之前即无罪’这一格言在1800年之前的任何英国法院案例或者法学论述中都找不到。”因此，我们只能说克莱门蒂的上述论证只能作为无罪推定思想的一个来源，而非“被证明有罪之前即无罪”这一格言的来源。

1215年，英国大宪章保障了被告人在被赦免或者定罪之前被审判的权利。这是英国无罪推定思想的进一步发展。根据英国大宪章的规定，“除非经同等人的合法审判或者根据本国法律行事，否则，任何自由人不得被监禁、剥夺财产、被宣布为不受法律保护、流放或加以任何其他损害”②。

二、作为格言的起源③

虽然无罪推定的思想相当广泛地存在于世界上大多数法律制度中，但是，“被证明有罪之前即无罪”的格言起源于13世纪晚期和14世纪早期的欧洲大陆。罗马教会的红衣主教，一位法国人，教会法学家，约翰内斯·莫纳克斯（Johannes Monachus）首先提出

---

① Kenneth Pennington, *Innocent until Proven Guilty*: *The Origins of a Legal Maxim*, 63 Jurist 106（2003）.

② 25 Edw. I, c. 29（1297）（1215）.

③ See generally, Kenneth Pennington, *Innocent until Proven Guilty*: *The Origins of a Legal Maxim*, 63 Jurist 106（2003）; Walter Ullmann, *The Defence of the Accused in the Medieval Inquisition*, 63 The Irish Ecclesiastical Rec. 481, 486（1950）（cited in Jerome E. Janssen, The Legal Procedure of the 13th Century French Inquisition 53（1954）（unpublished Ph. D. dissertation, University of Wisconsin））; Gaines Post, *Ancient Roman Ideas of Law*, in 2 Dictionary of the History of Ideas: Studies of Selected Pivotal Ideas 689（Philip P. Wiener ed., 1973）; Kenneth Pennington, The Prince and the Law, 1200-1600: Sovereignty and Rights in the Western Legal Tradition 157（1993）.

“被证明有罪之前即无罪”这一格言。虽然肯尼斯·彭宁顿等人认为无罪推定的格言可以从上帝对亚当审判的逻辑中推导出来,[①] 但是,笔者认为这一推导有些牵强,至少不能推导出“被证明有罪之前即无罪”这一格言表述。从无罪推定格言的起源看,无罪推定具有很深的宗教(基督教)背景,受到罗马法的深刻影响,教会法学家(欧洲共同法的法学家)在其中起到了极其重要的作用,甚至可以说,是中世纪欧洲共同法的法学家创造出了无罪推定的格言。

要探究无罪推定格言的起源,需从欧洲共同法谈起。欧洲共同法(Ius commune)是12—17世纪普遍适用于欧洲地区的法律。它是由罗马法、教会法以及后来的封建法在中世纪欧洲的神学院和法庭中偶然结合而成的。其出现在欧洲大陆的法律实践正在发生重大变革的时代。法律正由非成文的作为习惯的使用逐渐发展为成文的习惯法和制定法。欧洲大陆当时的司法程序处于不断的变动中。12世纪之前,神示证据制度(judicial ordeal)是欧洲大陆普遍的证明模式。12世纪,特别是在南欧,神示证据制度被法定证据制度(ordo iudiciarius)代替。法定证据制度是一种基于罗马法,但规则是由欧洲共同法学家确立的证明模式。

从基于神明裁判的证明模式到借鉴罗马法程序标准的证明模式的改变对于12世纪的欧洲社会来讲极其令人不安,因为程序是任何法律制度的核心部分,一个社会的正义感与其证明模式紧密相联。由于法定证据制度是由基督教会和世俗权威强加给欧洲法庭的,因此,证据清楚地表明欧洲社会各阶层对其合法性产生疑问。

为此,12世纪的法学家需要证明这些彻底的程序变革的正当性。令人十分惊奇的是,他们在《圣经·旧约》中找到了其合理性并精巧地将法定证据制度的起源追溯到上帝在天堂对亚当和夏娃

---

① Kenneth Pennington, *Innocent until Proven Guilty*: *The Origins of a Legal Maxim*, 63 Jurist 106, 113-6 (2003).

的审判中。如此，他们创造了一个强有力的神话以证明法定证据制度的正当性，并将其解释力保持到了17世纪。

这一神话可以让我们洞察12世纪欧洲大陆的司法精神活动。其发起人是一位叫作帕卡派利亚（Paucapalea）的法学家。他是第一个将法定证据制度与亚当和夏娃联系起来的人。大约在1150年，他在对《格拉提安教会法》（*Gratian's Decretum*）的评注中记载了法定证据制度起源于亚当在天堂对上帝的有罪指控提出无罪的申辩。在《创世纪》3.9–12中，上帝冲进天堂并查问：亚当，你在哪里？（Adam ubi es?）可能有人注意到对于一位神来讲，上帝的这个问题显得不太无所不知。亚当回应上帝对于非法摘取苹果的指控，抱怨道："你赐给我的妻子给的我苹果，我就吃了。"换句话说，当上帝赐给亚当妻子时，上帝陷害了亚当。帕卡派利亚的观点是精细微妙的，但是并没有被后世的法学家所遗忘。虽然上帝无所不知，但是，他也必须传唤被告人并听取其辩解。帕卡派利亚增加了另一条证明法定证据制度起源于《圣经》的证据。当摩西（Moses）规定必须根据两个或者三个证人的证言才能认定事实时，他宣布了一条基本证据规则并确认了一项为上帝本身所接受的程序制度的古老性。① 肯尼斯·彭宁顿认为对于无罪推定问题最重要的是，帕卡派利亚的评论的潜台词明显意味着如果上帝必须传唤诉讼当事人以为其自身辩护，那么，普通人类也必须传唤他们并且假定每个被告人在被当庭证明有罪之前无罪。② 笔者认为，虽然肯尼斯·彭宁顿的这一观点前半部分有一定的道理，但是，后面的这个"假定每个被告人在被当庭证明有罪之前无罪"应当说只是他的想法，从"帕卡派利亚的评论"中得不到这样的"潜台词"，因为"帕卡派利亚的评论"只是说明应当给予当事人被传唤权，辩护权

① 《申命记》19.15：人无论犯什么罪、作什么恶，不可凭一人之口作见证，总要凭两三个人之口作见证才可定案。

② Kenneth Pennington, *Innocent until Proven Guilty*: *The Origins of a Legal Maxim*, 63 Jurist 106, 113 (2003).

和未经审判不得被定罪的权利，但是，即便有了这些权利也并不意味着在不能当庭证明有罪时要假定当事人无罪，赋予当事人这些权利的理由也可能是为了查清案件事实真相，一旦经过这些程序仍旧查不清案件事实真相，由以上这些也不能必然得出假定当事人无罪的结论。因此，笔者认为所谓“帕卡派利亚的评论”包含了“人类必须假定每个被告人在被当庭证明有罪之前无罪”的潜台词只是作者肯尼斯·彭宁顿一厢情愿的想法。只能讲，“帕卡派利亚的评论”包含了“每个人在被审判之前被假定为无罪”的潜台词而非“人类必须假定每个被告人在被当庭证明有罪之前无罪”或者“每个人在被依法定罪之前被假定为无罪”的潜台词。

自12世纪中期开始，法学家将法定证据制度的合理性建立在其起源于《圣经》上。[①] 毫无疑问，这一做法后来为12世纪后半期法定证据制度被教会法庭以及一些世俗法庭所一般接受提供了正当性支持。虽然无罪推定的一般原则早已在13世纪初期欧洲共同法的法学中确立，然而，这一权利还远未绝对化。当时的法学家并没有认识到如果上帝必须传唤亚当进行审判，那么逻辑上必然只能要求每个被告人都必须被传唤进行审判。他们当时普遍认同如果一个罪行令人发指、臭名昭著，那么法官可以不经审判而作出对被告人不利的裁决。13世纪中期，当时最著名的法学家之一塞古西奥的亨里克斯（Henricus of Segusio）在宣称臭名昭著的罪行（特别是那些针对教会的罪行）不需要正式的司法审查时，总结了当时的法律思想。

在无罪推定成为一项绝对的权利之前，还需要一个更加关键的变革。这一变革在很大程度上是由帕卡派利亚关于法定证据制度起源于《圣经》的主张带来的。13世纪之前，法学家接受君主或者

① Richard Helmholz, *The Bible in the Service of Canon Law*, 70 *Chicago Kent Law Review* 1557-1581（1995）；idem，The Spirit of Classical Canon Law（Athens，Georgia-London：1996）passim.

法官无视司法程序规则的权力，因为他们认为法律程序是国家法律的一部分，是实定法，因此完全处于君主或者法官的权力之下。帕卡派利亚和教会法学家引进了一种不同的学说和一个不同的范式。他们的主张在逻辑上不可阻挡地导致的必然结论就是，如果法定证据制度可以首先在《旧约》中找到，并且如果上帝必须尊重被告人的权利，那么，程序规则必然超越实定法。如此一来，这就为作为程序规则的无罪推定成为君主或者法官必须遵守的法律规则奠定了法理上的基础。

帕卡派利亚新范式的影响在13世纪的法学中缓慢地发展着。《圣经》毕竟是人们对神法理解的基石。自格拉提安以来，法学家将神法和自然法等同。因此，在帕卡派利亚的影响下，1250年至1300年，法学家开始主张司法程序和程序标准并非来自国家法，而是来自自然法或者国际法、万民法（ius gentium）。因此，程序的基本规则不能被君主或者法官忽视。被告人就其案件在法庭上接受审判的权利是绝对的，而不是可以随意更改的。

一旦法学家决定程序标准是自然法的一部分，他们马上就看到被告人的基本权利（程序权利）不能被侵犯。13世纪后期和14世纪早期关于被告人权利的法律思想最精致和最完整的总结被发现于一位去世于1313年的法国教会法学家约翰内斯·莫纳克斯（Johannes Monachus）的作品中。在注释教皇博尼费斯八世（Pope Boniface VIII）的一条教令时，他广泛地评论了被告人的权利。他首先提出以下问题：教皇能在没有传讯一个人的情况下，基于此教令控诉这个人吗？约翰内斯的结论是教皇仅在实定法之上，而非自然法之上。既然传唤由自然法确立，教皇就不能对其无视。他主张除非被告人出庭，没有哪个法官，即便是教皇，能够作出公正的裁判。当罪行令人发指、臭名昭著时，法官可以对某些诉讼环节进行简化，但是，传唤和裁判必须被遵守。他主张传唤到庭（citatio）和判决（sententia）是司法程序的主要部分，因为《创世纪》3.9-12证明二者都是有必要的。上帝有义务传唤亚当，人类法官必须同样这样做。然后，他以下述字眼确切地提出了一种关于被告人对审判和正当程序权利的表述：一个人在被证明有罪之前被假定为无罪（item quilbet presumitur innocens nisi probetur nocens）。[①]

然而，笔者认为，从上帝对亚当的审判中推导出“一个人在被证明有罪之前被假定为无罪”的无罪推定格言的逻辑是牵强的，因为从上帝对亚当的审判中并不能必然得出无罪推定格言所述的结论。相反，笔者认为彭宁顿在其论文《法定证据制度发展中的正当程序，社会和君主》（*Due Process, Community, and the Prince in the Evolution of the Ordo indiciarius*）中的说法更加合适，即无罪推定的格言是约翰内斯·莫纳克斯对中世纪正当程序概念所作的进一步引申。[②] 确切地说，实际上是约翰内斯·莫纳克斯提出了无罪推定的格言。“在被证明有罪之前被假定为无罪”这一格言并非上帝对亚当的审判本身应有之义。

---

① Johannes Monachus, Gloss on Pope Boniface VIII's Decretal Rem non novam (1303) (ca.1310). Johannes Monachus cited Innocent III's decretal Dudum (X 2. 23. 16) to justify his assertion. The last sentence of the decretal *Dudum* reads as follows: "*cum primailacie praesumaturidoneus: nisi aliud in contrarium ostendatur.*" *See* Decretales D. Gregoriipapae IX: Suae Integritati Und Cum Glossis Restituae: Ad Exemplar Romanum Diligenter Recognitae 796 (Lyon, 1584). Monachus replaced "*idoneus*" with "*innocens*" and applied the maxim to criminal matters.

② Kenneth Pennington: Due Process, Community, and the Prince in the Evolution of the Ordo iudiciarius, http://faculty. cua. edu/pennington/Law508/procedure. htm#Establishment%20of%20Ordo, last visited on March 11, 2015. "... Johannes took medieval conceptions of due process one step further: Everyone is presumed innocent unless they are proven culpable; the law is more inclined to absolve than to condemn."

其他的教会法学家对被告人的权利发挥了充分的想象。[①] 他们杜撰出一条谚语称上帝甚至必须给予撒旦当庭审判。[②] 约翰内斯对于教皇博尼费斯八世教令（Rem non novam）的评论最终成为中世纪后期一部被称作《〈格拉提安教会法〉未包含之常见教令》(*Extravagantes Communes*)[③] 的教会法集本的常规注解。这一集本及其注解以数百份手稿和几十个印刷版的方式一直流传到17世纪。因此，第一个明确提出“一个人在被证明有罪之前即被假定为无罪”这一格言的人是法国的教会法学家约翰内斯·莫纳克斯。他的注解由于被直到贝卡利亚时代的欧洲共同法的法学家所阅读，因此，也是将这一格言传播给后代法学家的一个主要媒介。

第二节　无罪推定的发展

一、在大陆法系的发展

虽然学者特别是英美法系的学者认为无罪推定是英美法系区别

① Kenneth Pennington, The Prince and the Law, 1200-1600: Sovereignty and Rights in the Western Legal Tradition 163-4 (1993).

② 古留莫斯·杜兰蒂斯（Guilielmus Durantis）将被告人在被证明有罪之前被假定为无罪的权利附会到了极致，声称即便是撒旦也有权受到当庭审判。Kenneth Pennington: Due Process, Community, and the Prince in the Evolution of the Ordo iudiciarius, http: //faculty. cua. edu/pennington/Law508/procedure. htm # Establishment% 20of% 20Ordo, last visited on March 11, 2015. “...Guilielmus Durantis stretched this norm to its ultimate extreme: even the devil should have his case heard in court.”

③ Corpus Juris Canonici - Wikipedia, http://en. wikipedia. org/wiki/corpus Jnris Canonici, last visited on March 2.2019.

于大陆法系的特色,[①] 但实际上，至少从无罪推定的起源来看，无罪推定思想在欧洲大陆的起源要早于英美法系国家，无罪推定格言并非起源于英美法系国家，而是起源于欧洲大陆的法国。

自从约翰内斯·莫纳克斯于 13 世纪末明确提出无罪推定格言后，这一格言得到了广泛的传播。然而，在随后的几个世纪中，无罪推定在大陆法系的发展经历了一个曲折的过程。一方面，在部分司法实践或者是理论上，无罪推定的精神得到了一定的彰显。犯罪嫌疑人除非被当场抓获或者可能逃跑，只能在有法官经完全调查后签发的适当的逮捕证的情况下被逮捕。[②] 法律要求法官对有利于和不利于被告人的证据都要审查,[③] 如果存疑，被告人必须被宣判无罪。[④] 法庭反复地撤销没有预先调查而签发的逮捕令[⑤]或者将被追

① Francois Quintard-Morénas, *The Presumption of Innocence in the French and Anglo-American Legal Traditions*, 58Am. J. Comp. L. 107 (2010). D. Clementi, *The Anglo-Saxon Origins of the Principle "Innocent until Proven Guilty"*, Herrschaftsvertrge, Wahlkapitulationen, Fundamentalgesetze (Gottingen: 1977) 68-76. Sir John Scott on Criminal Procedure, TIMES (London), May 25, 1900, at 11 ("At the Society of Arts, yesterday, Sir John Scott ... was glad that the British presumption of innocence had prevailed over the Latin presumption of guilt ..."); People v. Molineux, 168 N. Y. 264, 291 (1901) ("... that jealous regard for the liberty of the individual which has distinguished our jurisprudence from all others, at least from the birth of Magna Charta. It is the product of that same humane and enlightened public spirit which, speaking through our common law, has decreed that every person charged with the commission of a crime shall be protected by the presumption of innocence ..."). Innocence and Guilt, WALL ST. J. EUR., May 26, 2000, at 12 ("The lack of a presumption of innocence in the French legal system has long set it apart from the Anglo-American systems of justice").

② Ordon. 1670, tit. 10.

③ Ordon. 1670, tit. 4, art. 1.

④ Ordon. 1670, tit. 25, art. 12.

⑤ Pierre Brillon, Dictionnaire Des Arrests; Ou, Jurisprudence Universelle Des Parlemens De France, Et Autres Tribunaux 536 (Paris, 1727) (citing a deision of the Parlement of Grenoble dated July 28, 1628 and a decision of the Parlement of Provence dated Mar. 11, 1666).

诉人描述成罪犯的逮捕令①。1536年，巴黎最高法院提醒法官在逮捕令中将犯罪嫌疑人描述成杀人犯、奸夫或者小偷是非法的；② 只允许提及犯罪嫌疑人已被指控犯罪，③ “否则，我们将说得好像被追诉人已被定罪，那只有在明确的判刑后才被允许”④。相似地，教会监察（monitoires）⑤ 根据法官的命令鼓励犯罪案件的证人主动站出来时不能通过名字使人辨认出犯罪嫌疑人⑥或者以会无疑地确定他们身份的方式描述他们⑦，因为“没有比在定罪前就给某人造

---

① Jean Papon, Recveil D' Arrestz Notables Des Covrs Sovveraines De France 568 (Lyon, 3d ed. 1559).

② Jean Papon, Recveil D' Arrestz Notables Des Covrs Sovveraines De France 568 (Lyon, 3d ed. 1559) (citing a decision of the Parlement of Paris dated May 26, 1536).

③ Jean Papon, Recveil D' Arrestz Notables Des Covrs Sovveraines De France 568 (Lyon, 3d ed. 1559) (citing a decision of the Parlement of Paris dated May 26, 1536).

④ Antoine Bruneau, Observations Et Maxims Sur Les Matieres Criminelles 103 (Paris, 1715).

⑤ *Monitoires* were letters written by church officials and affixed to the door of churches and other public spaces. See 1 Daniel Jousse, Traite de la justice criminelle en France 119 (Paris, 1771).

⑥ Ordon. 1670, tit. 7, art. 4. The Criminal Ordinance of 1670 imposed a fine of 100 livres on offenders. See 1 Daniel Jousse, Traite de la justice criminelle en France 126 (Paris, 1771) (stating that the purpose of this law was to prevent anyone “from injuring the honor or reputation of an individual that could be innocent”). 可见，这一法律对无罪之人权利的保护还是相当强的，对无罪推定精神的彰显力度很大。

⑦ Ordon. 1670, tit. 7, art. 4. See also Pierre Brillon, Dictionnaire Des Arrests; Ou, Jurisprudence Universelle Des Parlemens De France, Et Autres Tribunaux 395-96 (Paris, 1727) (citing a decision of the Parlemnet of Bretagne dated Apr. 14, 1572, a decision of the Parlement of Dijon dated Mar. 27, 1575, a decision of the Parlement of Provence dated Nov. 23, 1664 and decisions of the Parlement of Paris dated Feb. 5, 1564 and June 16, 1625).

成伤害更大的丑行了”[①]。负责执行逮捕命令的官员被要求谨慎地选择逮捕的时间和地点以使这一逮捕几乎不可避免地会给犯罪嫌疑人造成的不满最小。[②] 牧师、法官或者学校老师不能在履行职务的时候被逮捕。[③] 结婚典礼不能因逮捕新郎或者新娘而被扰乱。[④] 法庭也执行这一原则，证据是一位警佐因粗暴地逮捕刚完成诵经的牧师而被定罪。[⑤] 一旦被逮捕，法律禁止没收犯罪嫌疑人的财产，以免妨碍他们行使自我辩护权。这一原则于 1697 年被梅茨最高法院重申。[⑥] 因为一个人“可能被指控犯罪而且非常无辜”，所以，被告人被允许进行商业活动。正如罗马法所规定的，犯罪嫌疑人可以继承、赠与、立遗嘱、还账、卖商品或者土地，只要其未被指控犯有

---

① Antoine Bruneau, Observations Et Maxims Sur Les Matieres Criminelles 83 (Paris, 1715). Actions to protect the reputation of individuals facing criminal justice did not cease upon conviction. In the sixteen the century, a court ordered the jurist Jean Papon to remove from his case law report any reference to cases involving plaintiffs whose convictions of embezzlement were later reversed. See Pierre Brillon, Dictionnaire Des Arrests; Ou, Jurisprudence Universelle Des Parlemens De France, Et Autres Tribunaux 279 (Paris, 1727) (observing that "the urge to cite cases should not compromise the honor of families, [and] often the honor of persons unjustly accused [and] without proof").

② Antoine Bruneau, Observations Et Maxims Sur Les Matieres Criminelles 105 (Paris, 1715).

③ Antoine Bruneau, Observations Et Maxims Sur Les Matieres Criminelles 105 (Paris, 1715).

④ Antoine Bruneau, Observations Et Maxims Sur Les Matieres Criminelles 105 (Paris, 1715).

⑤ See 3 Daniel Jousse, Traite de la justice criminelle en France 119 (Paris, 1771) (citing a decision dated Dec. 31, 1563).

⑥ *Arrest de la Cour de Parlement, Portant Reglement pour l' execution des Decrets de Prise de corps* (Metz, 1697) ("[O]ne shall not at the same time seize the Body [and] the Goods of an Accused; that this Jurisprudence which is uniformly applied in the whole Kingdom, is based on the Rules of equity; because accused persons would almost be prevented from defending themselves if at the same time as we seize their Body, we take their Goods; ... one shall always incline towards leniency in the interpretation of penal laws.") (on file with the Bibliotheque nationale de France).

叛国罪并且其善意地从事这些交易。1552 年，巴黎最高法院以同一原则提醒一位牧师被控告之人不能被阻止参加告解礼（sacrament of penance）或者在复活节接受圣餐。[①] 然而，“一个人在被证明有罪之前即被假定为无罪”的无罪推定格言和无罪推定精神逐渐被另外一条不利于被告人的格言所压倒——“宽恕有罪之人就是惩罚无辜者”[②]。刑讯、秘密指控和任意的程序不公逐渐成为常规和普遍化。一般认为，法国旧制度时期的刑事诉讼完全忽视犯罪嫌疑人定罪前被视为无罪的权利，如 1670 年的《刑事法令》（*Criminal Ordinance of* 1670）规定，有公职的人一旦被逮捕或者传唤，其职务将被自动暂停。法官将不再是法官，牧师将被禁止主持婚礼。这种对无罪推定的忽视，因为一种现实的考虑获得正当性，即被指控的公职人员履行职务的行为将会受到不断的质疑，因此可能导致“日常的尴尬和冲突”[③④]。对于这种忽视的另一种解释是当时的法院有惩罚犯罪的责任感，这是一个公用事业问题，获得“真实”的程序捷径，如刑讯是这些法院实现其责任的手段。[⑤] 至于寻求公职的个人，指控将阻止他们竞选成功。[⑥] 早在 12 世纪，法国就有数个省份确立

---

① 2 Dictionnaire de Jurisprudence et des Arrets, ou Nouvelle Edition du Dictionnaire de Brillon 336 (Lyon, 1772) (citing a decision of the Parlement of Paris dated Mar. 21, 1552).

② Pierre-Francois Muyart de Vouglans, Lettre de l'auteur des loix criminelles 26 (1785) (citing Seneca's maxim "*Qui malis parcit, bonis nocet*").

③ *Proces verbal des conferences tenues par ordre du Roi, pour l'examen des articles de l'ordonnance civile du mois d'avril*, 1667 *et de l'ordonnance criminelle, du mois d'aout*, 1670, at 115 (Paris, 1709).

④ Francois Quintard-Morénas, *The Presumption of Innocence in the French and Anglo-American Legal Traditions*, 58Am. J. Comp. L. 107, 118 (2010).

⑤ Kenneth Pennington, *Innocent until Proven Guilty: The Origins of a Legal Maxim*, 63 Jurist 106, 117 (2003).

⑥ *See* 5 *Recueil general des anciennes lois francaises depuis l'an* 420 *jusqu'a la revolution de* 1789 *par MM. Jourdan, Decrusy, Isambert* 497 (Paris, 1822). (citing letters from King Charles V dated Jan. 1378 stating that a criminal defendant could not be elected consul in the town of Ouveillan, Languedoc).

了被告人通过申请保释而避免被拘留的权利。然而，由于在一个被暴力困扰的国家，镇压犯罪的需要成为王权的优先考虑，因此，预防性羁押逐渐成为规则和常态。① 只有轻微犯罪的犯罪嫌疑人被允许保释。② 虽然法律要求法官在嫌疑人被抓捕后的 24 小时内进行讯问，③ 但是，长期羁押（有时长达数月或者数年）④ 变得越来越普遍。未决犯经常被与已决犯一起关押在污秽的监狱里，⑤ 因此遭受着法律本身所禁止的惩罚。⑥ 然而，最公然违反无罪推定的是酷

① Adhemar Esmein, A History of Continental Criminal Procedure with Special Reference to France 174 (John Simpson trans., Augustus M. Kelley Publ. 1968) (1913). Persons of modest condition and vagrants accused of a crime would almost inevitably be detained without bail. See 3 Daniel Jousse, Traite de la justice criminelle en France 571 (Paris, 1771).

② See 3 Daniel Jousse, Traite de la justice criminelle en France 571 (Paris, 1771).

③ Ordon. 1670, tit. 14, art. 1. The most important law court in France had previously ordered first-level judges or *prgv6ts* to interrogate prisoners within twenty-four hours of their capture. *See* Pierre Brillon, Dictionnaire des arrests; ou, Jurisprudence universelle des parlemens de France, et autres tribunaux 869 (Paris, 1727) (citing a decision of the Parlement of Paris dated Oct. 30, 1565). The right of the accused to be heard in criminal matters was recognized in France as early as the sixth century. See Jourdan, Decrusy, Isambert, 7 Recueil general des anciennes lois francaises depuis l'an 420 jusqu'a la revolution de 1789 par MM 60 (Paris, 1822) (citing a constitution of King Clotaire I (497-561): "*Si quis in aliquo crimine fuerit accusatus, non condemnatur penitus inauditus. ...*").

④ 2 *Oeuvres de M. Duplessis* 17-18 (Paris, 1728) (observing that the Parlement of Paris regularly admonished judges who failed to abide by the Criminal Ordinance).

⑤ Charles Eleonor Dufriche de Valaze, Loix penales, dediees a Monsieur, frere du Roi 301 (Alencon, 1784) (pleading for a dual prison system, one for accused individuals and one for convicted criminals). 3 David Houard, Dictionnaire analytique, historique, etymologique, critique et interpretatif de la Coutume de Normandie 613 (Rouen, 1781).

⑥ Ordon. 1670, tit. 13, art. 1 ("Jails shall be safe and arranged in such a way that the health of prisoners is not affected"). King Louis XVI reiterated the prohibition of insalubrious jails by declaring that suspects would not "endure beforehand a rigorous punishment by their detention in gloomy and unwholesome places." *See* Jean-Marie Carbasse, Historie Du Droit Penal Et De La Justice Criminelle 367 (2000) (citing the Declaration of Aug. 30, 1780 establishing new prisons).

刑这一早在13世纪的法国就已确立的实践的合法化。[①] 酷刑逐渐被限制于证明标准极高的死刑案件,[②] 也被视为一种迫使被认为善于撒谎之人招供的必要手段。[③] 法国法学家奥古斯丁·尼古拉斯(Augustin Nicolas)在一本献给国王路易十四(King Louis XIV)的书[④]中对违反“总是支持无罪的假定”[⑤]、“在恶劣的窘困之事中惩罚先于定罪”[⑥] 的实践进行了谴责。民众对被指控犯罪之人所处困境的相对冷漠[⑦]与法学家普遍持有的酷刑并非惩罚[⑧]以及人道的刑

① Ordon. 1254, art. 22 (cited in Jean-Marie Carbasse, Historie Du Droit Penal Et De La Justice Criminelle 169 (2000)).

② Ordon. 1670, tit. 19, art. 1.

③ Louis Lassere, L'art de proceder en Justice, ou La science des regles judiciaires, pour decouvrir la Verite, tant en matiere Civile, que Criminelle 198 (Paris, 2d ed. 1680).

④ Augustin Nicolas, Si la Torture est un moyen seur a verifier les crimes secrets (Amsterdam, 1682) (cited in Adhemar Esmein, A History of Continental Criminal Procedure With Special Reference to France 352 (John Simpson trans., Augustus M. Kelley Publ. 1968) (1913)).

⑤ Augustin Nicolas, Si la Torture est un moyen seur a verifier les crimes secrets (Amsterdam, 1682) (cited in Adhemar Esmein, A History of Continental Criminal Procedure With Special Reference to France 84 (John Simpson trans., Augustus M. Kelley Publ. 1968) (1913)).

⑥ Augustin Nicolas, Si la Torture est un moyen seur a verifier les crimes secrets (Amsterdam, 1682) (cited in Adhemar Esmein, A History of Continental Criminal Procedure With Special Reference to France 46 (John Simpson trans., Augustus M. Kelley Publ. 1968) (1913)). On torture as punishment, see John H. Langbein, Torture and the Law of Proof: Europe and England in the Ancient Regime 66 (1977).

⑦ Adhemar Esmein, A History of Continental Criminal Procedure With Special Reference to France 178 (John Simpson trans., Augustus M. Kelley Publ. 1968) (1913).

⑧ *See Proces verbal des conferences tenues par ordre du Roi*, *pour l'examen des articles de l'ordonnance civile du mois d'avril*, 1667 *et de l'ordonnance criminelle*, *du mois d'aout*, 1670, at 224 (Paris, 1709). ("[T] orture is not ordered as a punishment and the one that suffers it is not rendered infamous ....") (Cited in Adhemar Esmein, A History of Continental Criminal Procedure With Special Reference to France 235 (John Simpson trans., Augustus M. Kelley Publ. 1968) (1913).

事诉讼程序将鼓励犯罪①的观点结合在一起，导致了酷刑这一实践得以维持。法国直到 17 世纪末才逐渐放弃这一实践。② 如果在侦查程序末期，被追诉人是否有罪仍旧存疑，那么，法官通常会没有任何法律依据地要求进一步调查，③ 因此导致对被追诉之人的羁押延长，而如果无罪推定的格言被遵守的话，这些人本该已被宣布无罪。④ 虽然没有招供的犯罪嫌疑人偶尔被从监狱中释放，但是，法官都很谨慎，不会宣布他们无罪，因为害怕被指控司法不公。⑤ 既非完全无罪，又非完全有罪，他们遭受着被定罪的罪犯才应该承受的污名。⑥ 至于面对酷刑设法做到不招供的被追诉人，也有可能根

---

① 2 Pierre-Francois Muyart de Vouglans, Les loix criminelles de France, dans leur ordre naturel 319 (Paris, 1781).

② Antoine Astaing, Droits et garanties de l´accuse dans le proces criminel d´Ancien Regime XVIe et XVIIIe siecles: Audace et pusillanimite de la doctrine penale francaise 32-3 (1999).

③ *See, e. g., Arret de la Cour de Parlement qui ordonne un plus amplement informe pendant trois mois, contre Jean Magre, Claude Marechal et Marie Louise Thibault pendant lequel temps, lesdits Magre et Marechal tiendront prison et ladite Thibault mise en liberte* (Paris, 1722).

④ Mohammed-Jalal Essaid, La presomption d' innocence 33 (1971).

⑤ Jean Boutiller, Somme rural, ou, Le grand coustumier general de practique civil et canon 229 (Paris, 1603).

⑥ *Oeuvres de M. Le Chancelier d´Aguesseau contenant les plaidoyers prononces au Parlement en qualite d´Avocat General, depuis le mois d´avril* 1696, *& dans les annees* 1697, 1698 & 1699, at 451 (Paris, 1764) ("If we add the public noise, the judgments of the people, this voice ... that does not wait for the accusation to discover the culprit, [and] that designates the victim a long time before the sacrifice ..."); Charles Eleonor Dufriche de Valaze, Loix penales, dediees a Monsieur, frere du Roi 302 (Alencon, 1784) (pleading for a dual prison system, one for accused individuals and one for convicted criminals) ("Public opinion forms a considerable part of the punishment. It prolongs its duration, [and] renders the reparation of the innocent almost impossible").

据法官的裁量而被惩罚。[①] 教会监察也未能总是做到遵从无罪推定的原则行事。在著名的卡拉斯（Calas）案中，监察排除了被告人简·卡拉斯（Jean Calas）之长子马克·安托万·卡拉斯（Marc Antoine Calas）自杀的可能性，假定了简·卡拉斯负有谋杀其长子之罪，结果，简·卡拉斯（Jean Calas）因被宣称谋杀其长子而被执行死刑。

程序规则被破坏和权利被侵犯最经常发生在法官面对刺激社会最敏感神经的犯罪时。过去如此，如今仍旧如此。约翰内斯·莫纳克斯于13世纪末明确提出无罪推定格言后的几个世纪中，欧洲大陆案件中反复讨论无罪推定问题的案件主要是涉及边缘群体，特别是异教徒、女巫和犹太人的案件。[②] 西方无罪推定的发展过程与对特定边缘群体的司法待遇有关：某些边缘群体能否获得与基督徒一样的正当程序，能否享有无罪推定的权利等都成为争议的问题。这与我国确立无罪推定的推动力量主要是冤假错案对社会的影响以及社会对冤假错案产生原因的反思而非与某些特定的社会群体有关不同。当15世纪和16世纪的法官和法学家自问这一问题时，理论上的答案总是一样的：犹太人享有和基督徒同样的正当程序权利。如果无法证明，那么，他们被假定为无罪。诚然，这一理论并未总是在法庭上得到体现，但是，这些规则在发给地方法官和宗教法庭的教皇指令中被反复提及。1469年，教皇保罗二世（Pope Paul II）批准了皇帝腓特烈三世（Emperor Frederick III）的请求，赦免参与涉及犹太人案件的基督徒法官、司法人员和书记员的罪行。一些基督教牧师曾经拒绝赦免他们的罪行，除非他们为其在法庭上帮助犹

① Ordon. 1670, tit. 19, art. 2. The Criminal Ordinance of 1670 codified a practice permitted by the courts. *See* Hyacinthe de Boniface, 1Arrests notables de la Courde Parlementde Provence, Cour des Comptes, Aydes & Finances du mesme Pays 7 (Paris, 1670) (citing a decision of the Parlement of Provence dated June 17, 1667).

② Kenneth Pennington, *Innocent until Proven Guilty*: *The Origins of a Legal Maxim*, 63 Jurist 106, 117 (2003).

太人的作用而赎罪。[①] 从罗马教廷在接下来的50年间重复这些警告的次数来看，欧洲大陆当时关于无罪推定的理论和实践可能并非总是很好地相符。[②]

虽然在实践中无罪推定的贯彻并不尽如人意，但是在理论上，无罪推定仍旧得以保存和发展。辩护权、获得律师帮助权以及行使辩护权的手段是"被证明有罪之前即无罪"这一格言所尊奉的权利的明显扩展。1535年，教皇保罗三世宣布："任何人都不应当被剥夺由自然法确立的辩护权。"[③] 对于欧洲共同法中的刑事实体法和程序法来说，16世纪是一个伟大的时代。16世纪，法学家综合了欧洲共同法的法学理论，并写出了关于刑事被告人权利的伟大篇章。在这一发展中的伟大人物之一是普洛斯彼罗·法里纳奇（Prospero Farinacci，1544–1618）。他于1581年开始写作他最重要的作品《刑事理论与实践》（*Praxis et Theorica Criminalis*），于1601年完稿。法里纳奇的论文充满了无罪推定的激情，将无罪推定视为法

---

① Kenneth Pennington, *Innocent until Proven Guilty*: *The Origins of a Legal Maxim*, 63 Jurist 106, 118 (2003).

② Kenneth Pennington, *Innocent until Proven Guilty*: *The Origins of a Legal Maxim*, 63 Jurist 106, 119 (2003).

③ Theodore F. T. Plucknett, A Concise History of the Common Law 410 (4th Ed. London 1948). Cf. James A. Brundage, Medieval Canon Law 149 (London–New York: 1995) n. 50. French jurisprudence continued to follow the dictates of the lus commune: Procez verbal des confrences tenues par ordredu roi, entre messieurs les commissairesdu con- seil et messieursles diputdsduparlement de Paris, reprinted in Code Louis: Ordonnance criminelle (1670) (Testi documenti per lastoria del processo, edd. Nicola Picardi and Alessandro Giuliani (Milan: 1996) 163: "ce conseil qu´on a acoatumd de donner aux acusez n´est point un privilge acord6 par les Ordonnances ni par les Loix que c´6toit une libert6 aquise par le droit naturel, qui est plus ancien que toutes les Loix humaines. Que le nature enseignoit Al´homme d´avoir recours aux lumieres des autres, quand il ne n´en avoit pas assez pour se conduire et d´emprunter du secours, quand il ne se sentoit pas assez fort pour se drfendre... Que si on vouloit comparer n6tre procedure criminelle Acelle des Romains et des autres Nations, ou trouveroit qu´il n´y en voit point de si rigoureuse, que celle qu´on observe en France, particulirrement drpuis l´Ordonnance de 1539."

律特权，永远不能被制定法废除。另外一个刑事诉讼中伟大的理性呼声是腓特烈·冯·施佩（Frederick von Spee，1591-1635）。他是一位批评不宽容和愚昧的法学家。他谴责酷刑、对女巫的迫害和触怒君主及乌合之众的其他犯罪。他对酷刑的谴责是不容置疑的。他继承了法里纳奇的观点。他的激昂之言鼓舞了一个世纪后的贝卡利亚：在酷刑下不坦白的被告人可以被定罪吗？施佩写道："我认为没有人可以被判刑，除非他的罪行是确定的；无罪之人不应被处死。每个未被认定有罪之人都被假定为无罪。"① 其实，这三句话可以被视为逻辑上相扣的三个环节："没有人可以被判刑，除非他的罪行是确定的"并不意味着"被告人是无罪的"，且和第二句"无罪之人不应被处死"衔接不上。这一环节的缺失由第三句"每个未被认定有罪之人都被假定为无罪"补上。于是，这三个环节连在一起后得出的结论就是"每个未被认定有罪之人都被假定为无罪，并不应被处死"。17 世纪和 18 世纪，无罪推定获得了进一步的发展。1748 年，孟德斯鸠在《论法的精神》中说：一个人，即使是最卑微的公民的生命也应当受到尊重。他的荣誉和财产，如果没有经过长期的审查，是不得剥夺的；他的生命，除了受国家的控诉之外，是不得剥夺的。1764 年，意大利的法学家贝卡利亚所著的《论犯罪与刑罚》一书提出："在法官判决之前，一个人是不能被称为罪犯的。只要还不能断定他已经侵犯了给予他公共保护的契约，社会就不能取消对他的公共保护"，明确提出无罪推定的刑事司法原则。贝卡利亚的这一著作对无罪推定思想的传播产生了深远的影响。与此同时，被告人被假定无罪的权利经常被谴责刑事诉

① Kenneth Pennington, *Innocent until Proven Guilty: The Origins of a Legal Maxim*, 63 Jurist 106, 119-22 (2003).

讼实践中虐待问题的法国法学家援引①并享沐法国皇家的恩泽。国王路易十六（King Louis XVI）在《1788年5月宣言》中将其称为"刑事问题中首要的原则",② 同时禁止使用侮辱性的审讯椅（sellette),③ 禁止犯罪嫌疑人穿囚服,④ 强制公开无罪判决⑤以恢复被

---

① 17世纪的如 Laurent Jovet, La bibliotheque des arrests de tous les parlemens de France 175（"This prescription has been introduced in favor of innocence, for which we always presume ..."）; *Oeuvres de M. Le Chancelier d'Aguesseau contenant les plaidoyers prononces au Parlement en qualite d'Avocat General, depuis le mois d'avril* 1696, *& dans les annees* 1697, 1698 & 1699, at 422（Paris, 1764）（"Would you leave these innocents groan in fetters and in the horror of a jail during the uncertain course of a long instruction? ... Until then the law always presumes in favor of innocence ..."）. 18世纪的如 Comte de Mirabeau, *Des Lettres de cachet et des prisons d'Etat. Ouvrage posthume, compose en* 1778, at 344（Hambourg, 1782）（"An accusation does not negate the presumption of innocence, and until condemnation there is no culprit."）; Jean-Baptiste Janety, Journal du Palais de Provence, ou Recueil des Arrets rendus depuis les derniers Journalistes, par le Parlement & la Cour des Aides de cette Province. Annees 1775, 1776, 1777 & 1778, at 161（Aix, 1785）（"Does a public officer not enjoy his condition until a judgment of condemnation? The presumption is always in favor of innocence" declared the lawyer of Me. Jerome, notary, in a case in which the Parlement of Provence, in a decision dated May 27, 1777, quashed the disciplinary decision of a College of Notaries taken without Me. Jerome being heard）.

② Declaration Du Roi, Relative a L'ordonnance Criminelle 5（Versailles, 1788）（"This formality openly offends the first of all principles in criminal matters that provides that an accused, even if sentenced to death in the first instance, is always presumed innocent in the eye of the Law until his sentence is confirmed on appeal."）（cited in Jean-Marie Carbasse, Historie du droit penal et de la justice criminelle 368（2000））. The "formality" in question was the *sellette*.

③ Declaration Du Roi, Relative a L'ordonnance Criminelle 8（Versailles, 1788）. The *sellete* was a low wooden stool in which the accused was seated during interrogation. It was particularly humiliating for the accused, who was forced to stand lower than the judges in an uncomfortable posture.

④ Declaration Du Roi, Relative a L'ordonnance Criminelle 9（Versailles, 1788）.（"It shall be prohibited to strip defendants of the clothes distinctive of their status⋯."）. Cf. Dig. 48. 20. 2（Callistrate, De Cognitionibus 6）（stating that a detainee will only be stripped of his clothing after conviction）.

⑤ Declaration Du Roi, Relative a L'ordonnance Criminelle 10（Versailles, 1788）.

追诉人的公共名誉。[1] 几个月后，当国民代表获得机会在凡尔赛宫议会表达他们的不满时，[2] 他们提及无罪推定以要求对犯罪嫌疑人更好的对待[3]以及在证据不充分的情况下无罪推定得到完全绝对的实施。[4] 在1789年8月22日的巴黎国民议会上，一位名为阿德里安—让—弗朗索瓦·迪波尔（Adrien-Jean-Francois Duport）的年轻贵族代表，吃惊于法国定罪前惩罚的“野蛮使用”，提议将无罪推定题写在《人权宣言》中，这一提议被一致通过。[5] 在《人权宣言》中，无罪推定的表述如下：“所有人在被宣布为有罪之前即被假定为无罪；如果认为有逮捕他的绝对必要，那么法律应严厉禁止任何形式的为抓获其人身所不必要的严厉手段。”[6] 这是无罪推定的格言第一次被明确纳入立法。

此后，大陆法系对于无罪推定的态度发生了摇摆。1792年，

---

① Declaration Du Roi, Relative a L´ordonnance Criminelle 7（Versailles, 1788）.

② Albert Desjardins, Les cahiers des Etats Generaux en 1789 et la legislation criminelle XXIX（Paris, 1883）.

③ Mohammed-Jalal Essaid, La presomption d' innocence 39（1971）.

④ Albert Desjardins, Les cahiers des Etats Generaux en 1789 et la legislation criminelle xxix 317（Paris, 1883）.

⑤ Eugene Blum, La declaration des droits de l´homme et du citoyen: texte avec commentaires 202（1902）. For an earlier codification, see Constitutionum Regni Siciliarum Libri iii 261（Naples, Vol. 1, 1773）（1231）（“*Si tamen accusator in crimine prius offerat se probare per testes, & si in eorum probatione deficiat, tunc inquisitionis, & pugnae probatione minime locum habente, reus qui nocens non convincitur, & praesumitur innocens, absolvatur*”）.

⑥ Declaration Des Droits De L´homme Et Du Citoyen. Decretes par l´Assemblee Nationale dans les seances des 20, 21, 23, 24 et 26 aout, 1789, acceptes par le Roi. Article 9. As all persons are held innocent until they shall have been declared guilty, if arrest shall be indispensable, all harshness not essential to the securing of the prisoner's person shall be severely repressed by law.（Tout homme étant présumé innocent jusqu´à ce qu´il ait été déclaré coupable, s´il est jugé indispensable de l´arrêter, toute rigueur qui ne serait pas nécessaire pour s´assurer de sa personne doit être sévèrement réprimée par la loi.）有法律史学者强烈谴责法国《人权宣言》没有提及将无罪推定视为一项证据规则。*See*, *e. g.*, Jean-Marie Carbasse, Histoire du droit penal et de la justice criminelle 374（2000）.

巴黎对路易十六的审判是对无罪推定的第一次明显背叛。因在革命小册子中被刻画成一位暴君，路易十六还未被审判就已被定罪。法国大革命之后紧接着的数年内，“被告人”和“罪犯”的区分被废除了。甚至在法官开始阅卷之前，被追诉人就已经受到了严厉的惩罚。1793 年 9 月 17 日通过的《犯罪嫌疑人法》授权对通过行为、社团、评论或者作品从事与自由为敌的活动或者无法为其生活手段或者公民义务的履行进行辩护的任何人进行羁押。对于无故受到指控或者已被无罪释放的人，该法允许将其作为“嫌疑犯”进行无限期的羁押。在德雷福斯（Dreyfus）一案中，法国陆军上尉犹太人阿尔弗雷德·德雷福斯（Alfred Dreyfus）就被错误地指控犯有叛国罪。无罪推定的实践和理论出现了背离，并且在法国大革命之后的一百年里被追诉人的境遇都没有得到改善。法国大革命后的刑事诉讼程序依旧保留了旧制度时期的许多弊病，包括强迫自证其罪、对犯罪嫌疑人的长期审前羁押、缺乏辩护律师等。定罪的动力战胜了对被追诉人的保护，对案件真实的追求压倒了对无罪推定的遵从。19 世纪末期和 20 世纪的法国对被追诉人的保护有了缓慢的进步。1897 年的一项法律赋予了被追诉人在预审法官讯问期间的律师在场权。在被指责为专制和压迫的压力下，1958 年通过的新刑事诉讼法典将审前羁押作为一项例外。1970 年，“预防性羁押”的术语被替换为“有条件羁押”。虽然在刑事诉讼法典中没有被明确提及，但无罪推定这一宪法性原则经常被法国法院用来谴责警察权力滥用或者提醒控诉方其负有证明责任。1988 年，法国启动了一场刑事诉讼程序改革。改革委员会重申了无罪推定的双重维度——证明规则和防范提早惩罚，并指出审前羁押仍应作为例外并且应当采取措施避免压力下的供述——包括告知犯罪嫌疑人保持沉默的权利。对于一位社会党的原财政部长的腐败指控促成了落实 1993 年改革的社会立法。于是，被警方拘留的犯罪嫌疑人首次有了获得律师帮助权。虽然这次立法并没有确立警察告知犯罪嫌疑人保持沉默的义务，但是，确立了逮捕或者转送时不被戴上手铐的权利。其中一项重要改革是在《法国民法典》中加入了一条规定，将无罪推定提升为一项人格权。1995 年，法国总统换届引发了一系列新的改革，主要关注如何进一步加强司法独立和无罪推定。改革委员会于 1997 年发布了一份报告，建议从警方羁押开始，被追诉人就有权请求辩护律师在场，同时建议剥夺预审法官对犯罪嫌疑人进行审前羁押的决定权，将无罪推定作为一项人格权扩展到接受询问或者初步调查的任何人，以及警方有告知犯罪嫌疑人保持沉默权的义务。这些改革最终在 2000 年被落实。在被证实有罪之前犯罪嫌疑人有权被假定为无罪现在已被庄严地写入《法国刑事诉讼法典》。① 此外，如今法国对无罪推定的保护并不局限于刑事诉讼领域。作为对 1789 年法国《人权宣言》第 9 条所包含的对被追诉人保护的扩展，法国民法典如今认可了定罪前不被公开描绘为有罪的权利。从犯罪嫌疑人法到德雷福斯（Dreyfus）案，再到媒体经常将被追诉人描绘为罪犯，法国对无罪推定表现出了非常矛盾的心态。这一矛盾心态经常被外国评论人谴责。为此，法国最近实施改革以加强无罪推定。② 在其他大陆法系国家或地区，无罪推定的观念也在逐步发展，在很多国家或地区被纳入本国宪法和刑事诉讼法典中。例如，俄罗斯联邦宪法第 2 章第 49 条规定："1. 每个被控犯罪者在其罪名未经联邦法律规定的程序以证实和已经生效的法院判决所确认之前均为无罪。2. 被告人没有证明自己无罪的义务。3. 无法排除的有罪的怀疑应作出有利于被告人的解释。"俄罗斯 2001 年新刑事诉讼法典第 1 章第 14 条规定："1. 刑事被告人在未依照本法典

① Criminal Procedure Code of the French Republic, First Part: Legislative Preliminary Article "III. Every person suspected or prosecuted is presumed innocent as long as his guilt has not been established. Attacks on his presumption of innocence are proscribed, compensated and punished in the circumstances laid down by statute." Article 304 "... to remember that the accused is presumed innocent and that he has the benefit of the doubt; ..."

② Francois Quintard-Morénas, *The Presumption of Innocence in the French and Anglo-American Legal Traditions*, 58Am. J. Comp. L. 107 (2010).

规定的程序被证明有罪并由已经发生法律效力的刑事判决确定其有罪以前，应被认为无罪。2. 犯罪嫌疑人或刑事被告人没有义务证明自己无罪。证明对被告人的指控和推翻为犯罪嫌疑人或刑事被告人辩护理由的责任由控诉方承担。3. 依照本法典规定的程序不能排除对被告人有罪的所有怀疑，均应作对被告人有利的解释。4. 有罪判决不得根据推测作出。”意大利宪法第 27 条第 1 款规定：“在最终判决确定之前，不得认定被告人有罪。”葡萄牙宪法第 32 条第 2 款规定：“任何被告人在证明其有罪以前应被推定为无罪。”韩国宪法第 27 条规定：“……（4）刑事被告人在被判为有罪之前，应推定为无罪。”1982 年土耳其宪法第 38 条规定：“任何人在法院证明其有罪前推定无罪。”1999 年 12 月 20 日起实施的澳门特别行政区基本法第 29 条规定：“……澳门居民在被指控犯罪时，享有尽早接受法院审判的权利，在法院判罪之前均假定无罪。”我国台湾地区 2003 年修订的“刑事诉讼法”第 154 条第 1 项规定：“被告未经审判证明有罪确定前，推定其为无罪。”

现如今无罪推定在大陆法系的适用范围进一步扩大，不仅适用于法庭之上，而且适用于法庭审理之前，甚至适用于整个社会。其内涵也非常丰富，蕴含着一系列权利要求，可以说是一系列权利的基础。大陆法系无罪推定的内涵包含以下要求：在被依法证明并被合法的法庭认定有罪之前任何人有权被视为无罪；控诉方承担证明有罪的责任，被控诉方不承担证明自己无罪的责任；任何人在被定罪前都不应被公开描绘为有罪；防范提早惩罚，反对刑讯逼供，反对强迫自证其罪；被追诉人享有保释权、沉默权、辩护权、获得律师帮助权，获得公开、公正、无偏倚审判权及上诉权；禁止任意逮捕和拘禁；非法证据应当予以排除；无罪推定是一项人格权，适用于任何人；等等。

二、在英美法系的发展

早在 13 世纪，英国法院就裁决被指控犯有重罪的个人不能被当作重罪犯对待[①]，因为“在经审判被认定为犯有某一罪行前任何人都不被确定犯有该重罪”[②]。由此，在定罪前，犯罪嫌疑人不会丧失其财产或者土地被没收。[③] 这一项罗马法原则[④]在 15 世纪时成为英国制定法的一部分。[⑤⑥]

1260 年，布莱克顿（Bracton，1210-1268）引述过一句非常接近无罪推定格言一般表述的话：“在被证反之前，每个人都被假定是好人”（de quolibet homine presumitur quod sit bonus homo donec probetur in contrarium）。[⑦] 布莱克顿也常强调监狱只为安全监禁而非惩罚。[⑧] 罗马法和教会法对布莱克顿的影响自此被确立。[⑨] 根据

① 1 The Earliest English Law Reports 128（Paul A. Brand ed.，Selden Society 1996）（citing a decision of the Court of Common Pleas of 1283）.

② 2 Year Books of the Reign of King Edward the First：Years XXI and XXII 56-57（Alfred J. Horwood ed.，Longman & Co. 1873）（citing a decision of the Court of Common Pleas of 1293）.

③ Abraham Fraunce，The Lawiers Logike，Exemplifying the Praecepts of Logike By the Practise of the Common Lawe 151（London，1588）.

④ See DIG. 48. 21. 3. 7（Marcian，De Delatoribus）. See also 2 FLETA 66（London，Bernard Quaritch 1955）（1290?）. Fleta was written in the thirteenth century by an anonymous author. See *Fleta*，73 Eng. Hist. Rev. 672（1958）.

⑤ 1 Rich. III，c. 3（1483）（Eng.）.

⑥ Francois Quintard-Morénas，*The Presumption of Innocence in the French and Anglo-American Legal Traditions*，58Am. J. Comp. L. 107，126（2010）.

⑦ Bracton，193. Thayer cited Bracton（1210-1268）as the source of the maxim：“But let us observe it in its earlier history. In Bracton，say in 1260，we find it in the most general form - de quolibet homine presumitur quod sit bonus homo donec probetur in contrarium.” James Bradley Thayer，*The Presumption of Innocence in Criminal Cases*，6 Yale L. J. 185，190（1897）.

⑧ 2 Bracton，on the Laws and Customs of England 299（Cambridge，Harvard University Press 1968）（1260?）. See also The Mirror of Justices Edited for the Selden Society by William Joseph Whittaker 52（London，Bernard Quaritch 1895）（1290?）（“And because it is forbidden that anyone be tormented before judgment the law wills that no one be placed among vermine or putrefaction，or in any horrible or dangerous place，or in the water，or in the dark，or any other torment ...”）

⑨ See，e. g.，Gaines Post，*A Romano-Canonical Maxim，“Quod Omnes Tangit，” in Bracton*，4 Traditio 197，215-17（1946）.

盖恩斯·波斯特（Gaines Post）的观点，“现在似乎很明确，布莱克顿有时意译一些关于 quod omnes tangit 这一术语所表达的共同或者一致同意的罗马法，或者使用这些罗马法中的关键性词汇。也许因为他既没有逐字引用这些法条，也没有标明出处，现代权威并未将其列于他的罗马资料，也没有在‘罗马法当时存在的流行形式，而非《查士丁尼学说汇纂》的纯粹学术形式’所述的文段中注意到它。[①] 但如果我们将与布莱克顿相关的文段与罗马法逐一对照，我们一眼就可以看出布莱克顿使用了一些最终来自国法大全的术语。”[②] 此外，犯罪嫌疑人有权获得保释，这一“刑事被告人被假定为无罪的必然后果”[③] 早在 1275 年就被规定在制定法中。[④] 此后，奥卡姆的威廉（William of Ockham，1285-1349）再次引述了无罪推定的思想。[⑤]

15 世纪时，英国大法官弗特斯克（Fortescue）说：“我宁愿希

---

① Plucknett, Com. Law2 233: “We may probably assume, therefore, that when Bracton used foreign law he had a fairly good idea of what he was about.” Similarly, Vinogradoff, Rom. Law 117f: “If we want definite traces of it (Roman Law) we have to look out not for references but for maxims, some of which, besides, had passed through the medium of Canon law. The only real test of its character and extent is afforded by the development of juridical ideas, and in this respect the initial influence of Roman teaching on English doctrines will be found to be considerable. On many subjects the judges and legal writers of England were, as it were, prompted by their Roman predecessors, and this intercourse of ideas is nowhere as conspicuous as in the frequent cases when English lawyers did not simply copy their Roman models, but borrowed suggestions from them in their own way.”

② Gaines Post, *A Romano-Canonical Maxim*, “*Quod Omnes Tangit*,” *in Bracton*, 4 Traditio 197, 238-39 (1946).

③ Daines Barrington, Observations on the Statutes Chiefly the More Ancient, from Magna Charta to the Twenty-First of James The First 263 (London, 1766).

④ 3 Edw. I, c. 15 (1275) (Eng.), available at http://en.wikisource.org/wiki/Prisoners_and_Bail_Act, last visited on July 2, 2015.

⑤ William of Ockham (1285-1349), Dialogus (Paris, 1476) (“Quia sicut unusquisque presumitur bonus nisi probetur contrarium ...”) (on file with the Northwestern University Library).

望二十个犯人通过怜悯而逃脱死刑，也不愿意一个人被不公正地判处。”①

16 世纪后半叶，马修·黑尔（Matthew Hale）提出“五个有罪之人被无罪释放好过一个无辜之人被定罪”。②

17 世纪早期，无罪推定思想正式进入英国流行文化。其证据是乔治·赫伯特（George Herbert, 3 April 1593-1 March 1633）在其作品《异域箴言》（*Outlandish Proverbs*）中的记录：“所有人在被发现犯有错误之前都被假定是好人。”③ 也继续有一些法学家引述无罪推定的思想。例如，威廉·巴洛（William Barlow）在其作品中提到“法律假定每个人都是好人直到其明显不是”④。1624 年，在英国下议院，埃德温·桑迪斯爵士（Sir Edwyn Sandys）担心对财政大臣克兰菲尔德（Lord Treasurer Cranfield）的腐败指控会使他产生偏见，提醒每个人一条“古老的法则，每个人都被假定是无罪的直到被证明并非如此”，并要求迅速对这一问题进行审查，⑤ 间接地实质上提到了无罪推定的格言。爱德华·科克爵士（Sir Edward Coke，1552-1634. 9. 3）曾在其《英格兰法律总论》（*Institutes of the Laws of England*）中宣称“英格兰法律是仁慈的法

---

① De Laudibus legume Angliae（1st edn 1545-6），c. 27. Fortescue wrote De Laudibus circa 1468-71 and this is not necessarily the earliest example of this mode of expression. See William S. Holdsworth，III History of English Law，620（1925）.

② Matthew Hale，Pleas of the Crown，or A Brief but Full Account of Whatsoever Can Be Found Relating to that Subject，289（1678）.

③ George Herbert，Outlandish Proverbs（London，1640）（“944. All are presumed good，till they are found in a fault.”）See also George Herbert，http：//en. wikipedia. org/wiki/George_ Herbert，last visited on March 6，2016.

④ William Barlow，An Answer To A Catholike English-Man 349（London，1609）（“The Law presumes every man to be good till hee bee apparantly naught ...”）.

⑤ Francois Quintard-Morénas，*The Presumption of Innocence in the French and Anglo-American Legal Traditions*，58Am. J. Comp. L. 107，127（2010）.

律（Lex Angliae est lex misericordiae）[1]，理由有三：一是无辜者不会被长期的监禁所消磨和虚耗，而是迅速接受审判。二是刑事被告人接受审判时被人性化对待。……三是法官应当规劝被告人无惧地应答，并给予其公正的裁判”[2]。这体现了反对定罪前进行惩罚的观念。

1649年，在英国李尔本（Lilburne）叛国案中，李尔本发表了一段关于无罪推定的演说：“虽然我被指控犯有臭名昭著的罪行，但是在我被依法宣告犯有被指控的犯罪事实或者罪名前，在英国法律的眼中，我是一个无辜的人，和那些称我为叛徒的人一样无辜；因此，大人，我恳求你停止对我的诽谤，因为你这样做会对我既不公平也不合法。”最终，李尔本精彩的自我辩护赢得了陪审团对他的无罪宣判。

1657年，美国马萨诸塞州议会提出“在法律眼中，每个人都是诚实无辜的，除非被依法证明相反”[3]。这可能是无罪推定最早在美国被提及。

1680年，在英国对五个天主教议员进行的审判中，斯塔福德议员（Lord Stafford）据引证（代表自己）说：“一千个罪人逃脱好过一个无辜之人被处死。”[4]

1696年，爱德华·西摩尔爵士（Sir Edward Seymour）在论及

① See also 4 Jac. I, c. 1, § 16 (1606) (Eng.) “Ilt is most juste and necessarie to pvide as well that the guiltie shalt not escape, as that the innocent shall not be condemned ...”

② Sir Edward Coke, The Second Part of the Institutes of the Laws of England 315 (London, 1669).

③ *Records of Massachusetts*, iii. 434-435. Cited by James Bradley Thayer in A Preliminary Treatise on Evidence at the Common Law 552 (Little Brown, 1898) “The operation and exact scope of this maxim, both in civil and criminal cases, was very neatly expressed by the General Court (the Legislature) of Massachusetts so long as 1657, as follows: ‘... and so it is also in a criminal case, for, in the eye of the law every man is honest and innocent, unless it be proved legally to the contrary.’ ”

④ Howell, 7 *State Trials*, 32 Charles II at 1529.

《剥夺公权法案》（*Bill of Attainder*）时说："我和罗马人的观点一致……宁愿十个有罪之人逃脱，也不愿一个无辜之人受罚。"[①]

18世纪，无罪推定的思想在英国进一步发展。法学家托马斯·布兰奇（Thomas Branch）在1753年记录了有关无罪推定的格言："任何人都被假定是诚实正派的；疑案应以有利于被告人的方式解决。"（Quisquis praesumitur bonus; et semper in dubiis pro Reo respondendum.）[②] 约翰·阿尔蒙（John Almon）在一封信中说道："你的律师没有在没进行任何证明之前……努力使公众对威尔克斯先生（Mr. Wilkes）产生偏见或者反对威尔克斯先生吗？这在一个每个人在被定罪之前都依法被假定为无辜的国家是公平的吗？他们没有对他进行预断吗？没有谴责他吗？"[③] 布莱克斯通（Blackstone）在谈及重罪时说，"法律认为，十个有罪之人逃脱好过一个无辜之人受罚"。[④] 美国著名政治家及科学家本杰明·富兰克林（Benjamin Franklin）在其1785年给本杰明·沃恩（Benjamin Vaughan）的一封信中提到："一百个有罪之人逃脱好过一个无辜之人受罚。"（It is better a hundred guilty persons should escape than one innocent person should suffer.）[⑤]

18世纪晚期至19世纪早期，爱尔兰人伦纳德·麦克纳利（Leonard MacNally，1752–1820）大力弘扬无罪推定的精神和思想，并积极地将其应用到司法实践中。他于1802年在都柏林和伦敦发

① See Glanville Williams, The Proof of Guilt 187 (London: Stevens, 3rd edn. 1963).

② Principia Legis & Aequitatis, Being an Alphabetical Collection of Maxims, Principles Or Rules, Definitions and Memorable Sayings in Law and Equity 92 (London, 1753).

③ John Almon, A Letter to the Right Hon. George Grenville 15 (London, 1763) ("Have not your advocates, before any kind of proof is made ... endeavoured to bias, and set the public against Mr. Wilkes? Is this fair, in a country, where, by the laws, every man is supposed to be innocent till convicted? Have they not prejudged him? condemned him?").

④ William Blackstone, IV Commentaries Book 4, Ch. 27, 358 (1765).

⑤ Letter from Benjamin Franklin to Benjamin Vaughan (Mar. 14, 1785), in II The Works of Benjamin Franklin 11, at 13 (John Bigelow, ed., fed. Ed., 1904).

表了作品《刑事诉讼证据规则》(*The Rules of Evidence on Pleas of the Crown*, *Illustrated from Printed and Manuscript Trials and Cases*),引用贝卡利亚在其名著《论犯罪与刑罚》中的话来论证无罪推定的合理性。[①] 该作品在出版后立即被传播到大西洋对岸并于1804年在美国费城出版,1811年再版,成为美国19世纪上半叶关于证据和推定问题的必读论文。[②] 19世纪的许多论文清楚地表达了无罪推定原则,如威廉·威尔斯(William Wills)的《论间接证据》(*On Circumstantial Evidence*),西蒙·格林利夫(Simon Greenleaf)的《论证据法》(*On the Law of Evidence*),以及威廉·贝斯特(William Best)的《论推定》(*On Presumptions*)。在这些法学家中,只有威廉·贝斯特在其论文中明确表达了这是一条"法律格言,每个人在被证明有罪之前必须被假定为无罪"。[③]

美国《1798年罗德岛权利法案》第10条明确提出了无罪推定格言的表述:"任何人在被依法宣布为有罪之前都被假定为无罪。"[④] 由于该条文的表述与法国1789年《人权宣言》第9条的相关表述几乎一字不差,有学者认为《1798年罗德岛权利法案》第

---

① 伦纳德·麦克纳利在论述叛国案件中的双证人规则时,引用贝卡利亚的话说:"In Beccaria's judgment, one witness is not sufficient; for whilst the accused denies what the other affirms, truth remains suspended, and the right that every one has to be believed innocent turns the balance in his favour." See Leonard MacNally, The Rules of Evidence on Pleas of the Crown 19 (London-Dublin: 1802).

② Kenneth Pennington, *Innocent until Proven Guilty*: *The Origins of a Legal Maxim*, 63 Jurist 106 (2003).

③ Kenneth Pennington, *Innocent until Proven Guilty*: *The Origins of a Legal Maxim*, 63 Jurist 106, 108-9 (2003).

④ *The Public Laws of the State of Rhode-Island and Providence Plantations*, *As Revised by a Committee*, *and Finally Enacted by the Honourable General Assembly*, *At Their Session In January*, 1798, at 79-81 (Providence, 1798) ("*An Act declaratory of certain Rights of the People of this State* ... Sec. 10. Every man being presumed to be innocent, until he has been pronounced guilty by the law, all acts of severity that are not necessary to secure an accused person ought to be repressed").

10 条的起草者可能抄袭了法国 1789 年《人权宣言》第 9 条的相关内容。[①] 1842 年罗德岛宪法沿袭了该条，明确规定："在被依法宣告为有罪之前，每个人都被假定为无罪。为有效控制被告人所不必要的严厉行为将不被允许。"[②]

18 世纪末，体现无罪推定思想的表述在各种戏剧和滑稽剧中的使用证明无罪推定思想在英格兰已变得家喻户晓。19 世纪上半叶，边沁（Bentham）在其《司法程序原则》（*Principles of Judicial Procedure*）中讨论错放和错罚的比例问题时，提到过 100∶1（即宁可错放 100 个，不能错罚 1 个）。当然，其提出这一比例的目的是对其进行评论，而非主张。在 1935 年英国沃明顿诉皇家检察署署长（Woolmington v. DPP）一案中，桑基 L. C. 子爵（Viscount Sankey L. C.）宣称："纵贯英国刑法之网，总是可以看到一条金线，即证明被告人之罪是公诉方的责任……"其在发言的后半部分明确提到了"无罪推定"。[③] 在美国，亚历山大·汉密尔顿（Alexander Hamilton）在谴责 1784 年的一次纽约效忠宣誓时，将

① "Section 10 of the Rhode Island Bill of Rights of 1798 reproduces almost word for word the provision contained in Article 9 of the French Declaration of Rights of 1789. The similarities between the two texts can hardly be a coincidence. We can assume that the drafters of the Rhode Island Bill of Rights were familiar with the text of the French Declaration, which was published in English and American newspapers shortly after its adoption. *See*, *e. g.*, *Copy of the Declaration of Rights as Finally Decreed by the National Assembly of France on Thursday*, *August* 27, TIMES (London), Sept. 3, 1789, at 2; *Copy of the Declaration of Rights*, THE PENNSYLVANIA GAZETTE, Oct. 28, 1789; *National Assembly of France. Declaration of the Rights of Man and of Citizens*, The Providence Gazette and Country Journal, June 11, 1791, at 1." See Francois Quintard-Morénas, *The Presumption of Innocence in the French and Anglo-American Legal Traditions*, 58Am. J. Comp. L. 107, 125 (2010), n. 172.

② R. I. CONST. art. I, § 14 ("Every man being presumed innocent, until he is pronounced guilty by the law, no act of severity which is not necessary to secure an accused person, shall be permitted").

③ [1935] AC 462, 481 - 2, HL. Available at http://www.bailii.org/uk/cases/UKHL/1935/1.html, last visited on July 14, 2015. Viscount Sankey makes explicit reference to the "presumption of innocence" only once, and almost in passing, near the end of his speech.

其称作“一次对一项伟大的社会安全原则的颠覆：即每个人在被证明有罪之前将被假定为无罪”[1]。到19世纪中期，美国已确立起对刑事案件陪审团强制说明无罪推定的制度。[2] 虽然美国宪法没有提及，但是，美国最高法院在1972年库尔诉美国（Cool v. United States）一案中裁定无罪推定“植根于宪法中”。[3] 1982年加拿大宪法第11条规定：“关于刑事的与刑罚的诉讼被指控犯罪的人享有下述权利：……（四）在独立的不偏袒的法庭举行公平的公开审判中，根据法律证明有罪之前，应推定为无罪；（五）如果没有正当的理由，不得被拒绝合理保释；……”[4] 英国在1998年颁布了人权法，在其附表1第6条关于“接受公平审判的权利”中规定：“二、被控告刑事犯罪的每个人均应被假定无罪，直到依据法律证明其为有罪。”[5]

纵观整个17世纪和18世纪，英美法系和大陆法系的法律人对于无罪推定格言的理解都是一样的：一个人在被定罪之前在法律上是无罪的，他（她）不能被当作罪犯来对待或者被描绘成一个罪犯。[6] 此后，在普通法系，无罪推定逐渐演化为没有审前效力的单纯的证据规则。这一转变起始于19世纪并以美国1979年的贝尔诉

---

① Article 1, Section 9, Clause 3 - Alexander Hamilton, A Second Letter from Phocion, http://press-pubs.uchicago.edu/founders/print_documents/a1_9_3s6.html, last visited on August 16, 2015.

② See generally, Tom P. Conom, *Bulwarks of Liberty: Presumption of Innocence and Reasonable Doubt*, 45 Wash. St. B. News 39 (1991).

③ Cool v. United States, 409 U.S. 100, 104 (1972).

④ 参见百度百科“加拿大宪法”词条，http://baike.baidu.com/link? url=cqv__woujxpfbdsu5o3ulhznrvkgukex4h7ezqn-d-yjbimkh5iotjgqptczfmy7zxnbcbufqvraotclrhj4gq, last visited on march 15, 2016.

⑤ 《世界各国宪法》，中国检察出版社2012年版。

⑥ Francois Quintard-Morénas, *The Presumption of Innocence in the French and Anglo-American Legal Traditions*, 58Am. J. Comp. L. 107, 124-5 (2010).

伍尔菲什（Bell v. Wolfish）[①] 案告终。19世纪下半叶，从格林利夫（Greenleaf）到罗斯科（Roscoe）、沃顿（Wharton）、贝斯特（Best）和斯蒂芬（Stephen），当时的法学权威都将无罪推定简单地视为传统的将排除合理怀疑地证明有罪的责任分配给控诉方原则的另一种表达方式。美国的一些州立法也明确规定推定的效果仅限于证明责任的分配。例如，1872年，美国加利福尼亚州刑法典第1096条对无罪推定的内涵进行了规定，同时明确说明“推定的效果仅为将排除合理怀疑地证明被告人有罪的责任分配给公诉方”。[②] 美国最高法院在1895年科芬诉美国（Coffin v. United States）一案中将无罪推定区别于“合理怀疑”标准时，将其表述为一种“证明手段”。[③] 这些法律学者是故意忽略掉无罪推定防范定罪前施加惩罚的维度，还是本来就不知道这一维度，目前不得而知。有人认

---

① Bell v. Wolfish, 441 U. S. 520, 545 (1979) (6-3 decision) (“The presumption of innocence is a doctrine that allocates the burden of proof in criminal trials. ... But it has no application to a determination of the rights of a pretrial detainee during confinement before his trial has ever begun.”) . *See also* Black's Law Dictionary 1225 (8th ed. 2004) . *Contra* The Director of Public Prosecutions v. Broderick [2006] I. E. S. C. 34 (Ir.) (citing O'Callaghan v. Attorney General [1966] I. R. 501, 513: “The presumption of innocence is a very real thing and is not simply a procedural rule taking effect only at the trial.”); R. v. Pearson, [1992] 3 S. C. R. 665, 683 (Can.) (Lamer, C. J. : “This operation of the presumption of innocence at trial ... does not, in my opinion, exhaust the operation in the criminal process of the presumption of innocence as a principle of fundamental justice.”) .

② See CAL. PENAL CODE § 1096, http: //www. leginfo. ca. gov/cgi-bin/displaycode? section=pen&group=01001-02000&file=1093-1130, last visited on March 15, 2016. “1096. A defendant in a criminal action is presumed to be innocent until the contrary is proved, and in case of a reasonable doubt whether his or her guilt is satisfactorily shown, he or she is entitled to an acquittal, but the effect of this presumption is only to place upon the state the burden of proving him or her guilty beyond a reasonable doubt.” Joseph N. Sorrentino, *Demystifying the Presumption of Innocence*, Glendale Law Review, 1996, vol. 15, p. 19.

③ Coffin v. United States, 156 U. S. 432. “The court noted that reasonable doubt is the result of proof, not the proof itself; whereas the presumption of innocence is one of the instruments of proof, going to bring about the proof, from which reasonable doubt arises. ”

为，可能是因为担心通过将无罪推定扩展到法庭之外来恢复其生命力将有损于对犯罪的打击。20 世纪大部分时间盛行的观点是将无罪推定简化为一种证据规则。美国 20 世纪 60 年代的联邦保释制度改革引起了无罪推定的支持者和反对者之间的激烈争论。最终，美国司法部主张无罪推定仅仅是一项证据规则，并不适用于审前程序，从而终止了这场争论。后来，美国最高法院对于无罪推定问题也产生了争论。在一份罕见的公开表达不满的意见中，瑟古德·马歇尔大法官（Justice Thurgood Marshall）批评了最高法院的意见，强调“最高法院判决认为无罪推定根本不存在”。法律史学者哈罗德·伯尔曼（Harold Berman）谴责对于无罪推定进行“不必要的限制”。一些法院也因此与贝尔诉伍尔菲什案的判决保持一定的距离。虽然对于无罪推定的内涵范围问题，英美法系国家内部存在不同的观点并产生了激烈争论，但事实是贝尔诉伍尔菲什案判决 30 年后，在美国，被告人和罪犯之间的区分令人难以置信地模糊了。英国也出现了类似的趋势。

无罪推定具有证据规则和防范过早惩罚的双重维度。然而，现代英美法系尚未在此双重维度上正式完整地认可无罪推定。① 现如今，在英美法系，无罪推定的适用范围仍旧主要局限于法庭审理，作为传统证明规则的另一种表达方式。其内涵主要包括：控诉方承担排除合理怀疑地证明有罪的责任，被控诉方不承担证明自己无罪的责任；疑罪从无，即控诉方提出的证据不足以认定被告人有罪时，应当做无罪处理；禁止强迫自证其罪，即被控诉方不得被强迫证明自己有罪，也没有义务证明自己无罪。然而，也有个别地区通过立法对此观念进行调整。例如，1997 年 7 月 1 日实施的香港特别行政区基本法第 87 条第 2 款规定：“任何人在被合法拘捕后，享有尽早接受司法机关公正审判的权利，未经司法机关判罪之前均假

① Francois Quintard-Morénas, *The Presumption of Innocence in the French and Anglo-American Legal Traditions*, 58Am. J. Comp. L. 107 (2010).

定无罪。” 2000 年，美国俄勒冈州成为美国继罗德岛后第二个承认无罪推定为防范过早惩罚保障的州。该州宪法规定：“……民主社会的一条基本宗旨是一个人在被证明有罪之前被假定为无罪且不应被惩罚。”① 与此相反，英国作出了一些影响无罪推定的变革，规定被告人的前科在一定情况下会被泄露给陪审团，虽然嫌疑犯在被正式逮捕后并不被强迫回答问题，但不提供信息现在可能会在审判中对其不利。②

三、在其他法系和国家或者地区的发展

伊斯兰法系中也存在着无罪推定的思想。伊斯兰先知穆罕默德说：“如果仅据某些人的指控就相信有人要求属于他人的人员和财务，那么指控者有义务提供积极证据。”③ 伊斯兰刑法因此将证明责任重重地扔给控诉方，并且如果没有这种证明，被告人必须被宣判无罪。关于证明标准，穆罕默德还有进一步的格言。疑罪将被按照有利于被告人的方式处理，因为穆罕默德教导：“预防在存疑的情况下进行惩罚。如果可能的话要释放被告人，因为统治者错误的宽恕要好过错误的惩罚。”④ 近代以来，信仰伊斯兰教各国的律法进行了一定的世俗化改革。例如，1971 年的《阿拉伯联合酋长国临时宪法》确认了保护权利和自由的法律原则，包括罪刑法定原

---

① *See* OR. CONST. art. XV, § 10（2）（stating that the property of a person should not be forfeited by the government prior to conviction because a “basic tenet of a democratic society is that a person is presumed innocent and should not be punished until proven guilty.”）.

② Cf. Gregory W. O′reily, *England Limits the Right to Silence and Moves towards an Inquisitorial System of Justice*, 85 J. Crim. L. & Criminology 402（1994-1995）.

③ Transmitted from Ibn Abbas by al-Bukhari, Muslim and others; see Bassiouni, 1982, p. 67. Cited by C. G. Weeramantry in Islamic Jurisprudence: An International Perspective 78（Macmillan Press, 1988）.

④ Transmitted from Ibn Abbas by al-Bukhari, Muslim and others; see Bassiouni, 1982, p. 67. Cited by C. G. Weeramantry in Islamic Jurisprudence: An International Perspective 78（Macmillan Press, 1988）.

则、无罪推定原则、禁止酷刑原则等。其他伊斯兰教国家的宪法也不同地宣布和确认了这些权利和自由。①

印度法系是公元5世纪至7世纪以前古代印度奴隶制法及以其为基础的古代缅甸、锡兰（今斯里兰卡）、暹罗（今泰国）、菲律宾等国法律的统称，是古印度法及受古印度法影响的东南亚各国法所组成的法系。该法系在历史上曾有较大影响，但随着15世纪最后一个印度化王国的灭亡而成为“死法系”。现在上述各国，包括印度在内，均已不再采用印度古代法。由于印度法系主要是以《摩奴法典》和佛教经典等宗教戒律为渊源的庞杂的体系，在内容上具有极为浓重的理想主义和幻想的色彩，其中许多法律内容并不试图在社会实际生活中发生效力，而是出于宗教理想对应然规则的预期与构想。鉴于印度法系本身的庞杂性，具体考证其是否确有无罪推定思想的内容尚存困难，但考虑到其内容的特点，基本可以认为其并不包含无罪推定的内容。当前，印度法系已成为历史名词，但在习惯中还保留有一些遗迹。②

在社会主义法系中，无罪推定精神也在法律性文献或者学术著作中得到体现。例如，南斯拉夫社会主义联盟共和国宪法第181条规定：“凡未经法院作出有法律效力的判决，任何人不得被认为犯有刑事罪。”1946年苏联最高法院全体会议决议曾指出：“被告人在他的罪过未经根据法定的程序加以证明之前，不得被认为是犯罪人。”切里佐夫在《苏维埃刑事诉讼》（1951年出版）中引用了苏联最高法院全体会议决议后指出：“苏联最高法院所提出的这一原

① 高鸿钧：《伊斯兰法：传统与现代化》，清华大学出版社2004年版，第301-302页。

② 参见百度百科“印度法系”词条，http://baike.baidu.com/view/801311.htm，最后访问时间：2016年3月16日；百度文库“世界主要法律体系　第七讲印度法系”，http://wenku.baidu.com/link? url=dr03qvomakmds29q_hzxljdzsyonqmrmiblpv-ijrbu9inmew_d11pm4nugpzlcinjnv5r5wtym6e73ksemthmihrvdx8q0wvnja72ggzss，最后访问时间：2016年3月16日；高鸿钧：《伊斯兰法：传统与现代化》，清华大学出版社2004年版，第26-27页。

理就是苏维埃刑事诉讼中无罪推定原则中的内容”（中译本第 209 页）。1958 年公布的《苏联各加盟共和国刑事诉讼纲要》第 7 条则规定：“非经法院判决，任何人不能被认定为犯罪人并受到刑事惩罚。”[①] 1977 年苏联《苏维埃社会主义共和国联盟宪法》第 160 条规定：“非经法院判决和根据法律，任何人都不能被认为是罪犯和受刑事惩罚。”[②] 1978 年苏联最高法院全体会议 6 月 16 日决议指出：“被告人（受审人）在其罪责未依法定程序被证明并被已发生法律效力的判决所确定以前，被视为无罪。”此外，苏联还不止一次地支持宣告无罪推定的国际条约。[③] 当然，对于无罪推定也有反对的声音。例如，1958 年苏联就有最高苏维埃代表公开指责无罪推定为“陈旧教条的资产阶级学说”。[④]

四、在中国的发展

（一）古代

在我国古代，除了前文所述的《尚书·夏书》、《尚书·虞书·大禹谟》和《左传》中有关于无罪推定思想的记载外，《礼记·王制》和《尚书·吕刑》中也有关于无罪推定思想的记载。《礼记·王制》云：“疑狱，汜与众共之；众疑，赦之。”《尚书·吕刑》云：“五刑之疑有赦，五罚之疑有赦，其审克之。”后世主张对疑罪作有利于被告人解释和处理的学者不少。西汉贾谊认为“诛赏之慎焉，故与其杀不辜也，宁失于有罪也。故夫罪也者，疑

① 陈光中：《应当批判地继承无罪推定原则》，载《法学研究》1980 年第 4 期，第 35 页。

② 《苏维埃社会主义共和国联盟宪法》，http：//www. cccpism. com/book/lilun/1977fa. htm ，最后访问时间：2016 年 3 月 16 日。

③ 文玮：《论无罪推定原则》，载《南华大学学报》（社会科学版）2003 年第 4 期，第 59 页。

④ Cf. Hock Lai Ho, *The Presumption of Innocence as a Human Right* in Paul Roberts and Jill Hunter（eds）, Criminal Evidence and Human Rights – Reimagining Common Law Procedural Traditions 277–8（Oxford：Hart Publishing, 2012）.

则附之去已”[①]。在文中，贾谊继续宣扬《夏书》中的疑罪处理观点，并将这一观点直接表述为罪疑从去，亦即从无，同时还强调了这一模式的慎刑价值。此外，刘向通过一则故事也表达了罪疑应当从去的观点。“梁尝有疑狱，群臣半以为当罪，虽梁王亦疑。梁王曰：‘陶之朱公以布衣富侔国，是必有奇智。’乃召朱公而问曰：‘梁有疑狱，狱吏半以为应罪，虽寡人亦疑。吾子决是，奈何？’朱公曰：‘臣，鄙民也，不知当狱。虽然，臣之家有二白璧，其色相如也，其径相如也，然其价一者千金，一者五百金。’王曰：‘径与色泽相如也，一者千金，一者五百金，何也？’朱公曰：‘侧而视之，一者厚倍，是以千金。’梁王曰：‘善！’故狱疑则从去，赏疑则从与。梁国大悦。由是观之，墙薄则亟坏，缯薄则亟毁，酒薄则亟酸。夫薄而可以旷日持久者，殆未有也。故有国、蓄民、施政教者，宜厚之可耳！”[②] 在文中，刘向除了继续主张狱疑从去的观点，还称赞施政从厚的德政，赋予罪疑从无模式新的意义。东汉班固则言“罪疑者予民”[③] 及“罪疑从轻”。[④] 晋代关于疑罪处理的例文名称是“罪疑从轻”。[⑤] 罪疑从无不只是儒家知识分子观点的表达，在制度上亦有一席之地。前述《尚书·吕刑》中的相关记载包含有疑罪处理模式的规定。其中“五刑疑各入罚”，伪孔传称“出金赎罪”。这一做法可以视为罪疑从轻。此外，《吕刑》还规定“五罚不服，正于五过”。而“正于五过”的含义，伪孔传解释为“从赦免”。据此，蒋铁初认为，《吕刑》主张的疑罪处理模式有从轻与从无两种：从轻的表现是出金赎罪；从无则是赦免。问题在于何种情况下应从轻，何种情况下应从无。对此，蒋氏认为，

---

① 贾谊：《新书》卷四，文渊阁四库全书本，卷695，上海古籍出版社2003年版，第411页。

② 刘向：《新序·杂事第四》，湖北人民出版社1986年版，第125页。

③ 《汉书·刑法志》。

④ 《汉书·于定国传》。

⑤ 《晋书·王湛传附王坦之传》。

由于《吕刑》主张五刑疑入于五罚，而五罚疑入于五过，入于五过的条件是被告人从轻人按五罚处理仍然有疑问。由此可以推断，五过的有罪可疑程度低于五罚的可疑程度。亦即有罪嫌疑程度高的，从轻处理；有罪嫌疑程度低的，从无处理。《礼记·王制》主张“疑狱，汜与众共之；众疑，赦之”。对于此处的疑罪处理模式的定性及其是作者的观点还是疑罪处理制度的问题，蒋氏认为它应是疑罪处理制度，因为这段话中无“应”或“当”等文字，作者不是说他认为疑狱应当如何处理，而是直接指出处理模式，因此是对现行或历史制度的记载。据此，蒋氏认为可以将“众疑，赦之”视为先秦时期疑罪处理制度。关于此处的“从赦”究竟是从无还是从轻的问题，蒋氏认为因为《吕刑》中关于五刑疑各入罚及五罚疑入于五过还有一段总结性的文字，即五刑之疑有赦，五罚之疑有赦，但两种“赦”的含义并不一样，刑疑之赦是入刑，即从赎，而罚疑之赦则是赦免，依此为参照，《礼记》中的“众疑，赦之”也可能有罚与赦两种情形，即在没有新资料的情况下，从无、从轻皆可。稍显不足的是，罪疑从无模式虽在理论上不乏主张者，在制度上亦有规定，但在司法实践中竟然一案难求。这种情形出现的原因一方面可能是史料散佚，另一方面也是罪疑从无的做法极少发生，这说明罪疑从无模式在司法实践中没有得到司法官员的普遍认可。[①] 无罪推定思想萌芽于我国上古时期，留存于学者的论述中，但在长达数千年的封建历史中并没有被普遍贯彻到司法实践中，令人遗憾。我国长期的封建社会刑事诉讼仍旧主要采用有罪推定模式，实行纠问式诉讼，被告人只是诉讼客体，是被拷问、逼取口供和追究罪刑的对象。[②]

---

① 蒋铁初：《中国古代的罪疑惟轻》，载《法学研究》2010 年第 2 期。

② 参见文玮：《论无罪推定原则》，载《南华大学学报》（社会科学版）2003 年第 4 期，第 60 页。

（二）近现代

1. 清末改制时期

鸦片战争后，西方列强打开了封闭已久的封建帝国的大门，开始对中国进行疯狂的掠夺。由于中国的封建法制不能满足他们攫取经济、政治利益的需要，以及中西法律在原则和制度上的冲突，尤其是中国不重视诉讼程序和被告人在刑事诉讼中的无权利、无地位状况，因此，西方列强一方面强烈要求清政府变革法制；另一方面凭此借口乘机取得了在华的"领事裁判权"，分割了中国的司法主权。[①] 在连年的对外战争中，清政府接连战败。与此同时，国内革命运动风起云涌。清政府在内忧外患的局势下，为了挽救统治危机，被迫进行了法制改革。

在清末进行的法制改革过程中，随着西方近代司法理念的传入，无罪推定的理念也开始在中国落地生根。作为无罪推定理论基础之一的被告人诉讼主体学说被引入中国。宣统三年（1912 年）熊元襄出版的《刑事诉讼法》将诉讼主体定义为："诉讼主体，乃作诉讼行为者，即裁判所及原被告，原被告即诉讼当事者。"[②] 1906 年，沈家本主持制定了《大清刑事民事诉讼法草案》（以下简称刑民诉讼法），这是中国有史以来第一部独立的诉讼法，但是由于中央和地方主政官员的阻挠和羁绊，该法典未能颁行。1910 年，又将刑事诉讼法和民事诉讼法分立，分别制成《大清刑事诉讼律草案》（以下简称刑诉律）和《大清民事诉讼律草案》，但由于辛亥革命的爆发，这两部草案还没有来得及审议和颁行，就与清王朝一起灭亡了。[③] 在清末修律大臣沈家本与伍廷芳的主持与倡导之下，刑民诉讼法和刑诉律对刑事诉讼程序进行了完整的规定，体现了很

---

① 参见张华：《无罪推定原则的历史演进》，中国人民大学 2008 年博士学位论文，第 131 页。

② 熊元襄：《刑事诉讼法》，安徽法学社 1911 年刊印，第 24 页。转引自尤志安：《清末司法改革研究》，中国人民公安大学出版社 2004 年版，第 126 页。

③ 姜田龙：《无罪推定论》，中国检察出版社 2014 年版，第 108 页。

强的时代性和先进性。特别是刑诉律第346条第1款第4项“犯罪不能证明即被告人之行为不为罪者，谕知无罪”的规定实际上在证据规则维度上规定了无罪推定原则。这是中国立法史上的一个重大进步，但是由于刑诉律从未进入中国的法律实践，其所包含的无罪推定原则自然也从未随之进入中国的法律实践。此外，刑民诉讼法与刑诉律还包含了许多以无罪推定思想为指导的规定，如禁止刑讯（刑民诉讼法第17条之“凡审讯一切案件，概不准用仗责、掌责及他项刑具或语言威吓、交逼，原告、被告及各证人偏袒供证，致令淆乱事实”；刑诉律第66条之“讯问被告人，禁用威吓及诈罔之言”）、辩护制度（刑民诉讼法第199条至第207条，刑诉律第55条至第61条）、审前羁押的限制及保释制度（刑民诉讼法第44条，第45条之“犯人无论所犯何罪，被虏之后立即送公堂审讯。自被虏至审讯之时，拘留不得逾二十四小时”，第46条之“凡人被虏，如因人证不齐或因他故不能于二十四小时内审讯，准由承审官展限至多不过七日，期满即将该犯提堂审讯。若人证尚未齐集或因有合理事故不能审讯者，准将该案再行展限。惟每次展限均不得逾七日，统计展期亦不得逾十次，尚不能审判者，公堂应将被告人取保释放”，第47条至第49条，刑诉律第100条至第118条）、证据定罪（刑诉律第326条第1款之“认定事实应依证据”）等。此外，1906年《大理院审判编制法》还规定了作为无罪推定得以实现前提的司法独立原则。该法第6条规定：“自大理院以下及本院直辖各审判厅局关于司法裁判权不受行政衙门干涉，以重国家司法独立大权，而保人民身体财产。”这是我国法律文件首次规定司法独立原则，具有重大的历史意义。①

2. 民国时期

虽然由于清政府迅速垮台，刑民诉讼法和刑诉律这两部法律草

---

① 张华：《无罪推定原则的历史演进》，中国人民大学2008年博士学位论文，第134页。

案没有得到实施，但是其所确立的无罪推定等司法精神被民国继承了下来。伍廷芳在民国初年的“姚荣泽案”[①]中更是明确地提出无罪推定原则：“外国法家有恒言曰：未经裁判所判决，指为有罪之人，皆不得谓之有罪。”[②]并在该案中极力主张贯彻无罪推定原则。[③] 1914年的李侃侵占日本邮便局包裹案[④]则是疑罪从无原则在我国司法实践中的首次运用，“淋漓尽致地展现了对清末民初刑法典精神的全面彻底实行”，“造就了正确施行新刑事诉讼程序制度的全新气象”，“在涉外强势和重大压力面前，以法抗衡，维护了当事人的合法权益，是一起令人拍案惊奇、十分扬眉吐气的经典案

---

① “姚荣泽案”发生于1911年11月。此案的被害者周实、阮式系南社社员、同盟会会友，奔走革命事业多年。二人于1911年11月14日宣布淮安脱离清朝而独立，以响应武昌起义。11月17日，二人被光复后任县司法长的姚荣泽令县团练杀害。1912年年初，根据周实、阮式家属的告发，沪军都督陈其美以“旧官僚残杀革命志士的严重事件”向孙中山电请把姚荣泽押解来上海按照军法进行审讯。此案中伍廷芳和陈其美围绕着“司法独立”、“外国律师出庭”、“审判组织”进行了激烈的争论。参见张礼恒：《从西方到东方——伍廷芳与中国近代社会的演进》，商务印书馆2002年版，第259-268页。

② 伍廷芳著，丁贤俊、喻作凤编：《伍廷芳集》，中华书局1993年版，第509页。

③ “查阅原电含有原告性质，语意之间，似坐实姚荣泽为有罪。天下岂有先坐实彼造之人为有罪，而对于此造不生危险之理？”参见伍廷芳著，丁贤俊、喻作凤编：《伍廷芳集》，中华书局1993年版，第509页。

④ 1914年，受雇于天津日本邮便局办理小包事宜的李侃因该局屡次发生小包财物被盗事件受到怀疑，被天津的日本警察署拘押讯供，并传讯李侃之父。李侃及其父均承认盗窃事实并承诺照数赔偿。后因多日未能缴纳赔偿款，日本警察署遂将李侃及相关证物移转至天津警察厅，请代为追还款项。在天津警察厅提讯李侃时，李侃翻供，称之前在日本警察署所作口供系害怕受刑讯而为，并非实情。天津警察厅在追款未得的情况下，将该案移转至天津地方检察厅向同级审判厅提起公诉，天津地方审判厅一审以侵占罪判处李侃徒刑。李侃对天津地方审判厅所作之一审有罪判决不服，上诉至直隶高等审判庭。直隶高等审判庭严格依据案件事实和逻辑推理，以日本邮便局未能提出李侃犯罪之充分证据，且拒绝配合法院调查，拒绝提交对认定案情有重要意义的邮局簿记证据，认定李侃犯罪不能证实是事实，依照诉讼法对李侃宣告无罪。参见《华洋诉讼判决录》，中国政法大学出版社2003年版，第330-333页。

例”[①]。无罪推定原则在此案中不仅发挥了保障人权的作用，而且成为抗击外辱的法律武器，产生了很大的影响。[②]

民国初期，无论是南京临时政府还是北洋政府、广州政府，要么规定法院可以直接援用刑民诉讼法和刑诉律这两部法律草案中的条文，要么以这两部法律草案为蓝本略加修改制定刑事诉讼法。例如，北洋政府于1921年11月14日公布了《刑事诉讼条例》，从1922年7月1日起在全国施行。它是在清末刑诉律的基础上制定的，也是中国正式公布施行的第一部刑事诉讼法典。《刑事诉讼条例》第338条规定：“法院认为被告之犯罪嫌疑不能证明或其行为不成犯罪者，应论之无罪判决。”这包含了证据规则维度上无罪推定的精神，是具有无罪推定原则特点的法律规范在中华大地上第一次进入施行阶段。[③]

国民政府于1928年公布实施了刑事诉讼法，并于1935年进行大幅度修正。修正后的刑事诉讼法完善了辩护（第27条至第34条）、证据（条文散布于勘验、人证、鉴定及通译各章）、羁押与具保（第101条至第121条）、疑罪从无（第293条第1款）等制度。自此，无罪推定所要求的各项制度在立法中初步建立起来。

然而，立法上所取得的成就并不意味着司法实务的洗心革面。实际上，在清末、民国时期，有罪推定观念仍牢牢地钳制着众多司法者和民众，司法实践与立法严重脱节。实践中刑讯盛行，司法擅断，冤假错案接连不断，“军统”等国民党特务组织令人闻之色变。国民党政府还在统治期间制定了《惩治盗匪暂行条例》、《反革命案件陪审暂行法》、《暂行反革命治罪法》、《共产党人自首法》、《特种刑事案件诉讼条例》、《特种刑事法庭审判条例》等单

① 郭成伟等著：《清末民初刑诉法典化研究》，中国人民公安大学出版社2006年版，第358页。

② 张华：《无罪推定原则的历史演进》，中国人民大学2008年博士学位论文，第141页。

③ 参见姜田龙：《无罪推定论》，中国检察出版社2014年版，第108-109页。

行法，公开践踏资产阶级民主和法制，为对共产党人、进步人士进行法西斯镇压披上了合法的外衣，使得国民党在镇压人民、镇压共产党员时根本不需要适用刑事诉讼法。在“宁可错杀一千，不可放过一人”的口号下，这种赤裸裸的镇压已将无罪推定破坏殆尽。①

3. 新中国成立前中国共产党领导的新民主主义革命政权时期

新中国成立前，中国共产党领导的新民主主义革命政权对无罪推定进行了积极的探索，集中体现在解放战争时期解放区的立法实践中。解放战争时期，一些解放区在立法中确立了疑罪从无原则。例如，1946 年的《冀南区诉讼简易程序试行法》第 32 条后段规定：“被告犯罪事实不能证明，或证明后不应受刑事处分者，应为无罪之判决。”② 1948 年华北人民政府作出的《关于县、市公安机关与司法机关处理刑事案件权责的规定》指出：“若被告人仅有嫌疑，没有积极的证据可以证明被告人确有犯罪时，即不能论罪判刑。”1949 年 1 月的《华北人民政府为清理已决未决犯的训令》规定：“嫌疑证据不足，又无法继续再找证据的，应登记教育释放，并通知该犯原籍的公安机关注意其行动”；“一部罪行能确定，一部罪行不能确定时，其不能确定部分应宣告无罪。”③ 1949 年 5 月颁布的《关于清理积案并研究减少积案颁发的训令》再次指出：“嫌疑不足和证据不足的，赶快进行解释和释放……”由于受历史和现实条件的限制，这些立法中有限的关于无罪推定的规定并未在司法实践中得到完全的落实，新中国成立前新民主主义革命政权的

---

① 参见程远：《无罪推定原则在我国的命运》，南京师范大学 2007 年硕士学位论文，第 8-10 页。

② 武延平等编：《刑事诉讼法学参考资料汇编》，北京大学出版社 2005 年版，第 506 页。

③ 武延平等编：《刑事诉讼法学参考资料汇编》，北京大学出版社 2005 年版，第 615-616 页。

立法和司法实践同样存在着脱节的问题。[①]

4. 中华人民共和国成立后

(1) 1949—1978 年。

新中国成立前夕，中共中央宣布彻底废除国民党政府的六法全书，包括无罪推定在内的原有一切刑事审判制度均被否定。1950 年，针对实践中出现的如何处理疑罪问题，周恩来总理曾代表中央政府签署发布过一个具有积极进步意义的政令。其内容为“有犯罪嫌疑而证据不足，且无法再寻求证据者，除反革命犯外，应分别案情，予以教育释放，或交保释放”。该政令是无罪推定在新中国历史上的一个标志性政令。[②] 然而，由于新中国成立初期法律尚不完善，刑事审判基本沿用了解放区的司法实践，其中也包含了有罪推定的做法。1952 年的全国司法改革运动清除了审判队伍中的大批“旧法人员”，然而调任充当审判员的革命干部许多缺乏基本的法律常识，[③] 更不用说具备无罪推定的法律理念。同时，全国各地掀起对“旧法观点”大批判的活动，《人民日报》发表署名文章对“司法独立”、“办案须制定和遵循一套完备的司法程序”、“司法不

---

① 事实上，中国共产党历史上的许多惨痛教训（如红军肃反、“文化大革命”等运动中发生的冤假错案）都与违背无罪推定、大搞个人专断、主观主义、刑讯逼供、轻信口供、忽视事实和证据有关（参见百度百科“红军肃反”词条，http://baike.baidu.com/item/红军肃反/3994156？fr=aladdin#reference-[2]-5147258-wrap，最后访问时间：2017 年 8 月 4 日）。以致后来毛泽东同志在延安审干时提出了“一个不杀，大部不抓”，“重证据，不轻信口供”的方针，就是对这一惨痛教训的深刻总结。有了这一原则方针，以后的历次政治运动中就不杀头了，留下了平反昭雪的余地，这不能不说是一个重大的决策（《毛泽东在苏区被架空原因：在组织路线上失人心》，http://news.ifeng.com/history/zhongguojindaishi/detail_2010_03/10/364839_0.shtml，最后访问时间：2017 年 8 月 4 日）。

② 张华：《无罪推定原则的历史演进》，中国人民大学 2008 年博士学位论文，第 144，145 页。

③ 参见陆锦碧、铁犁：《建国初期司法改革的得失》，载郭道晖等主编：《中国当代法学争鸣实录》，湖南人民出版社 1998 年版，第 19-20 页。

能搞运动”等所谓的“旧法观点”进行激烈的抨击。[①] 在这种背景下，无罪推定的发展受到一定的阻碍。

1954 年，我国第一部宪法经第一届全国人民代表大会第一次会议全票通过，标志着我国进入社会主义社会法制建设的启动阶段。1956 年，中国共产党第八次全国代表大会在京召开。会议明确提出“要逐步系统地制定完备的法律，健全社会主义法制”。董必武在中共八大的发言中也强调了健全社会主义法制的重要性，他指出：“工人阶级领导的国家必须建立健全的法制，才能更有效地发挥国家的职能和保障人民的权利。”[②] 在 1954 年宪法和中共八大社会主义法制建设的背景下，理论界开始反思新中国成立后法制建设上的种种失误，主张对无罪推定等合理的法律制度进行继承。陈光中先生发表于 1955 年第 2 期《政法研究》的《苏联的辩护制度》一文在 20 世纪 50 年代的中国学术界最早明确支持无罪推定，其本人后来也成为中国支持无罪推定时间最恒久的学者。陈光中先生的这篇文章是附带性地论述无罪推定的，它旨在回答，“有的同志说，被告人既然是犯罪者，甚至是反革命分子，给他们以辩护权，岂非有失革命立场”！陈光中先生为此很直白地宣称：“很显然，这种认识是不正确的，因为被告人虽然被控诉犯罪，但法院审理结果，可能判有罪也可能判无罪；因此，在法院判决有罪之前，还不能认为被告人已经是真正的犯罪者，而应该假定他为无罪的公民（这是刑事诉讼中无罪假定原则的要求）。”陈光中先生还说无罪假定原则是民主精神的体现。[③] 杨兆龙先生发表于 1956 年第 3 期《法学》的《法律的阶级性和继承性》一文自全国各地批判旧

① 李光灿、李剑飞：《肃清反人民的旧法观点》，载《人民日报》1952 年 8 月 22 日第 3 版。

② 陈光中、张佳华、肖沛权：《论无罪推定原则及其在中国的适用》，载《法学杂志》2013 年第 10 期，第 5 页。

③ 张成敏：《20 世纪 50 年代的无罪推定学术观点》，载《政法论丛》2010 年第 1 期，第 75-76 页。

法观点以来首次明确主张应当继承旧法中合理的内容；此外，还有刘庆林先生的《怎样对待刑事案件的被告人》一文虽然没有明确提出无罪推定原则，但通篇孕育着无罪推定的精神；[①] 等等。1957年黄道在《法学》上发表的《略论刑事诉讼中的无罪推定原则》一文成为新中国成立后发表的第一篇直接论述“无罪推定”原则的文章。[②] 黄道从证据学的角度论证了无罪推定原则在司法工作中的重要性，认为无罪推定原则有利于发现案件真实，有利于保障被告人的合法权利。文章还对当时理论界的几种错误认识，如该原则仅仅是客观真实原则的重复，保障被告人有权获得辩护原则可以代替无罪推定原则，该原则会使侦查人员和审判人员的思想产生混乱，该原则是资产阶级提出的在我们社会主义国家不能适用等做了辨明。文章同时提出了无罪推定原则引申出的三条具体诉讼规则：第一，不能以被告人对侦查人员和审判人员的态度不好，就对他们作出有罪的结论；第二，不能以被告人的沉默作为他有罪的根据，同时也无权强迫被告人陈述；第三，不能以被告人的虚伪陈述作为他有罪的根据，被告人对虚伪陈述，只要未构成诬陷罪，是不负刑事责任的。[③] 进而指出这个原则已很自然地成为批判和反对“主观臆断”的思想作风的具体途径之一，在司法人员中发生了威力，起到了指导实践的作用，从而积极地主张在我国刑事诉讼中确立无罪推定原则。[④] 1957年5月27日，杨兆龙先生在复旦大学第四次科学报告讨论会上做了题为“刑事法律科学中的无罪推定与有罪推定问题”的发言，指出：“无罪推定是社会主义民主与法治的一

---

① 程远：《无罪推定原则在我国的命运》，南京师范大学2007年硕士学位论文，第14-15页。

② 参见黄道、铁犁：《无罪推定在新中国的命运》，载《法学》1997年第7期，第2页。

③ 参见张华：《无罪推定原则的历史演进》，中国人民大学2008年博士学位论文，第146-147页。

④ 黄道：《略论刑事诉讼中的无罪推定原则》，载《法学》1957年第5期，第52页。

种保证，同时也是社会主义民主与法治的一种具体表现。”其基本含义为“民主原则、法治原则、人道主义原则、公私原则”。寄希望于用无罪推定原则实现新中国民主法治梦。[1] 黄道的《略论刑事诉讼中的无罪推定原则》和杨兆龙的《刑事法律科学中的无罪推定与有罪推定问题》这两篇文章揭开了全国范围内无罪推定大讨论的序幕。这一时期国内的政法刊物上还发表了多篇与无罪推定密切相关的文章，如曲夫的《略谈刑事诉讼中被告人的诉讼地位》，罗荣的《试论刑事诉讼中的被告人》，庄惠辰的《刑事诉讼中审判与侦查起诉的关系问题》，吴磊的《关于我国刑事诉讼中辩护人诉讼地位的研究》等。[2]

20 世纪 50 年代中国大陆地区学术界触及无罪推定论题的文章

（依据“全国报刊索引数据库”）[3]

陈光中	《苏联的辩护制度》（该文最早明确支持无罪推定）	《政法研究》1955 年第 2 期
吴磊	《驳“无罪推定论”》	《光明日报》1957 年 12 月 13 日
H. H. 波梁斯基 陈光中译	《苏维埃刑事诉讼中的无罪推定》	《教学简报》1957 年第 26 期
M. JI. 希夫曼 张保成译	《无罪推定和证明责任》	《法学》1957 年第 5 期

---

① 参见张华：《无罪推定原则的历史演进》，中国人民大学 2008 年博士学位论文，第 147 页。张成敏：《20 世纪 50 年代的无罪推定学术观点》，载《政法论丛》2010 年第 1 期，第 76 页。

② 参见程远：《无罪推定原则在我国的命运》，南京师范大学 2007 年硕士学位论文，第 14-15 页。

③ 张成敏：《20 世纪 50 年代的无罪推定学术观点》，载《政法论丛》2010 年第 1 期，第 75 页。

续表

黄道	《略论刑事诉讼中的无罪推定原则》	《法学》1957年第5期，未入报刊索引数据库
杨兆龙	《刑事法律科学中的无罪推定与有罪推定问题》	1957年5月27日在复旦大学第四次科学报告讨论会上的发言，已成文稿，当时未出版发表，但已为批判者所掌握
洁人	《什么叫“无罪推定”，为什么必须驳斥这种谬论?》	《解放日报》1958年1月15日
张子培	《驳“无罪推定论”》	《政法教学》1958年第1期
黄道	《应该彻底批判“无罪推定”的谬论——对〈略论刑事诉讼中的无罪推定原则〉一文的初步检查》	《法学》1958年第1期
张子培	《驳资产阶级的“无罪推定”原则》	《法学》1958年第1期
巫宇甦	《批判资产阶级“无罪推定”原则》	《政法研究》1958年第2期
吴耀辉	《揭穿杨兆龙的〈刑事法律科学中的无罪推定与有罪推定问题〉一文的反动本质》	《学术月刊》1958年第3期

1957年草拟的《刑事诉讼法（草案）》第5条规定：“被告人在有罪判决发生法律效力以前，应当假定为无罪的人。”这是新

中国迄今为止在立法草案中明确规定无罪推定原则的唯一草案。但可惜只是昙花一现，在其后进行的整风反右运动中，该原则被定性为“资产阶级反动原则”而遭到批判并在1963年被废除。[①] 这次整风反右运动对无罪推定作出的“结论是：无罪推定是以主观唯心主义为思想基础的，是为犯罪分子张目，应当像对其他资产阶级旧法观点一样，彻底抛弃它”。[②]

“文化大革命”期间，法律虚无主义盛行，自由被严重践踏，公检法都被砸坏，更谈不上在司法制度中确立无罪推定原则。公民本应享有的基本权利缺乏应有的保障，很多习以为常的法律理念和原则遭到了批判和诋毁，如“公民在法律面前一律平等”被指责为抹杀法的阶级性，敌我不分；如果强调依法办事就被看成是“法律至上”的资产阶级观点，也是不要党的政策和与人民作对的表现；辩护制度、律师制度被批判成为罪犯开脱的反动观点。正常的法学教育和研究活动在批判资产阶级观点、旧法观点和修正主义观点的环境中已经不可能正常运作。民法、行政法、劳动法等课程被取消，法学研究在重重的思想束缚中陷入了停滞状态。在这种情况下，无罪推定当然被认为是资产阶级腐朽反动的法律观点，是无原则地同情阶级敌人，是放纵犯罪等，是应该被加以批判和扫荡的歪理邪说。[③] 林彪、江青反革命集团在迫害广大干部群众的过程中大肆采用“办案要立足于有，着眼于是”，“一人供听，二人供信，三人供定”等有罪推定的做法，鼓吹“大棒子底下出材料”，大搞刑讯逼供、非法搜查、非法拘禁的法西斯专政，造成了大量冤、

---

① 陈光中、张佳华、肖沛权：《论无罪推定原则及其在中国的适用》，载《法学杂志》2013年第10期，第5-6页。

② 陈光中：《刑事诉讼法学五十年》，警官教育出版社1999年版，第11页。

③ 刘倩：《文革时期法律虚无主义盛行的表现及根源》，载《新余高专学报》2007年第1期，第43页。转引自姜田龙：《无罪推定论》，中国检察出版社2014年版，第112页。

假、错案，对人权的践踏到了无以复加的地步。[①] 特别是“四人帮”横行时期，封建法西斯专政和有罪推定的做法被进一步强化，不少人一被点名，便成罪人，刑讯逼供，锻炼成狱，致使冤、假、错案遍于国中。[②] 新中国成立以后“反右”扩大化和“文化大革命”可以说将有罪推定发挥到了极致，以致出身、宗教信仰、个人历史、言论等都可能被作为有罪的根据，私刑滥用。[③]

（2）1979 年刑事诉讼法颁布实施时期。

“文化大革命”结束后，我国开始了法制重建的历程。在“解放思想、实事求是”方针的指导下，在刑事诉讼法领域，时隔 20 年后，无罪推定的问题被重新提出，并引起国内学者纷纷对其重新进行反思和探讨。1979 年，《人民日报》发表了题为《一个值得研究的问题》的文章，指出可以将无罪推定原则规定在正在起草的刑事诉讼法中，或者至少应当汲取它的精神和某些内容。[④] 其后，《西南政法学院学报》和复刊后的《法学研究》也纷纷发表论文，表达不同的观点。由于观念上存在分歧，无罪推定原则未能被 1979 年 7 月 1 日通过、1980 年 1 月 1 日施行的新中国第一部刑事诉讼法典采纳。然而，该法颁布后，学术界对无罪推定的争论更加激烈，演变为新中国成立后对于无罪推定问题的第二次大讨论。这次大讨论主要集中于三个问题：第一，关于无罪推定的表述问题。多数学者认可法国《人权宣言》对无罪推定的表述，即“所有人在被宣布为有罪之前即被假定为无罪”。但也有学者认为无罪推定还有其他两种表述，即“在没有作出有罪判决以前，任何人都不

---

① 张华：《无罪推定原则的历史演进》，中国人民大学 2008 年博士学位论文，第 149 页。

② 参见陈光中：《应当批判地继承无罪推定原则》，载《法学研究》1980 年第 4 期，第 34 页。

③ 张华：《无罪推定原则的历史演进》，中国人民大学 2008 年博士学位论文，第 149 页。

④ 田采：《一个值得研究的问题》，载《人民日报》1979 年 2 月 17 日。

能被认为是罪犯”，“被告人未经依法确定有罪以前，应假定其无罪”。第二，关于无罪推定是否适用于我国刑事诉讼的问题。针对这一问题，学界形成了三个阵营：否定派、肯定派和折中派。否定派“认为我国刑事诉讼中不宜采用无罪推定原则，理由是：以无罪的先入为主来防止有罪的先入为主，同样是唯心主义的，与‘以事实为依据，以法律为准绳’的原则相违背，并与依法逮捕、起诉、审判被告人等诉讼行为相矛盾；引入无罪推定原则，可能导致放纵犯罪；我国法律对被告人权利保护作了具体规定，无须借助于无罪推定来保障被告人的权利；存在冤假错案的原因很多，绝非无罪推定原则所能防止”。① 否定派的代表性作品有晓华发表于《法学研究》1980 年第 1 期的《“无罪推定”原则与我国刑事诉讼实践格格不入》，于志发表于《民主与法制》1980 年第 3 期的《无罪推定不能作刑事诉讼的指导思想》，张子培发表于《法学研究》1980 年第 3 期的《“无罪推定”原则剖析》。肯定派“认为我国应当确立或已经采用了无罪推定原则。理由是：无罪推定的核心是指控的犯罪必须得到证明，否则不得以有罪论处或久押不决，它可促使司法人员深入调查，全面收集证据，防止先入为主、刑讯逼供，有助于保护无辜，准确地惩罚犯罪；无罪推定并非无罪认定，与对被告人实施逮捕、起诉、审判等诉讼行为并不矛盾；无罪推定是保证实现客观真实原则的手段，是实事求是的必要补充，是维护权利的思想基础，与实事求是和‘以事实为依据，以法律为准绳’的原则并不矛盾；只有确立无罪推定才能否定有罪推定，两者之间非此即彼，那种既反对有罪推定，又反对无罪推定的主张，在逻辑上说不通，在实践上也是有害的”②。肯定派的代表性作品有赵虹、窦继样发表于《法学研究》1979 年第 3 期的《对“无罪推定”原则的理解》，蓝全普发表于《民主与法制》1979 年第 4 期的《无

① 陈光中：《刑事诉讼法学五十年》，警官教育出版社 1999 年版，第 24–25 页。
② 陈光中：《刑事诉讼法学五十年》，警官教育出版社 1999 年版，第 24–25 页。

罪推定原则有利于正确执行刑事诉讼法》，宁汉林发表于《中国社会科学》1982 年第 4 期的《论无罪推定》，王秉新、赵虹发表于《未定稿》1983 年第 21 期的《论无罪推定中的几个问题》。折中派“在吸收、继承无罪推定原则合理成分的同时，主张摈弃其中的糟粕：一是认为无罪推定原则的传统表述不准确，容易导致逻辑上的混乱，既然推定无罪，为什么还要对其实施逮捕、起诉呢？主张采用否定式的表述方式，即‘任何人在被法院宣判有罪之前，不能被认为是罪犯’，但也不认为其是无罪的。二是认为无罪推定原则要求控方承担举证责任，从而推导出被告人不应承担如实供述的义务不合理，容易导致放纵罪犯，被告人在享有诉讼权利的同时理应承担相应的诉讼义务”①。折中派的代表性作品有陈光中发表于《法学研究》1980 年第 4 期的《应当批判地继承无罪推定原则》，林欣发表于《中国社会科学》1983 年第 3 期的《“无罪推定”还是“无罪假定”?》。遗憾的是，官方当时始终支持否定无罪推定的观点，并对无罪推定进行了点名批评。第三，关于疑案处理的问题。对于这一问题，学界也提出了三种主张：多数学者主张应做无罪处理；少数学者主张“疑罪从轻”；另有一部分学者主张采取撤销案件或者终止诉讼的方式。

1983 年至 1984 年，随着“严打”斗争的开始，全国又发起了反对精神污染和自由化的运动，将无罪推定当作资产阶级自由化的精神污染进行批判。个别学者也出来著文批判。关于无罪推定问题

① 张华：《无罪推定原则的历史演进》，中国人民大学 2008 年博士学位论文，第 150-151 页。

的讨论再次陷入低潮。[①]

虽然1979年刑事诉讼法未能采纳无罪推定原则，但是，这次新中国成立后对于无罪推定问题的第二次大讨论“仍然具有相当的积极意义：一是学者对无罪推定原则的具体内容、相关保障和实践问题有了更深入的了解；二是这些讨论也进一步影响到立法机关对无罪推定的理解和立场，为未来的立法采纳奠定了理论基础；三是实务部门，尤其是从事刑事辩护工作的律师团体在刑事诉讼实践中的相关经验和教训得以学理化和系统化。这些均为1996年修正刑事诉讼法工作提供了宝贵的资料和借鉴”[②]。

（3）1996年第一次修正刑事诉讼法前后。

1996年刑事诉讼法修正之前，我国刑事诉讼法学界又出现了对于无罪推定问题的第三次大讨论。由于改革开放逐步深入，特别是1992年邓小平同志南方谈话之后，人们的思想观念逐步解放，中国法学研究的学术氛围越来越宽松，这次讨论相对于前两次讨论已经不再政治化，而主要局限于学术范围内。在这次讨论中，大多数学者对无罪推定原则持肯定态度。最终在1996年刑事诉讼法第12条规定：“未经人民法院依法判决，对任何人都不得确定有罪。”然而，这一规定并没有终止我国法学界对于无罪推定问题的讨论。这条法律条文的文字表述使法学工作者对无罪推定原则的讨论从纯粹的理论争论与探讨上升到对法律规范的理解与阐释，也就是说，1979年刑事诉讼法没有确立无罪推定原则这一结论无可置疑和辩

① 参见《王汉斌答新华社记者问——就有关审判林江反革命集团案的几个法律问题》，载《人民日报》1980年12月12日。“按照《刑事诉讼法》的规定，我国的诉讼程序不是‘无罪推定’，也不是‘有罪推定’。而是以事实为根据，以法律为准绳。”《加强社会主义法制的有力措施——刘复之同志答（法律与生活）记者问》，载《中国法制报》1984年1月20日。“在所谓‘社会主义异化论’和资产阶级人道主义思想的影响下，有的人不积极宣传我国社会主义法制的原则，如‘以事实为根据，以法律为准绳’……而是宣言杀人有理、犯罪有理、无罪推定、有利被告等谬论，造成某些思想混乱。”

② 姜田龙：《无罪推定论》，中国检察出版社2014年版，第114页。

驳，而1996年修正后的刑事诉讼法关于这一问题的答案却难以让学者很快得出清晰的结论。[①] 这一方面是由于1996年修正后的刑事诉讼法第12条的规定与《公民权利和政治权利国际公约》中无罪推定原则的部分内容相契合；另一方面是由于该条表述并非国际惯用的无罪推定原则的规范表述，且立法者在立法时的初衷并非通过该条规定在我国正式确立无罪推定原则，而仅仅是肯定人民法院的唯一定罪权。这一点从参与刑事诉讼法修改工作的陈光中教授的表述和全国人大法工委主任顾昂然在向全国人大所做的《关于〈中华人民共和国刑事诉讼法修正案（草案）〉的说明》（以下简称《说明》）以及全国人大常委会法制工作委员会刑法室编著的《中华人民共和国刑事诉讼法释义》（以下简称《释义》）对第12条的解释中可以得到证实。陈光中教授认为1996年修正后的刑事诉讼法并没有完全确立无罪推定，只是采纳了无罪推定的部分内容，并明确指出第12条与《公民权利和政治权利国际公约》第14条第2款规定的无罪推定原则不具有等同性，恰恰相反，1996年修正后的刑事诉讼法具有另外的含义，第12条的规定未采用国际公约的表述就是为了防止带来无罪推定原则的争议。[②] 陈光中教授将之归纳为三点："1. 任何人在被法院判决有罪之前，不能被认为是罪犯；2. 不能证明被告人有罪，就应推定其为无罪；3.（以及）对疑难的情况，应作有利于被告人的解释。……对无罪推定原则，应批判继承，既不能全部搬用，也不应一概否定。"[③]《说明》以"不经人民法院判决不得定罪"概括了第12条及相关部分的内容，突出了人民法院的定罪权，而没有提及无罪推定。《释义》解释第12条时称："我们反对有罪推定，但也不是西方国家的那种无罪推定，而是实事求是地进行侦查，客观地收集有罪或无罪、罪轻或罪

---

① 姜田龙：《无罪推定论》，中国检察出版社2014年版，第115页。

② Chen Jianfu, Chinese Law: Context and Transformation 312 (Martinus Nihoff Publishers, 2008).

③ 陈光中：《中国刑事诉讼法学40年（下）》，载《政法论坛》1989年第5期。

重的各种证据，在人民法院作出有罪判决以前，我们不称被告人为罪犯，但也不说他没有罪或假定他无罪，如果假定他无罪，那么侦查机关对他进行侦查、采取强制措施就没有根据了。”①

（4）第二次修正刑事诉讼法过程中的讨论及后续发展。

虽然1996年刑事诉讼法第12条的规定体现了无罪推定的精神内核，但是，该条规定并未能全面准确地体现出无罪推定的内涵。随着经济、社会的发展及人权和法治观念的提升，学者对无罪推定原则立法化的呼声越来越高。陈光中教授主持的《中华人民共和国刑事诉讼法——再修改专家建议稿与论证》第10条规定了两款内容，其中第1款规定：“在人民法院依法作出生效裁判确定有罪以前，任何人应当被推定为无罪”，第2款规定：“不能认定犯罪嫌疑人、被告人有罪或无罪的，按无罪处理；不能认定犯罪嫌疑人、被告人罪重或罪轻的，按罪轻处理。”② 陈卫东教授主持的《模范刑事诉讼法典》（第二版）第4条规定了“无罪推定原则”，该条规定：“任何受到追诉的人，在被人民法院依法最终判决有罪之前，推定其无罪。”③ 另外，其他相关论著也主张将无罪推定原则载入刑事诉讼法典。④ 通过搜索“中国知网”，2005年至2012年“篇名”包含“无罪推定”的文献达518篇。其中，绝大部分主张无罪推定原则应当立法化。2012年修正的刑事诉讼法进一步贯彻和彰显了无罪推定原则和精神，但是，仍然没有正式确立无罪推定原则。该法颁布后，学术界继续保持对无罪推定立法化的热情。“中国知网”的搜索结果显示，2012年以来⑤“篇名”包含“无罪

① 胡康生、李福成主编：《中华人民共和国刑事诉讼法释义》，法律出版社1996年版，第15页。

② 参见陈光中主编：《中华人民共和国刑事诉讼法——再修改专家建议稿与论证》，中国法制出版社2006年版，第4页。

③ 陈卫东主编：《模范刑事诉讼法典》（第二版），中国人民大学出版社2011年版。

④ 例如，陈瑞华、田文昌：《〈中华人民共和国刑事诉讼法〉再修改律师建议稿与论证》，法律出版社2007年版。

⑤ 截至2017年11月18日。

推定”的文献达130篇，“主题”涉及“无罪推定”的文献更是超过了2400篇。党的十八大以来，以习近平同志为总书记的党中央高度重视司法体制改革，将依法治国提到了一个新的高度。2014年10月23日，中国共产党第十八届中央委员会第四次全体会议通过了《关于全面推进依法治国若干重大问题的决定》，明确提出要“加强人权司法保障”，“健全落实疑罪从无、非法证据排除等法律原则的法律制度。完善对限制人身自由司法措施和侦查手段的司法监督，加强对刑讯逼供和非法取证的源头预防，健全冤假错案有效防范、及时纠正机制”。对无罪推定精神在中国的彰显起到了一定的推动作用。2016年6月27日，中央全面深化改革领导小组第二十五次会议通过了《关于推进以审判为中心的刑事诉讼制度改革的意见》(以下简称《意见》)，最高人民法院、最高人民检察院、公安部、国家安全部、司法部于2016年7月20日印发了关于《意见》的通知（法发〔2016〕18号)。《意见》重申了刑事诉讼法第12条的规定，要求认定犯罪事实要坚持证据裁判原则，要求完善讯问制度，防止刑讯逼供，不得强迫任何人证实自己有罪，明确要求“证据不足，不能认定被告人有罪的，应当按照疑罪从无原则，依法作出无罪判决”。① 2017年2月17日，最高人民法院发布了《关于全面推进以审判为中心的刑事诉讼制度改革的实施意见》(以下简称《实施意见》)（法发〔2017〕5号)。《实施意见》明确要求“坚持证据裁判原则”，“坚持非法证据排除原则，不得强迫任何人证实自己有罪”，“坚持疑罪从无原则，认定被告人有罪，必须达到犯罪事实清楚，证据确实、充分的证明标准。不得因舆论炒作、上访闹访等压力作出违反法律的裁判”，“人民法院作出有罪判决，对于定罪事实应当综合全案证据排除合理怀疑”，“定罪

① 《深改丨两高三部：关于推进以审判为中心的刑事诉讼制度改革的意见》，http://dy.163.com/v2/article/t1397720048954/btg4ae580521007n，最后访问时间：2017年11月19日。

证据确实、充分，量刑证据存疑的，应当作出有利于被告人的认定”，“坚持程序公正原则”。① 这些司法改革的成果进一步彰显了无罪推定精神，为在法律中正式规定无罪推定原则奠定了良好的基础。2018 年，我国对刑事诉讼法进行了第三次修正，但是仍然没有正式确立无罪推定原则。

（5）对新中国成立后无罪推定在中国发展过程中遇到挫折的简评。

虽然无罪推定思想广泛起源于世界各古老的法系，无罪推定格言起源于 13 世纪晚期和 14 世纪早期的欧洲大陆，由法国教会法学家约翰内斯·莫纳克斯（Johannes Monachus）首先提出，但是其得到大力宣扬和推广则是在 1764 年意大利法学家贝卡利亚出版《论犯罪与刑罚》以及 1789 年法国颁布《人权宣言》之后，也就是欧洲思想启蒙运动之后。前者为无罪推定得到大力宣扬和推广提供了思想理论上的基础，后者为无罪推定得到大力宣扬和推广提供了立法上的借鉴。无罪推定是随着资产阶级革命和文化潮流的兴起而广泛传播的，是资产阶级在反对封建专制主义的过程中提出的法制上的要求。因此，新中国成立后一段时期将其视为资产阶级思想是有一定原因也是可以理解的。

实行无罪推定有时会导致错放有罪，会使得无罪推定看起来像是保护真正罪犯的工具。特别是在以阶级斗争为纲的新成立尚未成熟的社会主义国家中，无罪推定有时会成为保护真正罪犯（阶级敌人——资产阶级等反动势力残余或者走资派）的工具这一点与当时阶级斗争的要求相悖，因此会被强烈地斥责为“资产阶级反动原则”、“精神污染”和“资产阶级自由化”② 的腐朽思想。然

---

① 《最高人民法院关于全面推进以审判为中心的刑事诉讼制度改革的实施意见》，http://www.court.gov.cn/zixun-xiangqing-36422.html，最后访问时间：2017 年 11 月 19 日。

② 参见程远：《无罪推定原则在我国的命运》，南京师范大学 2007 年硕士学位论文，第 15、17、20 页。

而，虽然无罪推定有时会导致释放真正的阶级敌人，不利于阶级斗争，但这也不是仅在社会主义国家中才会出现的问题，在任何国家和社会制度中，只要彻底贯彻无罪推定，都难以绝对避免不错放有罪。这是由无罪推定的内在法律认识和运行机理决定的，并非由于其带有某种阶级属性，也就是说，在实行无罪推定的条件下出现错放有罪的原因是一个法律问题而不是政治问题。正因为如此，新中国成立后相当一段时期以无罪推定不利于打击革命对象为由将无罪推定归属为政治问题是认识不清和盲目的表现，阻碍了我国法治和社会的进步。

无论实施什么政治主张，无论这种政治主张多么正义，都需要通过公正的程序来实现——这是中国历史的基本教训。无罪推定是程序正义的要求。公正的程序是正义的政治主张得以实现的保障。无论实施什么政治主张，采用类似“文化大革命”的方法肯定是不对的，无论这种政治主张多么正义。没有法治，没有公正的程序，再正义的目的也无法保证实现，还可能附带出严重的恶。交流非常重要，各方都要有交流的态度。任何一方企图以势压人，而不是以理服人都有可能造成结果的不正义。如何使各方都有交流的态度，并且能够交流好，则成了一个大问题。“文化大革命”的方法确实有效，也确实高效，但更适于战争时期，而不适于和平时期。正如“战时共产主义”政策在战争时期起到了积极的作用，但到了和平建设时期，却带来了很大的弊端。因为战争时期形势瞬息万变，时间就是生命，时间就是胜利，不可能有太多的时间去纠结于每一个细节，因此效率至上。而在和平时期，人们相对更加看重公正的价值。虽然“迟来的正义非正义”，但是“迟来的正义”也总要好于“早到的非正义”。

虽然无罪推定先由资产阶级明确提出和广泛宣传，但是其在当时反对封建专制主义的斗争中具有积极进步的意义，并且其并非资产阶级的专利，也可以被用来为广大人民和社会主义服务，保护好每个人的人权。因此，对于无罪推定，不应因资产阶级主张过就上纲上线，而应理性分析，实事求是，以社会主义理论对其进行重新诠释，使其为社会主义服务，为广大人民群众服务。

五、在国际法上的认可

第二次世界大战后，基于对战争中法西斯暴行的反思，世界各国人民开始积极探索切实保障人权、防止再次出现人道主义灾难的有效机制。为此，以维护世界和平、促进世界发展为己任的联合国应运而生。联合国在成立后，与其所属机构一起推动制定了一系列旨在保障人权的国际文件，形成了国际人权法律体系。无罪推定被载入这些国际人权法律文件，成为一项重要的国际刑事司法准则。在联合国人权法律体系中，处于基础性地位的是《世界人权宣言》。《世界人权宣言》是联合国大会于1948年12月10日通过的一份旨在维护人类基本权利的文献。[①] 其首次在联合国文件中确认了无罪推定的权利，为在国际社会推广这一权利提供了法律依据。《世界人权宣言》第11条规定，凡受刑事控告者，在未经获得辩护上所需的一切保证的公开审判而依法证实有罪以前，有权被视为无罪。虽然《世界人权宣言》并非强制性的国际公约，但由于其是由联合国大会通过且实际上是之后两份具有法律强制性的联合国人权公约——《公民权利和政治权利国际公约》和《经济、社会及文化权利国际公约》——的法律基础，因此许多学者、律师和法庭依然经常引述《世界人权宣言》中的相关条款来证明自己立场的正当性。然而，《世界人权宣言》与公约、条约等正式国际法律文件相比还是缺乏直接强制力，只能“作为所有人民和所有国家努力实现的共同标准，以期每一个人和社会机构经常铭念本宣言，努力通过教诲和教育促进对权利和自由的尊重”，还需要“通过国家的和国际的渐进措施，使这些权利和自由在各会员国本身人

① 联合国大会第217号决议，A/RES/217。

民及在其管辖下领土的人民中得到普遍和有效的承认和遵行”。[①]在这些渐进措施中，最重要的方式是制定国际公约，以法律强制力保障包括无罪推定在内的所有《世界人权宣言》倡导的人权标准能得到成员国的切实执行。为此，1952 年联合国大会第 375 次全体会议作出了“拟具人权盟约草案”的决议，要求人权委员会起草两个人权公约，以备大会第七届会议审议。“该二盟约，一载列公民、政治权利，一载列经济、社会、文化权利，以便大会同时核准，同时备各国签署。”[②] 1966 年 12 月 16 日，联合国大会以第 2200A（XXI）号决议通过了《公民权利和政治权利国际公约》并开放给各国签字、批准和加入。按照该公约第 49 条的规定，该公约已于 1976 年 3 月 23 日生效。该公约对公正司法的国际标准进行了详细列举，再次确认了《世界人权宣言》所倡导保护的无罪推定权利。该公约第 14 条第 2 款规定：“凡受刑事控告者，在未依法证实有罪之前，应有权被视为无罪。”自此，无罪推定不仅在宣言性的国际文件中得到认可，也得到正式国际公约的正式确认，成为国际公约的正式内容。同时，无罪推定也作为所有人类家庭成员应当享有的一项公民权利和政治权利，成为该公约各缔约国国内刑事司法所必须遵守和采取必要措施加以尊重和保障的一项重要人权标准。迄今，《公民权利和政治权利国际公约》的成员国和已经批准实施的国家覆盖了全世界绝大部分国家，成为世界上绝大多数国家共同认可和遵守的国际法律规范。中国于 1998 年 10 月 5 日签署了该公约，但至今没有批准实施。中国各地社会精英多年来一直在多种场合下进行呼吁，要求人大尽快批准实施该公约，以促进我国刑事司法改革和刑事司法文明进步。2016 年全国“两会”前，又有数百名精英“上书”“两会”，其中律师、法学家等司法界专业人士占有比例较高。他们提出六条要求，其中第一条就是批准履行联合国

① 参见《世界人权宣言》序言部分。

② 决议号：A/RES/543（VI）。

《公民权利和政治权利国际公约》。①

1998 年 7 月 17 日，联合国设立国际刑事法院全权代表外交会议通过了以保护国际人权，打击国际犯罪为宗旨的《国际刑事法院罗马规约》（*Rome Statute of the International Criminal Court*）（以下简称《规约》）。《规约》作为《联合国宪章》的重要组成部分于 2002 年 7 月 1 日生效。《规约》第 66 条专门就无罪推定问题进行了规定："（一）任何人在本法院被依照适用的法律证明有罪以前，应推定无罪。（二）证明被告人有罪是检察官的责任。（三）判定被告人有罪，本法院必须确信被告人有罪已无合理疑问。"同时，为保障无罪推定得到贯彻落实，《规约》还在第 67 条"被告人的权利"第 1 项对相关配套权利作了专门规定："在确定任何指控时，被告人有权获得符合本规约各项规定的公开审讯，获得公正进行的公平审讯，及在人人平等的基础上获得下列最低限度的保证：……7. 不被强迫作证或认罪，保持沉默，而且这种沉默不作为判定有罪或无罪的考虑因素；8. 作出未经宣誓的口头或书面陈述为自己辩护；和 9. 不承担任何反置的举证责任或任何反驳责任。"

1955 年，第一届联合国"防止犯罪和罪犯待遇大会"在日内瓦举行，大会通过了《囚犯待遇最低限度标准规则》。该规则第 84 条第 2 款规定："未经判罪的囚犯视同无罪，并应受到如此待遇。"此外，联合国防止犯罪和罪犯待遇大会先后通过的《关于司法机关独立的基本原则》、《关于检察官作用的准则》、《关于律师作用的基本原则》等都明确认可了《世界人权宣言》第 11 条所宣示的无罪推定原则，并将其作为基本指导原则，要求各国考虑和遵守。1988 年，联合国第 76 次全体会议核准了《保护所有遭受任何形式

① 《人大代表呼吁批准实施〈公民权利和政治权利国际公约〉》，http://www.mala.cn/thread-13378056-1-8.html，最后访问时间：2016 年 3 月 17 日。

拘留或监禁的人的原则》。[①] 原则 36-1 规定："涉嫌或被控犯有刑事罪行的被拘留人，在获得辩护上一切必要保证的公开审判中依法确定有罪之前应被视为无罪。"

在对涉及刑事司法的未成年人权利保护方面，1989 年 11 月 20 日第 44 届联合国大会第 25 号决议通过了《儿童权利公约》（*Convention on the Rights of the Child*）。该公约于 1990 年 9 月 2 日生效。该公约第 40 条第 2 款规定："为此目的，并鉴于国际文书的有关规定，缔约国尤应确保：（a）任何儿童不得以行为或不行为之时本国法律或国际法不禁止的行为或不行为之理由被指称、指控或认为触犯刑法；（b）所有被指称或指控触犯刑法的儿童至少应得到下列保证：（一）在依法判定有罪之前应视为无罪……" 此外，联合国还在其他未成年人司法国际准则中特别强调无罪推定问题。1985 年，联合国第 96 次全体会议决定在第 41 届会议临时议程中列入"预防犯罪和刑事司法" 项目[②]，同时制定通过了《联合国少年司法最低限度标准规则》（《北京规则》）[③]。《北京规则》第 7.1 条规定："在诉讼的各个阶段，应保证基本程序方面的保障措施，诸如假定无罪指控罪状通知本人的权利、保持沉默的权利、请律师的权利，要求父亲或母亲或监护人在场的权利、与证人对质的权利和向上级机关上诉的权利。" 1990 年通过的《联合国保护被剥夺自由少年规则》[④] 第 17 条规定："被逮捕扣押的少年或待审讯（"未审讯"）的少年应假定是无罪的，并当作无罪者对待……"[⑤] 再次重申了无罪推定原则。此外，无罪推定也是联合国一些国际刑事法庭的重要审判原则。比如，《前南斯拉夫问题国际刑事法庭规约》第 21 条第 3 款，卢旺达问题国际刑事法庭规约第 20 条第 3 款都明确

① 决议号：A/RES/43/173。

② 决议号：A/RES/40/32。

③ 决议号：A/RES/40/33。

④ 决议号：A/RES/45/113。

⑤ 决议号：A/RES/45/113。

规定："在根据此规约条款被证实有罪之前，被告人应当被推定为无罪。"

除了联合国关于人权保障和刑事司法准则的文件规定和认可了无罪推定以外，一些地区性的关于人权保障和刑事司法准则的国际文件也规定和认可了无罪推定。例如，1950 年 11 月 4 日在欧洲委员会（The Council of Europe）的主持下，《欧洲人权公约》（*European Convention on Human Rights*，*ECHR*）（全名为《欧洲保障人权和基本自由公约》（*Convention for the Protection of Human Rights and Fundamental Freedoms*））得以签署，并于 1953 年 9 月 3 日正式生效。该公约第 6 条第 2 款规定："凡受刑事罪指控者，在未经依法证明为有罪之前，应当推定为无罪。"为了保障无罪推定得以切实落实，《欧洲人权公约》还在第 2 条至第 6 条详细规定了相应的保障措施，主要包括如下几个方面：（1）非经法院依法定罪并执行，不得故意剥夺任何人的生命；（2）禁止对任何人施以酷刑或者使其受到非人道的或者侮辱的待遇或者惩罚；（3）未经法定程序，不得使任何人从事强制或者强迫劳动；（4）除非有合理怀疑，并经合法逮捕或监禁，不得限制任何人的人身自由；（5）已经被逮捕或监禁者，享有被立即带至法官处，并在合理期限内获得审查、保释，以及提请解除监禁的权利；（6）在刑事诉讼中有权获得公正审判；（7）被指控者有权自我辩护或由律师帮助辩护，符合条件者有权获得法律援助，应给予充分的时间和条件准备辩护；等等。经 2009 年 12 月 1 日正式生效的《里斯本条约》（*Treaty of Lisbon*）修订的《欧洲联盟条约》（*Treaty on European Union*，TEU）第 1 章"一般规定"F 条第 2 款规定："联盟必须将尊重《欧洲保障人权和基本自由公约》所保护的基本权利作为共同体法律的基本原则，因为这些权利源自成员国共同的宪法传统。"从而间接认可了无罪推定。同时，《欧盟基本权利宪章》第 48 条还专门规定了"无罪推定和被告人的权利"，根据该规定，"在依法被证实有罪之前，任何被指控者都应被推定为无罪；任何被指控者的辩护权都应当得到尊重和保护。”

1948年5月2日美洲国家第九次国际会议通过的《美洲人的权利和义务宣言》（*American Declaration of the Rights and Duties of Man*）在第26条“正当法律程序权利”（Right to due process of law）中规定：“在被证明有罪之前，所有被指控者都被推定为无罪。所有被指控者都有权获得公正、公开的听证，并有权获得已经依现行法成立的法庭审判，并且不得受到残忍的、不名誉的或者非常规的惩罚。”可见，该宣言将无罪推定视为正当法律程序权利的一部分，将其作为正当法律程序权利予以保护。1969年，美洲国家组织特别人权会议通过的《美洲人权公约》（*American Convention on Human Rights*）最后文本第8条第2款规定：“被指控犯有罪行的每一个人，只要未依法证实有罪，有权被认为无罪。”同时，规定了保证无罪推定得以真正落实的条款：“在诉讼的过程中，人人都有权完全平等地享有下列最低限度的保证：（1）如果被告人不懂或者不会说法庭或者法院所使用的语言，他有权无偿地接受一位翻译或者口译的帮助；（2）将对被告人的指控事先详细地通知他；（3）为准备辩护所需要的适当的时间和手段；（4）被告人有权亲自为自己辩护或者由他自己挑选的律师来协助，并自由地和私下与律师联系；（5）如果被告人不亲自为自己辩护或者在法律规定的时间内未聘请自己的律师，他有不可剥夺的受到国家所指派的律师帮助的权利，并按照国内法律规定自付费用或者不负担费用；（6）被告人一方有权查询在法院出庭的证人，并有权请专家或者其他能说明事实真相的人出庭作为证人；（7）有权不得被迫作不利于自己的证明，或者被迫服罪；（8）有权向更高一级的法院提起上诉。”

1986年10月生效的《非洲人权和民族权利宪章》（*African Charter on Human and Peoples' Rights*）第7条第1款规定：“人人享有对其诉讼案件要求听审的权利。此项权利包括：（1）对侵犯由公约、法律、法规和习惯有效地确认和保障的权利的行为，有权向有管辖权的国家机关起诉；（2）在由有管辖权的法院或法庭证实有罪之前，有权被视为无罪；（3）有权为自己辩护，包括请由自己选择的律师辩护；（4）有权要求公平无私的法院或法庭在一个适当的时间内予以审判。”

1990 年《开罗伊斯兰世界人权宣言》（*Cairo Declaration on Human Rights in Islam*）第 19 条规定：“1. 所有个人在法律面前一律平等，没有统治者与被统治者之间的区别；2. 人人诉诸司法审判的权利受到保障；3. 责任在本质上是个人性质的；4. 除伊斯兰教法规定的以外，不应有犯罪或刑罚；5. 被告人在未经公正审判证实有罪之前，是无罪的，在公正审判中，应给予被告人一切辩护保证。”

1993 年 9 月 20 日至 25 日东南亚国家联盟（简称东盟）议会组织通过了《吉隆坡人权宣言》（*Kuala Lumpur Declaration on Human Rights*），该宣言第 14 条规定：“在被依法证实有罪之前，每一个受到刑事指控者都有权被推定为无罪。”（Everyone charged with a criminal offence has the right to be presumed innocent until proven otherwise according to law.）2005 年，在泰国帕塔举行的亚洲议会和平协会第六届年会通过了《亚洲国家人权宪章》（*Asian Human Rights Charter*），该宪章第 3. 7 条规定了死刑案件中的被告人应当享有无罪推定权。2004 年 5 月 22 日，阿拉伯国家联盟理事会（Council of the League of Arab States）通过了新版《阿拉伯人权宪章》（*Arab Charter on Human Rights*）。该宪章于 2008 年 3 月 15 日生效。该宪章第 16 条明确规定：“在依据法律作出最终判决有罪之前，每个受刑事指控者都应当被推定为无罪。”为了实现这一权利，“在侦查与审判过程中，受指控者应当享受如下最低限度的保障：（1）以其能理解之语言被及时、详细告知所受指控的权利；（2）有充分的时间和便利条件准备辩护，并允许与家人联络；（3）在普通法院受审，有权自我辩护或通过其选定的，可自由、秘密交流的律师代为辩护；（4）如果无法自我辩护或为司法利益之要求，有权获得律师的免费帮助，如果无法理解法庭语言，有权获得免费翻译；（5）有权自己或经由其律师与控方证人对质，有权根据控方证人的情况进行辩护；（6）有权不被强迫自证其罪或认罪；（7）如果被判有罪，有权依法向高级别法庭提出上诉；（8）在任何情况下，其人身安全和隐私都应当得到尊重。”

当前，世界各国和地区都普遍在其刑事诉讼法或者宪法性文件中规定了无罪推定原则，许多国际人权公约也对此予以规定，[①] 无罪推定已成为一项世界普遍认可的基本刑事司法准则。

---

① 根据谢里夫·巴西奥尼的考证，截至1993年，已有至少5个国际公约和67个宪法性文件规定了无罪推定原则。See M. Cherif Bassiouni, *Human Rights in the Context of Criminal Justice: Identifying International Procedural Protections and Equivalent Protections in National Constitutions*, 3 Duke Journal of Comparative and International Law 235, 266-267 (1993).

第二章　无罪推定的内涵

第一节　"无罪推定"还是"无罪假定"——无罪推定的措辞辨析

作为本书的基础概念，"无罪推定"的表述其实存在着一定争议。有人认为，如果从其本义来讲，似乎"无罪假定"的表述更准确。[①] 中国过去的学术和法律等文献在涉及"无罪推定"的概念时也曾使用"假定"一词，如 1966 年 12 月 9 日在纽约开放签字的《公民及政治权利国际盟约》[②] 第 14 条第 2 款就规定："受刑事控告之人，未经依法确定有罪以前，应假定其无罪。"巫宇甦在翻译介绍"无罪推定"时，把法国 1789 年《人权宣言》第 9 条翻译为"任何人在其未被宣告为犯罪以前，应当被假定为无罪，即使认为必须予以逮捕，但为扣留其人身所不需要的各种残酷行为都应受到法律的严厉制裁"；把 1976 年生效的《公民权利和政治权利国际公约》第 14 条第 2 项翻译为"被告人未经依法确定有罪以前，应

① 参见林欣：《"无罪推定"还是"无罪假定"?》，载《中国社会科学》1983 年第 3 期；裴苍龄：《论无罪推定》，载《河北法学》2015 年第 1 期，第 8-10 页；徐灿：《论腐败案件中明知的推定规则在中国的确立》，载《澳门法学》2015 年第 14 期，第 81-82 页；何家弘：《论推定概念的界定标准》，载《法学》2008 年第 10 期，第 41 页。

② 该版本是由台湾蒋介石集团派代表参与制定的。1971 年，中华人民共和国提议将原来的《公民及政治权利国际盟约》修改为《公民权利与政治权利国际公约》。后来，该公约的名称被进一步修改为《公民权利和政治权利国际公约》，并成为当前最流行的版本。

假定其无罪"[1]。张子培也把法国1789年《人权宣言》第9条翻译为"任何人在未被法院宣告有罪之前，应当被假定为无罪"。[2] 林欣经过论证认为无罪推定"这个译法是不确切的，根据它的原意和实际内容，应该译为'无罪假定'"[3]。然而，在大多数相关文献中，人们还是约定俗成地使用无罪推定这一称谓。那么，什么是"推定"？它与"假定"有着怎样的关系？下面将逐一解读。

一、"推定"的内涵解读

"推定的概念十分混乱。可以肯定地说，迄今为止，人们还不能成功地阐明推定的概念。"[4]"有人大胆提出主张，认为除了其同辈'证明责任'之外，'推定'是法律术语家族中最难以捉摸的成员"[5]，以至于成为一个"魔术词语"（"magic words"[6]）。据史料记载，作为一项成文规则，推定最早始于罗马法。据粗略考证，罗马法上的推定大致包含死亡的推定、婚生子女的推定、要式买卖的推定、善意的推定、占有为所有的推定、占有意思的推定等。[7] 然而，最早在法律上对推定进行定义的则是1804年的《法国民法典》。该法典第1349条规定："推定为法律或法官从已知的事实推

① 巫宇甦主编：《证据学》，群众出版社1983年版，第98页。

② 张子培：《评"无罪推定"》，载《中国政法大学学报》1983年第4期，第14页。

③ 林欣：《"无罪推定"还是"无罪假定"?》，载《中国社会科学》1983年第3期，第173页。

④ ［德］莱奥·罗森贝克：《证明责任论》，庄敬华译，中国法制出版社2002年版，第206页。

⑤ Kenneth S. Broun, 2 McCormick On Evidence 675（［St. Paul, Minn.］: Thomson Reuters, 2013, Seventh Edition）.

⑥ Charles V. Laughlin, *In Support of the Thayer Theory of Presumptions*, 52 Mich. L. Rev. 195（1953）.

⑦ 参见叶自强：《论推定法则》，载陈光中、江伟主编：《诉讼法论丛》（第2卷），法律出版社1998年版，第467-468页。

论未知的事实所得出的结论。”①《美国统一商法典》第1-206款对推定作了专门的规定。该款规定：“当本法典就某一事实创制‘推定’或者规定某一事实‘被假设’时，事实的审理者必须认定该事实的存在，除非并且直至提出支持认定该事实不存在的证据。”《加利福尼亚州证据法典》在第600条（a）款中给推定下了明确的定义：“推定是一种根据法律要求从另一被认定或者在诉讼中确定的事实或事实组中作出的对于事实的假定。”在理论上对推定的界定，长期以来，亦可谓众说纷纭。查尔斯V. 拉夫林（Charles V. Laughlin）教授通过对司法实践中“推定”一词的使用情况进行考察，列举了“推定”一词有八种不同的用法：指法庭的一般倾向；作为一种权威性的推理原则；作为一项实体法规则；作为一种确定说服责任的规则；指一种可以容许的推论；表述一种符合立法规定的初步成立案件；指司法认知的一项命题；作为一种转移举证责任的规则。② 由此可见，对于推定这一概念的认识角度也是多种多样的。综合对于推定概念的主要认识，大致可以分为以下几种：

第一，认为推定是描述某一事实或若干事实与另一事实或若干事实之间的关系。

美国学者摩根（Edmund M. Morgan）认为：“一般说来，使用推定即在描述某一事实或若干事实与另一事实或若干事实之间的关系。某一事实称为基础事实（甲），而另一事实称为推定事实（乙）。”③ 英国学者保罗·罗伯茨（Paul Roberts）和艾德里安·扎克曼（Adrian Zuckerman）在其著作《证据法》（第2版）中指出：

---

① 《法国民法典》第1349条法文原文为：“Article 1349-Les présomptions sont des conséquences que la loi ou le magistrat tire d´un fait connu à un fait inconnu.”

② Charles V. Laughlin, *In Support of the Thayer Theory of Presumptions*, 52 Mich. L. Rev. 195, 196-209 (1953).

③ Edmund M. Morgan, Basic Problems of Evidence 31 (September, 1962) (Philadelphia: Joint Committee on Continuing Legal Education of the American Law Institute and the American Bar Association, 1963).

"……最常遇到的推定是议会附加给特定的法定罪行的推定。……这些推定遵从一个常见的模式。在每个案件中，一旦特定的触发事实被证实……则进一步的事实被当作被证实，'除非相反的情况被证明'（或者'表明'等）。"[Whilst common law presumptions sometimes arise in criminal proceedings, the most frequently encountered presumptions are those attached by Parliament to particular statutory offences. ... (These presumptions) follow a familiar pattern. In each case, once certain triggering fact (s) have been established ... further fact (s) are treated as established 'unless the contrary is proved' (or 'shown', etc)][①] 还有人认为"推定就是指由法律直接规定或法官按照经验法则所确立的某一事实或若干事实与另一事实或若干事实之间的一种充分条件关系，其中某一事实或若干事实为基础事实，另一事实或若干事实为推定事实"[②]。

第二，将推定视为推论。

美国"谨慎之法官与学者均主张适当之术语应为'推论'而非'推定'"。[③] 英国学者一般认为，推定"在证据法中，指从其他已经确定的事实必然或可以推断出的推论或结论"[④]。英国18世纪著名法学家杰弗里·吉尔伯特在其著作《证据法》中对推定下的定义是："从一个确定的事物中所作推测，为另一个具有确定性的事物所支持，它被视为真实。"当一个事实本身不能被证明时，推定"最接近于证明，是对该事实通常所需情况的证明，因此被称为推定，而不是称为证明，它们替代对事实的证明，直到相反的

① Paul Roberts & Adrian Zuckerman, Criminal Evidence 234 (OUP, 2nd edn. 2010).

② 王学棉：《论推定的逻辑学基础——兼论推定与拟制的关系》，载《政法论坛》2004年第1期，第170页。

③ 参见[美]摩根：《证据法之基本问题》，李学灯译，台湾世界书局1960年版，第57页。

④ [英]戴维·M. 沃克编：《牛津法律大词典》，北京社会与科技发展研究所组织翻译，光明日报出版社1988年版，第714页。

情况被证明”①。在我国，也有人认为，“推定即推测判断。推定作为法律上的术语，是指法律或司法机关从已知的事实推论未证事实所得出的结论，亦即从前提事实的成立推论待证事实的成立，其意在表示某一事实或若干事实，与另一事实或若干事实之间的内在联系”②。当然，在这种主张中，根据对推论是一种行为还是一种结果的认识不同，又可分为作为行为的推论，如杰弗里·吉尔伯特的观点；作为结果的推论，如英国学者的一般观点。1804 年的《法国民法典》第 1349 条更是明确地指出：“推定为法律或法官从已知的事实推论未知的事实所得出的结论。”③

第三，将推定视同假定。

美国学者塞耶、威格莫尔和美国法学会“一般均主张，并且许多（美国）法院也认同，推定一词，应仅用以表示若干事实于诉讼中一经确立，除非并直至另有特殊条件构成，即必须假定另一（组）事实存在”④。在中国，也有人认为，“所谓推定，是指根据某一事实（基础事实）的存在而作出的另一事实（推定事实）存在的假定”⑤。《加利福尼亚州证据法典》第 600 条（a）款对推定的定义也支持这一主张。

第四，认为推定是一种处理证据的规则。

其中，根据处理证据的依据是否必须为法律性规范，又可分为

① Geoffrey Gilbert, The Law of Evidence 160-1 (London, 1756). 转引自［美］巴巴拉·J. 夏皮罗：《对英美“排除合理怀疑”之历史透视》，熊秋红译，载王敏远主编：《公法》（第 4 卷），法律出版社 2003 年版，第 109 页。

② 万选才、肖秀敏：《论推定规则在刑事审判中的运用——兼论我国刑事立法确立推定规则的必要性》，载《法学家》2001 年第 5 期，第 95 页。

③ 《法国民法典》第 1349 条法文原文为：“Article 1349-Les présomptions sont des conséquences que la loi ou le magistrat tire d´un fait connu à un fait inconnu.”

④ Edmund M. Morgan, Basic Problems Of Evidence 32 (September, 1962) (Philadelphia: Joint Committee on Continuing Legal Education of the American Law Institute and the American Bar Association, 1963).

⑤ 赵钢、刘海峰：《试论证据法上的推定》，载《法律科学》1998 年第 1 期，第 90 页。

两种。一种认为推定必须依据法律性规范进行。例如，“所谓推定，是指根据法律的规定，从已证事实直接认定另一事实的存在，除非被追诉者提出反证加以推翻”[①]。“推定，是指依照法律或某种法规，基于某一确定事实，而推知和确定另一不明事实的存在。”[②]有学者指出，自从威格摩尔的证据法著作问世以来，英美法学界及判例已经就“推定”达成了比较一致的意见，认为严格意义上的推定只能是法律推定。[③] 另一种观点认为，推定不仅包括法律推定，也包括事实推定。例如，“所谓推定，乃指由法律规定或者法院按照经验法则，从已知的前提事实推断未知的结果事实存在，并允许当事人举证推翻的一种证据法则”[④]。美国学者华尔兹认为：“推定是关于某事实存在与否的推断，而这推断又是根据其他基础或基本事实来完成的。”[⑤] “推定产生于下面这种思维过程，即根据已知的基础事实的证明来推断出一个未知的事实，因为常识和经验表明该已知的基础事实通常会与该未知事实并存。”[⑥] “推定是指基于事物之间的普遍的共生关系，或者说是常态的因果联系，由基础事实推出待证事实（又称推定事实）的一种证明规则。”[⑦] “推定是指依照法律规定或者由法院按照经验法则，从已知的基础事实推

① 陈光中主编：《刑事诉讼法》（第五版），北京大学出版社、高等教育出版社2014年版，第181页。

② 肖中华、张少林：《刑事推定与犯罪认定刍议》，载《法学家》2002年第3期，第14页。

③ 参见孙长永：《探索正当程序——比较刑事诉讼法专论》，中国法制出版社2005年版，第221页。转引自赵俊甫：《刑事推定研究》，吉林大学2008年博士学位论文，第13页。

④ 江伟主编：《证据法学》，中国人民大学出版社2000年版，第178页。

⑤ ［美］乔恩·R. 华尔兹：《刑事证据大全》（第二版），何家弘等译，中国人民公安大学出版社2004年版，第395页。

⑥ ［美］乔恩·R. 华尔兹：《刑事证据大全》（第二版），何家弘等译，中国人民公安大学出版社2004年版，第397页。

⑦ 樊崇义、王建明主编：《〈联合国反腐败公约〉与我国职务犯罪侦查研究》，中国方正出版社2011年版，第314页。

断未知的事实存在，并允许当事人提出反证予以推翻的一种证据法则。”①“推定是指依据法律直接规定或经验规则所确立的基础事实与待证事实之间的一种充分条件关系（即常态联系），当基础事实确证时，可认定待证事实存在，但允许受不利推定的当事人举证反驳的一项辅助证据证明的标准化规则。”②

第五，认为推定是一种认定事实的方法。

例如，“推定是指通过对基础事实与未知事实之间常态联系的肯定来认定案件事实的特殊方法”③。“推定是司法证明的一种重要的辅助性方法，其以肯定基础事实与推定事实之间的常态联系为基础，通过对基础事实的证明来实现对推定事实存在状态的认定。”④“推定是基于某一确定事实而推知和确定另一不明事实的存在的一种案件事实的认定法则或者认定方法。”⑤

笔者认为，第一种观点将推定视为基础事实和推定事实之间的关系，看到了推定涉及的两个重要方面，也涉及了推定存在的重要原因之一——通过严格的证明从基础事实到达推定事实的困难，但是没有把握住推定的目的或者本质——一种特殊的认定案件事实的方法或者途径，因此作为对推定概念的界定似有不妥。第二种观点将推定视为推论，看到了推定与推论在结构上的相似性——都在一定程度上契合三段论的基本逻辑推理结构，但是推定毕竟不是一般的推论，它是基于法律的规定或者经验法则而进行的具有一定“跳跃性”的推论，不一定是严密的逻辑推论，具有一定的盖然性。这种盖然性来源于推定依据的基础——法律规定或者经验法则。经验法则是人们从大量的实践经验中归纳总结出来的具有高度盖然性的法则，代表着大多数情况，但还远没有达到公理所要求的

① 王明高、曾志雄：《论贿赂推定》，载《湖湘论坛》2008年第2期，第85页。
② 赵俊甫：《刑事推定研究》，吉林大学2008年博士学位论文。
③ 裴苍龄：《再论推定》，载《法学研究》2006年第3期，第120页。
④ 张云鹏：《刑事推定论》，吉林大学2007年博士学位论文，第12-13页。
⑤ 贺志军：《论明知的推定》，湖南师范大学2003年硕士学位论文，第9页。

极高度的盖然性（或者说是必然性）。由于其毕竟只是对一般经验的归纳和总结，忽略了特殊的情况，因此经验法则又不具有绝对性，不能排除例外的存在。正是基于此，根据经验法则作出的判断（推定）可能与事实不符，因此理应允许被举证推翻。作为推定基础的法律规定实际上是对实践中的经验法则通过立法的形式予以认可而上升为法律的形式，是对实践中经验法则的法律肯认和固化。它使得据其作出的推定具有了明确的法律依据，从而获得了较高的正当性和权威性。但实质上无论是基于法律规定的法律上的推定还是基于经验法则的事实上的推定，从根源上来讲都是基于实践中的经验法则，都具有一定的盖然性而不是绝对性，因此都是可以通过举证予以推翻的。而推论却不一定具有这样的特点，如直接基于自然规律和公理而进行的基本推论一般情况下就不能通过举证予以推翻[①]。因此，将推定视同推论的观点也不能作为推定的概念。第三种观点将推定视同假定，似乎看到了推定结论与通过严格证明而得出的结论相比所具有的某种“相对基础事实的脱离性”，但实质上假定忽略了推定基础事实的存在及其必要性。推定不是毫无根据的推定，而是基于一定的基础事实和经验法则或者法律根据的，而假定却并不以基础事实和经验法则的存在为必要。假定是认识的起点，而推定则是认识的结果。因此，可以说推定与假定是两个截然不同的概念，将推定视同假定明显不妥。第四种观点认为推定是处理证据的规则，看到了推定运行的一般特征，抓住了推定在外在表现形式上的特点，但是没有看到推定存在的价值或者目的。推定的

---

① 关于此点，中华人民共和国最高人民法院（以下简称最高人民法院）于 2001 年 12 月 6 日通过的《关于民事诉讼证据的若干规定》第 9 条就表达了类似的观点：“下列事实，当事人无需举证证明：（一）众所周知的事实；（二）自然规律及定理；（三）根据法律规定或者已知事实和日常生活经验法则，能推定出的另一事实；（四）已为人民法院发生法律效力的裁判所确认的事实；（五）已为仲裁机构的生效裁决所确认的事实；（六）已为有效公证文书所证明的事实。前款（一）、（三）、（四）、（五）、（六）项，当事人有相反证据足以推翻的除外。”最高人民法院于 2002 年 6 月 4 日通过的《最高人民法院关于行政诉讼证据若干问题的规定》第 68 条表达了相同的意见。

存在是为了在特殊情况下对事实予以认定，是认定事实的一种方法或者手段，是证明这种认定事实一般方法的辅助或者补充。因此，对于推定概念的这种认识也不够准确。第五种观点将推定视为一种认定事实的方法，看到了推定的本质及推定存在的目的和价值，但是对推定依据的认识不够全面，大都忽略了法律上的推定和基于经验法则的推定之间的区别，而且没有指明推定的可反驳性，因此也不够科学。

笔者在综合辨析上述观点的基础上提出以下“推定”的概念：推定是指在为确定权利、义务、责任等所必要的事实不明而又难以证明的情况下，为了确定该不明事实的状态，而依据法律规定或者经验法则，直接从已证的基础事实认定不明事实的状态，并允许当事人反驳的一种辅助证明的认定案件事实的特殊方法。

关于推定的分类，由于对推定的概念认识不同，分类的方法可能也不同。在上述“推定”概念的前提下，可以将推定分为法律推定和事实推定，而法律推定还可以进一步分为强制性法律推定和选择性（可为性）法律推定。例如，英国 1991 年《危险犬类法》（Dangerous Dogs Act 1991）第 5 条规定：“……如果在诉讼中公诉方声称上述第 1 款或者第 2 款项下的命令适用于一条狗，则推定这是一条这样的狗，除非被告人以法庭认为充分的证据表明情况并非如此。”（“… (5) If in any proceedings it is alleged by the prosecution that a dog is one to which section 1 or an order under section 2 above applies it *shall be presumed* that it is such a dog unless the contrary is shown by the accused by such evidence as the court considers sufficient …”）英国 1996 年《教育法》（*Education Act* 1996）第 445 条（与逃学有关的年龄的推定）规定：“……（2）……当事儿童将随时被推定已达强制就学年龄，除非父或母提出相反证明。”（“…（2）… the child in question *shall be presumed* to have been of compulsory school age at any time unless the parent proves the contrary.”）英国 1994 年《刑事司法和公共秩序法案》第 51 条

(通过威胁证人或者陪审团成员来干预司法）规定：“……（7）如果在因上述第（1）款罪行而对一个人提起的诉讼中经证明其在（b）节所要求的明知或者相信的情况下实施了（a）节所规定的行为，那么除非有相反证明，其将被推定以该款（c）节所要求的意图实施了该行为。（8）如果在因上述第（2）款罪行而对一个人提起的诉讼中经证明其在相关的时期内在（b）节所要求的明知或者相信的情况下实施或者威胁实施了（a）节所规定的行为，那么除非有相反证明，其将被推定以该款（c）节所要求的动机实施了该行为。”（“... (7) If, in proceedings against a person for an offence under subsection (1) above, it is proved that he did an act falling within paragraph (a) with the knowledge or belief required by paragraph (b), he shall be presumed unless the contrary is proved, to have done the act with the intention required by paragraph (c) of that subsection. (8) If, in proceedings against a person for an offence under subsection (2) above, it is proved that he did or threatened to do an act falling within paragraph (a) within the relevant period with the knowledge or belief required by paragraph (b), he shall be presumed , unless the contrary is proved, to have done the act with the motive required by paragraph (c) of that subsection.”）英国 1916 年《预防腐败法》（*Prevention of Corruption Act* 1916）第 2 条（政府合同回扣中的腐败）规定：“以受贿罪被起诉之人，当其被证明在王室或者任何政府部门或者公共机构供职中的任何现金、礼品或者其他报酬是由或来自于或者寻求与王室或者任何政府部门或者公共机构签订合同的人员或者其代理人所支付或者给予或者接受时，该现金、礼品或者其他报酬应当被认为是上述法律所说的作为诱导或者回报而贿赂地支付、给予或者接收，但反证被证实的除外。”（“Where in any proceedings against a person for an offence under the Prevention of Corruption Act 106, or the Public Bodies Corrupt Practices Act 1889, it is proved that any money, gift, or other consideration has been paid or given to or received by a person in the employment of His Majesty or any Government Department or a public body by or from a person, or agent of a person, holding or seeking to obtain a contract from His Majesty or any Government Department or public body, the money, gift, or consideration shall be deemed to have been paid or given and received corruptly as such inducement or reward as is mentioned in such Act unless the contrary is proved." ）英国 2003 年《性犯罪法》第 75 条（关于同意的证据性推定）规定："（1）如果在因适用该条的犯罪而提起的诉讼中，经证明（a）被告人实施了相关的行为，（b）存在第（2）款所标明的任何情况，和（c）被告人知道那些情况存在，那么，原告将被推定并未同意该相关行为，除非援引充分的证据以提出其是否同意的问题，并且被告人将被推定未合理地相信原告同意，除非援引充分的证据以提出其是否合理地相信的问题。（2）……"（"（1）If in proceedings for an offence to which this section applies it is proved-（a）that the defendant did the relevant act，（b）that any of the circumstances specified in subsection（2）existed，and（c）that the defendant knew that those circumstances existed，the complainant is to be taken not to have consented to the relevant act unless sufficient evidence is adduced to raise an issue as to whether he consented，and the defendant is to be taken not to have reasonably believed that the complainant consented unless sufficient evidence is adduced to raise an issue as to whether he reasonably believed it.（2）..."）上述几条都是法律推定，并且都可以称为强制性法律推定。强制性法律推定要求法庭必须直接推出结论，通常会附加说明可以反证推翻。其他的法律推定仅是选择性法律推定：允许但不强求作出特定的推定。选择性法律推定在导致超出严格的常识推理范围的事实结论的情况下与我们的推定概念完全吻合，也是真正的推定。例如，英国 2000 年《恐怖主义法》第 57 条就规定了选择性的（可为性的）法律推定，赋予法庭选择推定被告人占有案件所涉物品的权力。该条规定："（1）如果一个人在

某种情况下持有一项物品，而该种情况会引起其是为了与实施、准备或者鼓动恐怖主义行为相关的目的而持有的合理怀疑，那么该人犯有罪行。（2）被指控犯有本条所规定罪行的人可以以证明其持有该物品并非为了与实施、准备或者鼓动恐怖主义行为相关的目的为自己辩护。（3）在因本条所规定罪行而提起的诉讼中，如果经证明一项物品——（a）与被告人同时处于某一房屋，或者（b）处于被告人占有或者并非作为一名公众成员而惯常使用的房屋，那么，法庭可以推定被告人占有该项物品，除非其证明其不知该物品存在于该房屋或者其对该物品没有控制。”（“（1）A person commits an offence if he possesses an article in circumstances which give rise to a reasonable suspicion that his possession is for a purpose connected with the commission, preparation or instigation of an act of terrorism. （2）It is a defence for a person charged with an offence under this section to prove that his possession of the article was not for a purpose connected with the commission, preparation or instigation of an act of terrorism. （3）In proceedings for an offence under this section, if it is proved that an article—（a） was on any premises at the same time as the accused, or（b） was on premises of which the accused was the occupier or which he habitually used otherwise than as a member of the public, *the court may assume* that the accused possessed the article, unless he proves that he did not know of its presence on the premises or that he had no control over it.”）①

推定的后果是发生举证责任倒置，原来的证明责任主体不再承担部分举证责任，而将其转移给其他的诉讼主体，因此缓解了原来证明责任主体的部分举证责任，同时可以通过调整举证责任在不同诉讼主体间的分配来实现一定的立法或者司法目标。正如保罗·罗

① Cf. Paul Roberts & Adrian Zuckerman, Criminal Evidence 239（OUP, 2nd edn. 2010）.

伯茨和艾德里安·扎克曼所指出的，“（推定的）典型结果是控诉方被免除了证明可能特别不便于或者难于证明的犯罪构成要素的责任，无论这些要素是犯罪行为（*actus reus*）要素还是犯罪意图（*mens rea*）要素。在控诉方被免除其责任的同时，被告方被分配相应的基于盖然性反驳推定的举证责任”。(The typical effect, as in these three examples, is to relieve the prosecution of the burden of proving offence elements which are likely to be especially inconvenient or difficult to prove, whether *actus reus* elements or *mens rea* elements. At the same time as the prosecution is relived of its burden, a corresponding probative burden is placed on the accused to rebut the presumption, on the balance of probabilities.)①

还需指出的是，“推定”一词在英文中的表达也较为混乱。推定在英文中的表达一般为 presumption 或者 infer。前者如新加坡《1993 年预防腐败法》第 8 条的英文表述“Presumption of corruption in certain cases”。后者如《联合国反腐败公约》第 28 条的英文表述“Knowledge, intent or purpose required as an element of an offence established in accordance with this Convention may be inferred from objective factual circumstances.”然而，presumption 本身含义也不唯一。例如，presumption 除了有推定的含义外，还有假定等含义。“Presumption of innocence”中文一般翻译为无罪推定，但实际上准确的翻译应当是“无罪假定”②，因为无罪推定中的“推定”并非以存在某种基础事实为条件的推定，而是诉讼一开始就进行的假定。龙宗智教授在其发表于《法学研究》2008 年第 1 期的《推定的界限及适用》一文中对《联合国反腐败公约》

① Paul Roberts & Adrian Zuckerman, Criminal Evidence 234 (OUP, 2nd edn. 2010).

② 参见何家弘：《论推定概念的界定标准》，载《法学》2008 年第 10 期，第 41 页；裴苍龄：《论无罪推定》，载《河北法学》2015 年第 1 期，第 8 页。

英文版第 28 条[①]和《联合国打击跨国有组织犯罪公约》英文版第 5、6 条[②]中 “infer（red）” 一词被翻译为 “推定” 表示异议，认为该词应当译为 “推论”，而非 “推定”，这两个公约的中文版[③]将该词翻译为 “推定” 是误译。[④] 其实，这是一种误解。infer 这一英文单词本身就包括推定的含义。要探求该英文单词的真实含义，最好求助于权威的英文词典原文。牛津大学出版社的《牛津学习词典》（*Oxford Learner's Dictionaries*）对 infer 作出解释，即 “基于可获得的信息得到一种观点或者决定某事是真实的”，（“1. to reach an opinion or decide that something is true on the basis of information that is available.”）并在第 2 点通过用法举例说明其含义，即

---

① 《联合国反腐败公约》英文版第 28 条表述为 “Article 28. Knowledge, intent and purpose as elements of an offence” “Knowledge, intent or purpose required as an element of an offence established in accordance with this Convention may be inferred from objective factual circumstances.” 网址：http：//www. unodc. org/documents/treaties/UNCAC/Publications/Convention/08-50026_ E. pdf，最后访问时间：2017 年 11 月 19 日。

② 《联合国打击跨国有组织犯罪公约》英文版第 5 条第 2 款表述为 “2. The knowledge, intent, aim, purpose or agreement referred to in para- graph 1 of this article may be inferred from objective factual circumstances.” 第 6 条第 2 款 f 项表述为 “（f）Knowledge, intent or purpose required as an element of an offence set forth in paragraph 1 of this article may be inferred from objective factual circumstances.” http：//www. unodc. org/documents/treaties/UNTOC/Publications/TOC%20Convention/TOCebook-e. pdf，最后访问时间：2017 年 11 月 19 日。

③ 《联合国反腐败公约》中文版第 28 条表述为 “作为犯罪要素的明知、故意或者目的” “根据本公约确立的犯罪所需具备的明知、故意或者目的等要素，可以根据客观实际情况予以推定”。http：//www. unodc. org/documents/treaties/UNCAC/Publications/Convention/08-50025_ C. pdf，最后访问时间：2017 年 11 月 19 日。《联合国打击跨国有组织犯罪公约》中文版第 5 条第 2 款表述为 “2. 本条第 1 款所指的明知、故意、目标、目的或约定可以从客观实际情况推定”。第 6 条第 2 款 f 项表述为 “（f）本条第 1 款所规定的作为犯罪要素的明知、故意或目的可根据客观实际情况推定。” http：//www.unodc.org/documents/treaties/UNTOC/Publications/TOC% 20Convention/TOCebook-c.pdf，最后访问时间：2017 年 11 月 19 日。

④ 龙宗智：《推定的界限及适用》，载《法学研究》2008 年第 1 期，第 115-116 页。

“间接表明某事是真实的”。（“2. infer（that）... | infer something（non-standard）to suggest indirectly that something is true.”）[①]《牛津学习词典》对 inference 的解释更直接地表明了该词的推定内涵，即“可以从已知事物间接查明的事物”。（“something that you can find out indirectly from what you already know”）[②] 而关于 indirectly 的含义，《牛津学习词典》的解释为：“1. 不是作为某事物的主要目的、原因或者结果，而是除其之外；不是以直接的方式。2. 以一种并不清楚或者明显的方式。”（“1. not as the main aim, cause or result of something, but in addition to it; not in a direct line or manner. 2. in a way that is not clear or obvious.”）[③] 按照龙宗智《推定的界限及适用》一文的说法，推论即证明[④]，如果将《联合国反腐败公约》英文版第 28 条和《联合国打击跨国有组织犯罪公约》英文版第 5、6 条中的“infer（red）”一词翻译为“推论”的话，那么《联合国反腐败公约》第 28 条的意思就是说“根据本公约确立的犯罪所需具备的明知、故意或者目的等要素，可以根据客观实际情况予以证明”。《联合国打击跨国有组织犯罪公约》第 5 条第 2 款的意思就是说“本条第 1 款所指的明知、故意、目标、目的或约定可以从客观实际情况证明”。第 6 条第 2 款 f 项的意思就是说“本条第 1 款所规定的作为犯罪要素的明知、故

---

① “infer verb - Definition, pictures, pronunciation and usage notes | Oxford Advanced Learner's Diction”, http://www. oxfordlearnersdictionaries. com/definition/english/infer? q=infer，最后访问时间：2017 年 11 月 19 日。

② “inference noun - Definition, pictures, pronunciation and usage notes | Oxford Advanced Learner's Dic”, http://www. oxfordlearnersdictionaries. com/definition/english/inference? q=inference，最后访问时间：2017 年 11 月 19 日。

③ “indirectly adverb-Definition, pictures, pronunciation and usage notes | Oxford Advanced Learner's”, http://www.oxfordlearnersdictionaries.com/definition/english/indirectly? q=indirectly，最后访问时间：2017 年 11 月 19 日。

④ 龙宗智：《推定的界限及适用》，载《法学研究》2008 年第 1 期，第 106、109 页。

意或目的可根据客观实际情况证明”。这明显不合常理：即便两个公约不作出这样的规定，对于明知、故意或者目的等要素，也依旧可以根据客观实际情况予以证明，这是不言自明的，两个公约没必要多此一举专门对此予以规定。我们没有理由相信，作为由众多国家参与的严肃的国际条约会作出多此一举的规定。因此，将《联合国反腐败公约》英文版第28条和《联合国打击跨国有组织犯罪公约》英文版第5、6条中的“infer（red）”一词理解为（证明意义上的）推论是不合适的，而只能理解为推定。这也与加大对腐败和跨国有组织犯罪的打击力度、适度缓解控诉方部分举证责任的立法目的相符。

关于“在认定故意杀人的案件中，被告人不承认有杀人的故意，审判人员根据被告人使用的凶器、打击的部位等事实判断其是否有杀人故意”等做法是推定还是推论的问题，不同的学者对此有不同的看法。有的认为是推定①，有的认为是推论而非推定②。关于这类案件审理者根据案件事实对待证事实进行认定的行为是推定还是推论的问题，笔者认为，这一切都基于事实审理者对于用现有证据对待证事实进行证明能否达到证明标准的判断：如果能达到证明标准，那么此时认定待证事实的方法就是证明；如果不能达到证明标准，而仅是现有证据在一定程度上支持待证事实，那么此时如果仍旧认定待证事实，那么这种认定方法就是推定；如果现有证据对待证事实起不到支持作用，而仍旧认定待证事实，那么此时的认定方法就只能是假定或者拟制，并且此时如果待证事实可以反驳，则为假定，如果待证事实不能反驳，则为拟制（关于“推定”、“拟制”、“假定”与“证明”几个概念之间的关系详见下文）。

---

① 李玉华：《刑事诉讼证明中事实推定之运用》，载《现代法学》2005年第3期，第74页；贺平凡：《论刑事推定规则》，载《政治与法律》2003年第2期。

② 龙宗智：《推定的界限及适用》，载《法学研究》2008年第1期，第111-112页。

此外，在司法实践中，经常会遇到推定，特别是事实上的推定问题。如何正确对待和恰当处理这些问题对于维护当事人的合法权益、实现司法的公平正义具有重要意义。如前所述，根据推定所依据的基础不同，可以将推定分为法律上的推定和事实上的推定。前者有明确的法律依据，是基于法律规定的推定，因此又称为立法推定或者法律推定；后者没有明确的法律依据，是司法人员基于经验法则的推定，因此又称为事实推定。关于在司法实践中应当如何对待事实推定的问题观点不一。在英国刑事司法中，事实推定起着非常重要的作用，法官应该告知陪审团有权从被告人的违禁行为中推定出被告人的心理状态。[①] 然而，有学者指出，自从威格莫尔的证据法著作问世以来，英美法学界及判例已经就“推定”达成了比较一致的意见，认为严格意义上的推定只能是法律推定。[②] 笔者认为，由于事实推定缺乏明确的法律依据，而对于经验法则的归纳和认定又存在着较大的弹性，特别是在我国尚未建立陪审团制度的情况下，事实推定极易成为法官滥用自由裁量权的工具。因此，只有在证明标准不是非常高的民事诉讼和行政诉讼中（民事诉讼的一般证明标准是优势证明标准，行政诉讼证明标准介于民事诉讼和刑事诉讼之间），为了提高诉讼效率，可以适用事实推定。在涉及当

---

① 英国学者理查德·卡德（Richard Card）指出：“事实推定有时被称作暂时推定。由于其往往是能够证明被告心理状态的唯一手段，因此，其在刑事司法中起着非常重要的作用。法官应该对陪审团作出这样的指示，即它有权从被告实施的违禁行为的事实中，推定出被告的明知、预见或者目的，如果被告未作任何辩解，则推定通常成立。”（Presumptions of fact are sometimes called provisional presumptions, and they play a very important part in the administration of the criminal law because they are frequently the only means by which the state of the accused's mind can be proved. The judge will tell the jury that they are entitled to infer knowledge, foresight or intent from the fact that the prohibited act was done by the accused, and if the accused offers no explanation the inference will usually be drawn. See Richard Card, Card Cross And Jones Criminal Law 94－5（Butterworths, London, Dublin, Edinburgh, 12th ed. 1992））.

② 参见孙长永：《探索正当程序——比较刑事诉讼法专论》，中国法制出版社2005年版，第221页。

事人生命、自由、财产等重大权利的刑事诉讼中，原则上只能进行法律推定，而不应进行事实推定。只有在不进行事实推定就可能给国家或者社会造成重大的损失或者负面影响的情况下，才可以进行事实推定。同时，为了实现法律推定的价值，保护公共利益，提高司法效率，应当积极总结司法实践中遇到的问题和经验，将其上升为立法推定。然而，何为“可能给国家或者社会造成重大的损失或者负面影响”？对此，可以通过最高人民法院及时总结实践经验，发布司法解释或者案例指导的方式予以解决。

在刑事诉讼中适用减轻控诉方举证责任的推定的证明标准问题主要涉及控方的证明标准和辩方推翻推定的标准。此处控方的证明标准是指控方对作为推定基础事实的证明所应当达到的标准。由于这种推定是对被指控人诉讼权利一定程度的弱化，是对被指控人作为公民的基本权利一定程度的限制，因此对于推定的适用要非常严格。反映到诉讼过程中，就是要对作为推定适用条件的基础事实的证明必须达到一般的证明标准，不应有所降低。刑事诉讼中一般的证明标准，从当今世界主要法系来看，主要有英美法系的“排除合理怀疑”和大陆法系的“内心确信”。在中国，这一标准是“事实清楚，证据确实充分”。笔者认为，实际上这三种标准具有内在的统一性：只有“排除合理怀疑”，才能做到“内心确信”；只有“内心确信”，才能做到“事实清楚”。反之，要做到“事实清楚”，必须达到“内心确信”；而要达到“内心确信”，必须“排除合理怀疑”。关于辩方推翻推定的标准，如前所述，推定都允许当事人反驳。然而，这一反驳要达到何种标准？这一问题可从推定成立的反面去理解。推定的结构包括“法律规定或者经验法则+基础事实+推定事实”。只有这三项都成立，推定才能成立。对于法律推定的情况，只要辩方能够指出控方对基础事实的证明未达到法定的标准（例如，尚未“排除合理怀疑”，没有达到“内心确信”，也不能做到“事实清楚”），或者指出控方的推定没有准确地适用法律，即可推翻这一推定。对于事实推定的情况，只要辩方能够指出控方对基础事实的证明未达到法定的标准（如前所述），或者指出该“经验法则”缺乏常态联系、违背事实、具有不合理性，即可推翻这一推定。当然，无论是法律推定还是事实推定，如果当事人能够举出证据证明与推定结论相反的事实且能达到不低于50%的证明标准（换言之，使原证明责任主体的证明达不到优势证明标准），也可以推翻控方的推定。

二、“推定”与“假定”的关系

为了更好地厘清“推定”和“假定”的关系，有必要对“推定”、“拟制”、“假定”与“证明”几个概念之间的关系进行一个全面的梳理。

如前所述，可反驳性是推定的一个基本特性。所谓不可反驳的推定，实际上是法律的特殊规定或者法律拟制。① 拟制是一个古老的概念，早在古罗马法中就已经存在。英国学者梅因在其名著《古代法》中对拟制的含义做了精湛的阐释：“‘拟制’在古罗马法中，准确地说是指申诉这一术语，表示原告一方的虚假陈述是不允许被告反驳的；如原告提出自己是一个罗马人的证言，而他实际上是一个外国人。这种‘拟制’的目的，当然是为了给予审判权……但现在我所使用的‘法律拟制’一词，是指用以掩盖或假装掩盖一个事实的任何假定，即一条法律规定已经发生改变，它的文字虽没有变化，但其运用却改变了这一事实。……我们不难理解为什么各种不同形式的拟制特别适合于社会的新生时代。它们能够满足并不十分缺乏的要求改进的愿望，同时又不触犯当时普遍存在的对于变更的迷信般的嫌恶。在社会进步的某一特定阶段，它们是

① 美国学者迈克尔·H. 格莱姆认为：“一项所谓的不可用证据反驳的推定，不是一种推定，而是一条实体法规则。”（See Michael H. Graham, Federal Rules Of Evidence In A Nutshell 51（2nd ed. 1987））笔者认为，将所谓的不可用证据反驳的推定仅归结为一条实体法规则似乎偏窄，因为其也可能是一条程序法规则，如关于诉讼时效的规定。因此，笔者倾向于将这种所谓不可反驳的推定视为法律的特殊规定或者法律拟制。

克服法律僵化的最有价值的权宜办法……”① 《牛津法律大词典》认为，“法律上的拟制指任何隐瞒或倾向于隐瞒一种法律规则已发生变化，即其文字虽未变，但其作用却被修改了的事实的拟制。简言之，将甲案件假定为乙案件，并在法律上如同乙案件的实例一样加以对待。拟制常用于避免使法典或法令发生障碍。在罗马法和英格兰法中，广泛地使用拟制作为发展法律的手段，将规则扩展至原来未包括在内的案件”②。德国学者卡尔·拉伦茨认为：“法学上的拟制是有意地将明知为不同者，等同视之。”③ 我国学者李学灯认为，所谓法律拟制是指“遇有甲事实之存在，法律上视为有乙事实之存在，使甲事实与乙事实发生相等或相同之效果”④。何家弘也认为：“所谓拟制，即法律在特定情况下把某种事实视为另一种事实并发生相同的法律效果。”⑤ 此外，我国还有人认为，“所谓法律拟制，是指立法者基于某种价值目的的考虑，不论事实上的真实性，有意用现有的法律概念、法律规范去解释和适用社会生活中出现的新情况、新问题，以将不同事物等同对待，赋予其相同的法律效果，从而达到既能适应社会需要又能体现法律基本价值之目的的立法技术或立法活动”⑥。法律拟制是指“基于社会价值因素的考量以及法律的限制，将两件不具有逻辑常态联系的情事赋予相同法效果的虚构性陈述”⑦。“由此可以看出，拟制的根本作用在于通过

---

① ［英］亨利·萨姆奈·梅因：《古代法》，高敏、瞿慧虹译，中国社会科学出版社 2009 年版，第 20-21 页。

② ［英］戴维·M. 沃克编：《牛津法律大词典》，北京社会与科技发展研究所组织翻译，光明日报出版社 1988 年版，第 335 页。

③ ［德］卡尔·拉伦茨：《法学方法论》，陈爱娥译，商务印书馆 2003 年版，第 142 页。

④ 李学灯：《证据法比较研究》，台北五南图书出版公司 1992 年版，第 249 页。

⑤ 何家弘：《论推定概念的界定标准》，载《法学》2008 年第 10 期，第 43 页。

⑥ 李振林：《刑法中法律拟制论》，华东政法大学 2013 年博士学位论文，第 13 页。

⑦ 隋钰南：《拟制问题研究》，苏州大学 2012 年硕士学位论文，第 7 页。

将甲事实看成是乙事实，从而扩大法律的适用范围。”① 拟制关注的不是事实真相。拟制主要是立法者基于某种价值目的或者公共政策考虑的结果，是法律的强制性规定，因此也不具有可反驳性。

与拟制不同，假定、推定和证明都关注事实真相，都具有可反驳性。然而，这三者之间亦有区别。首先，虽然这三者都关注事实真相，但是，除此之外，在是否关注价值层面及关注的程度方面存在差别。证明主要关注的就是事实真相。证明的主要使命就是通过运用证据来获取事实真相。其对除此之外的价值层面关注得较少。推定不同于证明。② 推定作为一种辅助证明的认定案件事实的特殊方法，虽也关注事实真相，但与证明在获取事实真相的途径和手段上不同。此外，推定还以特定的价值判断和选择为动力和指向，而证明却不具备这一点。其次，在获取事实真相时，如果能够达到一般证明标准（如排除合理怀疑、内心确信等），则应适用证明；只有在不能或者难以达到一般证明标准时才可适用推定。

与证明和推定相比，假定虽然也关注事实真相，但是其关注价值的程度更深。并且，假定与推定的基本结构也不同。推定的结构包括“法律规定或者经验法则+基础事实+推定事实”，而假定的基本结构包括“法律规定+假定事实”。例如，无罪推定，实际上是“无罪假定”③，其不需要基础事实，直接以被追诉人无罪的假定作为认识的起点，其原因主要不在于被追诉人实际无罪的可能性有多大，而在于正义、自由、民主、人权等的价值判断和价值选择。假定通常只有在较极端或者典型的情况下才会适用，并且通常必须由法律明确规定才可适用。

---

① 王学棉：《论推定的逻辑学基础——兼论推定与拟制的关系》，载《政法论坛》2004年第1期，第170页。

② 英国学者理查德·卡德指出：“证明可以得到某些推定的帮助”，Richard Card, Card Cross And Jones Criminal Law 94 (12th ed. 1992). 显然，在其看来，推定并非证明。

③ 参见何家弘：《论推定概念的界定标准》，载《法学》2008年第10期，第41页。

由以上分析可见，从“推定”和“假定”的内涵来看，“无罪推定”准确地讲其实应当叫“无罪假定”。然而，鉴于我国学术和司法实践中已经形成了“无罪推定”的话语习惯，笔者无意更改这一习惯，姑且继续在本书中沿用“无罪推定”的称谓传统。

第二节　无罪推定的内涵

如前所述，无罪推定的发展经历了一个曲折的过程。无罪推定的内涵也随之发生了变迁。纵观整个17世纪和18世纪，英美法系和大陆法系的法律人对于无罪推定格言的理解都是一样的：一个人在被定罪之前在法律上是无罪的，他（她）不能被当作罪犯来对待或者被描绘成一个罪犯。[①] 此后，在英美法系，无罪推定逐渐演化为没有审前效力的单纯的证据规则。而在大陆法系，无罪推定的内涵则逐渐演化为不仅涉及证据规则维度，也涉及防范过早惩罚维度。现如今在英美法系，无罪推定仍旧主要作为法庭审理的证据规则。其内涵主要包括：控诉方承担排除合理怀疑地证明有罪的责任，被控诉方不承担证明自己无罪的责任；疑罪从无，即控诉方提出的证据不足以认定被告人有罪时，应当做无罪处理；禁止强迫自证其罪，即被控诉方不得被强迫证明自己有罪，也没有义务证明自己无罪；等等。而在大陆法系，无罪推定的内涵包含以下要求：在被依法证明并被合法的法庭认定有罪之前任何人有权被视为无罪；控诉方承担证明有罪的责任，被控诉方不承担证明自己无罪的责任；任何人在被定罪前都不应被公开描绘为有罪；防范提早惩罚，反对刑讯逼供，反对强迫自证其罪；被追诉人享有保释权、沉默权、辩护权、获得律师帮助权，获得公开、公正、无偏倚的审判权及上诉权；禁止任意逮捕和拘禁；非法证据应当予以排除；无罪推

---

① Francois Quintard-Morénas, *The Presumption of Innocence in the French and Anglo-American Legal Traditions*, 58Am. J. Comp. L. 107, 124-5 (2010).

定是一项人格权，适用于任何人；等等。联合国等国际组织认为无罪推定的内涵不仅包含证明责任分配等证据规则内容，而且包含保障人权的其他内容。例如，联合国人权组织就认为，证明责任分配只是无罪推定的基本内容之一，并非无罪推定之全部内容。联合国人权事务委员会在 2007 年通过的第 32 号一般性意见就规定："无罪推定是保护人权的基本要素，要求检方提供控诉的证据，保证在排除所有合理怀疑证实有罪之前，应被视为无罪，确保对被告适用无罪推定原则，并要求根据这一原则对待受刑事罪行指控者。所有公共当局均有责任不对审判结果作出预断，如不得发表公开声明指称被告有罪。"①

综合英美法系、大陆法系和联合国等国际组织关于无罪推定的观点，可以看出，无罪推定的基本内容至少包含以下几点：

第一，控诉方承担证明有罪的责任，被控诉方不承担证明自己无罪的责任。这是无罪推定在证据规则维度上的一项重要内涵，也是无罪推定的应有之义。这一内涵确立了刑事诉讼中有罪证明责任的基本分配原则。有学者指出："当说到面对刑事指控的被告人被推定无罪时，它的真实内涵是控方承担证明被告人有罪的责任。"②作为无罪推定的基本内容之一，"证明被告人有罪的责任由控诉一方承担"意味着"诉讼的起点由被告人无罪开始，证明的天平首先向有利于被告人一侧倾斜，控方的责任是逐一搬出证明被告人有罪的砝码堆放在对被告人不利的一侧，直至天平完全向被告人有罪一侧倾斜达到法律要求的定罪标准。"③

---

① 参见《联合国人权事务委员会第 13 号一般性意见：第 14 条》，http://hrlibrary.umn.edu/chinese/CHgencomm/CHhrcom32.html，最后访问时间：2018 年 9 月 18 日。

② Glanville Williams, The Proof of Guilt: A Sdudy of the English Criminal Trial 184 (London: Stevens & Sons Limited, 3rd edition, 1963).

③ ［加］阿兰 · W. 麦威特：《外国刑事诉讼制度探微》，法律出版社 2000 年版，第 153–154 页。

第二，达到法定证明标准。无罪推定要求“有罪证明”应当达到法律规定的证明标准，如果不能达到法定的证明标准，不能确定任何人有罪。大陆法系的有罪证明标准为“内心确信”。英美法系的有罪证明标准为“排除合理怀疑”（beyond reasonable doubt）。联合国相关文件对这一法定证明标准的认定也是“排除合理怀疑”。所谓排除合理怀疑，是指要求事实裁判者对被告人有罪不存在任何符合常理的怀疑，即有一种坚定的信念（abiding conviction）。[①] 按照这一要求，对被告人作出有罪判决必须建立在确凿、充分的证据基础之上，在有罪证明未能排除无罪的合理怀疑的情况下，不得认定被告人有罪。其实，“排除合理怀疑”、“内心确信”的证明标准是统一的：只有“排除合理怀疑”，才能做到“内心确信”；而要做到“内心确信”，必须“排除合理怀疑”；“排除合理怀疑”是实现“内心确信”的必要手段。

第三，被刑事指控者被证实有罪之前应被“推定”无罪。这是无罪推定的关键内容。如前所述，“无罪推定”实际上是“无罪假定”，其不需要基础事实，直接以被追诉人无罪的假定作为认识的起点，其并不意味着被追诉人实际上无罪，也不是因为被追诉人实际无罪的可能性有多大，之所以假定无罪，其原因主要在于正义、自由、民主、人权等的价值判断和选择，是一个国家或者地区政治理念在法律领域的反映，是在法律领域作出的一种政策安排。

第四，存疑案件的处理应有利于被指控人。这既是无罪推定的基本内容之一，也是“存疑有利于被告人原则”的要求。在一定程度上可以讲，无罪推定是“有利于被告人”原则历史发展的合乎逻辑的结果。[②]“存疑有利于被告人”自然是无罪推定不可或缺

---

① 陈光中、张佳华、肖沛权：《论无罪推定原则及其在中国的适用》，载《法学杂志》2013 年第 10 期，第 4 页。

② 参见沈德咏：《论疑罪从无》，载《中国法学》2013 年第 5 期，第 6 页。

的内容。此处的“存疑有利于被告人”包含两层意思：一是“疑罪从无”，即对被追诉人是否有罪存疑时，应当做无罪处理。亦即在已有一定证据证明被追诉人有犯罪嫌疑，但全案证据尚不足以支持有罪证明达到排除合理怀疑等法定证明标准，尚不能确认被追诉人就是真正罪犯时，应当对被追诉人做无罪处理。二是“罪行轻重存疑从轻”，即在案件定罪确定的前提下，对被追诉人罪行轻重存疑时，应当做罪轻处理。陈光中教授主持的《中华人民共和国刑事诉讼法——再修改专家建议稿与论证》第 10 条对无罪推定问题进行了规定。该条第 2 款就规定：“不能认定犯罪嫌疑人、被告人有罪或无罪的，按无罪处理；不能认定犯罪嫌疑人、被告人罪重或罪轻的，按罪轻处理。”① 综观当今世界各大法系和联合国等国际组织关于无罪推定的观点，“疑罪从无”、“罪行轻重存疑从轻”无疑是无罪推定所应当包含的基本内容。

第三节　无罪推定的适用范围

无罪推定的适用范围主要是指无罪推定在什么范围内产生影响或者发生效用。由于无罪推定包含两个维度：证据规则和防范过早惩罚。因此，对于这两个维度的认可情况不同，也就导致对无罪推定的认识不同，进而也会在相当程度上影响对无罪推定适用范围的认识。仅认可证据规则维度者多数认为无罪推定仅适用于提起刑事指控后的刑事庭审阶段，不适用于庭审前的诉讼阶段，更不适用于

① 陈光中主编：《中华人民共和国刑事诉讼法——再修改专家建议稿与论证》，中国法制出版社 2006 年版，第 4 页。

诉讼程序之外，如英美法系的大多数学者和法官持这种观点。[1] 仅认可防范过早惩罚维度者多数认为无罪推定仅是指在法院判决有罪之前应被视为无罪，并不认为或者强调被告人不承担证明自己无罪的义务，如法国旧制度时期的一些法学家持这种观点。[2] 同时认可证据规则和防范过早惩罚双重维度者认为无罪推定不仅适用于庭审程序，也适用于庭审前的诉讼阶段，甚至适用于诉讼程序之外，如

① See Flores v. State, 1995 OK CR 9 (Okla. Crim. App., 1995); Larry Laudan, Truth, Error and Criminal Law: An Essay in Legal Epistemology 99, 103 (Cambridge, CUP, 2006). See e. g., Dick Cavett, An Innocent Misunderstanding, N. Y. TIMES, Mar. 28, 2007, available at http://cavett. blogs. nytimes. com/2007/03/28/an - innocent - misunderstanding, last visited on June 25, 2015. ("The P. of I. has nothing whatever to do with you and me. We can talk, write, broadcast and even put up a billboard (if so foolish) stating that the accused is the one who did it. It has to do with our system. If you find yourself accused of a crime, you do not have to prove your innocence. The burden is on the other side. The prosecution has to prove your guilt. That's about it. And it is not even a rule of law. It is a rule of evidence, relevant only to the judge and the jury.") (alteration in original). See, e. g., Dan Abrams, Presumed Innocent? Bernie Madoff?, WALL ST. J., Feb. 27, 2009, at A15 ("But unless I am sitting in the jury box armed with that power I, and any other nonjuror for that matter, have no obligation, moral or legal, to embrace that legal fiction."). On the debate generated by Abrams's article, see The Presumption of Innocence Belongs Only in the Courtroom. Discuss, available at http://blogs. wsj. com/law/2009/02/27/the-presumption-of-innocence-belongs-only-in-the-courtroom-discuss, last visited on June 25, 2015.

② Francois Quintard-Morénas, *The Presumption of Innocence in the French and Anglo-American Legal Traditions*, 58Am. J. Comp. L. 107, 108-9 (2010).

法国当前的理论和实践。[①] 在法国，对无罪推定的保护不限于刑事诉讼领域。如今，《法国民法典》扩展了 1789 年法国《人权宣言》第 9 条所包含的对于被告人的保护，认可了在定罪前不被公开描述为罪犯的权利。联想到巴黎最高法院在 16 世纪的法学主张，破毁裁判所（the Cour de cassation）在适用新法时裁定对被告人的有罪性没有留有余地的报刊文章违反无罪推定。相似地，一本书的作者不能用“杀人犯”这个词来描述一个尚未被判刑的人，广播或者电视报道不能暗示犯罪嫌疑人犯了被指控的罪行。[②] 于是，我们会

① Cass. le civ., July 12, 2001, Bull. civ. I, No. 222. See also Cass. le civ., Mar. 20, 2007, Bull. civ. I, No. 124 (holding that a press article expressly referring to the accused as "guilty" violates the presumption of innocence). On the tension between the presumption of innocence and the freedom of expression, see Allenet de Ribemont v. France, 308 Eur. Ct. H. R. (ser. A) at 38 (1995) (suspect accused of murder at a press conference held by the French Minister of Interior and senior police officers. The Court observed that if officials cannot be prevented from informing the public about pending criminal investigations, they must do so "with all the discretion and circumspection necessary if the presumption of innocence is to be respected"). On a similar directive for journalists, see Du Roy and Malaurie v. France, 2000-X Eur. Ct. H. R. 34 ("Journalists reporting on criminal proceedings currently taking place must, admittedly, ensure that they do not overstep the bounds imposed in the interests of the proper administration of justice and that they respect the accused's right to be presumed innocent ... ").

② Francois Quintard-Morénas, *The Presumption of Innocence in the French and Anglo-American Legal Traditions*, 58Am. J. Comp. L. 107, 140-1 (2010).

看到，在美国媒体上，专栏作家①和法律分析者②在报道分析刑事案件时会迅速提醒其受众无罪推定本质上是一种仅适用于法庭审理的程序以证明他们将被告人描绘成罪犯的行为是正当的。而类似的对待被告人的行为在法国会构成违法。③

主张无罪推定仅适用于庭审者的理由主要是担心将无罪推定的

---

① See e. g. , Dick Cavett, An Innocent Misunderstanding, N. Y. TIMES, Mar. 28, 2007, available at http://cavett. blogs. nytimes. com/2007/03/28/an - innocent - misunderstanding, last visited on June 25, 2015. ("The P. of I. has nothing whatever to do with you and me. We car talk, write, broadcast and even put up a billboard (if so foolish) stating that the accused is the one who did it. It has to do with our system. If you find yourself accused of a crime, you do not have to prove your innocence. The burden is on the other side. The prosecution has to prove your guilt. That's about it. And it is not even a rule of law. It is a rule of evidence, relevant only to the judge and the jury.") (alteration in original) .

② See, e. g. , Dan Abrams, Presumed Innocent? Bernie Madoff?, WALL ST. J. , Feb. 27, 2009, at A15 ("But unless I am sitting in the jury box armed with that power I, and any other nonjuror for that matter, have no obligation, moral or legal, to embrace that legal fiction.") . On the debate generated by Abrams's article, see The Presumption of Innocence Belongs Only in the Courtroom. Discuss, available at http://blogs. wsj. com/law/2009/02/27/the-presumption-of-innocence-belongs-only-in-the-courtroom-discuss, last visited on June 25, 2015.

③ Cass. le civ. , July 12, 2001, Bull. civ. I, No. 222. See also Cass. le civ. , Mar. 20, 2007, Bull. civ. I, No. 124 (holding that a press article expressly referring to the accused as "guilty" violates the presumption of innocence). On the tension between the presumption of innocence and the freedom of expression, see Allenet de Ribemont v. France, 308 Eur. Ct. H. R. (ser. A) at 38 (1995) (suspect accused of murder at a press conference held by the French Minister of Interior and senior police officers. The Court observed that if officials cannot be prevented from informing the public about pending criminal investigations, they must do so "with all the discretion and circumspection necessary if the presumption of innocence is to be respected."). On a similar directive for journalists, see Du Roy and Malaurie v. France, 2000-X Eur. Ct. H. R. 34 ("Journalists reporting on criminal proceedings currently taking place must, admittedly, ensure that they do not overstep the bounds imposed in the interests of the proper administration of justice and that they respect the accused's right to be presumed innocent ...").

适用范围扩展到法庭审理之外将对惩罚犯罪造成不利影响。① 另外，现实中存在的审前羁押制度以及办案机关有时可以拒绝保释等现象也从侧面证明无罪推定并没有扩展适用于法庭审理之外。而坚持无罪推定不仅适用于法庭审理，而且适用于庭审前的诉讼阶段，甚至适用于诉讼程序之外的人认为只有将无罪推定更广泛地适用于整个诉讼程序以至诉讼程序之外才能保证被追诉人的正常生活和工作不受到不利影响，才能够更广泛和贴心地保护人权。

笔者认为，将无罪推定的适用范围扩展到法庭审理之外确实会对惩罚犯罪造成一定的影响。然而，这是自古以来反对无罪推定者一贯的理由，随着人类刑事司法文明的发展，已经逐渐失去作为反对无罪推定理由的正当性和充分性。现实中存在的审前羁押只是为保证刑事诉讼顺利进行而采取的暂时强制性措施，办案机关拒绝保释也只是在特定情况下才发生，它们都是无罪推定原则的例外，而非常态。之所以现实中在法庭审理之前侦查机关对犯罪嫌疑人进行拘留、逮捕、侦查终结后将案件移送审查起诉，公诉机关提起公诉，是因为国家打击犯罪的基本刑事政策需要作出这样的专门制度安排，否则这一基本刑事政策将无法得到落实。但是，这并不妨碍无罪推定可以在法庭审理之外得以普遍地适用和执行，审前（强制）措施的适用应当确属必要并控制在对犯罪嫌疑人的公民权利减损最小的范围，不得在法庭审理之前就对犯罪嫌疑人进行惩罚。由于善恶有报的朴素道德观念，刑罚报应主义和道义论，以及惩罚犯罪的刑事政策，有罪应当受到惩罚从这些角度讲具有了正当性。这就导致在法院依法定罪之前的庭前诉讼阶段，被追诉人可能遭受刑讯，被侵犯人权；在诉讼程序之外，国家及其官员或者其他公民可能以假定对方犯有罪行或者可能将要从事犯罪的方式对待尚未被宣判有罪的人，给其正常生活或者工作带来不利影响，如一些媒体

---

① Francois Quintard-Morénas, *The Presumption of Innocence in the French and Anglo-American Legal Traditions*, 58Am. J. Comp. L. 107, 108-9 (2010) .

假定嫌疑人有罪的报道，工作招聘中的歧视，行政事务办理中的歧视等都会对尚未被依法判刑、可能无辜的被追诉人的正常生活和工作造成不利影响，造成潜在的侵犯人权和不公。所以，无罪推定的适用范围不应仅限于刑事庭审之上，还应扩展适用于庭审之外的审前诉讼阶段，甚至是诉讼程序之外。

第四节　无罪推定的概念

无罪推定的核心和基本精神就是“任何人在未被依法证明、审判并宣告有罪之前应被视为无罪”。然而，从不同的层次看，无罪推定又呈现出不同的内涵。无罪推定是一个具有多层次内涵的概念。它不仅是一种理念，也是一种制度、一项原则，还是一项权利。作为一种理念，无罪推定是一种思想观念，反映着人们对于刑事诉讼活动应具有某种价值的判断和选择。作为一种制度，无罪推定是一种体系的存在。它不仅包含了基本的原则，而且包含了一系列与之配套的原则、规则和权利，是由一系列原则、规则和权利构成的体系。作为一项原则，无罪推定是刑事诉讼活动普遍遵守的一项准则，是处理刑事诉讼活动中诸多问题的依据。作为一项权利，无罪推定是被追诉人一系列合法权益的保障，维护着当事人的尊严，不仅自身是人权的一部分，而且保障着人权的其他部分。虽然无罪推定权利更能凸显从当事人的角度表达无罪推定这一概念，但其并不能代替无罪推定作为一种理念、一种制度和一项原则所表达的内涵，也不具备完全替代和僭越上述层次无罪推定内涵的功能。同时，无罪推定权利本身并非自由、公平、正义等价值本身，其与无罪推定理念、制度及原则之间的关系也并非目的和手段的关系，其与无罪推定理念、制度及原则一起，与自由、公平、正义等价值之间仍旧是手段和目的、形式和内容、保障和被保障的关系，仍旧是“橘子的皮和瓤”的关系（在橘子的皮和瓤的关系上，皮的目的是保护瓤，保障瓤的价值及其实现。没有皮，瓤就得不到保护，容易受到损害。虽然皮很重要，但瓤才是皮存在的根本目的和价值之所在，没有瓤，则皮的存在将失去意义），仅是在不同的层次上保障着自由、民主、正义等价值的内核及其实现。其中，权利是最硬的外壳，是最具体和最有可执行力及请求力的保障。由表及里，首先是原则，其次为制度，再次是最为柔软的理念，最后就是上述内容所保障的“橘子的瓤”——自由、公平、正义等价值。例如，无罪推定作为一项权利对自由、公平、正义等价值的保护体现在与无罪推定权利相对应的义务的履行和违反义务的责任的承担。权利的实现要求与之对应的义务的履行。无罪推定权利的实现要求与之对应的不侵犯其无罪推定权利的义务的履行。当这种义务不被履行，无罪推定权利被侵害时，负有不侵犯该无罪推定权利义务的主体将承担相应的责任，以此来保障无罪推定权利的实现。无罪推定作为一项原则要求刑事诉讼相关主体应当遵从无罪推定的相关要求，保护被追诉人的无罪推定权利。无罪推定作为一项制度要求刑事诉讼活动所应遵守的各项原则、规则和权利的制定要体现无罪推定的精神。作为一种理念，无罪推定要求人们将无罪推定深植于心底，是自由、公正、民主、人权等价值的延伸和要求，保障和维护着人们对于这些价值信念的坚守。①

从当事人（被追诉人）的角度讲，无罪推定更多地表现为一项权利。从司法办案人员的角度讲，无罪推定更多地表现为一项原则。从整个刑事诉讼活动的角度讲，无罪推定更多地表现为一种理念和一种制度。那种将无罪推定仅归结为单一层次（如仅归结为一种原则或者权利）概念的认识是不恰当的。

无罪推定解决的仅是法律上的无罪推定问题。而实践中导致刑讯逼供的原因并非仅为法律上的有罪推定，而实际上是事实上的有

① 有学者将无罪推定权利与自由、公平、正义等价值一起与无罪推定原则之间的关系视为目的与手段的关系。笔者不同意这种观点。参见张小海：《无罪推定权利论》，中国民主法制出版社 2015 年版，第 2 页。

罪推定。如此一来，无罪推定对于防止刑讯逼供，保障人权的作用难以解释。然而，这与人们的直观感受和实践事实并不符合。因此，对无罪推定必须作出更加充分和科学的解释和界定，不仅不允许法律上的有罪推定，也不允许事实上的有罪推定。唯此，才能真正实现和弘扬无罪推定的初衷和精神，实现其本来的目的和功能。而不会因语言或者形式上的原因导致对无罪推定概念的误解和执行的偏差。

第三章　无罪推定的根据——一个多视角的探查

截至目前，关于无罪推定的论文可谓汗牛充栋，但是对于无罪推定根据的系统理论分析却寥寥无几。下文将从哲学、政治学、法学、伦理学、心理学和决策理论等角度对无罪推定的根据进行探索，以期填补我国学术界在这一令人熟知的刑事司法理念中的理论空白。

第一节　哲学视角下的无罪推定

无罪推定的哲学基础主要涉及认识论和价值论两个方面。认识论主要解决证据规则维度上推定的必要性问题，即“在证据规则维度上为什么要推定?”或者说“在法院认定是否有罪时为什么有时需要推定?”价值论既解决防止定罪前施加惩罚维度上推定的必要性问题，即“定罪前为什么要推定?”也解决“无罪”推定的正当性问题，即“为什么要推定为‘无罪’而不是推定为‘有罪’?”这几者之间的关系如下表所示：

	证据规则维度上	防止定罪前施加惩罚维度上
推定的必要性	认识论	价值论
推定为无罪的正当性	价值论	价值论

从英美法系狭义的无罪推定角度讲，认识论主要解决推定的必要性问题，价值论主要解决“无罪”推定的正当性问题，且这两个问题密切相联：前一问题是讨论后一问题的基础和前提，后一问题是前一问题实现的路径和保障。从大陆法系广义的无罪推定角度讲，认识论主要解决证据规则维度上推定的必要性问题，价值论既解决防止定罪前施加惩罚维度上推定的必要性问题，也解决证据规则和防止定罪前施加惩罚双重维度上“无罪”推定的正当性问题。防止定罪前施加惩罚维度上推定的必要性主要是基于以下三点：一是定罪前一个人是否有罪的法律状态可以分为不确定和确定两种，且确定的法律状态又可分为确定有罪和确定无罪两种。二是是否有罪不确定的法律状态会导致整个社会人人自危，毫无自由和安全可言，因为任何人都无法保证自己不会受到错误追诉，因此会变得异常脆弱、缺乏自信，这不仅会严重减损公民的自由和社会的福祉，损害基本人权，也与自由民主法治的现代社会文明发展方向相悖，因此必须排除这种未经依法定罪前是否有罪不确定的法律状态，亦即一个人在定罪前应当具有明确的法律地位。三是一个人是否有罪只能由法院来确定，而在程序上，由于尚未经过审判，因而无法确定该人在法律上是否有罪。因此，在这种情况下，对一个人是否有罪的法律状态只能进行推定。大陆法系广义的无罪推定中推定的必要性和“无罪”推定的正当性之间的关系与英美法系狭义的无罪推定情况类似，亦即前者是讨论后者的基础和前提，后者是前者实现的路径和保障。

无罪推定的认识论基础既可以是不可知论，也可以是辩证唯物主义认识论。不可知论认为除了感觉或现象之外，世界本身是无法认识的，人的认识能力不能超出感觉经验或现象的范围，不能认识事物的本质及发展规律。[①] 根据不可知论的观点，人类无法认识事

① 参见搜狗百科“不可知论”词条，http://baike.sogou.com/v1168190.htm? ch=ch.bk.innerlink，最后访问时间：2015 年 7 月 22 日。

物的本质及发展规律，无法认识世界本身，因此也无法通过证据认识案件的客观真实。正是由于人类无法真正准确认识案件客观真实，因此对于是否有罪的问题，只能进行推定。然而，将不可知论作为无罪推定的认识论基础是危险的，因为它将导致整个证据制度的崩解，使得整个诉讼程序的存在失去必要性。既然世界不可知，人的认识能力不能超出感觉经验或现象的范围，不能认识事物的本质及发展规律，那么就不可能通过证据来认识案件的原貌，哪怕是部分的还原也不可能。而证据制度是整个诉讼制度的基础，证据是“认识主体—办案人员与认识客体—案件事实之间不可或缺的桥梁”①。否定证据的作用和意义，就意味着否定整个诉讼制度存在的意义。辩证唯物主义认识论认为世界在实践的意义上是可知的，以实践为基础的认识活动，是主体对客体的能动反映，人通过实践能够正确反映客观实际，认识客观事物。② 然而，世界具有可知性，并不等于人类对世界的认识是静止的、绝对的。实际上，人类的认识是无限性与有限性的统一。一方面，人类能够正确认识无限发展着的客观世界；另一方面，人类对客观世界的认识具有阶段性。人类对客观世界的全面准确认识并不是一蹴而就的，而是有一个发展的过程。在特定的时间内，人类可能囿于各种条件的限制，暂时无法准确全面认识客观世界。因此，在有些刑事案件中，办案人员可能囿于证据不全等因素而暂时无法还原案件的本来面目，无法在有限的审限内全面认识案件的客观真实。③ 从认识论的角度讲，无罪推定的基础在于认识的有限性。证据规则维度上推定的必要性就在于认识的有限性，在特定的时点上，人类还不能做到全知全能。如果有一天，由于科技发展等原因，人类能够做到全知全

① 陈光中等：《诉讼真实与证明标准改革》，载《政法论坛》2009年第2期，第6页。

② 参见《马克思主义哲学》编写组：《马克思主义哲学》，高等教育出版社2009年版，第254页。

③ 参见沈德咏：《论疑罪从无》，载《中国法学》2013年第5期，第9-10页。

能，那么就可以不需要推定，更不需要无罪推定了。不可知论无法与现代诉讼制度并存，而马克思主义关于人类认识有限性与无限性相统一的辩证唯物主义认识论则可以与现代诉讼制度相容。无罪推定的存在并非因为人类不能认识客观真实，而是由于审判的有限性——一个案件的审理不能无限期拖延，而必须在一个合理有限的期限内基于现有的证据作出有罪或者无罪的明确结论，从无限纠缠的讼累中解脱。[①] 因此，无罪推定在认识论上的真正基础应当是辩证唯物主义认识论，而不是不可知论。无限性与有限性相统一的人类认识规律和审判必须在有限的时间内作出有罪或者无罪明确结论的限制构成了证据规则维度上推定存在的必要性。[②]

无罪推定虽以认识论为基础，但本身不是一个认知规则，而是一个标准原则，是一个价值判断和选择。实事求是是一个认知规则，属于认识论问题，不是价值判断和选择，亦非价值论问题。而且无罪推定的认识论基础即承认无限性与有限性相统一的辩证唯物主义认识论本身也要求实事求是。因此，实事求是与无罪推定完全可以共存。实事求是要求我们通过发挥主观能动性对客观事实和客观规律进行认识和研究。而无罪推定则要求在未依正当法律程序证明有罪并作出有罪判决前，任何人有权被视为无罪。无罪推定的要求既包含了有罪判决要依正当法律程序作出，又包含了有罪判决的证明必须达到一定的标准，如排除合理怀疑，内心确信，或者案件事实清楚、证据确实充分等。在一个被追诉人被依正当法律程序认定有罪之前，不是通过实事求是的方法确定其事实上是否有罪的问题，而是有无法律上的权威认定其是否有罪的问题，是法律地位问题，而非事实问题。当一个被告人经过法庭审理，是否有罪仍旧存

① 此处“审判的有限性”在无明确审限制度的国家主要是指审判必须根据现有证据作出有罪或者无罪的明确结论，从无限的讼累中解脱；在有明确审限制度的国家，除此之外，更主要的是指审判必须在审限内完成。

② Cf. Edna Ullman-Margalit, *On Presumption*, The Journal of Philosophy, Vol. 80, No. 3 (1983), pp. 154-157.

疑时，根据无罪推定原则对其作出的无罪判决只是在审理案件的时点对案件事实情况（暂时无法确认是否有罪）的承认，而非在认识论上承认案件事实无法认识。这里的存疑是对案件事实（是否有罪）阶段性的暂时认定，而非绝对地认为案件事实无法查清。之所以要承认疑罪并据此作出无罪判决，是基于司法效率和社会安宁等价值的现实考量：一个太久不能获得解决的案件即便经过极长的时间最终获得解决，也几乎会失去大部分意义——很多当事人甚至都已不在人世，结果意义上的价值（震慑整个社会以及罪犯个人潜在犯罪，维护社会安宁等）也会大打折扣。马克思主义尊重和保障个人价值①，这是马克思主义能够与无罪推定兼容的价值基础。而马克思主义同样强调实事求是，这是马克思主义对于认识论

---

① Karl Marx, "Capital Punishment", New York Daily Tribune (18 February 1853). "Punishment in general has been defended as a means either of ameliorating or of intimidating. Now what right have you to punish me for the amelioration or intimidation of others? And besides, there is history — there is such a thing as statistics — which prove with the most complete evidence that since Cain the world has neither been intimidated nor ameliorated by punishment. Quite the contrary. From the point of view of abstract right, there is only one theory of punishment which recognizes human dignity in the abstract, and that is the theory of Kant, especially in the more rigid formula given to it by Hegel. Hegel says: 'Punishment is the right of the criminal. It is an act of his own will. The violation of right has been proclaimed by the criminal as his own right. His crime is the negation of right. Punishment is the negation of this negation, and consequently an affirmation of right, solicited and forced upon the criminal by himself.' [Hegel, Philosophy of Right]" ["一般说来，刑罚应该是一种感化或恫吓的手段。可是，有什么权利用惩罚一个人来感化或恫吓其他的人呢？况且历史和统计科学非常清楚地证明，从该隐以来，利用刑罚来感化或恫吓世界就从来没有成功过。适得其反！从抽象权利的观点看，只有一种刑罚理论是抽象地承认人的尊严的，这就是康德的理论，特别是当黑格尔用了一个更严谨的定义来表述它的时候。黑格尔说：'刑罚是罪犯的权利。它是罪犯本身意志的行为。罪犯把违法说成是自己的权利。他的犯罪是对法的否定。刑罚是这种否定之否定，因而又是对法的肯定；这种法是罪犯自己要求的，并且是他强加于自身的。'（黑格尔：《法哲学原理》）"] See http://www.marxists.org/archive/marx/works/1853/02/18.htm, last visited on June 9, 2015. 本文是马克思用英文写的第一篇论文。中文版翻译参见中共中央马克思恩格斯列宁斯大林著作编译局：《马克思恩格斯全集》（第8卷），第578-579页。

的态度。实事求是与无罪推定是两个范畴内的问题，二者并不矛盾，可统一于马克思主义的哲学观中。

无罪推定不是绝对的。从证据规则的维度讲，无罪推定意味着证明有罪的责任在控诉方，被控诉方不承担证明自己无罪的责任，但享有反驳控诉方有罪指控的权利，即辩护权。然而证明不是绝对的，证明标准再高，也不可能排除一切无罪怀疑；否则，那将会是在有限的时间内不可能完成的任务，也违背认识具有阶段性的规律。实际上，在严格的意义上讲，证明总是与推定相伴相随。俗话说："人心隔肚皮。"这说明人的主观世界是难以准确全面认识的，更是无法完全证明的。由于主观世界无法完全证明，对于主观世界的证明或多或少都会含有推测的成分，或者讲对犯罪主观方面的认定或多或少都含有推定的成分，因此就对犯罪主观方面的认定方法而言，推定和证明的区别是相对的，而不是绝对的。即便对于其他犯罪构成要素而言，由于人类对客观世界的认识是处于发展过程中的，因此对其他犯罪构成要素的认定也是相对的，而不是绝对的。无罪推定从作为证明责任分配规则的意义上讲，相应地也不具有绝对性。反映在证明规则上，虽然控诉方承担证明有罪的责任，但是其并不承担绝对地证明构成犯罪所可能需要确认的一切要素的责任，特别是涉及犯罪主观方面的证明必然或多或少包含推定的成分。同时，对于犯罪的证明标准也不可能达到绝对排除一切无罪可能的程度，而只能尽量达到一个极高的程度（如排除合理怀疑）。对于这一极高的证明标准和案件待证事实（客观真实）之间的差距，或者说对于案件待证事实的最后认定只能依赖于推定。此时，所认定的"案件事实"实际上是"法律真实"，而非哲学意义上的客观真实。如果将证明比作在证据铺就的通往待证事实的道路上行走，而将推定比作从已知事实到待证事实的跳跃的话，那么证明所行走的道路也不一定路面平整、毫无缝隙，证明行进的脚步也会掠过路面的缝隙或者缺漏，而不是像压路机的光钢轮一样要连续地压过每一片路面。证明行进的脚步对路面缝隙或者缺漏的这种掠过本身就是一种推定，这也恰是对证明中推定成分的写照，因此也可以说，这样的掠过（推定）本身也是行走（证明）的组成部分，是行走（证明）的内在应有之义，证明本身就包含了推定的成分。同时，正是因为所有的证明都不是绝对的，都或多或少需要一定的推定作为补充才能认定待证事实，而推定又都是允许反驳的（所谓不可反驳的“推定”其实是“拟制”，而非推定）①，由此构成了诉讼中控辩双方“证明—反驳—证明”的循环往复。也正由此构成了纷繁复杂、千变万化的具体诉讼过程。法官（裁判者）正是在对这一过程的主持和把控中认定案件事实，亦即“法律真实”。这一过程生动体现了无罪推定的辩证唯物主义认识论基础，是辩证唯物主义认识论在诉讼证明过程中的鲜活运用。

由于无罪推定的价值论基础所涉及的自由、人权等内容与政治学、法学和伦理学等问题紧密相联，因此本书将主要在下文对这部分内容进行阐述。

第二节　政治学视角下的无罪推定

正如保罗·罗伯茨和艾德里安·扎克曼在其著作《证据法》（第2版）中所言，“只有通过探索无罪推定的政治道德才能意识到无罪推定真正的法学意义”。（“Only by exploring the political morality of the presumption of innocence can its true jurisprudential significance be appreciated”.）② 无罪推定的思想虽然自古有之，但是其在近代被资产阶级思想家明确提出却有其深刻的政治逻辑。欧洲文艺复兴时期，资产阶级思想家明确提出了“天赋人权”的政治学说，并以此为基础提出“主权在民”的政治主张，以对抗当时封建统

① 参见徐灿：《论腐败案件中明知的推定规则在中国的确立》，载《澳门法学》2015年第14期。

② Paul Roberts & Adrian Zuckerman, Criminal Evidence 221（Oxford：Oxford University Press，2010）.

治者的专制暴政。基于上述理论，资产阶级又提出了“社会契约论”的国家政治理论，主张国家是由拥有天赋权利的人们让渡自己的天赋权利和自由而结成的契约，因此国家有义务为让渡自己权利的人们提供公共保护。只要作为契约当事方的人们（国家公民）没有违反这一契约，国家就不能违反该契约取消对公民的公共保护。正是基于此，1764 年，意大利法学家贝卡利亚在其名著《论犯罪与刑罚》中提出：“在法官判决之前，一个人是不能被称为罪犯的。只要还不能断定他已经侵犯了给予他公共保护的契约。社会就不能取消对他的公共保护，”明确提出无罪推定的刑事司法原则。

无罪推定虽然由资产阶级明确提出在前，但是它并非资产阶级的专利。社会主义同样主张无罪推定，但其政治逻辑却有所不同。社会主义主张无罪推定的政治逻辑在于：人民在代表自己利益的政党的带领下，通过革命斗争夺取政权，建立起社会主义国家。因此，社会主义国家的一切权力属于人民，人民是国家的主人。人民通过选举自身利益的代表具体行使国家权力。因此，社会主义国家有义务为人民利益服务，为人民提供公共保护。只要作为人民一员的个人没有侵害人民的利益，没有成为人民的敌人，而始终作为人民的一员，社会主义国家就有对其提供公共保护的义务。因此，任何人在未被依法证明并宣告有罪之前，都不能被视为有罪。当然，社会主义国家是人民利益的代表，是对人民的敌人进行专政的工具。一旦被告人被依法证明并宣告有罪，那么被告人就不再属于人民的一员，就不再受到社会主义国家为人民提供的公共保护，就会受到法律的相应惩罚。

刑事司法与政治德性密切相关，因为通过刑事裁决评判刑事责任和实施惩罚完全是一项道德事业。证据搜集和审判中证明有罪的道德标准应当向公众保证合法的国家权威未被僭越并且错误定罪的风险已被降到可以容忍的水平——鉴于所有的人类努力都可能发生错误，错判无辜的风险永远无法被完全排除。[①] 错误定罪会导致国家取消对公民自由、自主和人身及财产安全等权利的公共保护，因此采取有力的保障措施避免因错误定罪而侵犯公民自由、自主和人身及财产安全相关权利就变得非常有必要。无罪推定要求控诉方承担证明责任，要求保释权，反对强迫自证其罪，反对刑讯逼供，因此，本身也是这样一种保障措施。[②]

无罪推定不是一个可能性或者概率的陈述，[③] 而是一个政治信仰的陈述，体现着一定的政治倾向和价值抉择，是自由的保障。可以说，无罪推定最根本的价值基础就是自由，自由是无罪推定正当性的根本支撑。一个人是否有罪的法律状态可以分为三种：一个是有罪，一个是无罪，还有一个是不确定。有罪和无罪都是确定的法律状态。在审前阶段，如果没有无罪推定，那么逻辑上被追诉人的法律地位必然是有罪或者是否有罪不确定。如果在没有定罪的情况下被追诉人就被假定为有罪或者是否有罪不确定，那么整个社会将人人自危，毫无自由和安全可言，因为任何人都无法保证自己不会被追诉，而且有罪假定在一定程度上会诱使办案人员对被追诉人进行刑讯逼供。无罪推定有利于减轻社会的压抑感。如果实行任何人在被依法判决有罪之前是否有罪不确定的法律制度，那么由于任何人都无法保证自己不被错误追诉，任何人都随时面临着进入自身是

---

① Paul Roberts & Adrian Zuckerman, Criminal Evidence 17 (Oxford: Oxford University Press, 2010).

② See generally Paul Roberts & Adrian Zuckerman, Criminal Evidence 14 (Oxford: Oxford University Press, 2010).

③ 虽然有些学者论及错放有罪和错判无辜人数之比例，但这种比例只是为了表明倾向于反对错判无辜的态度，其本身并不是确立无罪推定的基础，如布莱克斯通（Blackstone）主张传统上“宁愿错放十个，也不可错判一个”。早期的文献还有其他比例的陈述，如黑尔（Hale）主张这一比例是 5∶1，弗特斯克（Fortescue）主张这一比例是 20∶1，斯塔福德议员（Lord Stafford）甚至主张这一比例是 1000∶1。See Glanville Williams, The Proof of Guilt 186-8 (London: Stevens, 3rd edn. 1963); W. Twining, Theories of Evidence: Bentham & Wigmore 95-8 (London: Weidenfeld, 1985).

否有罪不确定状态的风险。这将扩展权力任性的范围，而限缩公民的自由。自由应当不仅仅是指身体自由，也指心理自由。如果一个人时刻处于是否有罪不确定的状态下，那么他就不可能有真正充分的自由。所以，自由是无罪推定的根本价值支撑，是无罪推定主张的真谛之所在。对待无罪推定的态度，在某种程度上反映着对待自由的态度。在审判阶段，如果没有无罪推定，那么被告人被错误定罪的风险将会大大增加。由于任何人都面临着被迫在法庭上证明自己无罪的风险，任何人的自由、安全和隐私都将无法得到保障，任何人都将可能为自己没有犯下的罪行而承担责任。这同样会造成整个社会人心惶惶，毫无自由和安全可言。无罪推定的根本在于要求对犯罪追诉机关执行刑法进行问责。不能在给不出正当理由，不能作出合理解释的情况下恣意执行刑法，实施惩罚。否则，自由和安全将不复存在。刑事诉讼程序总是敏锐地反映着一个国家或者一个地区当时的社会关系和政治关系。在自由受到严厉约束的社会，无罪推定经常被唾弃，被排除在刑事司法制度之外。例如，1958 年苏联就有最高苏维埃代表公开指责无罪推定为“陈旧教条的资产阶级学说”。20 世纪 50 年代我国进行的整风反右运动将无罪推定原则定性为“资产阶级反动原则”，并认为其与我国的社会主义司法制度不相容。“文化大革命”期间，自由被严重践踏，公检法都被砸坏，更谈不上在司法制度中确立无罪推定原则。[①] 有罪推定的社会是一个不宽容、缺乏信任、相互猜疑、暴戾和富有攻击性、不和谐的社会。相反，无罪推定的社会趋向于宽容、相互信任、温和与和谐。除了在社会中掌握了绝对的权力、财富等各种资源的人之外，谁会愿意生活在一个有罪推定的社会中？很显然，不宽容、缺乏信任、相互猜疑、暴戾和富有攻击性、不和谐等特征与现代民主

① Cf. Hock Lai Ho, *The Presumption of Innocence as a Human Right* in Paul Roberts and Jill Hunter (eds), Criminal Evidence and Human Rights - Reimagining Common Law Procedural Traditions 277-8 (Oxford: Hart Publishing, 2012).

社会格格不入，它们是专制社会的特征，而不是民主社会的特征。社会主义社会应当是一个人民依法享有自由权利的民主社会，不应当与上述那些特征共存，因此社会主义法制不能一般地接受有罪推定，而必须实行无罪推定。

无罪推定限制公权力随意侵犯个人自由，赋予个人对公权力的行使提出质疑的权利，使个人有权要求公权力对其寻求限制个人自由的行为在法庭上作出合理解释，确保个人安全不受公权力恣意不公的干涉，是个人自由的保障。① 然而，自由来自于安全，并从不受犯罪侵害的安全自信中获取力量。一个保障自由的政府必然同时竭力保障社会的安全和秩序，保证其人民能够自由地生活、出行、合法享用财产而不必担心其生命、健康、自由及财产会受到犯罪的侵害。② 刑事诉讼程序不仅要惩罚和震慑犯罪以保护人民的切身利益和伸张正义，而且要避免冤枉无辜，保证所有人不因错误定罪和惩罚而受到伤害。无罪推定正是为缓解这两方面因素之间的基本紧张关系而在综合权衡个人自由和社会利益后作出的程序上的平衡。③

此外，虽然无罪推定要求由控诉方而不是被告方承担充分证明被告方有罪的责任，因而是人们不被随意认定为有罪的自由的保障。然而，无罪推定并不意味着控诉方要主动证明所有可能的问题，（例如，无罪推定要求控诉方证明犯罪构成要素问题，但是并不要求控诉方主动提起并证明违法阻却事由问题）因此无罪推定虽是自由的保障，但并非纵容无限制的自由。从这个角度讲，无罪

① Hock Lai Ho, *The Presumption of Innocence as a Human Right* in Paul Roberts and Jill Hunter (eds), Criminal Evidence and Human Rights – Reimagining Common Law Procedural Traditions 279 (Oxford: Hart Publishing, 2012).

② Hock Lai Ho, *The Presumption of Innocence as a Human Right* in Paul Roberts and Jill Hunter (eds), Criminal Evidence and Human Rights – Reimagining Common Law Procedural Traditions 280 (Oxford: Hart Publishing, 2012).

③ Cf. Paul Roberts & Adrian Zuckerman, Criminal Evidence 244 (Oxford: Oxford University Press, 2010).

推定在保障人们自由的同时，也在寻求个体自由与社会公共利益之间的平衡。①

需要特别指出的是，强调和尊重自由不等于赞同政治自由主义。自由是基本人权之一，但是在涉及社会公共政策和公共福利的政治领域，特别是政治思想和制度领域，必须从社会公共福祉出发，基于民主（代表和保障最广大人民的根本利益）和集中（保障基于民主原则制定的政策的有效执行）原则来践行国家政治生活，而绝不能不负责任地丢给丧失原则、无法保障公共福祉的政治自由主义。因为一个国家存在的最重要的根据和正当性之一就是保障最广大人民的根本利益，保护和发展好公共福祉；否则，这个国家本身就失去了道义上的正当性，就失去了正义性。政治自由主义丧失原则，主张对政治自由完全放任，然而由于无论在哪种制度下的社会，政治和舆情都容易被操弄，并且在现代社会条件下，许多问题（如经济金融等决策问题）对于民众来讲过于专业，以致无法进行明智、理性、有效的选择。因此，对政治自由完全放任的政治自由主义无法保障公共福祉，是自由走向极端的一种表现形式（其消极自由有余，积极自由不足），甚至会导致政治和社会混乱，阻碍甚至危害社会进步，因而不应为政治生活所接受。就我国国情而言，追求共同富裕是我国的基本国策，也是由我国的社会主义国家性质所决定的。政治自由主义承认和尊重不同群体和利益集团的不同利益诉求，但是并不以追求共同富裕为目标而且并不特别在意这种既得利益获取的正当性。我国的贫富分化和由此形成的不同社会阶层则是在改革开放"让一部分人先富起来"的国策下形成的。换句话说，我国先富群体的形成得益于国家"让一部分人先富起来"的政策。然而，"让一部分人先富起来"并非我国政策的全部，更非我国政策制定的目的及初衷。我国这一政策的目的及初衷

① Paul Roberts & Adrian Zuckerman, Criminal Evidence 244-5 (Oxford: Oxford University Press, 2010).

在于“先富带动后富，最终达到共同富裕”。也就是说，“让一部分人先富起来”仅是暂时的、过渡性的手段，其本身并不是我们想要达到的结果，因此我国不可能承认这些先富群体作为社会利益主体基于先富的特殊地位而提出的诉求，更不可能承认通过贪腐等非法途径获得不正当利益的群体基于其因非法获利而获得的特殊条件所提出的诉求，也不可能承认对此予以认可和支持的政治自由主义的正当性。即便政治自由主义所主张的重叠性共识具有一定的正当性，但是其范围也势必会大大缩小，无法准确代表和反映最广大人民的根本利益和我国的国家性质。政治自由主义很容易导致社会的不公，并且在社会未实现完全公平的条件下实行政治自由主义，必然导致和进一步强化社会的不公，因为在社会未实现完全公平的条件下实行政治自由主义，其结果必然是居于强势地位的既得利益集团攫取政权，为了维护和巩固其既得利益，其必然实行维护和巩固其既得利益的政策，这只会进一步固化甚至恶化社会的不公平现状，违背社会最大多数人的最大和根本利益，违背社会整体福利最大化的目标，必然会带来不正义性。

政治自由主义不适合我国目前的国情，因为其无法保障公共福祉，无法保障全体民众的平等权利，易成为既得利益群体基于其不以公平为基础而获得的特殊地位操控政治的工具。由此，我们自然可以得出，就目前的中国国情而言，要获得政治上的正当性，就必须能够保障公共福祉，保障全体民众的平等权利，防止既得利益群体基于其不以公平为基础而获得的特殊地位操控政治。而如果执政党能够通过加强自身建设，以先进理论和完善制度提高其执政能力、确保其为人民服务的性质，通过加强和完善法治来增强人民、社会各界及相关国家机关的民主监督能力，确保执政党能够一直沿着正确的道路走下去、始终坚定地代表和维护最广大人民的根本利益，那么社会整体福利最大化的目标可实现，最大多数人的最大和根本利益得到充分和有效保护的目标可实现，正义也就可实现。因此，笔者的建议是执政党要有科学理论的指导和武装，不断完善和发展这一理论，使得执政党能够始终保持有效和良性的执政能力，同时不断完善相关制度，建设完善的法治国家和法治社会，提高人民、社会各界和相关国家机关对执政党的民主监督能力和效果，从而保障执政者始终代表最广大人民的根本利益、始终确保社会整体福利最大化、始终遵循和体现正义性、实现和维护正义。对于我国来讲，作为执政者的中国共产党对该问题给出的答案就是“三个代表”，即中国共产党要始终代表中国先进生产力的发展要求，始终代表中国先进文化的前进方向，始终代表中国最广大人民的根本利益（中国共产党所主张的其他相关理论与之都是一致的）。这是中国共产党的党建工作，亦即中国共产党要通过不断加强和改进党的建设使党始终符合上述“三个代表”的要求，始终符合上述执政正当性的要求。为此，中国共产党不断创新党建的理论和实践，不断完善党的制度和队伍建设，确保能够做到这些要求。近几年来，党中央强力反腐，并且不断完善反腐机制，使其常态化和制度化，不仅净化了党的队伍，完善了党的制度，而且使党的先锋作用和人民性更加突显，在执政的正当性上取得了很大的成效，获得了广大人民群众的一致好评。

特别提出一点：当社会中某一群体具有紧迫性的急切需求与其他群体一般性的需求之间产生冲突，特别是当社会中最需要获得帮助的底层民众的根本利益与其他阶层的利益发生根本冲突时，即便这部分急需帮助的底层民众在数量上达不到“最广大人民”的要求，也不能按照“始终代表中国最广大人民的根本利益”的要求而抛弃他们，因为从伦理学的角度看，“人类的苦难发出直接的道德要求，也就是获得帮助的要求，”① 只有优先关注和提供这种被紧迫需求的帮助才是符合道德价值的——政治的正当性应当符合道德的正义性。例如，虽然我国目前绝大部分人已经实现脱贫，但是

① Karl R. Popper, The Open Society and Its Enemies, Volume I, 284–85 n. 2 (Princeton: Princeton University Press, 5th rev. ed. 1966).

仍旧有1000多万人口[①]生活在贫困线以下。此时，虽然这部分人从占比上看还达不到“最广大人民”的要求，但是道德的正义性和我国社会主义的国家性质决定了我们必须努力帮助他们尽快脱贫，以实现政治的正当性。另外一个例子就是虽然冤假错案的受害人从总体数量的占比上看并不大，但是从政治的正当性和道德的正义性上看，也必须努力尽快纠正这些错误，以使他们摆脱亟须洗刷的冤屈，实现司法的公正。审判监督程序的设立在一定程度上就是基于这样的价值考量。

此外，由于国际政治和形势的影响，我们要实现中华民族伟大复兴的中国梦，在目前以及可预见的未来，只能寄希望于依靠和改善党的领导，加快做好各项改革，而不能盲目实行政治自由主义。至于何时可以实行政治自由主义，就我国的国情而言，至少要满足下面三个条件才有可能：一是我国的综合国力在国际上获得绝对优势，已不存在明显的外部威胁和挑战；二是已实现共同富裕；三是已建立起完善的法制并已建成完善的法治社会。即便这些条件已经成熟，也不意味着我国就应当实行政治自由主义，因为政治自由主义本身并不具有必然性，并非解决社会问题的终极良方；保障最广大人民的根本利益，实现社会的全面正义价值并非必须要实行政治自由主义；实际上政治自由主义也无法保障上述目标的实现——重叠性共识的主张听起来好听，但是也要以代表最广大人民的根本利益为前提，要具备正当性和正义性，而不能是庸俗的泛化的重叠性共识。我们党在着眼于我国的国情实际和放眼全球一切有益经验的基础上，不断地探求实现社会全面正义的方法，并在不断地取得一定的成效。我们没有理由否认，并且应当坚信，这一探索能够取得

---

① 参见《2017年末我国农村贫困人口减少到3046万人》，http://www.xinhuanet.com/politics/2018-02/01/c_1122353906.htm，最后访问时间：2018年7月9日。2018年，我国农村贫困人口减少1386万，异地扶贫搬迁280万人。参见《2019年国务院政府工作报告》，http://news.sina.com.cn/c/xl/2019-03-05/doc-insxncvf9915493.shtml，最后访问日期：2019年3月6日。

伟大的成功，能够找到一条符合我国实际的现代化道路，能够为人类文明的发展和多样性贡献我们的力量。

自由不是绝对的、无条件的。无罪推定并不意味着绝对的不受任何约束的自由，反之，无罪推定权利的全面保障还要求对自由进行一定的限制。例如，在被追诉人未被法院依法认定为有罪之前，法庭以外的任何组织和个人都不能视被追诉人为有罪。[①] 此外，作为一名中国共产党员和国家公职人员，既然已经选择加入该党派，选择成为一名国家公职人员，就应当遵守该党的纲领、政策和纪律，以服务国家和人民的根本利益为宗旨，而不应没有原则、无所顾忌地放任自己的言行。因为当一个人选择加入某党派时，他（她）就选择了放弃不遵守该党纲领、政策和纪律的自由；当一个人选择成为国家公职人员时，他（她）就选择了放弃不以服务国家和人民的根本利益为己任的自由。

作为一项社会主义核心价值观，民主是我国人民民主专政社会主义国家性质的内在要求。人民民主在司法领域的具体体现就是司法民主。司法民主要求司法活动必须充分吸收诉讼当事人和人民群众参与诉讼进程，尊重与保障诉讼当事人和其他诉讼参与人的各项合法权益。[②] 在刑事诉讼中，被追诉人在未被依法定罪以前，仍旧属于人民的一员，司法民主也特别表现为尊重与保障被追诉人的诉讼主体地位和其他合法权益，包括公正对待权、辩护权等。公正权是基本人权之一。任何人都有权在政治上获得基于历史和现实的相对公平合理的对待。刑事诉讼是对犯罪行为的国家追究。无罪推定正是基于国家追诉力量相对于被追诉人所具有的压倒性优势的实际，为了保持被追诉人的政治主体地位，尊重其作为人而应当享有的独立自主性，基于公正原则而在法律上作出的一种制度安排。实

---

① Francois Quintard-Morénas, *The Presumption of Innocence in the French and Anglo-American Legal Traditions*, 58Am. J. Comp. L. 107, 108-9 (2010).

② 沈德咏：《论疑罪从无》，载《中国法学》2013年第5期，第8页。

行无罪推定有助于保障被追诉人的诉讼主体地位和公正对待权、辩护权等其他合法权益。从政治的角度讲，无罪推定是对人民权利的保障，是人民所享有的依法打击犯罪、保障社会福利的社会权利与个人合法权益不受侵犯的个人权利之间的平衡器。它使得人民在享受国家追诉犯罪职能所带来的社会福利的同时，能够兼顾个人的福利，即个体人权得到保障，合法权益不受侵犯。无罪推定是公平价值的要求。此外，公正权的实现也需要民主做保障。没有民主就难以实现公正，难以落实无罪推定。在没有民主的条件下要实现公正，就只能依靠行为者自觉按照法律、规则和公平正义原则行事。然而，在生产力水平尚不能满足按需分配的现实条件下，我们无法假定所有人都是道德人，而只能假定所有人原则上都是理性人，即努力实现自身利益最大化的人。此外，如果行为者都是自觉按照法律、规则和公平正义原则行事的道德人，那么整个司法制度将没有必要存在，因为在道德人假设的条件下，所有的实体法律、政策都将被这些道德人完美有效地执行，也就没有真正不可调和的矛盾存在，不需要司法制度来解决这些矛盾。而这明显是不现实的，“文化大革命”砸烂公检法实践的失败也证实了这一点。道德人的假设是不成立的。司法既是公平正义的象征，也是贫困的象征。正是因为现实中还做不到按需分配，所以，才会产生纷争和犯罪，才需要司法定分止争和恢复社会正义。就像医疗既是救死扶伤的象征，也是生病和死亡的象征。正是因为人类还面临着生病和死亡的威胁，所以才需要医疗救死扶伤，挽救生命于危亡。作为法治国家的一项基本原则，司法民主还要求司法过程最大限度地实现公开化、透明化，确保公民的知情权、参与权、表达权，进而实现对司法工作的有效监督。[①] 法谚有云，“正义不仅要实现，而且要以看得见

① 沈德咏：《论疑罪从无》，载《中国法学》2013年第5期，第8页。

的方式实现"[1]。正是司法民主所要求的司法公开透明保证了司法受到人民监督，保证了包括无罪推定在内的正当法律程序得到遵守，保证了公正权以遵守包括无罪推定在内的正当法律程序的方式实现。

无罪推定是程序正义的要求。公正的程序是正义的政治主张得以实现的保障。无论实施什么政治主张，采用类似"文化大革命"的方法肯定是不对的，无论这种政治主张多么正义。没有法治，没有公正的程序，再正义的目的也无法保证实现，还可能附带出严重的恶。交流非常重要，各方都要有交流的态度。任何一方企图以势压人，而不是以理服人都有可能造成结果的不正义。如何使各方都有交流的态度，并且能够交流好，则成了一个大问题。"文化大革命"的方法确实有效，也确实高效，但更适于战争时期，而不适于和平时期。正如"战时共产主义"政策在战争时期起到了积极的作用，但到了和平建设时期，却带来了很大的弊端。因为战争时期形势瞬息万变，时间就是生命，时间就是胜利，不可能有太多的时间去纠结于每一个细节，因此效率至上。而在和平时期，人们相对更加看重公正的价值。虽然"迟来的正义非正义"，但是"迟来的正义"也总要好于"早到的非正义"。

无罪推定有利于促进社会的和谐。有罪推定可能会增加社会的戾气。一些原本可能中止的犯罪可能会因为有罪推定理论和实践的存在而演变为激情犯罪或者不计后果的严重犯罪。当一个人因为一个较轻的过错行为而可能导致日后被推定有较重的罪行时，这个人可能会铤而走险或者不计后果，干脆将较轻的过错行为发展为严重的犯罪行为，从而增加社会的戾气。因此，即便对于有罪的怀疑是合理的，也不能仅仅因为存在有罪的可能就推定某人有罪。

无罪推定关系到国家权力的分配和行使，关系到国家刑事政策

---

① Paul Roberts & Adrian Zuckerman, Criminal Evidence 16 (Oxford: Oxford University Press, 2010).

的制定，与政治密切相关。根据国家政治的需要和国家政策的变化，无罪推定的落实、具体内容和范围等也会发生相应的变化，如英国的保护被害人利益政策以及美国的反恐政策等就对无罪推定的内容和具体执行产生了一定影响。

无罪推定符合自由、民主、人权等价值标准，符合我们党的基本政策和宗旨，也与我国代表人民根本利益的社会主义国家性质相吻合。因此，在我国确立无罪推定的基本理念、制度和原则不仅具有政治上的正当性，而且与我国的国体、政体和执政党的政策及宗旨具有兼容性。

第三节　法学视角下的无罪推定

在刑事诉讼中，诉讼的一方是代表国家履行犯罪追诉职能的检察机关，诉讼的另一方是作为被追诉对象的自然人、法人或者其他组织。由于追诉方在物质和组织上具有巨大优势，控辩双方在诉讼能力上不可避免地会出现严重失衡。国家追诉机关（检察机关）不仅拥有审查起诉权和提起公诉权，而且（侦查机关）拥有侦查权和收集证据的相关机会。特别是拥有侦查权的机关可以拘留、逮捕、讯问犯罪嫌疑人以获得口供。被告人甚至会被还押候审。这一切都导致国家追诉机关在指控犯罪时具有相当的实践优势，这些优势又进而可能影响随后的审判结果。因而，有必要采取制度性的矫正措施以确保个体性的犯罪嫌疑人和被告人免于遭受国家追诉权滥用和严重错判的危害。① 公平正义是人类社会的永恒追求，更是司法的最高价值，是司法的生命。刑事司法的根本原则就是要追求公平正义。反映到刑事诉讼中，公平正义要求被追诉人有权获得公正审判，刑事诉讼双方要被平等武装，具备能够大致相互抗衡的诉讼

① Cf. Paul Roberts & Adrian Zuckerman, Criminal Evidence 14－5（OUP, 2nd edn. 2010）.

能力。证据规则维度上的无罪推定正是基于刑事诉讼中控辩双方证明能力严重失衡的现实和“平等武装”原则的要求而采取的一种折中性方案。只有实行无罪推定，才能尽量矫正国家追诉力量与被追诉人辩护力量的严重失衡，才能在制度上尽量防止国家追诉权滥用和错误定罪，才能真正做到公正审判，实现公平正义这个司法的最高价值。①

无罪推定是尊重司法规律的结果。人类对于客观事物的认识能力虽然从整体上来讲是无限的，但是在特定阶段和条件下却是有限的。因此，疑案的存在在特定的时空和物质技术条件下便成为可能。同时，司法不仅要追求公平正义，也要强调成本和效率，必须考虑司法资源有限性的客观现实。如果不计成本和效率，无限地追求案件客观真实，就可能失去诉讼程序的社会正义性，社会的整体利益反而会受到损害。因此，一个案件不能无限期拖延，而必须在有限的时间内结案。正如法谚所云，“迟来的正义非正义”。(Justice delayed is justice denied.）一个案件的裁判结果无论多么公正，如果它来得太迟，对于这一公正的应得者来说也如同被拒绝给予正义。此外，从逻辑上讲，任何一个人在法律上是否有罪，其答案只能是二选一的：或者有罪，或者无罪。特别是在一个人被卷入刑事诉讼程序后，这个问题就变得更加严肃和重要，必须在法律上有一个明确的答案，否则其基本人权和其他权益都可能受到侵害。面对疑案，法律必须在有限的时间内给出是否有罪的明确结论。法院没有拒绝裁判的权力，否则法院本身的存在将失去意义。法院也没有拒绝对案件给出有罪或者无罪明确结论的权力，因为在一个法治社会里，法院是有权回答这一问题的终极机关，没有任何其他组织或者个人比法院更有资格对该问题给出明确的结论。因此，无论

① Cf. Tom P. Conom, *Bulwarks of Liberty*: *Presumption of Innocence and Reasonable Doubt*, 45 Wash. St. B. News 38, 1991; Paul Roberts & Adrian Zuckerman, Criminal Evidence 14-5 (OUP, 2nd edn. 2010).

在证明有罪之前还是在出现疑罪的情况下，无罪推定都有其存在的必要性。

根据无罪推定所认定的案件事实是典型的法律真实。关于客观真实和法律真实之间的关系，存在不同的观点：有的认为应当客观真实优先，有的认为应当法律真实优先，还有的认为客观真实和法律真实应当（动态）并重。笔者认为，客观真实和法律真实（实体公正和程序公正）之间并不是相互独立或者对立的关系，而是目的和手段，对象和结果之间的关系。在诉讼中，客观真实和法律真实并不是并列的关系，讲“客观真实与法律真实（动态）并重”容易使人产生误解。在诉讼中，法律真实不能离开客观真实而独立存在，法律真实是在一定的法律（诉讼）规则下对客观真实的认识结果，没有客观真实，法律真实也就失去了认识对象，可谓“皮之不存，毛将焉附?”；在诉讼中，对客观真实的认识也离不开法律真实，法律真实是对客观真实认识的必然结果，没有法律真实（完全抛开法律真实），就无法认识客观真实。因此，客观真实和法律真实并不是并重的关系，而是协调一致完成诉讼使命、实现诉讼价值的关系。从诉讼的功能上讲，二者具有协调统一性。同时，我们也必须看到法律真实存在与客观真实相符的程度问题，有些法律真实与客观真实的相符程度更高，而有些法律真实与客观真实的相符程度更低，这取决于法律程序的优劣。优秀的法律程序能够使通过其获得的法律真实与客观真实更相符，而存有缺陷的法律程序则可能会使通过其获得的法律真实与客观真实相背离。客观真实具有客观性和确定性，而法律真实则具有主观性和不确定性，是诉讼参与者通过一定的诉讼规则而获得的对于客观真实的认识，并且通过不同的诉讼规则对于客观真实所获得的认识可能不同。因此，我们应做的不是将客观真实与法律真实作为两元来并重或者将谁优先，而是不断改进我们的法律程序，以使通过更优秀的法律程序所获得的法律真实更加符合客观真实，从而实现我们在诉讼中认识（法律真实）的真理性。

当然，需要指出的是，在既定的法律程序下，我们所讲的客观真实通常实际上是指最接近客观真实的认识结果，而法律真实是指通过该既定的法律程序对客观真实的认识结果。在这个意义上，所谓客观真实优先还是法律真实优先，抑或是二者（动态）并重，实际上主要是指在一定的法律程序下对客观真实的认识结果（法律真实）并非最接近对客观真实的认识结果，而另有比其更接近客观真实但不符合该既定法律程序要求的认识结果（即此处所谓的"客观真实"）的情况下，法律真实优先还是这种比法律真实更接近客观真实的认识结果（"客观真实"）优先，抑或是二者（动态）并重。笔者认为，在"客观真实"最接近客观真实的认识结果这个意义上，在既定的法律程序下，似乎"客观真实"和法律真实（动态）并重的观点更为合理，即如果法律真实优先会严重损害实体公正，而"客观真实"优先不会严重违反法定程序，则应当"客观真实"优先；反之，如果"客观真实"优先会严重违反法定程序，而法律真实优先不会严重损害实体公正，则应当法律真实优先；如果法律真实优先会严重损害实体公正，同时"客观真实"优先会严重违反法定程序，或者如果法律真实优先不会严重损害实体公正，同时，"客观真实"优先不会严重违反法定程序，则由法庭（裁判者）根据客观具体实际情况自由裁量法律真实优先还是"客观真实"优先。这主要基于以下两方面价值的权衡：一是从"客观真实"优先的方面看，主要在于：（1）实事求是的基本政策；（2）保障实体公正是公正程序的重要使命之一，也是程序公正的权威来源之一；（3）之所以出现法律真实与"客观真实"不符的情况，一个重要原因就是程序不够完善（程序的瑕疵或者不足是产生"客观真实"还是法律真实优先问题的一个重要根源）。二是从法律真实优先的方面看，主要在于违反法定程序，舍弃法律真实，会严重破坏程序稳定和法制权威，不利于法治社会的建立和公民法治精神的培养。

需要特别指出的是，这里存在一个重要的先决条件：在讨论

“客观真实”还是法律真实优先时，必须首先证明此处所谓的“客观真实”比法律真实更接近客观真实。这是可能影响法治社会建设的一个重要的关键性问题。如果在不具备这一先决条件的情况下讨论“客观真实”还是法律真实优先，甚至践行其结果，则可能导致司法实践中以追求“客观真实”为由，恣意践踏法律（法定程序），违反法律真实，破坏法治后果的出现，使得法治社会建设这一长期努力奋斗的成果化为乌有。而如何证明此处所谓的“客观真实”比法律真实更接近客观真实？笔者认为，在此种情况下，必须排除此种所谓的“客观真实”（最接近客观真实的认识结果）并非更接近客观真实的合理怀疑，唯此才能证明其更接近客观真实。当然，如果法律真实本身就是最接近客观真实的认识结果，那么此时法律真实与所谓的“客观真实”合二为一，不存在客观真实优先还是法律真实优先，抑或是二者（动态）并重的问题。

无罪推定是程序正义的要求。笔者认为，程序正义既包含要遵守实证法中的程序规则，也包含要遵守符合正义价值的程序规则。无罪推定既是符合正义价值的程序规则，也是实证法中应当确立的程序规则。无罪推定是建立实质法治国的要求。实质法治国不仅要求国家要受制定法的约束，还要求制定法要符合特定的正义价值，即认可个人的独立价值，并尊重由此衍生出的个人自由和平等。无罪推定恰恰体现了对个人独立价值的认可和尊重，是对个人自由和平等的保障，因此是符合正义价值的程序规则，是建立实质法治国的要求。特别需要指出的一点是，有人以建立实质法治国需要确立自由、人权、法治等价值观念为由，否定绝对真理，将绝对真理观念视为建立实质法治国的障碍。[①] 其实，这是一种偏见。绝对真理的对立面不是自由、人权、法治等价值观念，而是价值多元。绝对真理并不排斥个人的独立价值，也不是建成实质法治国逻辑上的障

---

① Cf. Dieter Grimm：《如何建成实质的法治国》，http://news.ifeng.com/exclusive/lecture/special/grimm/#_www_dt2，最后访问时间：2015 年 4 月 23 日。

碍。将绝对真理视为建成实质法治国的障碍是单纯的经验主义的结论，并没有逻辑上的必然性。价值多元也不是自由的逻辑必然结果。价值多元的根本原因是利益多元。自由充其量是价值多元的一个必要条件，而绝非价值多元的根本原因或者充分条件。绝对真理与承认和尊重法治的独立价值并不矛盾，可以并存。绝对真理可以容得下分权，二者之间并没有逻辑上的矛盾性。例如，在中国执政党中国共产党与司法机关之间的关系上，就是司法机关独立行使审判权、检察权，党对其领导是政治方向上的领导，而非具体业务上的领导。司法机关不仅行使审判权、检察权，而且在其职能范围内享有独立的权力，因此是事实上的分权。有罪推定会导致程序法的虚无，甚至整个法律体系的虚无。古人云："欲加之罪，何患无辞？"意思是只要想加罪于某人，就不用担心找不到借口。这是典型的有罪推定。在这一思想的指导下，"加之罪"具有了随意性，根本或者基本不需要什么法定程序，甚至所加之罪的罪名也可以随意确定。其结果必然是程序法，甚至整个法律体系的虚无，法律完全成了政治的工具，成了为实现自己的欲望而随意拿来使用的工具，是否"加之罪"不决定于是否有罪或者是否能证明有罪，而完全决定于需要。因此，在我国确立全面依法治国的国策背景下，确立无罪推定，不仅具有政治上的正当性，而且具有法律上的正当性。

需要阐明的一点是，承认和坚持马克思主义与承认和尊重法治的独立价值、主张建立法治国并不矛盾。因为马克思主义的世界观是辩证唯物主义和历史唯物主义。辩证唯物主义主张实事求是，承认世界的客观性，并主张人们通过发挥主观能动性来认识客观世界。良善的法治有利于人们认识客观世界。历史唯物主义主张人民是历史的主人和创造者。法治国的建立有利于保障人民的合法权益，彰显人民的历史主人翁和创造者的地位。而且，进一步完善和发展马克思主义需要明确承认和尊重法治的独立价值，认同建立法治国的理念。

无罪推定是准确和合理裁判的客观要求，是完成刑事诉讼法任务的保障。我国刑事诉讼法的任务之一就是“保证准确、及时地查明犯罪事实，正确应用法律，惩罚犯罪分子，保障无罪的人不受刑事追究”。英国也将“保护无罪者不被错误定罪”作为刑事证据法的基本原则之一。在刑事裁判中，准确和合理的判断非常珍贵。冤枉无辜是最严重的官方错误。这不仅会伤害无辜的人，是一种极大的不正义，而且事实上不仅无法起到预防犯罪的作用，反而会削弱这一作用，因为真正的罪犯会因此逃脱法律制裁，可能继续危害社会。当然，如果国家追诉机关已经尽力，而罪犯仍旧逃脱侦查或者定罪，那么国家通常不会因此而直接受到责备。但是，如果国家冤枉无辜，那么国家将是不幸的直接制造者，不论直接相关人怎么想，这种巨大的道德错误都将会对任何政治共同体造成严重影响。谎言即便无害也是错误的，然而，官方关于刑事归责的谎言不仅是错误的，而且几乎总是危害巨大。① 在许多冤假错案中，相关责任机关和个人就总是试图掩盖事实真相，捏造被追诉人有罪的证据，故意使被追诉人受到刑事追究，严重侵犯被追诉人人权，破坏刑事司法制度打击犯罪、保障人权的功能。实际上，无罪推定不能减少错案，相反可能还会增加错案，但其却能最大限度地减少冤枉无辜。因此，无罪推定并非一个一般的错案减少机制，而是一个冤枉无辜的错案减少机制。② 正是从减少冤枉无辜的角度讲，无罪推定有利于形成准确合理的刑事裁判。

无罪推定有利于防止刑讯逼供，保障人权。首先，从刑事政策上讲，有罪当罚，无罪不当罚。在所有的发达的刑法典中都可以找到哈特（Hart）所称的“分配的报应原则”，即任何人都不应为其没有实施、预备或者计划的犯罪行为受到处罚，任何人都不应为其

① Paul Roberts & Adrian Zuckerman, Criminal Evidence 13-4 (OUP, 2nd edn. 2010).

② Paul Roberts & Adrian Zuckerman, Criminal Evidence 14, 242 (OUP, 2nd edn. 2010).

没有犯意或者可免责的行为受到处罚。① 无罪推定明确了被追诉人在未被依法证明有罪并被法庭依法认定有罪前无罪的法律地位，使得对被追诉人进行的刑讯逼供违背上述刑事政策，同时也使得在控诉方未能达到法定证明标准证明被告人有罪的情况下对被告人的定罪处罚违背上述刑事政策。因此，从刑事政策的角度讲，无罪推定有利于遏制刑讯逼供，保障人权。其次，如前所述，无论在证明有罪之前还是在出现疑罪的情况下，关于是否有罪的推定都有其存在的必要性，而从逻辑上讲，任何一个人在法律上都只能或者有罪，或者无罪，因此有罪推定是否认无罪推定的逻辑必然结果。无罪推定对于防止刑讯逼供、保障人权的意义还在于：鉴于推定存在的必要性，如果没有无罪推定，则必然实行有罪推定，这就可能为刑讯逼供提供正当理由，因为量刑需要知道犯罪的细节，既然已经假定被追诉人有罪，那么要求被追诉人供出犯罪的细节以确定具体刑罚也无可厚非。如此，刑讯逼供就获得了合理性。而被追诉人可能实际上是无辜的。因此，有罪推定可能导致刑讯逼供和侵犯人权，只有放弃有罪推定而实行无罪推定才能避免这一问题。再次，遏制刑讯逼供的目的或者理由就是防止屈打成招，防止无罪的人被追究刑事责任，保护无辜者。如果实行有罪推定，则这一目的已无法实现。因此，有罪推定已不能成为遏制刑讯逼供的理由，不能合理地排除刑讯逼供，只有无罪推定才有利于遏制刑讯逼供，保障人权。最后，鉴于对是否有罪的法律状态进行推定的必要性，不实行无罪推定则必然实行有罪推定。这就容易造成刑讯逼供、冤枉无辜。对于无辜的人来讲，这将是天大的灾难。由于每个人都有可能成为追诉机关怀疑的对象，即便其实际上是无辜的，因此没有无罪推定将会使社会上人人自危，严重减损人们的自由权益。而无辜者不应受到刑事追究，人人享有自由的权利恰是基本人权。因此，无罪推定与保障人权密切相关，是保障人权的要求。那种以“有些搞刑讯

① Nigel Walker, Why Punish? 88 (Oxford University Press, 1991).

逼供的司法人员就这样讲：无罪的人不能严刑拷打，有罪的人总可以严刑拷打吧。”[①] 这种有罪推定的主张否认无罪推定和遏制刑讯逼供及保障人权之间关系的观点是站不住脚的。相反，恰恰是因为“有罪的人总可以严刑拷打”，但由于未经正当法律程序确定有罪，因而会侵犯人权，所以必须明确任何人未经正当法律程序依法证明并认定有罪之前必须被推定为无罪，即确立无罪推定。这也恰恰证明了无罪推定对保障人权、遏制刑讯逼供的重要作用。此外，没有哪项制度或者因素能够必然导致或者防止侵犯人权和刑讯逼供。保障人权和防止刑讯逼供是多种因素综合作用的结果，没有哪项因素起决定作用或者与之有必然关系。无罪推定对保障人权、防止刑讯逼供具有重要作用。以无罪推定与保障人权和防止刑讯逼供之间没有必然关系为由，否定无罪推定对于保障人权和防止刑讯逼供的重要意义，[②] 是不合适的。

无罪推定可以分为法律上的无罪推定和事实上的无罪推定。相应地，有罪推定也可以分为法律上的有罪推定和事实上的有罪推定。无论是法律上的有罪推定还是事实上的有罪推定都易招致侵犯人权、刑讯逼供，应当予以摒弃。认为“没有哪一个制度不是在事实上假定犯罪嫌疑人、被告人有罪。如果不是这样，刑事诉讼程序就无法推动”[③] 的观点是值得商榷的，也是不符合现实的。在当代的主要法系中，没有哪个制度在事实上假定犯罪嫌疑人、被告人有罪，而仅仅是将其作为嫌疑对象。如果说刑事诉讼程序的进行需要一定的推动因素，那么这个推动因素与其说是事实上的有罪推定，不如说是事实上的有罪怀疑。需要注意的是，“嫌疑”或者“怀疑有罪”绝不等于假定有罪。假定有罪的状态是暂时确定的，即有罪；而怀疑有罪的状态是不确定的，既可能有罪，也可能无

---

① 裴苍龄：《论无罪推定》，载《河北法学》2015年第1期，第10-11页。

② 裴苍龄：《论无罪推定》，载《河北法学》2015年第1期，第10页。

③ 易延友：《论无罪推定的涵义与刑事诉讼法的完善》，载《政法论坛》2012年第1期，第17页。

罪。二者之间的关系如下表所示：

	有罪状态是否确定
假定有罪	暂时确定（在符合一定条件时，可能被推翻）
怀疑有罪	不确定（可能有罪，也可能无罪）

正是因为在各个诉讼阶段推动诉讼程序进行的是事实上的有罪怀疑而非事实上的有罪假定，所以侦查机关不仅要收集对被追诉人不利的证据，也要收集对被追诉人有利的证据，不仅要将对被追诉人不利的证据移送审查起诉机关，也要将对被追诉人有利的证据移送审查起诉机关；审查起诉机关不仅要审查对被追诉人不利的证据，也要审查对被追诉人有利的证据，如果作出起诉决定，则不仅要向法庭出示对被追诉人不利的证据，也要向法庭出示对被追诉人有利的证据；法庭不仅要审查对被追诉人不利的证据，也要审查对被追诉人有利的证据。只有这样，审查起诉机关才能兼听则明地作出公正的关于是否起诉的决定，法庭才能兼听则明地作出公正的裁决。

需要指出的是，假定无罪与怀疑有罪是可以并存的。侦查阶段以事实上的无罪假定开始，当侦查机关获取足够的证据推翻事实上的无罪假定，而认定犯罪嫌疑人事实上有罪时，侦查阶段事实上的无罪假定阶段结束，从而进入移送审查起诉阶段。同样的，审查起诉阶段也以事实上的无罪假定开始，当审查起诉机关通过对案件证据的审查，认为事实上的无罪假定被推翻，应当依法提起公诉时，审查起诉阶段事实上的无罪假定阶段结束，从而进入审判阶段。审判阶段也以事实上的无罪假定开始，当法院经过审理，认为事实上的无罪假定应当被推翻，而认定被告人事实上有罪时，审判阶段事实上的无罪假定阶段结束。当然，在上诉审同时对事实问题进行审查的法律制度中，如果被告人提起上诉，则审判阶段事实上的无罪假定在终审判决生效时结束。此时，不仅事实上的无罪假定至此结束，而且此前一直存在的法律上的无罪假定也至此结束。换句话说，法律上的无罪假定最终随着审判阶段事实上的无罪假定的结束而结束。审判机关的最终生效裁决不仅结束了事实上的无罪假定状态，也结束了法律上的无罪假定状态。审判机关对于事实有罪的认定具有了法律上有罪的意义，就是法律上的有罪认定。在此之前，虽然事实上的无罪假定在各诉讼阶段都存在，但是这并不妨碍各个诉讼机关对于被追诉人事实有罪的怀疑。事实上的无罪假定与事实上的有罪假定不可并存，但与事实上的有罪怀疑可以并存。

第四节　伦理学视角下的无罪推定

“正当”（right）与“善”（good）可以说是伦理学的两个基本概念，它们之间的关系也成为伦理学的一个主要问题。长期以来，围绕着二者之间的关系，在西方伦理思想史上形成了目的论与义务论两大流派。目的论认为善是独立于正当的，是更优先的，是我们据以判断事物正当与否的根本标准（一种目的性标准）；正当则依赖于善，是最大限度地增加善或符合善的东西，而依据对善的解释不同，就有各种各样的目的论，如功利主义、快乐主义、自我实现论、完善论等。义务论则与目的论相反，认为正当是独立于善的，是更优先的，康德就是义务论的一个突出代表。① 从伦理学的角度讲，无罪推定的根据在于其符合正当和善的观念。无论在义务论还是目的论中，无罪推定都能找到支持其合理性的根据。

从义务论的角度讲，无罪推定的伦理学基础主要是尊重和保障人权及“自主性，人格尊严，基本自由，讲真话，公平对待，加强好的结果要服从道德约束”② 等基本价值。如前所述，在对是否有罪的法律状态进行推定的情况下，有罪推定是否认无罪推定的逻

① ［美］约翰·罗尔斯：《正义论》（修订版），何怀宏等译，中国社会科学出版社 2009 年版，译者前言。

② Cf. Eyal Zamir, Law, Psychology, and Morality: The Role of Loss Aversion 178-9 (Oxford: Oxford University Press, 2015).

辑必然结果。然而，有罪推定可能导致刑讯逼供甚至错误定罪，导致无罪受罚、冤枉无辜。任何人应且只应对自己应负的责任负责，这是自主性的应有之义和内在要求，也是人格尊严、自由、讲真话、公平对待、信守承诺的基础，是人权的基础和保障。有罪推定可能导致被追诉人为自己没有犯下的罪行负责，侵犯人的自主性、人格尊严和自由，也违背讲真话、公平对待和信守承诺的要求，是对基本人权的侵犯。人是目的，而非单纯的手段。康德在《道德形而上学原理》中指出“你的行动，要把你自己人身中的人性，和其他人身中的人性，在任何时候都同样看做是目的，永远不能只看做是手段”①。惩罚一个人只能因为这个人本身的原因，而不能仅因为他之外的原因。单纯为了刑事被追诉人以外的原因（如社会安宁或者社会福利）而对其进行有罪推定或者刑讯逼供，违背了“将人作为目的，而非单纯的手段对待”的康德实践命令的要求。②

有罪推定侵犯人的尊严。虽然对于社会整体而言，个人可能微不足道，个人遭受的冤屈和不公可能无足轻重，但是对于个人自身来讲，其本身就是他（她）的全部，这样的不公毁掉的将是他（她）的整个世界。犹太人有句谚语：拯救一个人就等于拯救了一个世界。③ 黑格尔也说：一个人就是一个世界。④ 佛经亦云：一花一世界，一叶一如来。因此，我们不能无视任何一个生命个体的价值，而对其肆意蹂躏。对于每一个生命，我们都有尊重和谨慎对待的义务，不能容忍冤枉无辜的存在。从马克思主义的观点看，世界

---

① ［德］康德：《道德形而上学原理》，苗力田译，上海人民出版社 1986 年版，第 81 页。

② See generally, Kant's Groundwork of the Metaphysic of Morals, translated by H. J. Paton as The Moral Law 90-1 (Hutchinson University Library, London, 1966).

③ 在电影《辛德勒的名单》中，最后被辛德勒拯救的犹太人集体送给辛德勒一枚戒指，上面用希伯来文写着一句取自《犹太法典》的话：“救人一命即救了整个世界。”

④ 参见［德］黑格尔：《美学》（第一卷），朱光潜译，商务印书馆 1979 年版，第 303 页：“每个人都是一个整体，本身就是一个世界。”

不仅是客观的，而且是可知的，人通过发挥主观能动性能够认识和改造客观世界，思维着的精神是地球上最美丽的花朵。世界的可知性建立在主观见之于客观的实践基础之上，离不开人的主观能动性。离开了人这个认识主体，客观世界也就无所谓可知。因此，尊重每一个人，尊重每一个生命个体，不仅不违背马克思主义世界客观性原理，而且是马克思主义辩证唯物主义世界观的内在要求和应有之义。

在有罪推定的条件下，所有人都可能无罪受罚，这样就没有自由可言。而在义务论者看来，自由是最高的道德价值。康德就在其《实践理性批判》中指出“自由是道德法则的条件”，并主张“道德法则是我们能意识到自由的条件”，“自由是道德法则的存在根据（ratio essendi），道德法则是自由的认识根据（ratio cognoscendi）。因为如果我们在自己理性内不预先清楚地想及道德法则，我们就绝不会认为自己有理由来假定自由这一回事（虽则自由本身并不自相矛盾）。但如果没有自由，我们就绝无可能追寻到自己心中的道德法则”[①]。由此可见，康德认为人的自由是终极的或者最神圣的道德价值，应当给予优先重视的地位，丧失自由就会丧失德性和伦理学上的正当性。有罪推定否定自由，违背义务论的最高道德价值，失去德性和伦理学上的正当性，因此是应当竭力避免的。

在《法的形而上学原理》中，康德认为自由本身是能被用来限制自由的唯一价值，因为诉诸其他任何价值（如实用）都将破坏自由价值的终极地位。[②] 罗尔斯也在其“公平的正义”理论中强调由正义所保障的自由权利绝不受制于政治的交易和社会利益的权衡，不管这种有损于自由的交易多么有利或将带来的社会利益多么

---

① Immanuel Kant, Critique of Practical Reason, translated and edited by Mary Gregor 4 (Cambridge University Press, Revised Edition, 2015).

② Immanuel Kant, The Metaphysical Elements of Justice, translated by John Ladd 35-6 (The Bobbs-Merrill Company, Inc., 1965).

大，自由只能为了自由本身的缘故而被限制。① 无罪推定虽然可能导致错放有罪，但不会侵犯无辜者的个人自由。罪犯即便被错放，也已被暴露在公众的“聚光灯”下，其对社会的危害性也会大打折扣。而有罪推定在限制个人自由的同时，并不能保证社会的安全和自由，相反，在因有罪推定而导致的刑讯逼供和冤错案件中，不仅被追诉人个人自由受到严重侵犯，而且由于真正的罪犯逃脱法网，仍处于隐秘状态，可能继续危害社会，社会安全和自由反而会受到严重危害。因此，有罪推定没有限制自由的正当理由。

无罪不应当受到惩罚是报应理论的要求。“善有善报，恶有恶报”不仅是一个朴素的常识，也是报应主义义务论伦理学的一项基本原则。② 一旦被假定有罪，刑讯逼供就具有了道德上的合理性，因为对一个有罪的人进行惩罚在道德上具有正当性。然而，假定有罪并不等于真正有罪。一旦有罪的假定是错误的，对无辜者的惩罚将不仅失去法学意义上的正当性，也将失去伦理学意义上的正当性，这将导致严重侵犯人权。报应理论不仅要求有罪当罚，也要求无罪不当罚。“用马克思的话讲，至少康德和黑格尔按照共同意志和社会契约论所阐释的报应理论的美德之一就是其彰显了对于人的权利、尊严和自主性的一种至少形式上或者抽象的尊重。”③ 因此，从这个意义上讲，无罪推定也是报应理论和保障人权的要求。

去除不公正的公共污名是人类的强烈情感。这是确立无罪推定的另一个重要理由。不公正的事情，即便再小，也会被人们深深地憎恶。那些为了洗清冤屈而不知疲倦地奔走申诉的人们就是人类这

① ［美］约翰·罗尔斯：《正义论》（修订版），何怀宏等译，中国社会科学出版社 2009 年版，译者前言。

② “To sum up, commonsense morality-prevailing, deeply held moral convictions-is compatible with moderate deontology.” See Eyal Zamir, Law, Psychology, and Morality: The Role of Loss Aversion 188 (Oxford: Oxford University Press, 2015).

③ Jeffrie G. Murphy, *Marxism and Retribution*, Philosophy & Public Affairs, Vol. 2, No. 3 (Spring, 1973), 231.

一强烈情感的明证。为了自己名声的清白，即便已刑满出狱，人们也认为值得为之继续奋斗。即便在蒙冤者死后，其亲友也会为了恢复其名誉而继续这份追求公正的事业。例如，英国的蒂莫西·埃文斯（Timothy Evans）案和德雷克·宾利（Derek Bentley）案①，中国的呼格吉勒图案等。虽然被告人已被执行死刑，但是家属依然没有放弃追求平反昭雪，直到法律还给这些被不公正处罚的人以清白。这一强烈情感最有力的明证也许是那些虽有机会通过认罪而获得假释，但仍坚称自己无罪的人，如媒体报道的孙善武案。孙善武在入狱后，宁愿放弃被假释的机会，冒着不符合“确有悔改表现”假释条件的风险，也要坚称对判决不服，一直申诉。② 人们为了平反昭雪而不惜走过的漫漫长路生动地展现了不公判决所激发的人们强烈的反抗情感。一个易于导致这种不公判决的法律制度甚至可能导致“每个走向绞刑架的恶棍都可能是一个无辜的受害者”③。这样的制度将不仅失去公众的信任，也无法经受最基本的伦理检验。④ 任何一项制度都应当具备基本的德性。即便有罪推定有利于从社会整体上镇压犯罪，维护社会安宁，取得社会的整体效益，达成这样的效益或者好的结果，也必须受到道德的约束。⑤

从目的论的角度讲，特别是从社会整体功利最大化的结果主义观点看，似乎有罪推定有利于破案，震慑和预防犯罪，无罪推定可

① See Ludovic Kennedy, 10 Rillington Place (Grafton, 1971 (1961)); R v Derek William Bentley (Deceased) (2001) 1 Cr App R 307, CA.

② 《孙善武：希望在秦城监狱问周永康 为何把我打成贪官》，http://finance.ifeng.com/a/20150313/13551917_0.shtml，最后访问时间：2015 年 5 月 3 日。

③ Sir Samuel Romilly, Observations on the Criminal Law of England (T. Cadell and W. Davies, 1810), Note D, quoted in T. B. Howell, 7 State Trials (32 Charles II, 1680), 1529.

④ Paul Roberts & Adrian Zuckerman, Criminal Evidence 240－2 (OUP, 2nd edn. 2010).

⑤ 我国当前司法过程中违背无罪推定行为的动因或者目的还不仅是为了实现社会的整体效益，甚至更重要的是为了实现某些人（包括司法人员等）的个人利益。因此，这些行为几乎完全是恶的表现，根本就谈不上符合义务论的要求。

能会错放罪犯，影响刑法和刑事诉讼法打击犯罪、实现社会利益最大化的功能，因此有罪推定比无罪推定更具有可接受性。但是，这只是短视的、一厢情愿的看法。实际上，有罪推定可能导致冤假错案，造成无法挽回的损失——人的青春无法挽回，人死更是不能复生。冤假错案还会严重损害司法威信，增加社会恐慌，反而不利于社会的稳定和长治久安，最终不利于社会整体功利的最大化。此外，刑罚的影响非常严重。一个人一旦被判定有罪将会面临极其严重的后果，“包括可能丧失人身自由，背负社会污名，遭受社会排斥，以及其他社会的、心理的和经济的伤害”①，甚至会丧失生命。而错放有罪之人产生的后果（对社会安全和福利的破坏力）则相对没有如此严重。因为错放实际有罪之人显然不会侵犯被释放人的权利。对于受害人来讲，由于犯罪造成的损害是“沉没成本”，已无法改变，定罪也主要是精神上的抚慰，无论是否错放实际有罪之人，都无法改变被害人已被犯罪侵害的事实。② 对于社会来讲，犯罪对社会秩序的破坏也是“沉没成本”，已无法改变。由于被错放的实际有罪之人已被公之于众，其对社会秩序的潜在危害也将大打折扣，并且在一定的条件（出现新证据等法定条件）下，国家还可以继续对其进行追诉。再者，冤枉无辜造成的痛苦无法用惩罚犯罪带来的幸福予以补偿。波珀（Popper）就曾指出，“从伦理学的角度看，苦难和幸福之间或者痛苦和快乐之间，没有对称性。……人类的苦难发出直接的道德要求，也就是获得帮助的要求，而增加处境还不错的人的幸福不管怎么说都没有类似的要求。……增加快乐不比减少痛苦重要，特别是增加一个人的快乐不比减少另一个人的痛苦重要”③，“所有道德的紧迫性都是基于解救苦难或者痛苦的

① R. v. Oakes (1986), 24 C. C. C. (3d) 321 (S. C. C.).

② Eyal Zamir, Law, Psychology, and Morality: The Role of Loss Aversion 178-9 (Oxford: Oxford University Press, 2015).

③ Karl R. Popper, The Open Society and Its Enemies, Volume I, (Princeton: Princeton University Press, 5th rev. ed. 1966), 284-5 n. 2.

紧迫性"，"在任何情况下，增加幸福都远不及给予遭受不幸的人以帮助以及努力避免苦难紧迫（后一任务无关'品味问题'，而前一任务与'品味问题'有重大关系）"，"正因如此，建议将功利主义'以最大多数人的最大幸福为目的'，或者简言之'幸福最大化'的公式替换为'所有人可避免的苦难最小化'，或者简言之'苦难最小化'的公式"。[①] 波珀的这一观点也为现代科学实验所证实。通过使用 fMRI（Functional Magnetic Resonance Imaging 功能性磁共振成像）扫描人脑获取的证据表明风险决策不遵循补偿性规则，[②] 获得所产生的效用不能补偿损失造成的负效用。因此，有罪推定带来的"社会安宁"并不能补偿其给人们带来的心理恐慌和不安。从结果主义的角度讲，有罪推定并不比无罪推定有优势。

从伦理学的角度讲，无罪推定具有促使人向善的功能：如果一个人一旦被指控就将被假定为有罪，而作为个体来讲，证明自己无罪通常并不容易，有时会十分困难，甚至不可能，那么人们关心更多的便不再是能否证明自己无罪，而是自己是否被"抓捕"、被指控。如此一来，是否犯罪、是否遵纪守法便不再是最关键的问题，而是否被抓、被指控便成了关键的问题。这样，人们便不再有动力去遵纪守法，而是将主要精力放在如何逃避法律的制裁上。刑法规范人们行为和引导人们守法的功能也将受到极大削弱。法律是最低的道德。法律引导人们守法的功能也在一定程度上是在道德上引导和促使人们向善。法律引导人们守法的功能被削弱，其促使人们向善的功能也将会消逝。无罪推定促使人向善的这一功能不仅适用于仅有少部分适格犯罪主体实际犯罪的情况，也适用于大部分适格犯罪主体实际犯罪的情况。例如，假使社会上有资格犯贪污贿赂罪的

---

① Karl R. Popper, The Open Society and Its Enemies, Volume I, (Princeton: Princeton University Press, 5th rev. ed. 1966), 235 n. 6 (2).

② Rao L-L, Zhou Y, Xu L, Liang Z-Y, Jiang T, et al. (2011) *Are Risky Choices Actually Guided by a Compensatory Process? New Insights from fMRI.* PLoS ONE 6 (3): e14756. doi: 10.1371/journal.pone.0014756.

主体中大部分都触犯了贪污贿赂罪，并且在追诉贪污贿赂犯罪的刑事诉讼中实行有罪推定，任何适格犯罪主体一旦被指控就将被假定有罪，那么适格的贪污贿赂犯罪主体所关心的将主要不再是能否证明自己有罪或者无罪，而是自己是否会被抓到。由此导致的结果就是，这些适格的贪污贿赂犯罪主体将不再对自己是否从事了贪污贿赂犯罪行为特别在意，因为即便自己实际没有从事贪污贿赂犯罪行为，一旦被抓捕、被指控，由于其难以保证能证明自己无罪，因此也可能最终被认定为有罪而被惩罚。这样，潜在的贪污贿赂犯罪主体在从事贪污贿赂犯罪行为时将不再有所顾忌，其所关心和防范的是自己的罪行不被发现，自己不被抓捕、被指控。这导致的结果就是刑法本来引导人们守法向善的功能消失，至少是被大大削弱了。结果是越反越腐，越反，腐败的手段越隐蔽，对腐败犯罪的侦查和证明越困难。因此，无罪推定的确立和贯彻落实不仅对有效反腐具有重要意义，对社会风尚的向善也具有重要的意义。

第五节　心理学和决策理论视角下的无罪推定——“无知之幕”背后的思想实验

从心理学和决策理论的角度看，人们倾向于无罪推定也具有其合理性。其主要根据在于人们在做风险决策时所表现出来的损失规避。损失规避（loss aversion）是心理学的一个重要概念。它是指“与参照点相比，损失比等量获益产生的心理效用更大”①，亦即一定量的损失所引起的心理感受总是强烈于相似量的获益所引起的心理感受。一般说来，人们都是损失规避的。损失产生的负效用比相

① Kahneman, D., Knetsch, J. L., & Thaler, R. H.（1991）. *The endowment effect, loss aversion, and status quo bias*. Journal of Economic Perspectives, 5, 193-206. 刘欢、梁竹苑、李纾：《行为经济学中的损失规避》，载《心理科学进展》2009 年第 4 期，第 788 页。

似大小的获得产生的效用要大。不丧失比获取被看得更有价值。损失、不幸、负效用和伤害比获得、幸福、效用和利益显得更加重要和突出。增加一个人的幸福或者效用不如减少一个人的不幸或者负效用重要。①

损失规避的正式理论是预期理论（prospect theory）。预期理论是当前最流行的有关风险决策的描述性理论。② 预期理论由卡内曼（Kahneman）和特沃斯基（Tversky）在 1979 年正式提出，③ 以实验证据作为基础并以数学公式的形式表达出来。卡内曼和特沃斯基（1979）通过实验证实：损失和获益期望值相等的赌博游戏（损失和获益的概率均为 50%）对大多数被试来说明显不具有吸引力，而且随着赌注的增加，不愿参加赌博游戏的被试比例普遍增大。用数学公式表达就是，设赌注（赌博游戏中获益损失绝对值）x 和 y，心理效用 U，当 $x>y\geqslant 0$ 时，$U(y)+U(-y)>U(x)+U(-x)$，也就是 $U(-y)-U(-x)>U(x)-U(y)$。若将 y 设为 0，则得到 $U(x)<-U(-x)$，即损失的心理效用大于等量获益的心理效用；当 y 趋近 x，就得到心理效用函数 U 在 x 点的导数，即 $U'(x)<U'(-x)$，即损失心理效用函数的斜率大于获益心理效用函数的斜率，亦即损失价值函数的曲线比获益价值函数的曲线更陡（如下图所示，引自卡内曼和特沃斯基，1979，p. 279）。

---

① Eyal Zamir, Law, Psychology, and Morality: The Role of Loss Aversion xiii, 189-90 (Oxford: Oxford University Press, 2015).

② Mohammed Abdellaoui, Han Bleichrodt, Corina Paraschiv, (2007) *Loss Aversion Under Prospect Theory: A Parameter-Free Measurement*. Management Science 53 (10): 1659-1674, 1659. http://dx.doi.org/10.1287/mnsc.1070.0711.

③ Daniel Kahneman, Amos Tversky, *Prospect Theory: An Analysis of Decision under Risk*, Econometrica, Vol. 47, No. 2 (Mar., 1979), pp. 263-92.

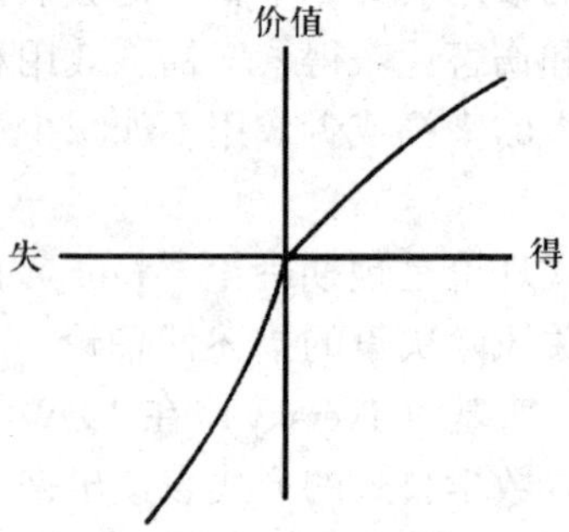

预期理论的价值函数曲线

据此，卡内曼和特沃斯基认为，损失和获益的心理效用并不相同，同等的损失与获益相比产生的心理效用更大，并把这种现象命名为损失规避。[①] 损失规避是卡内曼和特沃斯基（1979）预期理论（风险决策的描述性模型）的特点，它表明人们对损失比对所得更加敏感。得失与乐悲的情感密切相联。因此，一个选择的描述性理论必须顾及诸如对失去的痛苦和对错误的后悔的情感。实际上，通过使用 fMRI，神经学研究已经证明一般决策和具有损失规避特点的特别决策涉及大脑中诸如杏仁核等已知与情绪有关的区域。相似地，人们发现杏仁核损伤消除了金钱损失规避，在风险型和非风险型决策中，处理情感信息的能力不足与损失规避的减少都存在一一对应的关系。[②] 最新的神经科学研究使用 fMRI 技术发现，在与多巴胺系统相连的脑区中广泛发现了神经损失规避，且神经的损失规避与行为的损失规避呈显著相关。作者认为损失规避在行为和神经上的差异可能与个体在多巴胺功能上的差异有关。这说明损失规避

① 参见刘欢、梁竹苑、李纾：《行为经济学中的损失规避》，载《心理科学进展》2009 年第 4 期，第 788-789 页。

② Eyal Zamir, Law, Psychology, and Morality: The Role of Loss Aversion 15 (Oxford: Oxford University Press, 2015).

可能是人类或动物的一种基本机制。①

对于是否应当无罪推定的问题，人们同样表现出损失规避的特点。就一个已然发生的具体刑事案件而言，一个人如果本身是该案件中的被追诉人，那么他（她）很可能会更倾向于无罪推定；而如果他（她）本身不是被追诉人，那么面对严重的犯罪事实，他（她）可能会倾向于有罪推定。如果从抽象的面对整体制定政策的角度讲，一个人既有可能成为刑事案件中的被追诉人，也有可能不是该刑事案件中的被追诉人，即在每个人面前都存在一个关于自己身份的“无知之幕”，那么一个人在对于是否支持无罪推定的问题作出决定时，就会权衡作出这一决定的后果（利弊得失）。在不实行无罪推定的情况下，如果自己是刑事案件中的被追诉人，那么自己可能会被冤枉，从而为此丧失物质的和非物质的利益，包括青春甚至生命，因此可能遭受不可挽回的损失；如果自己不是该案件中的被追诉人，那么自己可能会从对被追诉人定罪处罚所带来的震慑潜在犯罪和社会安宁中获得一定的间接利益。在这种情况下，如果自己同时是刑事案件中的受害者，那么确实会从罪犯被定罪处罚中获得诸如经济赔偿、防止进一步受害的保护以及公众认可和证明带来的精神提振等好处。但是，总体来看，罪犯通常太穷以致无法进行有意义的赔偿，法院判决带来的保护性利益通常也很短暂，当充分意识到犯罪及其后果是一个人间悲剧时，打赢官司的味道似乎并不怎么甜蜜。个人能从刑事制裁中获得的利益实在寥寥无几。② 此时，由于人们损失规避的特点，相对于定罪处罚所带来的寥寥无几的利益，

---

① Tom, S. M., Fox, C. R., Trepel, C., & Poldrack, R. A. (2007). *The neural basis of loss aversion in decision-making under risk*, Science, 315, 515-8. 转引自刘欢、梁竹苑、李纾：《行为经济学中的损失规避》，载《心理科学进展》2009年第4期，第791页。

② Cf. Paul Roberts, *Double Jeopardy Law Reform: A Criminal Justice Commentary*, 65 Mod. L. Rev. 393, 403 (2002).

自己被冤枉甚至丧失青春和生命会显得更加令人敏感和不可接受，因此一个人会厌恶这种情况的存在。在实行无罪推定的情况下，如果自己是刑事案件中的被追诉人，那么可能会被错误释放，也就是有所获益；如果自己不是刑事案件中的被追诉人，即便错误释放被追诉人，自己也不会有什么损失，因为国家机器会一直对犯罪行为保持高压的追诉态势，在有新的证据等法定情况出现时，仍旧可以继续对该犯罪分子进行追诉。在这种情况下，即便自己是刑事案件中的受害者，如果错误释放被追诉人，自己也只是暂时丧失补偿自己已遭受的物质和精神损失的机会，但是犯罪所造成的损失已经是“沉没成本”，不会再因为错误的无罪释放而产生新的损失。因此，一个人相对不会厌恶这种情况的存在。因此，从制定政策的角度讲，人们会更倾向于无罪推定，确立无罪推定也是基于“无知之幕”背后思想实验的民主决策结果。

无罪推定还是有罪推定，这是一个风险型决策问题。作为一个一般的风险决策的描述性理论，预期理论同样适用于该问题。波珀关于快乐不能补偿痛苦，苦难而非幸福直接发出获得帮助的道德要求，减少痛苦比增加快乐更紧迫的观点与预期理论的结论相一致，与损失规避规律相吻合。将预期理论应用到无罪推定问题决策的结果就是与其选择有罪推定，不如选择无罪推定。这是获益（自身不是被冤枉人时）和损失（自身是被冤枉人时）的风险都明显存在时风险决策的普遍规律。由于任何人都不能保证自己不被冤枉，这两种风险都明显存在，因此无罪推定的决策结论也普遍成立。由于从广义上讲，预期理论应用到伦理学中，也属于目的论流派，因此即便从目的论的角度讲，也应当实行无罪推定，而不是有罪推定。

综上所述，无罪推定不仅有哲学、政治学上的基础，也有法学、伦理学、心理学以及决策理论上的基础，不仅有社会科学上的基础，也有自然科学上的基础，不仅有形而上学的基础，也有形而下学的基础。因此，无罪推定具有充分的根据与正当性，我们应当明确确立和加强无罪推定的理念、制度、原则和权利，促进司法文明的进步。

第四章 无罪推定与刑事诉讼相关范畴之间的关系

第一节 无罪推定与沉默权和反对强迫自证其罪

一、沉默权概述

沉默权，简言之，即保持沉默的权利[1]。关于沉默权的定义，林林总总，浩如烟海，不同的学者对其有不同的描述。例如，“沉默权，即拒绝陈述权”[2]。“沉默权，即拒绝供述的权利。”[3]“刑事沉默权，是指在刑事诉讼中，犯罪嫌疑人、被告人享有不自证其罪，可以对司法人员的讯问保持沉默的权利。”[4]“沉默权是指在刑事诉讼中，犯罪嫌疑人或被告人享有对司法人员，包括警察、检察

---

① 欧洲人权法院在芬克诉法国（Funke v. France）一案中也这样称呼这一权利（the right to remain silent）。See generally, John D. Jackson and Sarah J. Summers, The Internationalisation of Criminal Evidence: Beyond the Common Law and Civil Law Traditions 241 (Cambridge University Press, 2012).

② 陈光中、张建伟：《联合国〈公民权利和政治权利国际公约〉与我国刑事诉讼》，载《中国法学》1998 年第 6 期，107 页。

③ 周国均：《拒绝强迫自证其罪与沉默权》，载《法制日报》1999 年 1 月 2 日第 7 版。

④ 梅芳、尚进：《论刑事沉默权的诉讼价值及缺陷》，载《当代法学》1999 年第 5 期，第 21 页。

人员、法官的讯问保持沉默，不证明自己有罪的权利。"[1]“沉默权是指刑事诉讼中的犯罪嫌疑人、被告人以及可能成为刑事被告人的证人针对侦查人员、检察人员、审判人员的讯问享有的拒绝回答、保持沉默或作出陈述的权利。"[2] 作为刑事诉讼中“沉默权”的沉默，特指针对国家刑事司法机关的讯问，犯罪嫌疑人、被告人不回答任何不利于自己的问题或者所有问题的行为方式。[3] 沉默权“是指被追诉者（犯罪嫌疑人、被告人）对追诉者（警察、检察官、法官等）的讯问享有缄口不语的权利”[4]。“沉默权属于在沉默与供述之间进行自主选择的一项权利。关于权利的本质，黑格尔指出：‘法定的权利，不论是私人的或是国家的、市镇等公共的，原先就称之为‘自由’……每一个真正的权利就是一种自由。’[5] 任何一项法律权利，都表明自由的属性。沉默权作为权利主体的意志自由与行为自由的复合体，蕴含着三层含义：一是在明确供述后果的前提下，选择供述或是沉默，建立在意志自由的基础之上；二是在行为方面，可以选择沉默或供述两种方式；三是不得因沉默而导致不利的结论。"[6] 有的学者将沉默权分为消极的沉默权和积极的沉默权，并指出“消极意义上的沉默权是指犯罪嫌疑人享有在是否陈述之间进行选择的权利，任何司法官员都不得违背犯罪嫌疑人、被告人的意志而强迫犯罪嫌疑人、被告人作出供述。积极意义上的沉默权则是指犯罪嫌疑人、被告人享有如何进行陈述的权利，即在提

---

① 曾辉林：《简论沉默权对完善我国刑事诉讼制度的意义》，载《人民司法》1999 年第 6 期，第 38 页。

② 易延友著：《沉默的自由》，中国政法大学出版社 2001 年版，第 12 页。

③ 奚丹霓：《论无罪推定》，中国政法大学 2013 年博士学位论文，第 20-21 页。

④ 刘根菊：《在我国确定沉默权原则几个问题之研讨（上）》，载《中国法学》2000 年第 2 期，第 46 页。

⑤ 转引自周辅成：《从文艺复兴到 19 世纪资产阶级哲学家、政治思想家有关人道主义人性论言论选辑》，商务印书馆 1996 年版，第 681 页。

⑥ 白冬：《如实回答与沉默权的功能主义分析与文化解释》，载《法学杂志》2012 年第 2 期，第 114 页。

供不利于己的陈述与有利于己的陈述之间进行选择的权利。其中前一项权利是后一项权利的基础”①。有的学者从权利内容的角度指出“沉默权包括在警方对犯罪的调查中不与警方进行合作的权利和无论是否宣誓不在审判中作证的权利”。(This right to silence includes the right not to cooperate with the police in their investigation of a crime and the right not to give testimony at one's trial, whether or not given under oath.)②

这些概括都有一定的道理，只是有的简单扼要，有的比较具体，从总体上来讲，核心内涵分歧不大，但是在一些具体细节上有不同的看法。笔者认为，大体上可以将沉默权归结为以下几点：(1) 适用范围：学者们基本都认同沉默权的适用范围为刑事诉讼；(2) 适用主体：有的学者认为沉默权的适用主体为犯罪嫌疑人、被告人以及可能成为刑事被告人的证人，如易延友就认为“沉默权是指刑事诉讼中的犯罪嫌疑人、被告人以及可能成为刑事被告人的证人针对侦查人员、检察人员、审判人员的讯问享有的拒绝回答、保持沉默或作出陈述的权利”③。而大多数学者都认同沉默权的适用主体主要就是犯罪嫌疑人和被告人，即被追诉人。笔者认为，考虑到从沉默权的起源来看，沉默权的适用主体就是犯罪嫌疑人和被告人，而可能成为刑事被告人的证人在拒绝回答司法官员提出的问题时更多的是在援引反对强迫自证其罪的特权，因此沉默权的适用主体应当还是限于犯罪嫌疑人和被告人为宜；(3) 权利内容：权利在本质上是一种自由，即可以选择的自由。适用到沉默权，就是可以自主选择是否陈述以及陈述什么内容的自由。并且从后果上看，沉默权的行使人不会因为自己保持沉默、拒绝陈述的行

① 易延友：《沉默的自由（一）》，载《中国律师》2000年第1期，第50页。

② Barton L. Ingraham, *The Right of Silence, the Presumption of Innocence, the Burden of Proof, and a Modest Proposal: A Reply to O' Reilly*, Journal of Criminal Law and Criminology, Vol. 86, Issue 2 Winter (1996), Article 10, p. 564.

③ 易延友著：《沉默的自由》，中国政法大学出版社2001年版，第12页。

为而遭受对其不利的结果，办案机关也不能因为沉默权行使人保持沉默、拒绝陈述的行为而作出对其不利的决定。关于行为方式是针对讯问有权拒绝陈述还是有权拒绝供述，笔者认为有权拒绝陈述的表述更准确，更有利于保护被追诉人的人权。拒绝供述一般仅指对供认犯罪保持沉默，而拒绝陈述的范围则要广得多，既包括对供认犯罪保持沉默，也包括对辩解无罪保持沉默，还包括其他任何形式缄默不语的行为，[①] 但仅限于言语而不包括非言语的表达。拒绝非言语的表达方式应当归属于反对强迫自证其罪。概言之，可以将沉默权定义为在刑事诉讼中，被追诉者（犯罪嫌疑人、被告人）对追诉者（警察、检察官、法官等）的讯问享有自主选择是否陈述及陈述内容并不因拒绝陈述、缄默不语而遭受不利后果的权利。

从历史发展来看，在古罗马时期就已经产生了沉默权的萌芽。在罗马法中，原告负有举证责任（actori incumbit probatio）。[②] 如果原告不能证实案情，即便被告人保持沉默[③]或者否认指控的事实，

① 参见刘根菊：《在我国确定沉默权原则几个问题之研讨（上）》，载《中国法学》2000年第2期，第46页。

② William L. Burdick, The Principles of Roman Law and Their Relation to Modern Law 693 (1938). See also Samuel P. Scott, The Civil Law, including the Twelve Tables, the Institutes of Gaius, the Rules of Ulpian, the Opinions of Paulus, the Enactments of Justinian, and the Constitutions of Leo: Translated from the Original Latin, Edited, and Compared with All Accessible Systems of Jurisprudence Ancient and Modern 47-8 (Cincinnati, Vol. 13, 1932) ("The *onus probandi* rested on the plaintiff, who was obliged to establish his claim by affirmative evidence, as prescribed by the rule, '*Ei incumbit probatio qui dicit, non qui negat*,' a doctrine which has been adopted by all modern systems of jurisprudence").

③ William L. Burdick, The Principles of Roman Law and Their Relation to Modern Law 693 (1938). See also Samuel P. Scott, The Civil Law, including the Twelve Tables, the Institutes of Gaius, the Rules of Ulpian, the Opinions of Paulus, the Enactments of Justinian, and the Constitutions of Leo: Translated from the Original Latin, Edited, and Compared with All Accessible Systems of Jurisprudence Ancient and Modern 47-8 (Cincinnati, Vol. 13, 1932) ("The *onus probandi* rested on the plaintiff, who was obliged to establish his claim by affirmative evidence, as prescribed by the rule, '*Ei incumbit probatio qui dicit, non qui negat*,' a doctrine which has been adopted by all modern systems of jurisprudence").

被告人也应被宣告无罪（actore non probante, reus absolvitur）。[①] 但是通常认为，近代以来的沉默权起源于英美法系普通法，一般追溯至 1641 年英国星座法院（the Star Chamber）和高级专员公署（the High Commission）以及依职权宣誓程序（ex officio oath procedure）一起被废除之时。根据依职权宣誓程序，被告人被要求宣誓来回答所有的问题。[②] 当前，沉默权的积极意义得到世界绝大多数国家和地区的认可。一些国家通过立法认可了沉默权的精神，如《法国刑事诉讼法典》第 114 条规定："被告人有不作供述的自由。"《德国刑事诉讼法典》第 136 条规定："初次讯问开始时，要告诉被指控人所被指控的行为和可能适用的处罚规定。接着应当告诉他，依法他有就指控进行陈述或者对案件不予陈述的权利。"意大利新刑事诉讼法第 64 条规定："在开始讯问前，除第 66 条第 1 款的规定外，还应当告知被讯问者，他有权不回答提问。"《日本刑事诉讼法典》第 311 条规定："被告人可以始终沉默或对多个质问拒绝供述。"一些有关刑事司法的国际法律文件也对沉默权予以认可，如

---

① Code Just. 4. 19. 23（Diocletian & Maximian 304）. "23. The Same, and the Csesars, to Menelaus. A plaintiff who alleges that he cannot establish his claim does not compel the defendant to prove the contrary; for, in accordance with the nature of things, the denial of a fact is no evidence. Given on the eighth of the Kalends of January, during the Consulate of the Csesars, 304." Available at http://www. constitution. org/sps/sps13. htm, last visited on June 29, 2015. DIG. 22. 3. 2（Paul, Ad Edictum 69）. "2. Paulus, On the Edict, Book LX-IX. Proof is incumbent upon the party who affirms a fact, not upon him who denies it." Available at http://www. constitution. org/sps/sps05. htm, last visited on June 29, 2015.

② J. H. Wigmore, A Treatise on the Anglo-American System of Evidence in Trials at Common Law, vol. 8, §2250（Boston: Little, Brown, 3rd edn, 1940）; and P. Levy, The Origins of the Fifth Amendment: The Right against Self-Incrimination（Oxford University Press, 1968）. For a description of the ex officio procedure, see R. H. Helmolz, *The Privilege and the Ius Commune: The Middle Ages to the Seventeenth Century*, in R. H. Helmolz, C. M. Gray, J. J. Langbein, E. Moglen, H. E. Smith and A. W. Alschuler（eds.）, The Privilege against Self-Incrimination: Its Origins and Development（University of Chicago Press, 1997）17. Cited in John D. Jackson and Sarah J. Summers, The Internationalisation of Criminal Evidence: Beyond the Common Law and Civil Law Traditions 241, Cambridge University Press, 2012.

1994年9月10日世界刑法学协会第十五届代表大会通过的《关于刑事诉讼中的人权问题的决议》第16条建议各国立法规定“被告人有权保持沉默并且从警察或司法机关进行首次侦讯开始有权知悉受控的内容”。《联合国少年司法最低限度标准规则》（《北京规则》）第7条规定：“在诉讼的各个阶段，应保证基本程序方面的保障措施，诸如假定无罪指控罪状通知本人的权利、保持缄默的权利、请律师的权利、要求父或母或监护人在场的权利、与证人对质和盘诘证人的权利和向上级机关上诉的权利。”英美法系国家主要是通过司法判例或与司法相关的法律规定来直接确认沉默权，在其基本法中体现了沉默权的精神，但并未普遍在其基本法中对沉默权进行直接确认。尽管如此，一般说来，实行“对抗式”刑事诉讼模式的国家十分重视对于这一权利的保护和培育。[①] 例如，在英国，沉默权被视为一项基本权利和民主运行的必要条件之一。[②] 美国更是通过1966年联邦最高法院审查米兰达案确立的著名的“米兰达规则”而在美国联邦刑事司法领域确立了沉默权制度。

二、反对强迫自证其罪概述

反对强迫自证其罪起源于英美法系，在古罗马刑事诉讼法学中并没有相关的学说。[③] 18世纪末，伴随着对抗制刑事诉讼模式的兴

① Barton L. Ingraham, *The Right of Silence, the Presumption of Innocence, the Burden of Proof, and a Modest Proposal: A Reply to O' Reilly*, Journal of Criminal Law and Criminology, Vol. 86, Issue 2 Winter (1996), Article 10, p. 564.

② A. R. N. Cross, *The Right to Silence and the Presumption of Innocence-Sacred Cows or Safeguards of Liberty?*, 11 Society of Public Teachers of Law 66, 67 (1970-1971).

③ William L. Burdick, The Principles of Roman Law and Their Relation to Modern Law 694 (1938). “Our constitutional provisions of confronting one with the witnesses against him, and of immunity from self-incrimination were, however, unknown doctrines in Roman criminal procedure.”

起，反对强迫自证其罪正式出现，这是普通法系辩护律师的杰作。[①] 美国学者罗伯特·S. 格斯坦（Robert S. Gerstein）甚至将其称为"区分英美法系刑事司法制度与大陆法系刑事司法制度最典型、最独特的特征之一"。[②] 在英美法系中，反对强迫自证其罪通常被称为"反对强迫自证其罪特权"（privilege against self-incrimination）或者"反对强迫自证其罪权利"（right against self-incrimination）。根据《布莱克法律大辞典》的解释，反对强迫自证其罪是刑事被告人所享有的，除非其选择自愿作证，不得被法官或检察官讯问任何问题的权利。[③] 根据西方学者的解释，"任何人不受强迫自证其罪"包含如下几层含义：一是被追诉者无义务提供任何不利于己的供述或其他证据，国家追诉机关亦不得强迫其提供这样的证据。二是在讯问的过程中，国家司法官员应当告知被追诉人有权保持沉默。被追诉人有权拒绝回答所有讯问，且不会因此招致任何法律上的不利益。三是被追诉人在明知且明智的情况下，有权自愿作出不利于己的供述。但法院必须将那些非自愿的、受强迫而作出的不利的供述排除。[④] 美国最高法院裁定在刑事案件中，陪审团不能因被告人援引反对强迫自证其罪特权而作出对其不利的推论。在格里芬诉加利福尼亚州（Griffin v. California, 380 U.S. 609（1965））一案中，美国最高法院解释道，这将会是"对行使宪法特权的惩罚"。在米歇尔诉美国（Mitchell v. United States, 526 U.S. 314（1996））一案中，美国最高法院同样裁定在处刑时不能因在量刑

---

① John H. Langbein, *The Historical Origins of the Privilege against Self-Incrimination at Common Law*, Michigan Law Review, Vol. 92, No. 5 (Mar., 1994), p. 1047.

② Robert S. Gerstein, *The Self-Incrimination Debate in Great Britain*, The American Journal of Comparative Law, Vol. 27, No. 1 (Winter, 1979), p. 81.

③ See generally Black's Law Dictionary (8th ed. 2004), p. 3794. 转引自奚丹霓：《论无罪推定》，中国政法大学 2013 年博士学位论文，第 19 页。

④ Christopher Osakwe, "The Bill of Rights for the Criminal Defendant in American Law" in Human Rights in Criminal Procedure 274-5 (Martinus Nihoff Publishers, 1982). 转引自奚丹霓：《论无罪推定》，中国政法大学 2013 年博士学位论文，第 20 页。

程序中被告人未能作证而作出对其不利的推论。[①]

通说认为，反对强迫自证其罪萌芽于12世纪早期开始的英国教会法院和世俗法院的对立以及个人反对教会法院运用强迫宣誓程序作为获得自我归罪证据的斗争，起源于十六七世纪个人在世俗法院中反对官方纠问程序的斗争。1568年，英国普通上诉法院首席大法官戴尔在给一个被迫宣誓者签发人身保护令时，第一次宣布反对在当时的王座法院中进行的这种宣誓为有理。这一宣告后来成为一句名言，即“任何人都不得被强迫提供反对他自己的证据”。17世纪末，在国王詹姆斯二世诉七个主教违抗他关于取消所有反对极端主义法律的命令一案中，大主教圣克莱夫特在拒绝签发一个请愿书以保护该教会时，诉诸这样一句名言：“我有权拒绝回答任何可能使我自证其罪的问题。”这使得反对强迫自证其罪原则在英国牢牢站稳了脚跟。[②] 16世纪中期至18世纪晚期，普通法刑事审判的目的是为被告人提供亲自回应对其指控的机会。18世纪晚期，特别是19世纪，对刑事审判这一目的的看法发生了彻底的变化。在辩护律师的影响下，刑事审判开始被视为被告人律师检验控方指控的机会。在这种情况下，反对强迫自证其罪的特权作为这一深刻审判重组的一部分进入普通法程序。正是律师抓住刑事审判作为检验指控的机会和辩护使得拒绝自证其罪对于被告人来说才成为可能。[③] 1791年12月15日生效的美国宪法第五修正案明确规定了反对强迫自证其罪。该条规定：“任何人……不得在任何刑事案件中被迫自证其罪。”（No person shall be ... compelled in any criminal case to be a witness against himself.）

需要指出的是，反对强迫自证其罪与英国法中的另一项规

---

① Erwin Chemerinsky, Laurie L. Levenson, Criminal Procedure: Investigation 636-7 (2nd Edition).

② 易延友：《沉默的自由（一）》，载《中国律师》2000年第1期，第50-52页。

③ John H. Langbein, *The Historical Origins of the Privilege against Self-Incrimination at Common Law*, Michigan Law Review, Vol. 92, No. 5 (Mar., 1994), p. 1048.

则——“被追诉人不被讯问的权利”不同。根据“被追诉人不被讯问的权利”规则，除非被追诉人选择提供证据，无论是法官还是检察官在任何诉讼阶段都没有权力讯问被追诉人。反对强迫自证其罪适用于被追诉人及证人，拒绝回答的问题是“会导致自我归罪的问题”，而“被追诉人不被讯问的权利”仅适用于被追诉人，其不仅拒绝回答“会导致自我归罪的问题”，而且阻止问题被问及。被指控犯罪的人不仅有拒绝回答会导致自我归罪问题的自由，甚至免于被问及问题的尴尬。当证人在证人席上被问及问题时，其必须明确主张普遍适用于证人的反对强迫自证其罪特权；而被追诉人免于被讯问的自由阻止指控方要求（强迫性要弱得多）被追诉人进入证人席或向受审中的被追诉人提出问题。①

反对强迫自证其罪在大陆法系也有相应的体现。1897 年，法国制定新的法律规定：“预审法官在讯问犯罪嫌疑人时，应当告知犯罪嫌疑人有获得律师帮助和拒绝回答提问的权利，并在之后的每次讯问中，预审法官都必须事先通知辩护律师在场；在犯罪嫌疑人或辩护律师不在场的情况下，如果预审法官讯问证人，则应当在事后让犯罪嫌疑人或辩护律师尽快查阅讯问笔录。”这是法国第一次以书面形式对“拒绝回答提问权”作出了明确的肯定。② 自 1933 年开始，法国通过修改治罪法、颁布一系列法律和通过相关修正案，体现法律对人权的重视，不断改善犯罪嫌疑人和被告人的诉讼地位。目前，不得强迫自证其罪已成为法国刑事诉讼中的基本原则。

在国际法上，反对强迫自证其罪也得到广泛认可，如 1966 年 12 月 16 日联合国大会通过的《公民权利和政治权利国际公约》第 14 条第 3 款规定：“在判定对他提出的任何刑事指控时，人人完全

---

① Glanville Williams, The Proof of Guilt: A Sdudy of the English Criminal Trial 37-8 (London: Stevens & Sons Limited, 1963).

② 彭伶：《不得强迫自证其罪原则研究》，中国政法大学出版社 2007 年版，第 47 页。

平等地有资格享受以下的最低限度的保证：……（庚）不被强迫作不利于他自己的证言或强迫承认犯罪。"

我国2012年修正的刑事诉讼法第50条规定："审判人员、检察人员、侦查人员必须依照法定程序，收集能够证实犯罪嫌疑人、被告人有罪或者无罪、犯罪情节轻重的各种证据。严禁刑讯逼供和以威胁、引诱、欺骗以及其他非法方法收集证据，不得强迫任何人证实自己有罪。必须保证一切与案件有关或者了解案情的公民，有客观地充分地提供证据的条件，除特殊情况外，可以吸收他们协助调查。"我国2018年修正的刑事诉讼法保留了这一规定（作为第52条）。这标志着我国正式确立了"反对强迫自证其罪原则"。

需要指出的是，"反对强迫自证其罪"反对的是"强迫"自证其罪，而不包括"非强迫"或者说是"自愿"自证其罪。对于"自愿"自证其罪的证据，不管是何时产生的（立案前还是立案后），都不在被该特权排除之列。

三、沉默权和反对强迫自证其罪的关系

综观国内外关于沉默权和反对强迫自证其罪关系的论述，大体上可以将其分为两类：一类是"同一说"，即认为沉默权和反对强迫自证其罪是同一概念，如有学者经考证后认为，在英国证据法上，保持沉默的权利又被称为反对强迫自证其罪特权。[①] 还有学者认为，从权利受到保障来看，任何人不受强迫自证其罪原则体现为任何人不受强迫自证其罪特权；从权利的内容来看，该原则体现为沉默权。[②] 在英美法系国家，二者经常被作为同一概念使用。有的学者从沉默权的产生角度进行分析，认为"二者在本质上是一回

① 中国政法大学刑事法律研究中心：《英国刑事诉讼制度的新发展》，载陈光中、江伟主编：《诉讼法论丛》（第2卷），法律出版社1998年版，第366页。

② 宋英辉主编：《刑事诉讼原则》，法律出版社2010年版，第93页。

事，沉默权在法律上的本质就是不被强迫自我归罪特权”。[①] 有的学者认为：“在证据理论上，沉默权（right to silence）是与反对自我归罪特权紧密地联系在一起的，因此，沉默权又被称为反对自我归罪的特权（the privilege against self-incrimination）。”[②] 还有学者认为：“在现代刑事司法理论界和实务界，许多人不再区分不强迫自证其罪、任意自白规则和沉默权，因为广义的沉默权可以包括不强迫自证其罪和任意自白的内容，甚至可以与言论自由相联系，从而对于全部适用这三个概念，或广义沉默权的国家是可以的。”[③] 另一类是“区别说”，即认为沉默权与反对强迫自证其罪是两个不同的概念，如有学者认为反对强迫自证其罪包含沉默权，沉默权仅仅是前者的一个方面；[④] 有学者认为在大陆法系，沉默权和反对强迫自证其罪在主体、适用的证据范围、权利内容等方面存在区别；[⑤] 有学者认为，二者虽然有重要联系，但区别是主要的，它们在产生顺序、词语表述、立法规定、内容实质、适用对象范围等方面都不相同。[⑥] 还有学者认为，反对强迫自证其罪是一个总体原则，而沉默权则是实现这个原则的方法之一，但沉默权的某些方面

---

① 樊崇义：《沉默权与我国的刑事政策》，中国人民公安大学出版社 2002 年版，第 58 页。

② 易延友：《沉默的自由（一）》，载《中国律师》2000 年第 1 期，第 50 页。

③ 杨宇冠：《论不强迫自证其罪原则》，载《中国法学》2003 年第 1 期，第 132 页。

④ 参见陈光中、张建伟：《联合国〈公民权利和政治权利国际公约〉与我国刑事诉讼法》，载《中国法学》1998 年第 6 期，第 107 页；黄维智：《刑事证明责任分配的三项基本原则》，载《社会科学》2007 年第 3 期，第 96 页。

⑤ 易延友：《沉默的自由》，中国政法大学出版社 2001 年版，第 10-11 页。

⑥ 刘根菊：《在我国确立沉默权原则几个问题之研讨（上）》，载《中国法学》2000 年第 2 期，第 50-52 页。

又超越了反对强迫自证其罪的范围。[①]

笔者认为，由于沉默权和反对强迫自证其罪这两个概念的内涵都不是一成不变的，都随着时代的发展而演进，加之二者在内涵上存在着千丝万缕的联系，具有很大的重叠性，因此很多学者将二者等同也无可厚非。但是，除了共性以外，二者毕竟还有很多不同之处，因此不能将二者完全等同，而应当将它们视为一对既紧密相联又各有特点的概念。二者的密切联系表现在：（1）在近现代以来的英美刑事司法实践中，二者经常被作为同一概念使用。（2）在内容上，沉默权在很多国家的立法和学术理论中都被视为反对强迫自证其罪的重要组成部分，甚至其核心内容。因此，虽然从起源上看，反对强迫自证其罪最初并未明确包含沉默权的内容，但是在沉默权被明确提出来后，因其可以赋予个人权利直接对抗国家的强制讯问，比反对强迫自证其罪更具有直接性，因此其在内容上被纳入反对强迫自证其罪的范围。（3）在价值和实际功能上，二者具有一定的同一性。虽然沉默权是从保障个人权利的角度进行阐述，而反对强迫自证其罪包含了限制国家公权力的视角，但是在运用到实践的实际功能和效果上，二者具有一定程度的同一性，即都在一定程度上实现了保障个人权利和自由、限制国家公权力对个人进行非法侵害的效果。（4）从历史的角度看，二者在司法实践中的真正实施都与对抗制诉讼模式的兴起有关。只有当近现代“检验指控”理论（“testing the prosecution” theory）取代古老的“被告人说话”理论（“accused speaks” theory）时，被告人才享有实质的保持沉默、拒绝回答讯问、不被强迫自证其罪的权利。[②] 二者的区别表现在：（1）从起源来看，反对强迫自证其罪比沉默权要早。反对强迫自证其罪最早可以追溯到12世纪早期开始的英国教会法院和世

① 杨宇冠：《论不强迫自证其罪原则》，载《中国法学》2003年第1期，第131页。

② John H. Langbein, *The Historical Origins of the Privilege against Self-Incrimination at Common Law*, Michigan Law Review, Vol. 92, No. 5 (Mar., 1994), pp. 1066-1067.

俗法院的对立以及个人反对教会法院运用强迫宣誓程序作为获得自我归罪证据的斗争，而沉默权一般追溯至 1641 年英国星座法院（the Star Chamber）和高级专员公署（the High Commission）以及依职权宣誓程序（ex officio oath procedure）一起被废除之时。(2) 从适用的范围和主体来看，反对强迫自证其罪适用的范围和主体要比沉默权广泛。综观规定了反对强迫自证其罪的国际和各国国内立法条文，其表述基本都是“任何人”或者“人人”等类似的词语。例如，美国宪法第五修正案表述为：“任何人……不得在任何刑事案件中被迫自证其罪。”（No person shall be ... compelled in any criminal case to be a witness against himself.）《公民权利和政治权利国际公约》第 14 条第 3 款规定：“在判定对他提出的任何刑事指控时，人人完全平等地有资格享受以下的最低限度的保证：……（庚）不被强迫作不利于他自己的证言或强迫承认犯罪。”这表明反对强迫自证其罪至少适用于刑事诉讼中的犯罪嫌疑人、被告人和证人，甚至适用于非刑事诉讼程序中的当事人。在美国，联邦最高法院对第五修正案的解释是：“个人可以在大陪审团审判中、在民事审判中、在立法听证或行政听证中、在警察局接受讯问时，以及在诸多情形下援引第五修正案的特权，只要他将要提出的证言在美国刑事诉讼中可能被用作反对他的证据。”① 而沉默权一般仅适用于刑事诉讼中的被追诉人（犯罪嫌疑人和被告人），并不适用于证人，因为证人一般负有出庭作证的义务（依法享有作证豁免权者除外）。(3) 从内容上看，二者有所不同。沉默权赋予权利人拒绝回答所有问题的权利，既包括可能导致自我归罪的问题，也包括不可能导致自我归罪的问题；而反对强迫自证其罪只赋予权利人拒绝回答那些可能导致自我归罪的问题。有些人认为反对强迫自证其罪在适用的证据种类上不是仅限于言词证

---

① ［美］约书亚·德雷斯勒：《美国刑事诉讼法精解》（第 2 卷），魏晓娜译，北京大学出版社 2009 年版，第 251 页。

据，而是也适用于其他种类的证据，“范围上则涵盖了犯罪嫌疑人、被告人所提供的所有证据，包括其供述和其提供的其他所有实物证据”①。但实际上，这是一种误解。根据美国学界的通说，除非涉及强迫一个人作为反对自己的“证人”，否则就不涉及反对强迫自证其罪的问题。美国最高法院就此专门指出只有“言词证据”或者“谈话交流”才被美国宪法第五修正案（反对强迫自证其罪的特权）保护。②（4）从规则制定的出发点或者视角来看，二者也有所不同。虽然二者都有保障公民个人权利和自由免受国家公权力侵犯的作用，但是沉默权是从保障个人权利的角度进行阐述，赋予个人直接对抗国家公权力非法侵犯的权利，而反对强迫自证其罪则包含了限制国家公权力的视角，一方面，对于国家来讲，要反对国家强迫个人自我归罪；另一方面，对于个人来讲，个人有权拒绝国家强迫其自我归罪。

四、无罪推定与沉默权和反对强迫自证其罪的关系

无罪推定是沉默权存在的前提和基础。没有无罪推定，则不可能有真正完整意义上的沉默权。美国耶鲁大学教授约翰·H. 朗本（John H. Langbein）在论述普通法中反对强迫自证其罪特权的起源时指出，“自 16 世纪中期……至 18 世纪晚期，普通法刑事诉讼程序对被告人的基本保障不是保持沉默的权利，而是说话的机会。刑事审判的本质目的就是为被告人提供亲自回应对其指控的机会。在使刑事审判具有这一特性的程序属性中，最根本的就是禁止辩护律师的规则”③。笔者认为，虽然朗本教授准确

---

① 奚丹霓：《论无罪推定》，中国政法大学 2013 年博士学位论文，第 23 页。

② Charles H. Whitebread & Christopher Slobogin, Criminal Procedure: An Analysis of Cases and Concepts 421 (5th Edition, Foundation Press, 75th Anniversary, University Textbook Series).

③ John H. Langbein, *The Historical Origins of the Privilege against Self-Incrimination at Common Law*, Michigan Law Review, Vol. 92, No. 5 (Mar., 1994), p. 1047.

指出了16世纪中期至18世纪晚期普通法刑事诉讼程序将给予被告人说话的机会作为对其提供保护的手段，但是将禁止辩护律师的规则作为出现这一现象的根本原因则是不妥的。将为被告人提供亲自回应对其指控的机会作为对其进行保障的手段，这本身就暗含着（或者说预设了）一个前提，即若被告人不回应对其提出的指控，则会对其不利。这显然是有罪推定的意涵。换句话说，正是当时刑事诉讼程序中有罪推定的存在才使得被告人说话（自我辩护）的机会对其如此重要。有罪推定是这一现象存在的根源。相应地，正是无罪推定才为被告人不说话（保持沉默）并不因此而遭罪提供了条件和可能。

无罪推定与反对强迫自证其罪之间存在着密切的联系。这个联系的连接点就是“被告人没有义务对自己的言行作出解释：他有权袖手旁观并——如律师所言——通过坚持控方在获得辩方最低合作的情况下证明其对被告人的指控来‘让控方承担证明责任’”①。不确立无罪推定的思想，就容易过分看重认罪供述的价值，进而容易导致刑讯逼供，强迫嫌疑人自证其罪。无罪推定传入普通法系的过程就与反对酷刑、反对强迫自证其罪、保障人权密切相关。②

没有反对强迫自证其罪特权，侦查机关就可以强迫被追诉人或者证人自证其罪，就可能导致刑讯逼供、暴力取证等不正当行为，沉默权就会被侵犯，就违反了无罪推定的道义、实体和程序的要求。虽然一些人也许认为可能有时候折磨犯罪嫌疑人以

① Paul Roberts & Adrian Zuckerman, Criminal Evidence 244 (2nd Edition, OUP, 2010).

② K Pennington, *Innocent Until Proven Guilty: The Origins of a Legal Maxim*, 63 The Jurist 106, 124 (2003).

获取刑事犯罪情报是被允许的,[①] 但是，一般说来这样做是非法的。

沉默权在逻辑上必然要求不能强迫自证其罪。提高办案效率，节约司法资源，及时惩罚犯罪，维护好社会秩序是刑事诉讼法的基本任务，也是追诉机关的重要职责。而让被追诉人（犯罪嫌疑人和被告人）表达对其自身有利（开罪）的话可能会导致被追诉人有罪的嫌疑被排除（使被追诉人不存在有罪嫌疑），进而导致刑事追诉无法继续进行并且要释放被追诉人，结果造成对被追诉人的追诉错误，浪费有限的司法资源，破不了案，无法及时惩罚犯罪，维护好社会秩序。而这是追诉机关及其办案人员所不希望看到的结果。为了避免这样的结果出现，追诉机关必须设法证明被追诉人（犯罪嫌疑人和被告人）有罪。在口供是“证据之王”，获取口供是破案捷径的观念影响下，追诉机关必然试图从被追诉人（犯罪嫌疑人和被告人）那里获取有利于证明犯罪的口供，即希望被追诉人开口讲有利于追诉犯罪（对被追诉人不利）的话，而不是讲自我开罪（对被追诉人有利）的话。然而，如果被追诉人享有沉默权，那么追诉机关就不能强迫其作出任何陈述，当然也不能强迫其作出对其自身不利、可能导致其自我归罪的陈述，亦即不能强迫其自证其罪。因此，沉默权在逻辑上必然导致不能强迫自证其罪。

---

① See Michael S. Moore, *Torture and the Balance of Evils*, 23 Israel LR 280 (1989); reprinted in Moore, Placing Blame (OUP, 1997), ch 17. Cf. R. A. Duff, *In Defence of One Type of Retributivism: A Reply to Bagaric and Amarasekara*, 24 Melbourne University LR 411 (2000).

沉默权在逻辑上要求不能强迫自证其罪

让被追诉人（犯罪嫌疑人和被告人）表达对其自身有利（开罪）的话

↓

被追诉人有罪的嫌疑被排除（即被追诉人不存在有罪嫌疑）

↓

刑事追诉无法继续进行并且要释放被追诉人

↓

错误追诉，浪费司法资源，破不了案，无法及时惩罚犯罪，维护好社会秩序

提高办案效率，节约司法资源，及时惩罚犯罪，维护好社会秩序是刑事诉讼法的基本任务，也是追诉机关的重要职责

↓

追诉机关及其办案人员所不希望看到的结果

↓

避免这样的结果出现

↓

追诉机关必须设法证明被追诉人（犯罪嫌疑人和被告人）有罪

口供是“证据之王”，获取口供是破案捷径的观念影响

↓

追诉机关必然试图从被追诉人（犯罪嫌疑人和被告人）那里获取有利于证明犯罪的口供

主要希望被追诉人开口讲有利于追诉犯罪（对被追诉人不利）的话，而不是讲自我开罪（对被追诉人有利）的话

被追诉人享有沉默权

↓

追诉机关不能强迫其作出任何陈述

↓

追诉机关不能强迫其作出对其自身不利、可能导致其自我归罪的陈述：不能强迫其自证其罪

沉默权要求禁止酷刑。口供可以为追诉机关惩罚犯罪提供有用的信息来源（可以是直接证据，也可以是有用的破案线索）需要有两个前提条件：一个是口供主动提供者或者被讯问主体（被追诉人或者证人）是真正的罪犯或者确实掌握相关的案件信息，另一个是这些主体愿意提供（讲出）这些信息。如果这两个条件同时具备，那么将非常有利于破案和惩罚犯罪。因此，口供被视为“证据之王”，获取口供被视为破案和实现惩罚犯罪的捷径。也正因如此，追诉机关及其办案人员都想获取口供，让被追诉人开口讲话。而要实现此目的，就必须让被追诉人放弃沉默权。让被追诉人放弃沉默权的方法主要有以下四种：方法之一：当时采取强制措施：酷刑。根据酷刑作用的方式，又可将酷刑分为两种：一种是针对肉体实施的酷刑，又叫肉刑；另一种是针对人的精神实施的酷刑，又叫精神折磨。方法之二：告知被追诉人若其不说，则将发生其不希望发生的事：威胁。方法之三：告知被追诉人若其说，则将发生其希望发生的事：引诱。方法之四：审讯者明知方法二、方法三所承诺的结果不会发生或者并未打算让这种结果发生，仍旧作出该承诺：欺骗。上述四种方法又可以分为两类：一类是当时就发生被追诉人最关心（或最受影响）事件的方法，如方法一；另一类是非当时就发生被追诉人最关心（或最受影响）事件的方法，如方法二、方法三、方法四。其中，方法一、方法二或以方法二为背景的方法四即为强迫，主要是解决被追诉人愿意提供（讲出）案件相关信息的问题。而如果口供可以为追诉机关惩罚犯罪提供有用信息来源的另一个前提条件不存在，即被追诉人不是真正的罪犯且不掌握相关的案件信息，那么在这种情况下对被追诉人采取强迫措施，就可能造成冤假错案，造成的结果就是破坏司法公正：既侵犯人权，又不能有效惩罚犯罪。为了避免这种结果的出现，就必须保证“被追诉人不是真正的罪犯且不掌握相关的案件信息”和“强迫”这二者不能同时存在，即或者不能实施强迫，或者被追诉人是真正的罪犯或者掌握相关的案件信息。然而，由于人类认识的有限性（详见第三章“无罪推定的根据——一个多视角的探查”第一节“哲学视角下的无罪推定”）等主客观原因的存在，无法保证被追诉人是真正的罪犯或者掌握相关的案件信息，因此只能禁止实施强迫，即不能采取方法一、方法二或以方法二为背景的方法四，当然也不能采取方法一：酷刑，也就是要禁止酷刑。

沉默权要求禁止酷刑

<table>
<tr><td rowspan="16"></td><td colspan="4">口供主动提供者或者被讯问主体（被追诉人或者证人）是真正的罪犯或者确实掌握相关的案件信息</td><td colspan="2">这些主体愿意提供（讲出）这些信息</td></tr>
<tr><td colspan="6">⬇</td></tr>
<tr><td colspan="6">口供可以为追诉机关惩罚犯罪提供有用的信息来源（可以是直接证据，也可以是有用的破案线索）</td></tr>
<tr><td colspan="6">⬇</td></tr>
<tr><td colspan="6">有利于破案和惩罚犯罪</td></tr>
<tr><td colspan="6">⬇</td></tr>
<tr><td colspan="6">口供被视为“证据之王”，获取口供被视为破案和实现惩罚犯罪的捷径</td></tr>
<tr><td colspan="6">⬇</td></tr>
<tr><td colspan="6">追诉机关及其办案人员都想获取口供，让被追诉人开口讲话</td></tr>
<tr><td colspan="6">⬇</td></tr>
<tr><td colspan="6">让被追诉人放弃沉默权</td></tr>
<tr><td colspan="6">⬇</td></tr>
<tr><td colspan="6">让被追诉人放弃沉默权的方法</td></tr>
<tr><td colspan="2">当时采取强制措施：酷刑</td><td rowspan="2">告知被追诉人若其不说，则将发生其不希望发生的事：威胁</td><td colspan="2">审讯者明知威胁、引诱所承诺的结果不会发生或者并未打算让这种结果发生，仍旧作出该承诺：欺骗</td><td rowspan="2">告知被追诉人若其说，则将发生其希望发生的事：引诱</td></tr>
<tr><td>针对肉体实施的酷刑：肉刑</td><td>针对人的精神实施的酷刑：精神折磨</td><td>以威胁为背景的欺骗</td><td>以引诱为背景的欺骗</td></tr>
<tr><td colspan="2">当时就发生被追诉人最关心（或最受影响）的事件</td><td colspan="4">非当时就发生被追诉人最关心（或最受影响）的事件</td></tr>
</table>

续表

被追诉人不是真正的罪犯且不掌握相关的案件信息	强迫：主要是解决被追诉人愿意提供（讲出）案件相关信息的问题	
↓		
冤假错案		人类认识的有限性（详见第三章“无罪推定的根据——一个多视角的探查”第一节“哲学视角下的无罪推定”）等主客观原因的存在
↓		
破坏司法公正：既侵犯人权，又不能有效惩罚犯罪		
↓		
避免这种结果出现		
↓		
必须保证“被追诉人不是真正的罪犯且不掌握相关的案件信息”和“强迫”这二者不能同时存在		↓
或者不能实施强迫	或者被追诉人是真正的罪犯或者掌握相关的案件信息	无法保证被追诉人是真正的罪犯或者掌握相关的案件信息
↓		
禁止实施强迫：不能采取酷刑、威胁或以威胁为背景的欺骗方法		
↓		
不能采取酷刑方法，即禁止酷刑		

沉默权可以在一定程度上防止冤假错案。沉默权使被追诉人可以直接对抗强迫开口说话、自证其罪的要求，而强迫开口说话、自证其罪是导致冤假错案的一个重要原因。因此，沉默权可

以消灭造成冤假错案的一个重要原因，从而在一定程度上防止冤假错案。

沉默权可在一定程度上防止冤假错案

<table>
<tr><td>沉默权使被追诉人可以直接对抗强迫开口说话、自证其罪的要求</td><td rowspan="2">➡</td><td rowspan="2">沉默权可以在一定程度上防止冤假错案</td></tr>
<tr><td>强迫开口说话、自证其罪是导致冤假错案的一个重要原因</td></tr>
</table>

如果被追诉人开口讲话、作出陈述，那么其所作出的陈述可能对自己不利（导致自我归罪），可能对自己有利（导致自我开罪），也可能与是否对自己有利无关。这也就意味着被追诉人开口讲话既存在使自己有罪（自证其罪）的风险，也存在使自己无罪（自我开罪）的可能。如果实行无罪推定，任何人都被预先假定为无罪，都处在无罪的初始状态，那么被追诉人很自然不愿意开口讲话，希望享有沉默权。而如果实行有罪推定，任何人都被预先假定为有罪，都处在有罪的初始状态，那么被追诉人自然希望开口讲话，争取自我开罪的机会，从而不需要沉默权。因此，无罪推定为被追诉人行使沉默权提供了条件，使其不因不说而遭罪，是被追诉人希望拥有沉默权的原因。

无罪推定是沉默权的条件和原因

<table>
<tr><td rowspan="4">无罪推定：任何人都被预先假定为无罪，都处在无罪的初始状态</td><td colspan="3">被追诉人开口讲话、作出陈述</td><td rowspan="4">有罪推定：任何人都被预先假定为有罪，都处在有罪的初始状态</td><td colspan="3">被追诉人开口讲话、作出陈述</td></tr>
<tr><td colspan="3">↓</td><td colspan="3">↓</td></tr>
<tr><td>可能对自己不利（导致自我归罪）</td><td>可能对自己有利（导致自我开罪）</td><td>可能与是否对自己有利无关</td><td>可能对自己不利（导致自我归罪）</td><td>可能对自己有利（导致自我开罪）</td><td>可能与是否对自己有利无关</td></tr>
<tr><td>存在使自己有罪（自证其罪）的风险</td><td>存在使自己无罪（自我开罪）的可能</td><td></td><td>存在使自己有罪（自证其罪）的风险</td><td>存在使自己无罪（自我开罪）的可能</td><td></td></tr>
<tr><td colspan="4">↓</td><td colspan="4">↓</td></tr>
<tr><td colspan="4">被追诉人不愿意开口讲话，希望享有沉默权</td><td colspan="4">被追诉人希望开口讲话，争取自我开罪的机会，不需要沉默权</td></tr>
<tr><td colspan="8">↓</td></tr>
<tr><td colspan="8">无罪推定为被追诉人行使沉默权提供了条件，使其不因不说而遭罪，是被追诉人希望拥有沉默权的原因</td></tr>
</table>

综上所述，无罪推定是沉默权存在的原因，而沉默权具有反对强迫自证其罪、禁止酷刑和可在一定程度上防止冤假错案的重要意义。因此，无罪推定是沉默权的存在及实现其意义的源头：只有实行无罪推定，才能实现这一切。

无罪推定与沉默权和反对强迫自证其罪的关系

<table>
<tr><td rowspan="3">无罪推定为被追诉人行使沉默权提供了条件，使其不因不说而遭罪，是被追诉人希望拥有沉默权的原因</td><td colspan="3">无罪推定</td><td rowspan="5">➡</td><td rowspan="5">无罪推定是沉默权的存在及实现其意义的源头：只有实行无罪推定，才能实现这一切</td></tr>
<tr><td colspan="3">⬇</td></tr>
<tr><td colspan="3">沉默权</td></tr>
<tr><td rowspan="2">沉默权的重要意义</td><td colspan="3">⬇</td></tr>
<tr><td>反对强迫自证其罪</td><td>禁止酷刑</td><td>可在一定程度上防止冤假错案</td></tr>
</table>

第二节　无罪推定与正当法律程序

一、正当法律程序概述

正当法律程序这一术语是欧洲中世纪的创造物，首次出现在14世纪英国以法文书写的皇家法令集中。[①] 英国国王爱德华三世（King Edward III）统治期间的《六项法令》（1331—1369年通过）力图澄清《自由大宪章》（*Magna Carta*）的某些部分。特别是第三项法令于1354年重新定义了《自由大宪章》第29条，将“自由人”变成了“任何人，无分身份或情况”，并引进了词组“正当

① The earliest use of the term is in a statute of Edward III, 28 Edward III, c. 3 (1354): “saunz estre mesne en respons par due process de lei.” Cited in Kenneth Pennington: Due Process, Community, and the Prince in the Evolution of the Ordo iudiciarius, available at http://faculty.cua.edu/pennington/Law508/procedure.htm # Establishment% 20of% 20Ordo, last visited on March 26, 2016.

法律程序”（due process of law）以代替“同等人的合法审判或者根据本国法律行事”。① 这成为“正当法律程序”这一术语正式诞生的标志。“due process of law”（正当法律程序）这一表述来源于英国，在其他欧洲语言中并没有与之完全对应的表达。虽然这一短语无法被优雅地翻译成任何其他的欧洲语言，但是正当法律程序的观念是每个欧洲国家法律制度的一部分，因为欧洲共同法的法学家是在中世纪司法程序中发展正当法律程序观念的关键因素。②

正当法律程序的内涵较为宽泛和模糊。不同的学者对其也有不同的定义。英国著名法官丹宁勋爵认为：“‘法律的正当程序’，系指法律为了保持日常司法工作的纯洁性而认可的各种方法：促使审判和调查公正的进行，逮捕和搜查适当的使用，法律援助顺利的取得，以及消除不必要的延误，等等。”③《韦氏美国语世界新词典》将正当法律程序视为“由法律制度确立的保护个人权利的法律诉讼过程”④。根据《元照英美法词典》的解释，正当法律程序是个多义的宪法概念，既指法治、法律程序的公正，也指一项基本权利。正当法律程序权利（due process rights）是指要求遵循公平与正义的正当程序标准（due process standards of fairness and justice）具有根本性的所有权利，即公民享有的对抗危及剥夺生命、自由和财产的政府行为的程序上和实体上的权利。⑤ 国内有学者认为，

① Turner, Ralph (2003b). *Magna Carta: Through the Ages*. Routledge. ISBN 978-0582438262. p. 123. Cited at http://en.wikipedia.org/wiki/Magna_Carta, last visited on March 26, 2016.

② See generally Kenneth Pennington: Due Process, Community, and the Prince in the Evolution of the Ordo iudiciarius, available at http: //faculty.cua.edu/pennington/Law508/procedure.htm#Establishment%20of%20Ordo , last visited on March 26, 2016.

③ ［英］丹宁勋爵：《法律的正当程序》，李克强、杨百揆、刘庸安译，法律出版社 1999 年版。

④ To quote one dictionary's definition; Webster's New World Dictionary of the American Language (2nd College Edition; 1978).

⑤ 薛波：《元照英美法词典》，法律出版社 2003 年版，“正当法律程序”词条，第 448 页。

“正当法律程序”（due process of law）或称“正当程序”（due process），是指保证司法活动公正性，保护刑事活动涉及的每一个人，包括犯罪嫌疑人和被告人的生命权、自由权、财产权、隐私权等合法权利免受非法干涉的一系列规则。它要求国家行使刑事司法权力的部门在对个人的权利加以限制或剥夺时应当严格按照法律规定的程序，而且，这个程序本身必须是正当的和合理的。[①] 关于正当法律程序，有美国学者认为：“正当法律程序的意思还不是很清楚，许多最高法院最著名的决定都争论过这个问题。一般来说，正当法律程序是指无论何时诉讼，比如刑事诉讼，威胁人的生命，可能造成监禁或其他严重的丧失自由，或可能没收人们的金钱或财产时，政府必须使用公平的程序和标准。正当程序是所有个人享有的公平的最低限度标准。”[②] 美国著名学者约翰·V. 奥尔特认为：“正当法律程序很久以来就是我们宪法词汇的一部分，几乎没有比它更重要的短语了。但是，这个短语本身虽然具有提示性，但它不可能是不解自明的。法官和律师们已经从字面上努力了几百年，试图在具体的案例中赋予其内容。但是，他们努力的结果始终并未被普遍接受，即使取得共识，也极少能够持续很长时间。在不断变化的环境中试图实现这一理想可能是我们法律传统中不可缺少的一部分，而且由于这一传统，我们应当毫不逃避地断然宣告正当法律程序的需要已经一劳永逸地确定了。”[③] 即使美国联邦最高法院也未能给正当法律程序作出准确的定义，只是声称它愿意尊重司法的内涵与外延发展的规律，以一种渐进的过程对其加以适用。[④] 正如有

---

① 杨宇冠：《论构建我国刑事诉讼的正当法律程序体系》，载《杭州师范学院学报》（社会科学版）2004年第5期，第41页。

② ［美］爱伦·豪切斯泰勒·斯黛丽、南希·弗兰克：《美国刑事法院诉讼程序》，陈卫东、徐美君译，中国人民大学出版社2002年版，第70页。

③ ［美］约翰·V. 奥尔特：《正当法律程序简史》，杨明成、陈霜玲译，商务印书馆2006年版，中文版前言。

④ ［美］卡尔维因、帕尔德森：《美国宪法释义》，徐卫东、吴新平译，华夏出版社1989年版，第231页。

学者指出："究竟什么是'正当法律程序'？对此，并无统一的认识。——由于'正当性'涉及价值判断，主观色彩相当浓厚，'正当法律程序'也就成为一个人言人殊的'罗生门'式的问题。"①并指出"正当法律程序是一个具有高度灵活性的概念。与某些法律规则不同，正当法律程序并非具有固定的内涵，它和时间、地点、场合等因素有关。此外，正当法律程序还是一个不断进化的概念，过去的原则将在未来的经验下重新受到评判（J. Harlan）。②正当法律程序的灵活性和可变性使得它恰如一张博登海默（E. Bodenheimer）所说的'普洛透斯之脸'（a protean face）。当我们仔细查看这张脸并试图解开隐藏在其表面之后的秘密时，我们往往会深感迷惑③"④。

笔者认为，正当法律程序实际是指符合以人权保护为核心的价值标准并符合最低限度程序正义要求的一系列基本法律程序的总称。西方的判例和学术一再表明正当法律程序的价值性和基础性特征，并以之作为判定是否符合正当法律程序的根据。正当法律程序有以下两个主要特点：一是价值标准性，即正当法律程序的内容应符合以人权保护为核心的价值标准。二是基础性，即正当法律程序要符合最低限度的程序正义要求，是一系列重要的基本法律程序的总称，而不是所有法律程序的总称。"由于正当法律程序主要适用于没有法定程序的情形（否则即适用法定程序标准），所以正当法

① 刘东亮：《什么是正当法律程序》，载《中国法学》2010年第4期，第76页。

② 参见张千帆：《西方宪政体系》（上册·美国宪法），中国政法大学出版社2000年版，第221、226页。

③ 参见［美］E. 博登海默《法理学——法律哲学与法律方法》，邓正来译，中国政法大学出版社1999年版，第252页。

④ 刘东亮：《什么是正当法律程序》，载《中国法学》2010年第4期，第81页。

律程序实际上指的是某种程序是否‘合理’的问题。”① 正当法律程序包含了强烈的自然法色彩，是一定价值理念的体现和要求。

正当法律程序在美国宪法中一般指第五和第十四修正案。美国宪法第五修正案规定：“非经大陪审团提出报告或起诉，任何人不受死罪或其他重罪的惩罚，唯在战时国家危急时期发生在陆、海军中或正在服役的民兵中的案件不在此限。任何人不得因同一犯罪行为而两次遭受生命或身体伤残的危害；不得在任何刑事案件中被迫自证其罪；未经正当法律程序，不得剥夺任何人的生命、自由或财产；非有恰当补偿，不得将私有财产充作公用。”（No person shall be held to answer for a capital, or otherwise infamous crime, unless on a presentment or indictment of a Grand Jury, except in cases arising in the land or naval forces, or in the Militia, when in actual service in time of War or public danger; nor shall any person be subject for the same offence to be twice put in jeopardy of life or limb; nor shall be compelled in any criminal case to be a witness against himself, nor be deprived of life, liberty, or property, without due process of law; nor shall private property be taken for public use, without just compensation.）美国宪法第十四修正案第1款规定：“在合众国出生或归化合众国并受合众国管辖的人，均为合众国和他所居住的州的公民。无论何州均不得制定或实施任何剥夺合众国公民的特权或豁免权的法律；无论何州未经正当法律程序不得剥夺任何人的生命、自由或财产；亦不得拒绝给予在其管辖下的任何人以同等的法律保护。”（All persons born or naturalized in the United States, and subject to the jurisdiction thereof, are citizens of the United States and of the State wherein they reside. No State shall make or enforce any law which shall abridge the

① 刘东亮：《什么是正当法律程序》，载《中国法学》2010年第4期，第81页。“正当程序和法定程序在适用范围上具有互补性。正当程序主要适用于没有法律程序的明确规定（即法定程序）的情形。”刘东亮：《什么是正当法律程序》，载《中国法学》2010年第4期，第87页。

privileges or immunities of citizens of the United States; nor shall any State deprive any person of life, liberty, or property, without due process of law; nor deny to any person within its jurisdiction the equal protection of the laws.)

正当法律程序的内容较为宽泛，从不同的角度可以对其进行不同的描述。美国法学家贝尔斯认为，正当法律程序应当包含以下八项原则：和平、自愿、参与、公正——程序中的平等对待、可理解性、省时、得体、经济和道德上的花费低。① 美国学者们普遍认为正当法律程序包含以下基本内容：（1）任何人在被证明有罪之前推定为无罪；（2）任何人的身体、住所、财物不经法定程序不得被搜查、扣押或受侵犯；（3）在刑事程序中不得强迫自证其罪；（4）被告人享有律师帮助权，如果被告人无钱聘请律师，则需为他指定一名律师；（5）被告人有权知道被指控的性质、内容和理由，且享有由公正的陪审团迅速、公开审判的权利；（6）提起公诉时要求证明该案件的证据达到不容合理怀疑的程度，这一责任在起诉方；（7）被告人的同一罪行只能审判一次。② 在程序正义的最低标准方面，有学者将其总结为以下几条：（1）受刑事裁判直接影响的人应当充分而富有意义地参与裁判制作过程，即“程序参与原则”；（2）裁判者应在控辩双方之间保持中立，即“中立原则”；（3）控辩双方应受到平等的对待，即“程序对等原则”；（4）审判程序的运作应符合程序理性的要求，即“程序理性原则”；（5）法官的裁判应从法庭审判过程中产生，即“程序自治原则”；（6）程序应当及时产生裁判结果，并最终确定被告人是否担负法律责任，即“程序及时和终结原则”。并同时认为上述最低标准是无罪推定原则的应然要求。③

① 杨寅：《中国行政程序法治化》，中国政法大学出版社 2001 年版，第 45-46 页。

② 参见宋英辉主编：《刑事诉讼原理》，法律出版社 2003 年版，第 74 页，注[24]。

③ 陈瑞华：《刑事审判原理论》，北京大学出版 1997 年版，第 60-61 页。

正当法律程序是审判具有正当性的一个重要基础。即使一个实际上犯下了严重罪行的人也仅应当以一定的（公平的）方式定罪。公平不仅仅意味着准确认定所有的案件事实，而且意味着有罪判决应当依照正当法律程序作出。法庭不应是纯粹的定罪处刑的工具，而应当遵循一定的程序标准以使其审判具备正当性。“法院”和“惩治罪犯委员会”不是一回事，相似地，“定罪”也不仅仅意味着一群掌握权力的人满足于某人有罪的充分证据并利用国家权力对该人进行打击。真正的审判必须满足最低限度的程序标准。①

二、无罪推定与正当法律程序的关系

在正当法律程序的语境下，无罪推定是正当法律程序的一部分，并且是部分其他正当法律程序的根据。正如无罪推定权利是人权的一部分，并且是部分其他人权的根据一样。正当法律程序和无罪推定都既包含了权利的内容，也包含了义务的内容，在一定程度上都可以归属于制度的范畴；而无罪推定权利和人权属于权利的范畴，是在权利的层面上探讨问题。可以讲，无罪推定权利是从权利的视角观察无罪推定，人权是从人所应享有的权利的视角观察正当法律程序。无罪推定中义务主体（如追诉机关）所应承担的不得推定有罪的义务和正当法律程序中义务主体（如追诉机关）所应承担的配合和保证人权得以实现的义务则不在无罪推定权利和人权的观察焦点上。

无罪推定是正当法律程序的要求之一。它要求除非公诉方通过具有公正审判最典型特征（包括权利和保护措施）的程序证明某个人有罪，在此之前，国家不能宣告其有罪。法治的内在要求之一就是任何人享有在未被“依法”确定有罪之前被国家作为无罪之

① See generally Hock Lai Ho, *The Presumption of Innocence as a Human Right* in Paul Roberts and Jill Hunter (eds), Criminal Evidence and Human Rights – Reimagining Common Law Procedural Traditions 275 (Oxford: Hart Publishing, 2012).

人对待的权利。[①] 一些国际人权宣言明确将无罪推定作为正当法律程序的一部分予以规定。例如，1948 年 5 月 2 日美洲国家第九次国际会议通过的《美洲人的权利和义务宣言》（*American Declaration of the Rights and Duties of Man*）在第 26 条“正当法律程序权利”（Right to due process of law）中规定：“在被证明有罪之前，所有被指控者都被推定为无罪。所有被指控者都有权获得公正、公开的听证，并有权获得已经依现行法成立的法庭审判，并且不得受到残忍的、不名誉的或者非常规的惩罚。”

独立无偏倚的法庭是公正审判权的内容之一，是无罪推定的一方面，是正当程序的核心。正如英国的迪普洛克勋爵（Lord Diplock）指出的，无罪推定所要求的“依法”所依之法必须包含自然正义的基本规则，即正当法律程序的基本规则，其中之一就是强调罪行必须由独立无偏倚的法庭来决定。[②] 如果法官并非“独立无偏倚”，而是遵循控诉机关的判断，那么被告人就没有获得审判的完整利益。不能以批判态度审查侦查和公诉机关所移送的案件，就没有无罪推定。[③] 因此，可以讲没有审判机关的独立审判，就没有真正的无罪推定。审判机关不能因为公诉机关的意见而对案件产生先入为主的看法。刑事法庭的职能就是对控诉机关的控诉行为进行审查，要求公诉方对其定罪量刑建议的正当性进行解释和证明，包括向被告和社会解释刑罚的正当性。其他基本的程序标准或者说正当程序的要求都可由此推导出来，如被追诉人的被告知权、辩护

① See generally Hock Lai Ho, *The Presumption of Innocence as a Human Right* in Paul Roberts and Jill Hunter (eds), Criminal Evidence and Human Rights - Reimagining Common Law Procedural Traditions 276 (Oxford: Hart Publishing, 2012).

② See generally Hock Lai Ho, *The Presumption of Innocence as a Human Right* in Paul Roberts and Jill Hunter (eds), Criminal Evidence and Human Rights - Reimagining Common Law Procedural Traditions 268 (Oxford: Hart Publishing, 2012).

③ Hock Lai Ho, *The Presumption of Innocence as a Human Right* in Paul Roberts and Jill Hunter (eds), Criminal Evidence and Human Rights - Reimagining Common Law Procedural Traditions 276 (Oxford: Hart Publishing, 2012).

权、质证权、与证人对质权等。审判是一般地传达刑法标准的核心媒介。基于这一目的，审判的过程必须被公之于众，因此，我们要求公开的审判过程和透明的裁判。①

第三节　无罪推定与证据裁判原则

一、证据裁判原则概述

证据裁判原则是指“诉讼中司法人员认定案件事实必须以证据为依据”②。我国刑事诉讼法、民事诉讼法和行政诉讼法都未对该原则进行明确规定，但2010年最高人民法院、最高人民检察院、公安部、国家安全部和司法部联合颁布的《关于办理死刑案件审查判断证据若干问题的规定》第2条明确规定：“认定案件事实，必须以证据为根据。”在刑事诉讼中正式确立了证据裁判原则。党的十八届四中全会明确提出要“全面贯彻证据裁判规则”，将对证据裁判原则的重视提到了一个新的高度。

虽然证据裁判原则是现代法治国家刑事诉讼中认定犯罪事实时必须遵循的原则，但是大多数国家并没有在法律中明确规定证据裁判原则。欧洲大陆几个主要国家的刑事诉讼法典虽然规定了自由心证原则及其相关内容，但是并未将证据裁判作为独立的原则规定于条文之中，如现行的《法国刑事诉讼法典》、《德国刑事诉讼法典》、《俄罗斯联邦刑事诉讼法典》以及《意大利刑事诉讼法典》等。英美法系国家证据法非常发达，很多国家制定有专门的证据法典，如美国《联邦证据规则》、加利福尼亚州《证据法典》、加拿

① See generally Hock Lai Ho, *The Presumption of Innocence as a Human Right* in Paul Roberts and Jill Hunter (eds), Criminal Evidence and Human Rights - Reimagining Common Law Procedural Traditions 277 (Oxford: Hart Publishing, 2012).

② 陈光中、郑曦：《论刑事诉讼中的证据裁判原则——兼谈〈刑事诉讼法〉修改中的若干问题》，载《法学》2011年第9期，第3页。

大《证据法》、澳大利亚联邦《1995年证据法》、新西兰《1908年证据法》及其十三个修正法案，并且证据法学者也编著有大量的证据法学专著或教材，如《麦考密克论证据》、《墨菲论证据》，摩根教授所著的《证据法之基本问题》，以及近年来被大陆学者译成中文的乔恩·R.华尔兹所著的《刑事证据大全》，理查德·梅所著的《刑事证据》和罗纳德·J.艾伦所著的《证据法：文本、问题和案例》等。但是，英美法系这些立法和专著及教材中并没有关于证据裁判原则的规定，甚至英语中根本就没有与证据裁判原则准确对应的表达。①

虽然大多数国家并没有在法律中明确规定证据裁判原则，但是这些国家并非否认证据裁判原则。大陆法系国家虽然没有在法律中明确规定证据裁判原则，但是在其立法中却体现了证据裁判原则的精神。例如，《法国刑事诉讼法典》第427条规定："除法律另有规定外，犯罪得以任何证据形式认定，并且法官得依其内心确信作出判决。法官只能以在审理过程中向其提出的并在其当面经对席辩论的证据为其作出裁判决定的依据。"②《德国刑事诉讼法典》第244条第2款规定："为了调查事实真相，法院应当依职权将证据调查延伸到所有的对于裁判具有意义的事实、证据上。"③英美法系国家由于非常看重证据法及证据法学的价值，因此其将证据裁判原则作为默认的不言自明的道理，也就没有专门对该原则进行立法规定或者学术论述。

在法律条文上第一次明确规定证据裁判原则的是日本于1876年制定的《断罪依证律》。《断罪依证律》把《改定律例》规定的"凡断罪，依口供结案"修改为"凡断罪，依证据"，并规定"依

---

① 参见陈光中、郑曦：《论刑事诉讼中的证据裁判原则——兼谈〈刑事诉讼法〉修改中的若干问题》，载《法学》2011年第9期，第3、6、7页。

② 《法国刑事诉讼法典》，罗结珍译，中国法制出版社2006年版，第292页。

③ 《德国刑事诉讼法典》，李昌珂译，中国政法大学出版社1995年版，第101页。

证据断罪，完全由法官确定”。[①] 陈光中先生指出：根据其所掌握的资料，“这是法律文件对证据裁判原则的最早规定，将欧洲大陆的自由心证原则一分为二，区分了证据裁判原则和自由心证原则，也标志着证据裁判原则正式在法律上的确立。证据裁判原则的确立实际上也是对法官自由心证的一种限制。这一条文为现行的《日本刑事诉讼法典》所继承，该法第 317 条规定：‘认定事实，应当依据证据。’此外，这一规定也影响了亚洲其他国家或地区的立法，如韩国与我国台湾地区”[②]。

在刑事诉讼中，证据裁判原则有以下几点要求：（1）作为认定犯罪事实和作出裁判依据的证据必须具有客观性、关联性和可采性。（2）作为定案依据的证据必须按法定程序进行审查判断。（3）作为裁判依据的所有证据经过综合审查判断必须达到法定的证明标准。[③]

虽然证据裁判原则要求认定案件事实必须依据证据，而证据本身就包含口供（如证人证言，被害人陈述，犯罪嫌疑人、被告人供述和辩解等），但是证据裁判原则所强调依据的证据主要不是口供，而是口供以外的其他证据。理由主要有以下几点：第一，从历史渊源和立法目的的角度看，证据裁判原则是反对口供裁判主义的产物，因此，天然地排斥口供在认定案件事实中的主导地位。第二，从我国的立法情况看，在中国语境下，证据裁判原则中的证据也应当主要指口供之外的证据。我国刑事诉讼法第 55 条规定：“对一切案件的判处都要重证据，重调查研究，不轻信口供。只有

① 参见［日］松尾浩也：《日本刑事诉讼法》（下卷），宋英辉译，中国人民大学出版社 2005 年版，第 4 页。亦可参见［日］土本武司：《日本刑事诉讼法要义》，董璠舆、宋英辉译，台北五南图书出版公司 1994 年版，第 310~311 页。

② 陈光中、郑曦：《论刑事诉讼中的证据裁判原则——兼谈〈刑事诉讼法〉修改中的若干问题》，载《法学》2011 年第 9 期，第 7 页。

③ 陈光中、郑曦：《论刑事诉讼中的证据裁判原则——兼谈〈刑事诉讼法〉修改中的若干问题》，载《法学》2011 年第 9 期，第 8-9 页。

被告人供述，没有其他证据的，不能认定被告人有罪和处以刑罚；没有被告人供述，证据确实、充分的，可以认定被告人有罪和处以刑罚。”这一规定将“证据”与“口供”作了一定剥离，其中证据仅主要指除了口供之外的其他证据。①

关于口供与补强证据之间的关系，从我国刑事诉讼法第 55 条的规定来看，在我国刑事诉讼中，口供与补强证据之间不是主次关系，相反，补强证据已经超越口供成为定案的主要依据。②

二、无罪推定与证据裁判原则的关系

证据裁判原则强调的是认定案件事实的依据（即证据），也就是要依据证据而不是其他来认定案件事实，至于认定什么案件事实（即案件事实的内容），则在所不问。简言之，证据裁判原则只管认定的依据，而不管认定的内容。无罪推定是指任何人在未被依法证明并宣告有罪之前应被视为无罪。它要求由控方来证明被告人有罪的案件事实，即犯罪事实，而被告人无罪的案件事实不需要加以证明，只要控方没有证据证明被告人有罪或者证明被告人有罪的证据不充分，就应认定被告人无罪。从这个意义上讲，无罪推定为刑事诉讼中证据裁判原则所要求依证据认定的案件事实内容指明了方向，即要依证据认定的案件事实是有罪的事实（即犯罪事实），而不是无罪的事实。如果将无罪的事实也视为证据裁判原则所要求依证据认定的案件事实范围，则有违无罪推定的要求。当然，如果被告人能够并且愿意依证据证明无罪的案件事实，证据裁判原则对此也不排斥。因此，可以讲无罪推定补充了刑事诉讼中证据裁判原则所要求依证据认定的案件事实的内容。也正是基于此，“在刑事诉

---

① 参见陈光中、郑曦：《论刑事诉讼中的证据裁判原则——兼谈〈刑事诉讼法〉修改中的若干问题》，载《法学》2011 年第 9 期，第 9-10 页。

② 参见陈光中、郑曦：《论刑事诉讼中的证据裁判原则——兼谈〈刑事诉讼法〉修改中的若干问题》，载《法学》2011 年第 9 期，第 10 页。

讼中，就实体方面而言，证据裁判原则是指认定犯罪事实必须依据证据”①。

证据裁判是落实无罪推定的保证，是实现无罪推定的桥梁。根据无罪推定原则，对于一个刑事案件来讲，初始的假定状态是被追诉人无罪，然后根据证据裁判原则，通过证据来证明被追诉人有罪。如果不能依法证明被追诉人有罪，则审判机关只能作出无罪的认定。无罪推定与证明的关系密切，其要求国家对个人定罪处罚必须以证明其有罪为条件，任何人不得仅仅因为被怀疑有罪而被定罪处罚。② 证明是指利用证据来推理出待证事实的过程，本身就体现了证据裁判原则。因此，无罪推定的实现离不开证据裁判原则的落实。

无罪推定要求在“依法”证明和认定有罪之前应视为无罪，其中的“依法”包含了依正当法律程序的要求，而正当法律程序实际包含了举证责任和证明标准的内容和要求，因此，没有相应的恰当的举证责任和证明标准的保障，无罪推定将会是空谈和空中楼阁。在英美法系，无罪推定与证据裁判原则密切相连，无罪推定就是通过“举证责任”和“证明标准”的概念来阐述的。③

如上所述，证据裁判原则只是明确了认定案件事实的依据(即证据)，并没有明确所要认定的案件事实的内容，同样，证据裁判原则也没有明确认定案件事实的主体，即由谁去认定案件事实。在刑事诉讼中，对于这个问题，无罪推定同样给出了答案，即刑事诉讼中证明犯罪事实的主体是控方，被告人没有义务证明自己

---

① 陈光中、郑曦：《论刑事诉讼中的证据裁判原则——兼谈〈刑事诉讼法〉修改中的若干问题》，载《法学》2011 年第 9 期，第 8 页。

② See generally Hock Lai Ho, *The Presumption of Innocence as a Human Right* in Paul Roberts and Jill Hunter (eds), Criminal Evidence and Human Rights - Reimagining Common Law Procedural Traditions 262 (Oxford: Hart Publishing, 2012).

③ See generally Hock Lai Ho, *The Presumption of Innocence as a Human Right* in Paul Roberts and Jill Hunter (eds), Criminal Evidence and Human Rights - Reimagining Common Law Procedural Traditions 261 (Oxford: Hart Publishing, 2012).

无罪。这实际上就涉及刑事诉讼中关于案件事实的举证责任问题。

（一）无罪推定与举证责任

无罪推定意味着证明被追诉人有罪的责任不在被追诉人，而在于追诉方。在英美法系国家，鉴于由控方承担提供证据反驳每一个出罪的主张将导致大量的时间和金钱被浪费于证明一些并不真实存在争议的问题，同时，一些真正的罪犯将会仅仅因为控方不能证伪那些完全空想没有任何证据的理由和辩解而逃脱正义的定罪量刑，为了避免这种低效和潜在的不公正，有时会要求被告人承担提供证据责任。[①] 就中国司法制度而言，对于法定的犯罪构成要素原则上必须由公诉方予以证明，如果被告人或者法庭提出违法阻却事由问题，公诉方也必须对相关问题进行证明。非法定的违法阻却事由，在中国刑事法制中常常被当作酌定量刑情节进行考虑。只有“情节极其轻微，不认为是犯罪的”情况，本身已不再是简单的酌定量刑情节问题，而是一个决定罪与非罪的问题，如果被告人或者法庭提出该问题，公诉方必须予以相应证明。无论如何，被告人拥有要求控方承担充分证明被告人有罪责任的权利，控方也负有相应的义务。从这一角度讲，无罪推定无疑是人们不被随意推定或者认定为有罪的自由的保障。当然，无罪推定并不意味着控方要主动证明所有可能的问题，（例如，无罪推定要求控方证明法定的犯罪构成要素问题，但是并不要求控方主动提起并证明违法阻却事由问题），因此无罪推定虽是自由的保障，但并非纵容无限制的自由，而是在保障人们自由的同时，寻求个体自由与社会公共利益之间的平衡。[②]

在我国，不仅在公诉案件中，被告人不承担证明自己有罪的义务，在自诉案件中，被告人也不承担证明自己有罪的义务。我国刑

① Paul Roberts & Adrian Zuckerman, Criminal Evidence 244 - 5 (OUP, 2nd edn. 2010).

② Paul Roberts & Adrian Zuckerman, Criminal Evidence 244 - 5 (OUP, 2nd edn. 2010).

事诉讼法第51条规定：“公诉案件中被告人有罪的举证责任由人民检察院承担，自诉案件中被告人有罪的举证责任由自诉人承担。”

举证责任在刑事案件中具有战略意义，因为其决定着在争论的问题无法查清时，哪一方将从中受益。举证责任也是一个重要的“政策”问题，因为其决定着错误风险的分配。因此，控方必须以极高的证明标准（如排除合理怀疑，案件事实清楚、证据确实充分，等等）证明其指控这一通常规则意味着一种社会的、政治的或者道德的判断——我们更愿意忍受错放有罪而不是错判无辜。这一规则也具体定义了被告人有资格享有“无罪推定”权利的思想。①

在美国刑事诉讼中，“除非控方能够提出充分的证据使理性的陪审团排除合理怀疑地认定有罪，否则甚至不存在一个需要答辩的基本指控，并且被告人将被无罪释放，不用被传唤回应对其提起的指控。但是，公民义务可以说意味着被告人不应当被完全免除所有的举证责任。可以综合提出实用的和道德的考量以支持要求被告人在特定的情况下确立某些事实。因此，提供证据责任的分配，有时甚至说服责任的分配，都需要针对每个特定的指控具体说明”②。这一点其实不仅在美国司法实践中如此，在中国既往的司法实践中也是如此。例如，在腐败和毒品案件中，对于被告人主观状态的认定，很多时候实际上是法官对于举证责任在控辩双方之间分配的权衡。尽管如此，笔者认为为了增强在特定类型案件中将特定部分举证责任分配给被告人的说服力，有必要在立法中明确部分类型案件中部分犯罪要素的举证责任实行倒置（例如，在腐败案件中确立明知的推定规则），以增强司法的说服力和权威性。在具体个案

① John Kaplan, Robert Weisberg & Guyora Binder, Criminal Law: Cases and Materials 16 (Wolters Kluwer Law & Business, 7th Edition, 2012).

② Paul Roberts & Adrian Zuckerman, Criminal Evidence 244 (OUP, 2nd edn. 2010).

中，确实需要针对每个特定的指控具体说明提供证据责任的分配，有时甚至包括说服责任的分配，但是仅此还不够。如上所述，应当在一个更高的层次上进行一定的概括，并以立法或者司法机关审判规则的形式确立下来。否则，灵活性有余而使人信服性和权威性不足，特别是在我国还没有确立足够高的司法权威的情况下。

一言以蔽之，虽然无罪推定要求控诉方承担提出证据证明法定犯罪构成要素的责任，但是控诉方并不承担主动或者首先提出免责事由问题并承担相关证明或者反驳责任。控诉方只有在被告人或者法庭主动提出这些问题时，才承担相应的证明或者反驳责任。虽然被告人负有提出辩护理由的义务，但是被告人并不总是需要提出确定性的证据来履行这一义务。对于被告人来讲，有时候，指出公诉方证据的某一方面可能使陪审团从中推论出相关的无罪事实，或者至少对其产生一种合理怀疑，便已足够。虽然有时被告人有义务使某个问题成为审判者必须考虑和控方必须进行相应证明的问题，如自卫，“但是通过排除任何无罪的合理怀疑来证明被告人有罪的责任始终在控方”①。

对于被告人仅提出辩护意见但不提出任何证据的情况，笔者认为，应当根据辩护的种类来处理：如果被告人进行积极辩护，但不提出任何证据，那么这样的辩护就不应被考虑。但是，如果被告人进行消极辩护的话，就不能强迫被告人提出证据。换句话说，如果将辩护看作对控方有罪证明的反驳的话，那么积极辩护可视为通过反向证明进行的反驳，而消极辩护可视为通过攻击控诉方的有罪证明（即指出控诉方有罪证明的错误或者不合理之处，从而说明控诉方有罪证明不成立）进行的反驳。实际上，对于证明的反驳可以分为两种：一种是（反向）证明，如控诉方证明有罪，辩护方证明无罪；另一种是非证明的反驳，如指出原证明存在的问题，从而推翻原证明的结论。对于反向证明，应适用一般的证明规则，包

① Paul Roberts & Adrian Zuckerman, Criminal Evidence 229 (OUP, 2nd edn. 2010).

括提供证据，达到一定的证明标准等。对于非证明的反驳，则不必适用这些规则，可以采用其他方式进行反驳，甚至可以仅从逻辑上进行反驳。反驳（辩护）是当事人的权利，因此作为反驳种类之一的（反向）证明的反驳也是当事人的权利。当事人可以选择行使这项权利，也可以选择放弃这项权利，并不会因为未行使（反向）证明的反驳权利本身而承担任何不利的后果。但是，当法律规定（反向）证明是一项义务时，负有这项义务的当事人就必须履行这项义务，否则将承担相应的不利后果。此时的（反向）证明就成了举证责任倒置。也就是说，同样的（反向）证明行为，当其作为一项权利时，可以将其称为反驳（辩护）；当其作为一项义务时，可以将其称为举证责任倒置。由此，我们可以进一步得出结论：所谓举证责任倒置，是指某些由原证明方承担举证责任的问题的举证责任转移到对方当事人，由对方当事人负责提出证据进行反向证明。对方当事人进行反向证明不仅要提出证据，而且要达到一定的证明标准。其他不承担“提出证据并达到一定证明标准地证明”责任的诉讼行为不能被称为举证责任倒置。例如，我国刑事诉讼法第58条规定的“当事人及其辩护人、诉讼代理人……申请排除以非法方法收集的证据的，应当提供相关线索或者材料”的责任由于并非提供证据并达到一定证明标准地证明的责任（即举证责任），因此该条规定不属于举证责任倒置，而只可能与非证明的反驳有关。“申请排除以非法方法收集的证据”是“当事人及其辩护人、诉讼代理人”的权利，可以视为其反驳权（辩护权），具体说来属于反驳权中的非证明的反驳权。由于“应当”的措辞属于义务性规定，因此“应当提供相关线索或者材料”不属于一般的非证明的反驳，而只能将其视为对“申请排除以非法方法收集的证据”这项非证明反驳权的一个限制。由控方承担证明证据的合法性，否则将予以排除的非法证据排除规则并不意味着举证责任倒置，因为举证责任倒置要求原证明的存在，且发生举证责任的转移，承接转移举证责任的一方负有提出证据予以证明的义务。而该法第58条第2款规定的“当事人及其辩护人、诉讼代理人……申请排除以非法方法收集的证据的，应当提供相关线索或者材料”既不必是证据，也不必达到某种证明标准，因此原证明不存在，而控方本来就承担证明证据合法性的责任，这些关于控方证明证据合法性的规定并非举证责任倒置，而仅是对控方证明证据合法性责任的明确重申。

（二）无罪推定与证明标准

如前所述，无罪推定的实现需要相应的恰当的举证责任和证明标准的保障，然而并非任何程度的证明标准都能保障无罪推定的实现。要想保障无罪推定实现其价值和初衷，相应的证明标准（亦即刑事诉讼中的一般证明标准）必须达到一个很高的程度。这一程度的标准从当今世界主要法系来看，主要是英美法系的“排除合理怀疑”和大陆法系的“内心确信”。在中国，这一标准是“事实清楚，证据确实充分”。

虽然有很多学者大量论述了这三种证明标准之间的关系，特别是有一些学者非常关注三者之间的区别，主张一种证明标准优于或劣于其他的证明标准，试图以一种证明标准去否定另一种证明标准。这些论述对于详细了解这些证明标准的内涵具有积极的意义。但是，笔者认为，实际上这三种证明标准具有内在的统一性：只有“排除合理怀疑”，才能做到“内心确信”；只有“内心确信”，才能做到“事实清楚”。反之，要做到“事实清楚”，必须达到“内心确信”；而要达到“内心确信”，必须“排除合理怀疑”。只看到三者之间的区别，而看不到三者之间的统一性，不利于全面深刻把握这三者之间的关系，会导致在证明标准问题上的思想混乱。

排除合理怀疑等较高的刑事证明标准不仅为赢得社会对刑法适用的信任、维护刑法的道德力量所必不可少，也为赢得社会对刑事诉讼程序的信任、维护刑事诉讼程序的道德力量所必不可少。正如布伦南大法官（Justice Brennan）在温希普（In re Winship）一案中所评论的那样：“合理怀疑标准的使用对于赢得社会对刑法适用的尊重和信任是不可或缺的。刑法的道德力量不被使人们怀疑无辜之人是否被定罪的证明标准削弱是非常紧要的。”① 控方只有在履行了针对当庭提出的所有证据排除被告人无罪的所有合理怀疑的义务后才能获得一份有罪判决。②

实际上，从证明标准的意义上讲，无罪推定并非绝对，也不应当绝对，亦即控诉方对于无罪的证明并非必须排除一切怀疑，而只能是排除合理怀疑；裁判者对于有罪的内心确信是基于审判当时的认知水平和良心产生的内心确信，而不是基于审判以后发展了的认知水平产生的内心确信；裁判者作出的“案件事实清楚，证据确实充分”的判断是基于审判当时的认知水平和证据作出的判断，而不是基于审判以后发展了的认知水平作出的判断。否则，要求排除一切怀疑，基于人类终极认识能力的内心确信或者“案件事实清楚，证据确实充分”的判断不仅不现实，而且可能导致刑事实体法和刑事程序法打击犯罪功能的实际丧失，并最终导致社会混乱。③ 因此，无罪推定在不同的时代，基于不同的认知水平和主客观条件会有不同的表现，即便是同一个案件在不同的时代和主客观条件下进行审理，同样基于无罪推定的原则，也可能产生不同的结果。从这个意义上讲，无罪推定是历史的、动态的，而不是静止的、一成不变的。

综上，无罪推定与证据裁判原则的联系点主要在于无罪推定的证据规则维度与证据裁判原则的密切关联。二者的相同点在于都需要运用证据进行证明，即无罪推定在证据规则维度上遵循证据裁判原则。二者的区别则在于无罪推定在证据规则维度上规定了明确的

---

① In re Winship, 397 US 358, 364 (1970).

② See generally Hock Lai Ho, *The Presumption of Innocence as a Human Right* in Paul Roberts and Jill Hunter (eds), Criminal Evidence and Human Rights - Reimagining Common Law Procedural Traditions 260 (Oxford: Hart Publishing, 2012).

③ See generally Glanville Williams, The Proof of Guilt: A Sdudy of the English Criminal Trial 186-90 (London: Stevens & Sons Limited, 3rd edition, 1963).

证明内容，即要证明有罪，而证据裁判原则却没有这样的明确内容，仅是强调认定案件事实的依据（证据）。二者的另一个区别在于虽然无罪推定在证据规则维度上遵循证据裁判原则的要求，即要用证据来证明有罪，但是这一点又不是完全绝对的，无罪推定允许存在特定的例外。在特定情况下，在某些要素上不一定要完全依据证据进行证明，而是可以依法进行一定的推定，如巨额财产来源不明罪、医疗事故犯罪、食品安全犯罪等都存在一些理论上的犯罪构成要素被默认成立，除非被告人能提出相反的证明。[①] 此外，证据裁判原则要求以口供以外的证据作为认定案件事实的主要根据。因此，坚持证据裁判原则有利于减少对口供的依赖，进而有利于减少为获取口供而进行的刑讯逼供等强迫自证其罪的现象，有利于保障被追诉人的沉默权，有利于贯彻无罪推定。

① 参见徐灿：《论腐败案件中明知的推定规则在中国的确立》，载《澳门法学》2015 年第 14 期。

第五章　无罪推定在中国取得的成就和存在的问题以及进一步完善

第一节　无罪推定在中国取得的成就和存在的问题

一、已取得的成就——无罪推定精神在中国的彰显

新中国成立以来，虽然无罪推定在中国的发展命运坎坷，但是毕竟取得了一定的成就。我国现行有效的刑事诉讼法，即2018年10月26日第十三届全国人民代表大会常务委员会第六次会议审议通过并自修改决定公布之日起施行的刑事诉讼法就在多方面体现了无罪推定的精神。此外，关于无罪推定的理论研究、司法实践和社会意识等也取得了一定的成就。当前，无罪推定精神在中国的彰显主要表现在以下几个方面：

第一，在政策上，党和政府对于无罪推定和人权保障的问题高度重视。党的十八大以来，以习近平同志为总书记的党中央高度重视司法体制改革，将依法治国推到了一个新的高度。2014年10月23日，中国共产党第十八届中央委员会第四次全体会议通过了《关于全面推进依法治国若干重大问题的决定》，明确提出要“加强人权司法保障”，“健全落实疑罪从无、非法证据排除等法律原则的法律制度。完善对限制人身自由司法措施和侦查手段的司法监

督，加强对刑讯逼供和非法取证的源头预防，健全冤假错案有效防范、及时纠正机制”。对无罪推定精神在中国的彰显起到了一定的推动作用。2016 年 6 月 27 日，中央全面深化改革领导小组第二十五次会议通过了《关于推进以审判为中心的刑事诉讼制度改革的意见》，最高人民法院、最高人民检察院、公安部、国家安全部、司法部于 2016 年 7 月 20 日印发了关于该意见的通知（法发〔2016〕18 号）。该意见重申了刑事诉讼法第 12 条的规定，要求认定犯罪事实要坚持证据裁判原则，要求完善讯问制度，防止刑讯逼供，不得强迫任何人证实自己有罪，明确要求“证据不足，不能认定被告人有罪的，应当按照疑罪从无原则，依法作出无罪判决”。①

第二，在立法上，现行的刑事诉讼法（即 2018 年第三次修正的刑事诉讼法）第 12 条规定：“未经人民法院依法判决，对任何人都不得确定有罪。”虽然理论界和实务界对于该条是否是我国无罪推定之规定，观点并不完全一致，但是从字面逻辑解释的角度看，该条规定体现了无罪推定的精神内核。原因主要有以下几点：一是该条明确了定罪权的权力主体，即人民法院；规定了不得确定有罪的时间范围，即人民法院依法判决之前；将定罪权集中于审判机关符合无罪推定精神的要求。二是该条规定了人民法院确定任何人有罪，必须“依法”判决，结合刑事诉讼法第 51 条规定的控方承担有罪证明责任的内容，该条规定体现了有罪判决要以控诉方证明有罪为前提，体现了无罪推定精神的要求。此外，现行的刑事诉讼法还在以下几方面体现了无罪推定的要求：一是区分了“犯罪嫌疑人”、“被告人”与“罪犯”的称谓。被追诉人自侦查机关立案到检察院提起公诉前，称为“犯罪嫌疑人”，在人民检察院向人

---

① 《深改 | 两高三部：关于推进以审判为中心的刑事诉讼制度改革的意见》，http://dy.163.com/v2/article/t1397720048954/btg4ae580521007n，最后访问时间：2017 年 11 月 19 日。

民法院提起公诉后，称为“被告人”，在经过法院生效裁判确定有罪后，称为“罪犯”。二是明确由控诉方承担被告人有罪的举证责任。刑事诉讼法第 51 条规定：“公诉案件中被告人有罪的举证责任由人民检察院承担，自诉案件中被告人有罪的举证责任由自诉人承担。”因此，控诉方有责任或义务提出证据证明被告人有罪，并应使这一证明达到确实充分的程度，而被追诉人则没有证明自己有罪或者无罪的义务。三是确立了“疑罪从无”原则。疑罪从无是无罪推定的核心要求之一，是保障人权的要求和体现。刑事诉讼法第 175 条第 4 款规定：“对于二次补充侦查的案件，人民检察院仍然认为证据不足，不符合起诉条件的，应当作出不起诉的决定。”第 200 条规定：“在被告人最后陈述后，审判长宣布休庭，合议庭进行评议，根据已经查明的事实、证据和有关的法律规定，分别作出以下判决：……（三）证据不足，不能认定被告人有罪的，应当作出证据不足、指控的犯罪不能成立的无罪判决。”可见，根据刑事诉讼法的规定，当事实不清或者证据不足时，在审查起诉阶段，人民检察院作出不起诉的决定，在审判阶段，人民法院应当作出指控罪名不能成立，被告人无罪的判决。需要说明的是，在审查起诉阶段，人民检察院依法作出不起诉的决定并不侵犯第 12 条所规定的法院的定罪权，因为第 12 条所规定的法院的定罪权是指只有法院有权确定有罪，但并不意味着其他机关不能确定无罪。四是检察院在审查起诉阶段作出的酌定不起诉决定或者对未成年人作出附条件不起诉决定，其法律效果属于无罪的处理。因为按照刑事诉讼法第 12 条的要求，在法律上确定被追诉人有罪的主体只能是法院，其他任何机关无此权限。① 五是增加了反对强迫自证其罪的规定。刑事诉讼法第 52 条规定：“审判人员、检察人员、侦查人员必须依照法定程序，收集能够证实犯罪嫌疑人、被告人有罪或者无

① 陈光中主编：《刑事诉讼法》（第五版），北京大学出版社、高等教育出版社 2014 年版，第 108 页。

罪、犯罪情节轻重的各种证据。严禁刑讯逼供和以威胁、引诱、欺骗以及其他非法方法收集证据，不得强迫任何人证实自己有罪。必须保证一切与案件有关或者了解案情的公民，有客观地充分地提供证据的条件，除特殊情况外，可以吸收他们协助调查。”六是引进了非法证据排除规则的相关条文。除了第52条规定了“严禁刑讯逼供和以威胁、引诱、欺骗以及其他非法方法收集证据”以外，刑事诉讼法还在第56条至第60条规定了与排除非法证据有关的条文。第56条规定：“采用刑讯逼供等非法方法收集的犯罪嫌疑人、被告人供述和采用暴力、威胁等非法方法收集的证人证言、被害人陈述，应当予以排除。收集物证、书证不符合法定程序，可能严重影响司法公正的，应当予以补正或者作出合理解释；不能补正或者作出合理解释的，对该证据应当予以排除。在侦查、审查起诉、审判时发现有应当排除的证据的，应当依法予以排除，不得作为起诉意见、起诉决定和判决的依据。”第57条规定：“人民检察院接到报案、控告、举报或者发现侦查人员以非法方法收集证据的，应当进行调查核实。对于确有以非法方法收集证据情形的，应当提出纠正意见；构成犯罪的，依法追究刑事责任。”第58条规定：“法庭审理过程中，审判人员认为可能存在本法第五十六条规定的以非法方法收集证据情形的，应当对证据收集的合法性进行法庭调查。当事人及其辩护人、诉讼代理人有权申请人民法院对以非法方法收集的证据依法予以排除。申请排除以非法方法收集的证据的，应当提供相关线索或者材料。”第59条规定：“在对证据收集的合法性进行法庭调查的过程中，人民检察院应当对证据收集的合法性加以证明。现有证据材料不能证明证据收集的合法性的，人民检察院可以提请人民法院通知有关侦查人员或者其他人员出庭说明情况；人民法院可以通知有关侦查人员或者其他人员出庭说明情况。有关侦查人员或者其他人员也可以要求出庭说明情况。经人民法院通知，有关人员应当出庭。”第60条规定：“对于经过法庭审理，确认或者不能排除存在本法第五十六条规定的以非法方法收集证据情形的，对有关证据应当予以排除。”七是细化了定罪处刑的证明标准。我国定罪处刑的证明标准传统上就是“案件事实清楚，证据确实充分”。2018年刑事诉讼法对这一标准进行了细化，引进了排除合理怀疑的概念。刑事诉讼法第55条规定：“对一切案件的判处都要重证据，重调查研究，不轻信口供。只有被告人供述，没有其他证据的，不能认定被告人有罪和处以刑罚；没有被告人供述，证据确实、充分的，可以认定被告人有罪和处以刑罚。证据确实、充分，应当符合以下条件：（一）定罪量刑的事实都有证据证明；（二）据以定案的证据均经法定程序查证属实；（三）综合全案证据，对所认定事实已排除合理怀疑。”现行刑事诉讼法上述与无罪推定有关的规定实际上继承自2012年刑事诉讼法。在2012年刑事诉讼法通过后，最高人民法院和最高人民检察院分别通过了《关于适用〈中华人民共和国刑事诉讼法〉的解释》和《人民检察院刑事诉讼规则（试行）》，对2012年刑事诉讼法中与无罪推定要求相关的条款进行了细化。2017年2月17日，最高人民法院印发了《关于全面推进以审判为中心的刑事诉讼制度改革的实施意见》的通知（法发〔2017〕5号）。该实施意见明确要求要“坚持证据裁判原则”，“坚持非法证据排除原则，不得强迫任何人证实自己有罪”，“坚持疑罪从无原则，认定被告人有罪，必须达到犯罪事实清楚，证据确实、充分的证明标准。不得因舆论炒作、上访闹访等压力作出违反法律的裁判”，“人民法院作出有罪判决，对于定罪事实应当综合全案证据排除合理怀疑”，“定罪证据确实、充分，量刑证据存疑的，应当作出有利于被告人的认定”，“坚持程序公正原则”。[①] 通过近几年的司法改革，特别是通过“以审判为中心的诉讼制度”改革，我国的刑事侦查程序已经发生了重大变化，不仅

① 《最高人民法院关于全面推进以审判为中心的刑事诉讼制度改革的实施意见》，http://www.court.gov.cn/zixun-xiangqing-36422.html，最后访问时间：2017年11月19日。

犯罪嫌疑人的辩护权得到更为充分的保障，律师越来越普遍地进行介入，而且侦查程序越来越受到一系列程序的限制。例如，到2017年6月为止，我国刑事诉讼中的非法证据排除规则就多达数十条，仅适用于被告人供述的排除规则就多达十余条，常见的有：侦查人员通过刑讯逼供、威胁、非法拘禁、重复性供述、在非法地点讯问、没有依法录音录像等手段获取的供述，一律不得作为定案的根据。不仅如此，在拘留或者逮捕之后，嫌疑人应尽快被送交看守所羁押，讯问只能在看守所内的讯问场所进行。特别是律师介入之后，可以向侦查人员提出辩护意见，可以依法进行会见，可以进行必要的调查取证工作，可以申请变更强制措施，申请取保候审，申请进行羁押必要性审查，可以提供法律咨询，可以提出一定的申诉控告，等等。[①] 这些司法改革的成果进一步彰显了无罪推定的精神，为在法律中正式规定无罪推定原则奠定了更好的基础。

第三，在理论上，无罪推定的研究也取得了重大的进展，不仅关于无罪推定的论文大量出现，而且在刑事诉讼法修改前涌现出了优秀的刑事诉讼法修改专家建议稿，主张在刑事诉讼法中明确确立无罪推定。通过搜索“中国知网”，2005年至2012年“篇名”包含“无罪推定”的文献达518篇。其中，绝大部分主张无罪推定原则应当立法化。2012年刑事诉讼法颁布后，学术界继续保持对无罪推定立法化的热情。“中国知网”的搜索结果显示，2012年以来[②]“篇名”包含“无罪推定”的文献达130篇，“主题”涉及“无罪推定”的文献更是超过2400篇。在刑事诉讼法修改专家建议稿方面，陈光中教授主持的《中华人民共和国刑事诉讼法——再修改专家建议稿与论证》第10条规定了两款内容，其中第1款规定：“在人民法院依法作出生效裁判确定有罪以前，任何人应当

① 陈瑞华：《当监察法与刑诉法关系遭遇困境》，http://www.sohu.com/a/206189302_650721，最后访问时间：2017年11月25日。

② 截至2017年11月18日。

被推定为无罪。”第2款规定：“不能认定犯罪嫌疑人、被告人有罪或无罪的，按无罪处理；不能认定犯罪嫌疑人、被告人罪重或罪轻的，按罪轻处理。”① 陈卫东教授主持的《模范刑事诉讼法典》（第二版）第4条规定了“无罪推定原则”，该条规定：“任何受到追诉的人，在被人民法院依法最终判决有罪之前，推定其无罪。”② 另外，陈瑞华、田文昌主编的《〈中华人民共和国刑事诉讼法〉再修改律师建议稿与论证》也主张将无罪推定原则载入刑事诉讼法典。③

第四，在司法实践中，中国共产党第十八次全国代表大会以来，“平反冤假错案成为中国司法领域一个时常被提起的话题，各种冤假错案相继得到平反，一位位含冤受屈者走出了监牢”④。同时，我国冤假错案类型有了明显的变化，纠错由“真凶再现型”、“亡者归来型”转为“证据不足型”。在公众的印象中，典型的冤假错案，如佘祥林案、赵作海案，由于“真凶再现”或者“亡者归来”而真相大白。但是十八大以来纠正的冤假错案中，大多数是因为“证据不足”，如徐辉案、念斌案。2014年纠正的12起重大冤假错案中，仅有2起是因为出现了真凶。纠正的冤假错案在类型上由“真凶再现型”、“亡者归来型”转变为“证据不足型”说明“司法机关在司法理念上有了重大转变”。“人民法院敢于纠正

---

① 参见陈光中主编：《中华人民共和国刑事诉讼法——再修改专家建议稿与论证》，中国法制出版社2006年版，第4页。

② 陈卫东主编：《模范刑事诉讼法典》（第二版），中国人民大学出版社2011年版。

③ 陈瑞华、田文昌：《〈中华人民共和国刑事诉讼法〉再修改律师建议稿与论证》，法律出版社2007年版。

④ 李蒙：《为什么这么多冤案能够平反？——〈平反冤案这三年〉系列报道之二》，http：//blog. sina. com. cn/s/blog_ 5ff29ca40102w0rr. html，最后访问时间：2016年3月30日。《最高法院发布司法改革白皮书：十八大以来纠正重大刑事冤假错案34起》，http：//www. legaldaily. com. cn/zfzz/content/2017 - 02/28/content _ 7031724. htm? node=81122，最后访问时间：2017年11月13日。

这些冤假错案，说明其在依法独立公正行使审判权，落实尊重和保障人权、无罪推定、疑罪从无、证据裁判等理念方面有了长足的进步。"[①] 特别是 2016 年 6 月 6 日，最高人民法院决定依法提审原审被告人聂树斌故意杀人、强奸妇女一案，按照审判监督程序重新审判，[②] 在新中国的刑事司法历程中创下了最高人民法院对普通刑事案件进行提审的罕见案例，对于无罪推定精神在我国的彰显具有里程碑式的意义。"即便人已经死了，也要还给你一个公正。"这体现了最高人民法院对公平正义价值的执着追求，也是其本分和审判权本性的彰显。这是无罪推定精神在我国一定程度的彰显，是无罪推定的阶段性胜利。2016 年 12 月 27 日，最高人民法院发布了《中国法院的司法改革（2013—2016）》白皮书。在预防和纠正冤假错案方面，白皮书介绍，最高人民法院就健全防范刑事冤假错案工作机制提出指导意见，要求对于定罪证据不足的案件，应当依法宣告被告人无罪，不得降格或者变通作出"留有余地"的判决。颇受关注的聂树斌案被写进了白皮书中。2016 年 12 月 2 日，最高人民法院第二巡回法庭对原审被告人聂树斌故意杀人、强奸妇女再审案公开审判，宣告撤销原审判决，改判聂树斌无罪。最高人民法院认为，这起历时 22 年的重大疑难复杂案件得以纠正，彰显了对人权司法保障的高度重视和对证据裁判、疑罪从无等法律原则的坚定实践。[③] 此外，庭审改革也在一定程度上体现了无罪推定精神，

---

① 《十八大后纠正 23 起冤假错案 疑罪从无不再停留纸面》，http：//www. chinanews. com/gn/2014/12-17/6883197. shtml，最后访问时间：2014 年 12 月 16 日。《最高法院发布司法改革白皮书：十八大以来纠正重大刑事冤假错案 34 起》，http：//www. legaldaily. com. cn/zfzz/content/2017-02/28/content_ 7031724. htm? node = 81122，最后访问时间：2017 年 11 月 13 日。

② 《最高人民法院决定依法再审聂树斌故意杀人、强奸妇女一案》，http：//www. court. gov. cn/fabu-xiangqing-21751. html，最后访问时间：2016 年 6 月 8 日。

③ 《最高法院发布司法改革白皮书：十八大以来纠正重大刑事冤假错案 34 起》，http：//www. legaldaily. com. cn/zfzz/content/2017-02/28/content_ 7031724. htm? node = 81122，最后访问时间：2017 年 11 月 13 日。

长期以来被告人穿着“黄马甲”出庭受审的局面将彻底改变。2015年2月26日最高人民法院正式发布《关于全面深化人民法院改革的意见》（法发〔2015〕3号），其中，在强化人权司法保障机制方面明确规定：“禁止让刑事在押被告人或上诉人穿着识别服、马甲、囚服等具有监管机构标识的服装出庭受审。”同时，“加强对刑讯逼供和非法取证的源头预防，健全冤假错案的有效防范、及时纠正机制”。

第五，在社会观念上，随着我国法制教育的发展和人民群众法治意识的提高，与以前相比，更多的群众认识到无罪推定的内涵和意义。媒体与无罪推定相关的报道也比以前有很大的增加，客观上也有利于促进无罪推定基本意识的传播。① 无罪推定精神在群众的法治意识和舆论文化上得到了初步的彰显。

二、尚存在的问题——在中国无罪推定精神彰显所面临的困难

虽然当前我国在无罪推定精神的彰显方面取得了一定的成绩，但是仍旧存在一系列问题和困难。

虽然党的十八大以来大量的冤假错案得到纠正，但同时这也反映了我国在之前一段时期的司法实践中出现了相应的冤假错案，如云南杜培武、湖北佘祥林、河南赵作海、浙江张氏叔侄、安徽于英生等系列冤假错案，造成了很坏的社会影响，严重损害了司法公信力和司法权威。

在立法上，虽然刑事诉讼法第12条规定体现了无罪推定原则的基本精神，但是其并未能全面准确地体现出无罪推定的内涵，也并非国际惯用的无罪推定原则的规范表述。从国际惯用之无罪推定原则的表述来看，强调的是被指控人在刑事诉讼过程中所处的被推

① 如《〈民主与法制〉杂志社记者李蒙的〈平反冤案这三年〉专题系列报道》，http：//blog. sina. com. cn/s/blog _ 5ff29ca40102w0pd. html，http：//blog. sina. com. cn/s/blog_ 5ff29ca40102w0rr. html，等等。

定为无罪的地位，因此无罪推定原则要求在刑事诉讼中赋予被指控人推定无罪所应享有的诉讼权利；而我国刑事诉讼法第 12 条之规定所强调的是人民法院的定罪权，即强调只有法院有权对被告人进行定罪，侧重点并不在于强调被指控人在刑事诉讼中的境遇问题。这种侧重点的差异表明了中国只是吸收了无罪推定的核心内容，并未完全确立无罪推定原则，也反映了中国立法在被追诉人的人权保障问题上仍然有待完善和发展。此外，我国的“存疑有利于被指控人”原则之贯彻并不彻底。这种不彻底性的主要表现之一就是“证据不足”的“疑案”无罪判决是“有所保留”的结果。根据无罪推定原则的要求，当证据不足不能认定被告人有罪的，作出无罪判决与证明达到清白程度的同等看待。但是，根据我国刑事诉讼法要求作出的却是另眼看待的判决。我国刑事诉讼法第 200 条规定：“……（二）依据法律认定被告人无罪的，应当作出无罪判决；（三）证据不足，不能认定被告人有罪的，应当作出证据不足、指控的犯罪不能成立的无罪判决。”此条第（三）项规定的判决就是中国实务部门通称的“存疑无罪判决”。[①] 此外，现有关于无罪推定的立法中存在自相矛盾之处。例如，刑事诉讼法第 52 条规定了反对强迫自证其罪的原则，然而第 120 条中却规定“犯罪嫌疑人对侦查人员的提问，应当如实回答”。第 125 条却规定“询问证人，应当告知他应当如实地提供证据、证言和有意作伪证或者隐匿罪证要负的法律责任”。由于根据第 127 条规定，询问被害人，适用“询问证人”一节包括第 125 条在内的各条规定，因此询问被害人，也应当告知他应当如实地提供证据、证言和有意作伪证或者隐匿罪证要负的法律责任。同时，第 194 条第 1 款也规定：“证人作证，审判人员应当告知他要如实地提供证言和有意作伪证或者隐匿罪证要负的法律责任……”也就是说，刑事诉讼法一方

① 参见陈光中、张佳华、肖沛权：《论无罪推定原则及其在中国的适用》，载《法学杂志》2013 年第 10 期。

面规定了“不得强迫任何人证实自己有罪”；另一方面却使犯罪嫌疑人、证人、被害人负有如实回答的义务，从而造成刑事诉讼法在这一问题上的内部混乱。首先需要明确一点，反对强迫自证其罪要求确立沉默权，而沉默权与如实回答义务完全对立。一个人如果负有如实回答义务，那么就不可能享有沉默权。沉默权本身就免除了回答义务，更免除了如实回答义务。我国法律当前并未确立沉默权。然而，也许有人会提出，从实现实体公正的角度出发，可以调和反对强迫自证其罪与如实回答义务之间的矛盾：若被讯问人不是罪犯，则如实回答不会导致自证其罪；若被讯问人是罪犯，则如实回答会导致自证其罪。此时，虽然侵犯了被讯问人的不被强迫自证其罪的权利，但是此时能够实现实体公正，因此不妨取消被讯问人的不被强迫自证其罪的权利。其实，这是似是而非的观点，因为在实践中，不可能在自证其罪的供述和不导致自证其罪的供述之间进行明确的区分，很多时候，一个实际无罪之人的供述即便是如实供述，也可能最后实际上导致其被定罪。因此，上述理由仅在理论上成立，实践中根本行不通，不仅必然导致侵犯人权，而且无法保证实现实体公正。最后，中国也没有规定可以适用联合国国际刑事司法准则中的无罪推定。因此，对于被告人无罪推定权利的立法保障不够彻底。

在司法实践中，无罪推定原则也没有得到贯彻落实。事实上，对于有罪无罪存疑的案件，司法实践中往往采取“疑罪从轻”的做法，尤其是对于重罪案件更是如此。在一些死刑案件中，如果出现有罪无罪存疑时，司法机关有时会放弃“疑罪从无”原则，仍然判决被告人有罪，但又不判死刑，而是留有余地地判处死缓、无期或有期徒刑。正是由于这种“疑罪从轻”、“留有余地”的做法导致了冤假错案的发生，佘祥林案、赵作海案、浙江张氏叔侄案、萧山冤案等就是运用这种做法所形成的典型冤案。

在无罪推定相关制度的落实上缺乏完整配套符合实际的细则。当前已建立的一些无罪推定配套制度本身存有漏洞，以致无法落到实处，实现制度设立的初衷和目标。例如，虽然我国目前已经确立了非法证据排除规则，也有反对强迫自证其罪和全程录音录像等制度，但是这些规则和制度并未能相结合从而形成一张严密的防范刑讯逼供的网络，或者说这张网上仍旧有漏洞，以致各种规避这些规则和制度的做法在实践中层出不穷。譬如，一些侦查机关在讯问的过程中采用有选择的录音录像的做法，先以暴力、胁迫等非法方法摧垮被讯问人的意志，然后再对接下来的讯问过程进行录音录像，在法庭上只出示合法讯问部分的录音录像，以致全程录音录像制度成为摆设，不仅未能起到其应有的监督审讯人员以保证依法讯问的作用，反而成为公诉方“证明”讯问合法的工具。

很多人包括一些从事立法、司法、法学研究等的法律工作者对于无罪推定运行过程中遇到的一些问题认识不清。主要表现在以下几个方面：第一，一些人对于定罪前是否有罪不确定论的危害认识不清，对无罪推定与相关司法制度之间的关系也认识不清。例如，由全国人大常委会法制工作委员会编辑的《中华人民共和国刑事诉讼法释义》对刑事诉讼法第 12 条给予了这样的解释：“我们反对有罪推定，但也不是西方国家的那种无罪推定，而是实事求是地进行侦查，客观地收集有罪或者无罪、罪轻或者罪重的各种证据，在人民法院作出有罪判决以前，我们不能称被告人为罪犯，但也不能说他没有罪或假定他无罪，如果假定他无罪，那么侦查机关对他进行侦查、采取强制措施就没有根据了。”① 这实际上是一种定罪前是否有罪不确定论。其对公民自由、社会福祉和无罪推定的确立具有隐蔽、潜在和实质性的危害。其往往以实事求是为理论的幌子，具有很强的迷惑性，使人忽视其对自由、安全和公共福祉等价值的危害。是否有罪不确定的法律状态会导致整个社会人人自危，毫无自由和安全可言，因为任何人都无法保证自己不会受到错误追

① 胡康生、李福成主编：《中华人民共和国刑事诉讼法释义》，全国人大常委会法制工作委员会刑法室编著，法律出版社 1996 年版，第 15 页。

诉，因此会变得异常脆弱、缺乏自信，这不仅会严重减损公民的自由和社会的福祉，损害基本人权，也与自由民主法治的现代社会文明发展方向相悖。因此，必须排除这种定罪前是否有罪不确定的理论。另外，侦查机关对一个人进行侦查、采取强制措施与无罪推定并非不能共存，其可以以法律上的无罪假定和事实上的有罪怀疑为基础。[①] 侦查阶段对犯罪嫌疑人进行拘留、逮捕是因为侦查机关怀疑其有罪，侦查机关侦查终结、将案件移送审查起诉是因为侦查机关认为犯罪嫌疑人有罪；公诉机关提起公诉是因为公诉机关认为犯罪嫌疑人有罪。但是，无论是侦查机关认为一个人有罪，还是公诉机关认为一个人有罪，都仅代表它们各自自身认为这个人有罪，并不代表这个人在法律上有罪，因为一个人在法律上是否有罪只能由法律和审判机关说了算。在刑事诉讼中，侦控审三者之间的关系是“独立判断，递进审查”的关系（关于此点的解读详见下文），但这并不影响无罪推定在刑事诉讼中的适用。所以，虽然侦查机关对犯罪嫌疑人进行拘留、逮捕、侦查终结移送审查起诉，公诉机关提起公诉，但是这些都与无罪推定并不矛盾，因为无罪推定中的“无罪”仅是法律上的无罪，不是哪个（些）机关或个人认为无罪。之所以在无罪推定的情况下，也允许侦查机关对犯罪嫌疑人进行拘留、逮捕、侦查终结、将案件移送审查起诉，公诉机关提起公诉，是因为国家打击犯罪的基本刑事政策需要作出这样的专门制度安排，否则国家打击犯罪的基本刑事政策将无法得到落实。第二，我国刑事诉讼各阶段的证明标准具有统一性。我国刑事诉讼法对于侦查机关移送审查起诉，公诉机关提起公诉和法院有罪判决的证明标准都是“案件事实清楚，证据确实充分”。然而，有人对此很不理解，认为这样的标准对于侦查机关或者公诉机关来讲太高，甚至认为如果侦查机关或者公诉机关遵循的证明标准与审判机关一样，

① 关于此点，参见前文“法学视角下的无罪推定”部分关于假定无罪、假定有罪和怀疑有罪等概念之间关系的论述。

也是“案件事实清楚，证据确实充分”的话，那还需要后面的几道程序干什么？这显然是没有认清刑事诉讼设置侦查、公诉、审判三道程序的意义。之所以在证明标准统一的情况下还要设置三道程序，主要是基于以下几点考虑：一是民主原则和权力制衡。侦查权、公诉权和审判权一旦集于一体，这个权力主体将变得过于强大，难免导致权力专横和任性。多一道程序把关，有利于对事实的认定更谨慎、对犯罪的认定更准确。智者千虑必有一失，愚者千虑必有一得。多一个主体审查，就多一层保障。之所以要设置侦查、公诉、审判三道程序，就是因为坚守民主的理念，相信通过公检法三机关之间的相互制衡能够实现尽量准确认定案件事实、准确惩治犯罪、避免误伤无辜。二是保障被告人诉讼主体地位的要求。侦查权、公诉权和审判权一旦集于一体，被告人在刑事诉讼过程中就将沦为诉讼对象和客体，失去诉讼主体地位和作为主体应当享有的权利。只有侦控审相分离，才能保障被告人的诉讼主体地位和基本人权。三是对抗原则和保障被追诉人充分行使申诉权的要求。虽然在侦查和审查起诉阶段，被追诉人也会行使一定的申诉权，但是与审判阶段相比，申诉权行使得并不充分。只有在审判阶段，被追诉人的申诉权和控辩双方的对抗原则才能得到充分的保障和体现。第三，一些人对于中国刑事诉讼运行机制的基本特征认识不清。“侦查—公诉—审判”的刑事诉讼过程固然不是“上家端菜，下家只能吃上家端的菜”的“下家”遵循“上家”的流水作业，但是这几个环节之间也绝非并列的关系。审判中心主义强调审判的终局性和决定性，但绝非意味着侦查和公诉阶段不重要，一切都丢给审判阶段就可以，否则侦查和公诉阶段的存在将会失去意义。实际上，我国刑事诉讼侦控审各阶段之间是独立判断，递进审查的关系，亦即我国刑事诉讼各阶段在统一的证明标准之下，各自独立判断，后一阶段对前一阶段进行递进审查，最终由法院作出终局结论。对于这一过程及其运行机理认识不清，就会导致在刑事诉讼各阶段证明标准问题上的认识混乱，也看不到侦控审三阶段设置的民主价值和制度意义。第四，一些人对于中国刑事诉讼中公检法三机关的属性认识不清。诚然，侦查机关和行使公诉职能时的检察机关是“刀把子”，具有惩罚犯罪、保护人民的职能。但是，将行使审判职能时的法院以及行使审查起诉职能时的检察院也称为“刀把子”，就属于对这些机关的职能和属性认识不清。行使审判职能时的法院以及行使审查起诉职能时的检察院更主要的属性是公平正义，如果此时也将其称为“刀把子”，甚至要求其具有像“刀把子”一样专门打击犯罪的职能，则会使其存在失去意义，不如直接由其前一阶段决定结果。因此，笼统地将政法机关及其职能称为“刀把子”是对各个政法机关的职能和属性认识不清，不利于法院和检察院依法独立行使职权，特别是公正客观行使具有“审查”性质的职权，不利于刑事诉讼各有关机关职能的有效运行。

当前刑事诉讼庭审布局仍不够合理，让被告人站在法庭中央仰视审判席，公诉方和辩护人分列两边，带有明显的有罪推定色彩。同时，“被告人与其辩护人距离较远，辩护律师无法针对法庭审理的进展情况及时与被告人进行交流，并适时调整辩护策略，被告人在法庭审判过程中孤立无援，无法及时得到辩护人的有效帮助，辩护一方的力量处于分离、分散状态，严重影响了被告人辩护权的充分行使，也不利于发现案件中存在的问题，对审判质量产生了消极影响，难以有效防范冤假错案”①。虽然近年来部分地方法院积极探索庭审布局改革，将原来的“四方格”布局改为“三角形”布

① 赵红旗：《河南高院推进庭审布局改革》，http：//www. law－lib. com/fzdt/newshtml/yjdt/20131211161819. htm，最后访问时间：2016 年 3 月 30 日。参见李奋飞：《庭审布局：于细微处见法治》，载《检察日报》2014 年 7 月 2 日第 7 版。

局,[①] 但是目前尚未出台全国性的相关规定。

第二节　在中国进一步彰显无罪推定精神的建议

一、立法建议

（一）无罪推定应当入宪法还是入刑事诉讼法

虽然我国在刑事诉讼法第 12 条作出了“未经人民法院依法判决，对任何人都不得确定有罪”的规定，但是理论界和实务界对于该条是否就是我国无罪推定之规定，观点并不完全一致。笔者认为，我国应在立法上明确规定无罪推定，至少应当明确允许适用联合国国际刑事司法准则中的无罪推定，以促进无罪推定之精神在中国之彰显。

在无罪推定应当入宪法还是入刑事诉讼法的问题上，笔者认为无罪推定既应当入宪法，也应当入刑事诉讼法。理由主要有以下几点：一是从其他已经确立了无罪推定原则的国家立法来看，有的国家仅在宪法中规定了无罪推定而尚未在刑事诉讼法中规定无罪推定；在宪法和刑事诉讼法中都规定了无罪推定的国家中，大多是先在宪法中规定无罪推定，然后才在其刑事诉讼法典中规定无罪推定。例如，法国早在 1789 年的宪法性法律文件《人权宣言》第 9

---

① 例如，赵红旗：《河南高院推进庭审布局改革》，http：//www. law-lib. com/fzdt/newshtml/yjdt/20131211161819. htm，最后访问时间：2016 年 3 月 30 日；《改变庭审布局有利于维护辩护权利》，http：//sichuan. hexun. com/2015-05-07/175588672. html，最后访问时间：2016 年 3 月 30 日；《浙江法院改变刑案庭审格局 被告人将与律师同桌》，http：//news. xinhuanet. com/legal/2015-05/07/c_ 127772690. htm，最后访问时间：2016 年 3 月 30 日。

条即规定了无罪推定原则[①]，但法国 1808 年制定的世界上第一部刑事诉讼法典却没有规定无罪推定原则，直到 2000 年该原则才被正式写入刑事诉讼法典的序言，即序言第 3 项规定："每个犯罪嫌疑人或被告人在其被确定为有罪之前均推定为无罪。禁止侵犯其无罪推定的权利，否则，依据法律应当予以赔偿并处罚。"其他国家如俄罗斯，也是先在宪法中规定无罪推定，后在其刑事诉讼法典中规定无罪推定。[②] 之所以如此，有其深刻的原因。如前所述，"只有通过探索无罪推定的政治道德才能意识到无罪推定真正的法学意义"。无罪推定蕴含着丰富的政治价值，具有深厚的政治背景。历史上最晚从资产阶级明确提出和广泛传播无罪推定以与封建势力作斗争开始，无罪推定就被打上了深深的政治烙印，与政治有着千丝万缕的联系。而与刑事诉讼法这部"小宪法"相比，宪法与政治的关系显然更加密切。因此，从先入宪法后入刑事诉讼法的无罪推定立法世界普遍经验来看，无罪推定入宪法具有其内在合理性。当然，无罪推定作为刑事司法的一项重要原则，其入刑事诉讼法的合理性毋庸赘言。二是我国确立无罪推定的推动力量主要是冤假错案对社会的影响以及社会对冤假错案产生原因的反思，并非与政治斗争有关。然而，在我国现阶段，无罪推定仍旧具有重要的政治意义，仍旧有必要入宪。理由主要有二：一是无罪推定本身是一个基本人权，我国宪法也已明确规定"国家尊重和保障人权"，因此无罪推定入宪对于增强我国宪法的人权保障色彩具有重要意义；二是无罪推定有利于保障广大人民群众的个人自由，对于增加人民群众福祉、使人民群众中的每个个体都能享有更完整的幸福具有关键的

---

① 法国《人权宣言》第 9 条法文原文为："Article 9 - Tout homme étant présumé innocent jusqu´à ce qu´il ait été déclaré coupable, s´il est jugé indispensable de l´arrêter, toute rigueur qui ne serait pas nécessaire pour s´assurer de sa personne doit être sévèrement réprimée par la loi."

② 陈光中、张佳华、肖沛权：《论无罪推定原则及其在中国的适用》，载《法学杂志》2013 年第 10 期，第 3 页。

意义。

（二）监察法应否体现无罪推定精神

“国家监察体制改革是党中央作出的反腐防腐的重大决策部署，是事关全局的重大政治体制改革，是推进国家治理体系和治理能力现代化的重大举措。改革传承了自古以来独具特色的监察历史传统，借鉴了海外监察反腐制度的有益经验。”① 根据十九大报告，2017 年 11 月 4 日，全国人大常委会作出《关于在全国各地推开国家监察体制改革试点工作的决定》。2017 年 11 月 7 日，全国人大常委会正式公布《监察法（草案）》面向社会征求意见（2017 年 6 月第十二届全国人大常委会第二十八次会议审议稿）。② 2018 年 3 月 20 日，第十三届全国人民代表大会第一次会议通过了监察法。③ 然而，监察法并未明确无罪推定原则。一切国家行为都受到宪法的规制，监察也不例外。宪法明确了“国家尊重和保障人权”。监察涉及人权保障问题，也必须在宪法的范围内活动，因此也必须尊重与保障人权。监察涉及刑事诉讼，至少涉及与刑事诉讼的衔接。无罪推定涉及宪法和刑事诉讼法问题，在很多国家都被规定为宪法和刑事诉讼法的一项基本原则，因此监察法也涉及应否明确无罪推定问题。监察法第 1 条规定：“为了深化国家监察体制改革，加强对所有行使公权力的公职人员的监督，实现国家监察全面覆盖，深入开展反腐败工作，推进国家治理体系和治理能力现代化，根据宪

---

① 陈光中：《〈监察法〉的立法工作不能急于求成》，http://mp.weixin.qq.com/s/vbAs9Z5mnqV3IrpqviCC8A，最后访问时间：2017 年 11 月 25 日。

② 《中华人民共和国监察法（草案）面向社会征求意见（2017 年 6 月第十二届全国人大常委会第二十八次会议审议稿）》，http://www.ccdi.gov.cn/xwtt/201711/t20171107_111288.html，最后访问时间：2017 年 11 月 25 日。征求意见时间为 2017 年 11 月 7 日至 2017 年 12 月 6 日，参见《全国人大常委会法律草案征求意见》，载人大网，http://www.npc.gov.cn/npc/flcazqyj/node_8176.htm，最后访问时间：2017 年 11 月 25 日。

③ 《中华人民共和国监察法》，http://www.npc.gov.cn/npc/xinwen/2018-03/21/content_2052362.htm? from=timeline&isappinstalled=0，最后访问时间：2018 年 7 月 10 日。

法，制定本法。”可见，监察法“实质就是反腐败国家立法，为监察机关依法履职提供法治依据”①。鉴于腐败犯罪案件的复杂性和特殊性，在腐败犯罪案件中允许存在一些无罪推定的例外实属必要，也被国际公约所认可，如联合国大会于 2003 年 10 月 31 日通过的《联合国反腐败公约》第 28 条就允许对腐败犯罪所需具备的明知等主观要素根据客观实际情况进行推定。然而，“在追求高效率反腐的同时，国家监察制度的改革一定要重视现代化和法治化的问题。不能轻言反腐案件不会出错，一定要通过法治化建设防范冤假错案。通过公正的程序规制、监督和限制权力”②。作为国家监察体制改革重要成果之一的监察法从整体上仍旧应当体现无罪推定精神。

根据监察法第 3 条和第 11 条的规定③，监察机关的职能涉及对职务犯罪的调查。从其对职务犯罪调查的手段来看，这种调查其实就是刑事侦查，属于刑事诉讼活动的一部分，理应受到刑事诉讼法的规制，当然也应当适用无罪推定这一刑事诉讼的基本原则。不过，由于监察法只涉及对于职务犯罪的调查（侦查），不涉及对于职务犯罪的审判，因此不宜直接采纳无罪推定的一般表述，而只能在其规定中体现无罪推定精神，如证据裁判原则、人权保障原则、

---

① 《使党的主张成为国家意志》，http://csr.mos.gov.cn/content/2017-07/17/content_51847.htm，最后访问时间：2017 年 11 月 25 日。

② 吴尧：《陈光中：监察制度改革不能忽视程序法治》，http://news.caijingmobile.com/article/detail/327138? source_id=40，最后访问时间：2017 年 11 月 25 日。

③ 监察法第 3 条规定：“各级监察委员会是行使国家监察职能的专责机关，依照本法对所有行使公权力的公职人员（以下称公职人员）进行监察，调查职务违法和职务犯罪，开展廉政建设和反腐败工作，维护宪法和法律的尊严。”第 11 条规定：“监察委员会依照本法和有关法律规定履行监督、调查、处置职责：（一）对公职人员开展廉政教育，对其依法履职、秉公用权、廉洁从政从业以及道德操守情况进行监督检查；（二）对涉嫌贪污贿赂、滥用职权、玩忽职守、权力寻租、利益输送、徇私舞弊以及浪费国家资财等职务违法和职务犯罪进行调查；（三）对违法的公职人员依法作出政务处分决定；对履行职责不力、失职失责的领导人员进行问责；对涉嫌职务犯罪的，将调查结果移送人民检察院依法审查、提起公诉；向监察对象所在单位提出监察建议。”

非法证据排除规则和辩护权等。具体说来，国家监察机关调查和处置职务犯罪案件，必须以事实为根据，以法律为准绳。对职务违法和职务犯罪案件，应当进行调查，收集、调取被调查人有无违法犯罪以及情节轻重的证据，查明违法犯罪事实。依法收集、鉴别证据，形成相互印证、完整稳定的证据链。监察权的行使应当遵循惩治腐败与保障人权相平衡的原则。① 对此，监察法第 5 条规定："国家监察工作严格遵照宪法和法律，以事实为根据，以法律为准绳；在适用法律上一律平等，保障当事人的合法权益；权责对等，严格监督；惩戒与教育相结合，宽严相济。"第 40 条第 1 款规定："监察机关对职务违法和职务犯罪案件，应当进行调查，收集被调查人有无违法犯罪以及情节轻重的证据，查明违法犯罪事实，形成相互印证、完整稳定的证据链。"第 2 款规定："严禁以威胁、引诱、欺骗及其他非法方式收集证据，严禁侮辱、打骂、虐待、体罚或者变相体罚被调查人和涉案人员。"对留置等限制人身自由的措施应当设置具体的适用标准。比如，规定留置只适用于比较严重的职务犯罪案件，在有比较确实、充分的证据证明犯罪事实存在的情形下，才可采取留置；被留置后的 24 小时之内，通知被调查人的家属，后者有权通过监察人员向被调查人提供生活用品和药物；留置期间，应当保障被留置人员的饮食、休息，提供医疗服务；留置期间讯问被留置人员，严禁刑讯逼供和采用威胁、引诱、欺骗以及其他非法调查方法，讯问时应当合理安排讯问时间和时长，原则上应当全程录音录像；保障被调查人的辩护权，允许被调查人在被留置后聘请律师，以确保他具备必要的防御能力。② 对此，监察法第 22 条第 1 款规定："被调查人涉嫌贪污贿赂、失职渎职等严重职务违法或者职务犯罪，监察机关已经掌握其部分违法犯罪事实及证

---

① 陈光中、邵俊：《我国监察体制改革若干问题思考》，载《中国法学》2017 年第 4 期，第 31 页。

② 陈光中：《制定〈监察法〉应贯彻人权保障原则》，http://china.caixin.com/2017-08-17/101131939.html，最后访问时间：2017 年 8 月 17 日。

据，仍有重要问题需要进一步调查，并有下列情形之一的，经监察机关依法审批，可以将其留置在特定场所：（一）涉及案情重大、复杂的；（二）可能逃跑、自杀的；（三）可能串供或者伪造、隐匿、毁灭证据的；（四）可能有其他妨碍调查行为的。”第 2 款规定：“对涉嫌行贿犯罪或者共同职务犯罪的涉案人员，监察机关可以依照前款规定采取留置措施。”第 3 款规定：“留置场所的设置、管理和监督依照国家有关规定执行。”第 41 条第 1 款规定：“调查人员采取讯问、询问、留置、搜查、调取、查封、扣押、勘验检查等调查措施，均应当依照规定出示证件，出具书面通知，由二人以上进行，形成笔录、报告等书面材料，并由相关人员签名、盖章。”第 2 款规定：“调查人员进行讯问以及搜查、查封、扣押等重要取证工作，应当对全过程进行录音录像，留存备查。”第 44 条第 1 款规定：“对被调查人采取留置措施后，应当在二十四小时以内，通知被留置人员所在单位和家属，但有可能毁灭、伪造证据，干扰证人作证或者串供等有碍调查情形的除外。有碍调查的情形消失后，应当立即通知被留置人员所在单位和家属。”第 2 款规定：“监察机关应当保障被留置人员的饮食、休息和安全，提供医疗服务。讯问被留置人员应当合理安排讯问时间和时长，讯问笔录由被讯问人阅看后签名。”第 3 款规定：“被留置人员涉嫌犯罪移送司法机关后，被依法判处管制、拘役和有期徒刑的，留置一日折抵管制二日，折抵拘役、有期徒刑一日。”在留置之外，参照刑事诉讼法关于取保候审的规定，增设取保措施，期限可达 6 个月。①应参照现有刑事诉讼中已确立的非法证据排除规则，确立调查阶段的非法证据排除规则，“包括刑讯逼供、威胁、非法拘禁得来的口供一律排除，讯问没有在法定场所、调查终结前没有经过检察机关

① 陈光中：《〈监察法〉的立法工作不能急于求成》，http://mp.weixin.qq.com/s/vbAs9Z5mnqV3IrpqviCC8A，最后访问时间：2017 年 11 月 25 日。

核查程序的口供一律排除等”[①]，以及对实物证据的排除规则。对此，监察法第 33 条第 2 款规定：“监察机关在收集、固定、审查、运用证据时，应当与刑事审判关于证据的要求和标准相一致。”第 3 款规定：“以非法方法收集的证据应当依法予以排除，不得作为案件处置的依据。”

（三）无罪推定能否作为一项人格权予以规定

在法律上规定无罪推定的国家或者地区大都将无罪推定规定在宪法、刑事诉讼法等公法中，只有像法国这样的个别国家才在民法典中规定无罪推定，将无罪推定视为一项基本的人格权。然而，有没有必要将无罪推定作为一项基本的人格权规定在民法典中？这一问题值得我们深入思考。我们知道，无罪推定主要是指未被依法证明有罪之前应当被视为无罪，主要针对的是公权力、国家机关，因为只有国家才有权将某个人定罪，其他任何组织和个人都无此权力。因此，规定了无罪推定的国家或者地区大都是将无罪推定规定在宪法或者刑事诉讼法中，主要调整国家与公民之间的关系足矣，而非规定在主要调整平等主体之间人身和财产关系（民事主体之间私权利关系）的民法中。然而，如果将无罪推定作为一项基本的人格权予以规定，那么其意义就变成了无罪推定是一项基本的人格权，他人（包括国家、其他组织和个人）都不得对其进行侵犯。对于国家不得对其侵犯，这个我们比较容易理解，也正因如此，很多国家或者地区在其宪法或者刑事诉讼法中规定无罪推定。对于其他组织和个人不得对其进行侵犯，我们只能理解为在一个人未经依法证明有罪之前，其他组织和个人不得有将该人视为有罪的言行，在言行上只能将其视为无罪。这里就存在几个问题：（1）其他组织和个人是仅仅不能有将该人视为有罪的言行，在言行上只能将其

① 参见谭畅、郑可书、阚纯裕：《宪法、行政法、刑诉法三角度解读监察法草案 在法治轨道上，推进监察立法》（陈瑞华语），载《南方周末》2017 年 11 月 23 日，http://www.infzm.com/content/130895? from = groupmessage&isappinstalled = 0，最后访问时间：2017 年 11 月 25 日。

视为无罪，还是不仅如此，即便在思想上也不能将该人视为有罪？对于这个问题，笔者认为，由于思想自由是基本的人权，并且即便其他组织或者个人这样想，但没有相应的言行，也无法有效证明其这样想过，因此在思想上禁止其他组织和个人将该人视为有罪不仅缺乏正当性，也缺乏可行性。马克思就在《评普鲁士最近的书报检查令》中对追究思想的法律的不合理性进行了深刻的论述，指出："凡是不以当事人的行为本身而以他的思想作为主要标准的法律，无非是对非法行为的实际认可。与其把我要留胡子的想法当作剪胡子的标准，倒不如像那位俄国沙皇所做的那样，干脆让御用的哥萨克人把所有人的胡子统统剪掉。"① "只是由于我表现自己，只是由于我踏入现实的领域，我才进入受立法者支配的范围。对于法律来说，除了我的行为以外，我是根本不存在的，我根本不是法律的对象。我的行为就是法律在处置我时所应依据的唯一的东西……"②（2）其他组织和个人是不能将该人视为有罪，还是必须将该人视为无罪？换句话说，其他组织和个人能否在言行上视该人为可能有罪？这就涉及另外一个问题：侦查机关将某人或者组织视为犯罪嫌疑人，公诉机关将某人或者组织作为被告人向法院提起公诉，这都涉及将该人或者组织视为可能有罪的言行。然而，一般来说，应该没有人认为侦查机关或者公诉机关不能这么做，否则整个刑事诉讼制度将不复存在。然而，其他组织或者个人能否因此就可以将该人视为可能有罪呢？我们应当注意这二者之间的区别，即侦查机关和公诉机关这样做是依法打击犯罪、保护社会公共利益的需要，不这样做就无法有效打击犯罪，保护人民。而其他组织和个人这样做却并无这种必要性。因此，从这个角度看，其他组织和个人没有在言行上将该人视为可能有罪的理由。当然，将该人视为可能

① 中共中央马克思恩格斯列宁斯大林著作编译局：《马克思恩格斯全集》（第1卷·上册）（第二版），第120页。

② 中共中央马克思恩格斯列宁斯大林著作编译局：《马克思恩格斯全集》（第1卷·上册）（第二版），第121页。

有罪这种行为与公民和其他组织报案、控告、举报犯罪事实或者犯罪嫌疑人的行为之间是有区别的。后者已经涉及刑事诉讼程序，已经被纳入刑事诉讼法规制的范围，而前者则并非如此。（3）既然如此，为什么其他组织和个人不能有将该人视为有罪或者可能有罪的言行呢？因为无罪推定原则要求尚未经合法审判并依法证明有罪，任何人在法律上都是无罪的，将该人视为有罪或者可能有罪的言行违背了这一法律原则，侵害了该人的这项法律权利；另外，将该人视为有罪或者可能有罪的言行可能会给该人的正常生活带来很大的不便，侵害了该人正常生活的合法和切身利益，使该人遭受没有法律根据的痛苦。（4）如何认识“其他组织和个人不得有将该人视为有罪或者可能有罪的言行”与言论自由之间的关系？言论自由是基本人权之一，也是宪法明确规定的基本权利，但自由都是有边界的，自由的行使不能侵犯他人的合法权益，不能使他人为此而付出其合法权益受到侵害的代价，正如权利的行使不能侵犯他人的合法权益一样。应当将言论自由和仅仅存在于意识中尚未表现出来的思想自由区别开来。（5）无罪推定作为一项人格权设立的目的在于防止因未经证明的罪行而受到惩罚，因此对于因正在进行的犯罪而引起的将某人视为有罪或者可能有罪的言行不在无罪推定人格权的排除之列。正在进行犯罪的主体无权主张其无罪推定人格权。因正在进行的犯罪而被错误抓捕的主体不能针对无明显过错的因正在进行的犯罪而作出将前者视为有罪或者可能有罪言行的主体主张其无罪推定人格权；当然，有明显过错的例外。（6）是否侵犯无罪推定人格权应以是否损坏了权利主张人的名誉权和正常生活权益为判断标准，而非将所有未经依法证明有罪而将他人视为有罪或者可能有罪的言行都认定为侵犯他人无罪推定人格权。对于没有影响他人名誉及其正常生活权益的私下的将该人视为有罪或者可能有罪的言行，不能认定为侵犯该人的无罪推定人格权；否则，涉嫌侵犯言论自由权利，有违基本人伦。马克思就曾将监视普通人的私人谈话、私人邮件和在家里发表意见的行为视为最卑鄙的特务活动。[①]

综上所述，将无罪推定作为一项人格权进行规定具有积极的意义，是对无罪推定立法的创新和发展，应当予以肯定和支持。我国在无罪推定的立法中可以适当地对其进行借鉴。

二、处理好无罪推定与其例外之间的关系

无罪推定是否应当有例外，从伦理学的角度讲，涉及道德义务论是否应当绝对化的问题。道德义务论或者是绝对主义的，或者是温和主义的。[②] 当前，温和主义的道德义务论占主流。[③] 根据温和主义的道德义务论，道德的限制在为了促进公益等一定的情况下可以存在例外。[④] 这就为在一定的政策考量的基础上允许无罪推定存在例外提供了伦理学上的合理性根据。为了维护公共利益的迫切需要，国家可以立法规定一些无罪推定中的例外情况，包括反恐、反腐、禁毒等特殊案件中的一些无罪推定例外情况。

（一）无罪推定与反恐

对于恐怖主义犯罪中无罪推定适用的限制，笔者认为主要是考虑到两个因素：一个是恐怖主义犯罪对公共利益的危害；另一个是当前有效防范和应对恐怖主义犯罪措施的有限性以及侦查的难度。

---

① 参见中共中央马克思恩格斯列宁斯大林著作编译局：《马克思恩格斯全集》（第6卷），第405页。“新法案则企图把在私人谈话中、在自己房屋中、在自己家庭中、在私人通信中所发表的任何意见都置于警察局和检察机关的监督之下并加以惩治——也就是说，新法案企图组织最卑鄙的无孔不入的特务活动。”

② Shelly Kagan, Normative Ethics 78-84 (1998); Eyal Zamir & Barak Medina, Law, Economics, and Morality 46-74 (2010).

③ Even Robert Nozick has famously refrained from arguing that moral constraints are absolute, leaving open the possibility that they may be violated to avoid "catastrophic moral horror." Robert Nozick, Anarchy, State, and Utopia 30 n. * (1974).

④ Eyal Zamir, Law, Psychology, and Morality: The Role of Loss Aversion 179-80 (Oxford: Oxford University Press, 2015).

随着侦查技术的发展进步和恐怖主义对社会威胁程度的减轻，这些无罪推定的限制性措施应该可以逐步取消。也就是说，这些限制措施是历史的、暂时的、阶段性的。

对恐怖案件采取的应对措施虽然在一定程度上违背了无罪推定的精神，给民众的自由增添了一定的负担和限制，但是由于恐怖案件毕竟不是常态案件，这些应对措施对民众自由的影响也仅部分存在于特定类型的案件中，不会在一般意义上影响民众的自由。鉴于恐怖主义对整个社会的巨大威胁，特定的反恐措施即便在一定程度上会影响民众的自由，也是极其必要的。

为了防范和惩治恐怖活动，加强反恐怖主义工作，维护国家安全、公共安全和人民生命财产安全，2015 年 12 月 27 日第十二届全国人民代表大会常务委员会第十八次会议通过了反恐怖主义法。该法在一定程度上限制了无罪推定的适用。例如，该法第 12 条规定："国家反恐怖主义工作领导机构根据本法第三条的规定，认定恐怖活动组织和人员，由国家反恐怖主义工作领导机构的办事机构予以公告。"第 15 条第 1 款规定："被认定的恐怖活动组织和人员对认定不服的，可以通过国家反恐怖主义工作领导机构的办事机构申请复核。国家反恐怖主义工作领导机构应当及时进行复核，作出维持或者撤销认定的决定。复核决定为最终决定。"无罪推定要求任何人在被法院依法定罪之前应被视为无罪。这两条规定由国家反恐怖主义工作领导机构认定并复核最终决定恐怖活动组织和人员，实际上是对被认定为恐怖活动组织和人员者作出有罪评价，因此并不符合无罪推定的要求。该法第 14 条规定："金融机构和特定非金融机构对国家反恐怖主义工作领导机构的办事机构公告的恐怖活动组织和人员的资金或者其他资产，应当立即予以冻结，并按照规定及时向国务院公安部门、国家安全部门和反洗钱行政主管部门报告。"这种对被公告的恐怖活动组织和人员的资金或者其他资产立即予以冻结的做法其实也体现了一定的有罪推定，特别是这一做法的根据是国家反恐怖主义工作领导机构的办事机构公告，并非公安机关所为，因此也突破了传统上的侦查权限行使限制。由该法第五章“调查”的相关规定来看，恐怖主义犯罪的调查主体还是公安机关。当然，在加大打击恐怖主义犯罪力度的同时，该法也注意到了对人权的尊重和保障，体现了我国在反恐立法上的理性精神。如该法第6条规定：“反恐怖主义工作应当依法进行，尊重和保障人权，维护公民和组织的合法权益。在反恐怖主义工作中，应当尊重公民的宗教信仰自由和民族风俗习惯，禁止任何基于地域、民族、宗教等理由的歧视性做法。”

美国在“9·11”事件发生后很快就制定通过了《爱国者法案》，加强对恐怖主义犯罪的打击力度。该法采取的很多措施都涉及对基本人权的侵犯，因此也引起了很大的争议。甚至美国联邦调查局官员自身也对该法的合理性提出质疑。美国《爱国者法案》明确授权政府可以对公民进行跟踪和窃听，可以查阅公民的上网记录、私人信件和电子邮件等，还允许司法部门通过秘密法庭对一些恐怖主义嫌疑分子进行审判。[①] 为了打击恐怖主义犯罪，美国对传统的证据规则也创设了新的例外。例如，根据美国最高法院的解释，在有关恐怖主义犯罪的警察讯问中获得的证据在一定程度上不受传闻证据规则的限制。此外，美国在反恐案件中对米兰达规则的适用也进行了限制，在一定程度上降低了沉默权的保障，与无罪推定精神的落实存在一定的偏差。例如，在米兰达规则的公共安全例外应用于恐怖犯罪调查方面，美国司法部和联邦调查局就动了很大的脑筋。[②]《纽约时报》曾获取了一份未被签署的联邦调查局内部备忘录。该备忘录为执法官提供了关于在审讯恐怖主义犯罪嫌疑人的过程中何时告知嫌疑人其有保持沉默和讯问过程中拥有律师在场的所谓米兰达权利的指导。根据该备忘录……美国司法部和联邦调

① 傅达林：《反恐中的秩序与自由》，载《检察日报》2014年7月2日第7版。

② See generally, D. S. Kris, *Law Enforcement as a Counterterrorism Tool*, Journal of National Security Law and Policy, Vol. 5: 1, 2011, pp. 71-7.

查局相信可以通过继续坚持联邦调查局对在美国境内被捕的恐怖主义实施者[①]进行监禁下讯问时使用米兰达警告的政策来使实现目标的能力最大化：（1）如果适用，执法官应当在没有告知被逮捕人其米兰达权利的情况下询问任何所有为紧急的公共安全或者逮捕执行人员的安全考虑而合理提出的问题。[②]（2）在穷尽所有的公共安全问题之后，讯问人员应当告知被逮捕人其米兰达权利并寻求其在进一步审讯之前放弃那些权利，下面描述的特殊情况除外。（3）也许有这样的例外情况，即虽然已问过所有相关的公共安全问题，审讯人员仍旧作出结论认为继续无米兰达警告的讯问对于收集与紧急威胁无关但有价值和及时的信息是必要的，并且政府获取这一信息的利益超过了进行无警告讯问的不利。在这些情况下，审讯人员应当寻求批准以在公共安全问题问完后继续无警告地讯问。对特定的无警告讯问是否具有基于公共安全的正当性这一问题的决定必须基于所有的事实和条件进行个案判断。由于恐怖主义，特别是国际恐怖主义的巨大威胁，在恐怖主义犯罪中进行无米兰达警告的讯问比在普通刑事案件中要广泛和必要得多。[③] 小布什政府也主张虽然酷刑是被禁止的，但是强制讯问在与恐怖主义的斗争中是被允许也是必要的。《2006 年美国军事审判委员会法令》（*The Military Commission Act of* 2006）也支持这一观点。[④]

英国“反恐法”中规定了有关选择性的推定的内容，可在一定程度上视为无罪推定的例外。例如，英国 2000 年《反恐怖主义

---

① 为此目的，恐怖主义特工是指被合理相信为某个国际恐怖主义集团高层成员，或者个人实施或者试图实施威胁生命的恐怖活动，或者知晓将要发生的恐怖活动细节的个人的被逮捕者。

② 美国最高法院在纽约州诉夸尔斯（New York v. Quarles, 467 U. S. 649 (1984)）一案中确立了该规则。

③ http://www.nytimes.com/2011/03/25/us/25miranda-text.html?_r=0, last visited on May 15, 2015.

④ See generally Erwin Chemerinsky, Laurie L. Levenson, Criminal Procedure: Investigation 478 (2nd edition, Wolters Kluwer: Law and Business).

法》第57条就规定了选择性的（可为性的）法律推定，赋予法庭选择推定被告人占有恐怖主义犯罪所涉物品的权力。该条规定："（1）如果一个人在某种情况下持有一项物品，而该种情况会引起其是为了与实施、准备或者鼓动恐怖主义行为相关的目的而持有的合理怀疑，那么该人犯有罪行。（2）被指控犯有本条所规定罪行的人可以以证明其持有该物品并非为了与实施、准备或者鼓动恐怖主义行为相关的目的为自己辩护。（3）在因本条所规定罪行而提起的诉讼中，如果经证明一项物品——（a）与被告人同时处于某一房屋，或者（b）处于被告人占有或者并非作为公众而惯常使用的房屋，那么，法庭可以推定被告人占有该项物品，除非其证明其不知该物品存在于该房屋或者其对该物品没有控制。"英国上院2001年年底通过了新的《反恐怖主义、犯罪和保安法》，允许执法部门未经审判即可无限期拘留在英国居住但在外国出生的恐怖活动嫌疑人。2005年7月发生恐怖袭击后，绝大多数英国人赞同政府采取严厉措施打击恐怖主义威胁，86%的人同意给予警察更大权力拘捕策划恐怖袭击的嫌疑人。①

由此可见，在反恐案件中对无罪推定进行一定的限制也是一个世界趋势。

（二）无罪推定与反腐

腐败问题是一个世界性问题。腐败案件自身的特点又决定了在腐败案件中完全彻底贯彻无罪推定会对有效打击腐败造成极大的困难。因此，在腐败案件中实行一定的推定，对无罪推定进行一定的限制，就显得十分必要。腐败案件中的推定包括对犯罪主观方面的推定，对案件涉及财产性质的推定，以及刑事诉讼特别程序中对犯罪嫌疑人、被告人逃匿、死亡案件涉案财产性质的推定等。对犯罪主观方面的推定，如对腐败案件中明知、故意或者目的等的推定；对案件涉及财产性质的推定，如巨额财产来源不明罪中对差额部分

① 傅达林：《反恐中的秩序与自由》，载《检察日报》2014年7月2日第7版。

非法性质的推定；特别程序中对犯罪嫌疑人、被告人逃匿、死亡案件涉案财产性质的推定，如贪污贿赂犯罪中犯罪嫌疑人、被告人逃匿、死亡的，对相关涉案财产违法所得性质的推定。

我国目前已经在刑法中确立了巨额财产来源不明罪，对腐败案件中涉案财产的违法性质进行推定。例如，我国刑法第 395 条第 1 款规定："国家工作人员的财产、支出明显超过合法收入，差额巨大的，可以责令该国家工作人员说明来源，不能说明来源的，差额部分以非法所得论，处五年以下有期徒刑或者拘役；差额特别巨大的，处五年以上十年以下有期徒刑。财产的差额部分予以追缴。"我国刑事诉讼法已将对腐败案件中犯罪嫌疑人、被告人逃匿、死亡案件涉案财产违法性质的推定规定在刑事诉讼法第五编"特别程序"第四章"犯罪嫌疑人、被告人逃匿、死亡案件违法所得的没收程序"中。根据刑事诉讼法第 298 条规定，对于贪污贿赂犯罪案件，犯罪嫌疑人、被告人逃匿，在通缉 1 年后不能到案，或者犯罪嫌疑人、被告人死亡，依照刑法规定应当追缴其违法所得及其他涉案财产的，人民检察院可以向人民法院提出没收违法所得的申请。人民法院在必要的时候，可以查封、扣押、冻结申请没收的财产。第 300 条第 1 款规定："人民法院经审理，对经查证属于违法所得及其他涉案财产，除依法返还被害人的以外，应当裁定予以没收；对不属于应当追缴的财产的，应当裁定驳回申请，解除查封、扣押、冻结措施。"监察法也对腐败案件中被调查人逃匿或者死亡案件涉案财产的违法性质作出推定。监察法第 48 条规定："监察机关在调查贪污贿赂、失职渎职等职务犯罪案件过程中，被调查人逃匿或者死亡，有必要继续调查的，经省级以上监察机关批准，应当继续调查并作出结论。被调查人逃匿，在通缉一年后不能到案，或者死亡的，由监察机关提请人民检察院依照法定程序，向人民法院提出没收违法所得的申请。"此外，监察法还规定了限制出境等措施，涉及对人身自由等权利的限制，与无罪推定精神的要求存在一定的偏差，可被视为无罪推定的一种例外规定。监察法第 30 条规定："监察机关为防止被调查人及相关人员逃匿境外，经省级以上监察机关批准，可以对被调查人及相关人员采取限制出境措施，由公安机关依法执行。对于不需要继续采取限制出境措施的，应当及时解除。"监察法第52条规定："国家监察委员会加强对反腐败国际追逃追赃和防逃工作的组织协调，督促有关单位做好相关工作：（一）对于重大贪污贿赂、失职渎职等职务犯罪案件，被调查人逃匿到国（境）外，掌握证据比较确凿的，通过开展境外追逃合作，追捕归案；（二）向赃款赃物所在国请求查询、冻结、扣押、没收、追缴、返还涉案资产；（三）查询、监控涉嫌职务犯罪的公职人员及其相关人员进出国（境）和跨境资金流动情况，在调查案件过程中设置防逃程序。"对腐败案件中犯罪主观方面的推定我国目前的相关规定很少，仅有关于"转化型贪污罪"的司法解释中有对于非法占有公款目的的推定。例如，1998年5月9日最高人民法院颁布的《关于审理挪用公款案件具体应用法律若干问题的解释》第6条规定："携带挪用的公款潜逃的，依照刑法第三百八十二条、第三百八十三条的规定定罪处罚。"而刑法第382条、第383条是关于贪污罪的规定。也就是说，在"携带挪用的公款潜逃"这一基础事实成立的情况下，可以推定行为人主观上具有非法占有公款的目的，进而以贪污罪论罪科刑。① 对于腐败案件中明知的推定规则我国还迟迟没有建立，以致在很多腐败案件中，被告人都以对于其近亲属以及情人等中间人非法收受财物的行为不知情当作不具备犯罪故意的辩解理由，甚至成为某些被告人不服一审判决、提起上诉的重要理由，对我国反腐败斗争造成很大的负面影响。联合国大会于2003年10月31日通过的《联合国反腐败公约》第28条对腐败案件中的明知推定问题作出了明确规定。该条规定："根据本公约确立的犯罪所需具备的明知、故意或者目的等要素，可以根

① 赵秉志：《中国反腐败刑事法治的若干重大现实问题研究》，载《法学评论》（双月刊）2014年第3期，第7页。

据客观实际情况予以推定。”中国已于2005年10月27日审议并批准了该公约。[①] 因此，在坚持无罪推定总体原则的前提下，有必要尽快建立腐败案件中明知的推定规则，以进一步完善我国的反腐败法律体系，提高反腐败司法审判的公信力和权威性。[②]

上述几种推定都在一定程度上限制了无罪推定的适用，对被追诉人的自由造成了一定的减损。但是，这些推定都对打击腐败、促进政治清廉和社会清明具有重要积极的意义，因此是在特定问题上综合平衡个人自由和社会公共利益后作出的价值判断和选择，是一个公共政策考量问题。尽管如此，在适用或者确立这些推定时，要注重对人权的保障，不能滥用，以免造成侵犯人权的后果。例如，刑法第395条虽然将巨额财产来源不明罪中国家工作人员的财产、支出超过合法收入的差额部分推定为非法所得，但是允许该国家工作人员说明来源，只有其不能说明来源的，才将差额部分推定为非法所得，因此给了被追诉人申辩的机会，在一定程度上兼顾到了对其人权的保障。虽然根据刑事诉讼法第298条至第300条的规定，可以未经对被追诉人进行审判即将其占有的相关涉案财产认定为违法所得，并裁定予以没收（实际上就是未经审判间接认定被追诉人有罪，因而违反了无罪推定精神），但是刑事诉讼法对此也有一定的补救措施，如根据刑事诉讼法第300条第2款规定，犯罪嫌疑人、被告人的近亲属和其他利害关系人或者人民检察院对于人民法院依照该条第1款规定作出的对相关的违法所得及其他涉案财产予以没收的裁定不服的，可以提出上诉、抗诉。第301条规定：“在

---

① 2005年10月27日，第十届全国人大常委会第十八次会议审议并批准了《联合国反腐败公约》，同时声明：中国不受该公约第66条第2款的约束。自此，中国已经正式成为《联合国反腐败公约》的缔约国。这一行动在国内外引起强烈反响。http：//news. xinhuanet. com/politics/2005-11/08/content_ 3750946. htm，访问时间：2016年4月3日。

② 关于腐败案件中明知的推定规则问题，详见徐灿：《论腐败案件中明知的推定规则在中国的确立》，载《澳门法学》2015年第14期，第75-96页。

审理过程中，在逃的犯罪嫌疑人、被告人自动投案或者被抓获的，人民法院应当终止审理。没收犯罪嫌疑人、被告人财产确有错误的，应当予以返还、赔偿。”虽然根据监察法第 48 条规定，对监察机关调查的贪污贿赂、失职渎职等职务犯罪案件的被调查人可以未经审判即将其占有的相关涉案财产认定为违法所得并予以没收(实际上就是未经审判间接认定监察机关调查的贪污贿赂、失职渎职等职务犯罪案件的被调查人有罪，因而违反了无罪推定精神)，第 52 条也作出了限制被监察人员相关权利的措施，但是监察法对此也有一定的补救措施，如监察法第 49 条规定：“监察对象对监察机关作出的涉及本人的处理决定不服的，可以在收到处理决定之日起一个月内，向作出决定的监察机关申请复审，复审机关应当在一个月内作出复审决定；监察对象对复审决定仍不服的，可以在收到复审决定之日起一个月内，向上一级监察机关申请复核，复核机关应当在二个月内作出复核决定。复审、复核期间，不停止原处理决定的执行。复核机关经审查，认定处理决定有错误的，原处理机关应当及时予以纠正。”虽然监察法第 30 条规定：“监察机关为防止被调查人及相关人员逃匿境外，经省级以上监察机关批准，可以对被调查人及相关人员采取限制出境措施，由公安机关依法执行。”但是该条同时规定：“对于不需要继续采取限制出境措施的，应当及时解除。”以尽量避免对人权进行不必要的侵犯。在确立对腐败案件中主观方面的推定规则时，也应注意做好推定的补救措施。如在确立腐败案件中明知的推定规则时，一方面对作为推定适用条件的基础事实的证明必须达到一般的证明标准，不应有所降低；另一方面要允许被作出不利推定的被追诉人进行反驳。至于反驳要达到何种标准？这一问题可从推定成立的反面去理解。推定的结构包括“法律规定或者经验法则+基础事实+推定事实”。只有这三项都成立，推定才能成立。对于法律推定的情况，只要辩方能够指出控方对基础事实的证明未达到法定的标准（尚未“排除合理怀疑”，没有达到“内心确信”，也不能做到“事实清楚”），或者指出控方的推定没有准确地适用法律，即可推翻这一推定。对于事实推定的情况，只要辩方能够指出控方对基础事实的证明未达到法定的标准（如前所述），或者指出该“经验法则”缺乏常态联系、违背事实、具有不合理性，即可推翻这一推定。当然，无论是法律推定还是事实推定，如果当事人能够举出证据证明其确实不知情且能达到一般的证明标准，也可以推翻控方的推定。

（三）无罪推定与禁毒

当前，国际毒潮持续泛滥扩散，国内毒品问题正处于快速发展期，国际国内毒情相互交织、相互影响，我国毒品形势十分严峻复杂。禁毒工作关系国家安危、民族兴衰、人民福祉。因此，必须加大对毒品犯罪的打击力度，努力切除毒品犯罪这个社会毒瘤。然而，由于毒品犯罪隐蔽性强、复杂性高，犯罪证据收集难，如果完全贯彻无罪推定原则，在所有毒品犯罪案件中对每一个犯罪要素都通过证据证明到“案件事实清楚、证据确实充分”、“排除合理怀疑”的一般证明标准将会极其困难，也不利于对毒品犯罪的有效打击。为此，有必要在毒品犯罪案件中设置一些无罪推定的例外情况，在特定情况下允许存在一定的推定。

毒品犯罪中的推定主要包括主观明知的推定和毒品归属的推定。关于主观明知的推定问题，最高人民法院在 2008 年 12 月 1 日印发的《全国部分法院审理毒品犯罪案件工作座谈会纪要》（大连会议纪要）的通知（法〔2008〕324 号）中指出：“毒品犯罪中，判断被告人对涉案毒品是否明知，不能仅凭被告人供述，而应当依据被告人实施毒品犯罪行为的过程、方式、毒品被查获时的情形等证据，结合被告人的年龄、阅历、智力等情况，进行综合分析判断。具有下列情形之一，被告人不能作出合理解释的，可以认定其‘明知’是毒品，但有证据证明确属被蒙骗的除外：（1）执法人员在口岸、机场、车站、港口和其他检查站点检查时，要求行为人申报为他人携带的物品和其他疑似毒品物，并告知其法律责任，而行为人未如实申报，在其携带的物品中查获毒品的；（2）以伪报、藏匿、伪装等蒙蔽手段，逃避海关、边防等检查，在其携带、运输、邮寄的物品中查获毒品的；（3）执法人员检查时，有逃跑、丢弃携带物品或者逃避、抗拒检查等行为，在其携带或者丢弃的物品中查获毒品的；（4）体内或者贴身隐秘处藏匿毒品的；（5）为获取不同寻常的高额、不等值报酬为他人携带、运输物品，从中查获毒品的；（6）采用高度隐蔽的方式携带、运输物品，从中查获毒品的；（7）采用高度隐蔽的方式交接物品，明显违背合法物品惯常交接方式，从中查获毒品的；（8）行程路线故意绕开检查站点，在其携带、运输的物品中查获毒品的；（9）以虚假身份或者地址办理托运手续，在其托运的物品中查获毒品的；（10）有其他证据足以认定行为人应当知道的。”高贵君、王勇和吴光霞在《〈全国部分法院审理毒品犯罪案件工作座谈会纪要〉的理解与适用》一文中对于上述主观明知推定规定的背景作出介绍：“毒品犯罪隐蔽性强，犯罪分子往往具有较充分的反侦查、反制裁准备，因而在行为人拒不如实供述的情况下，极难取得证据有效证明其主观上明知行为对象系毒品，从而给毒品犯罪的认定带来困难。为了解决这一问题，《两高一部毒品犯罪意见》① 规定了可以认定明知的一些具体情形。《纪要》② 在此基础上，参考最高人民法院、最高人民检察院、海关总署 2002 年 7 月《关于办理走私刑事案件适用法律若干问题的意见》第 5 条‘关于走私犯罪嫌疑人、被告人主观故意的认定问题’的规定，结合司法实践经验，列举了可以认定被告人主观明知的具体情形。”③ 对于作出主观明知推定规定的

① 此处的《两高一部毒品犯罪意见》具体是指最高人民法院、最高人民检察院和公安部于 2007 年 11 月 8 日联合印发的《办理毒品犯罪案件适用法律若干问题的意见》（公通字〔2007〕84 号）——笔者注。

② 此处的《纪要》具体是指最高人民法院于 2008 年 12 月 1 日印发的《全国部分法院审理毒品犯罪案件工作座谈会纪要》（大连会议纪要）——笔者注。

③ 高贵君、王勇、吴光霞：《〈全国部分法院审理毒品犯罪案件工作座谈会纪要〉的理解与适用》，载《人民司法·应用》2009 年第 3 期，第 24 页。

原因，《〈全国部分法院审理毒品犯罪案件工作座谈会纪要〉的理解与适用》解释道："作出这一规定，一是出于公民基于法律法规而产生的义务。行为人在进行与自身相关的有关行为时，有责任审查被委托、雇佣携带、运输或者交接的物品是否属违禁品，不然，就要承担相应的法律责任。二是出于严惩毒品犯罪的需要。如果仅以行为人是否承认明知为标准，就难以认定毒品犯罪人的主观故意，严重影响惩治毒品犯罪活动。三是出于现行法律、司法解释和规范性文件对明知问题已作过类似规定。如刑法第219条第2款规定：'明知或者应知前款所列行为，获取、使用或者披露他人的商业秘密的，以侵犯商业秘密论。'最高人民法院、最高人民检察院2007年5月《关于办理与盗窃、抢劫、诈骗、抢夺机动车相关刑事案件具体应用法律若干问题的解释》第6条，最高人民法院、最高人民检察院、海关总署2002年7月《关于办理走私刑事案件适用法律若干问题的意见》第5条，都结合案件的具体情况规定了明知的认定问题。四是出于国际公约对明知事项的规定。《联合国禁止非法贩运麻醉药品和精神药物公约》第3条第1款规定了各种毒品的故意犯罪，其中第3款规定：'构成本条第1款所列罪行的知情、故意或目的等要素，可根据客观事实情况加以判断。'我国签署和批准了该公约（1990年11月11日在我国生效）。此外，《联合国打击跨国有组织犯罪公约》第5条第2款、《联合国反腐败公约》第28条也有类似规定。五是出于国外和我国香港地区关于毒品犯罪明知规定的借鉴。"[①] 关于判断是否明知应当注意的问题，《〈全国部分法院审理毒品犯罪案件工作座谈会纪要〉的理解与适用》指出："一是判断是否明知应当以客观实际情况为依据。尽管明知是行为人知道或者应当知道行为对象是毒品的心理状态，但是判断被告人主观是否明知，不能仅凭被告人是否承认，而应当

① 高贵君、王勇、吴光霞：《〈全国部分法院审理毒品犯罪案件工作座谈会纪要〉的理解与适用》，载《人民司法·应用》2009年第3期，第24页。

综合考虑案件中的各种客观实际情况，依据实施毒品犯罪行为的过程、行为方式、毒品被查获时的情形和环境等证据，结合被告人的年龄、阅历、智力及掌握的相关知识情况，进行综合分析判断。二是用作推定前提的基础事实必须有确凿的证据证明。首先要查明行为人携带、运输的东西确实是毒品，同时行为人有反常行为表现。三是依照上述规定认定的明知，允许行为人提出反证加以推翻。由于推定明知不是以确凿证据证明的，而是根据基础事实与待证事实的常态联系，运用情理判断和逻辑推理得出的，有可能出现例外情况。如果行为人能作出合理解释，有证据证明确实受蒙骗，其辩解有事实依据或者合乎情理，就不能认定其明知是毒品。”① 最高人民法院、最高人民检察院、公安部《关于办理毒品犯罪案件收集与审查证据若干问题的意见》（2017 年 4 月 25 日草案）吸收了大连会议纪要关于主观明知推定的精神，该草案第 44 条第 1 款规定：“具有下列情形之一，犯罪嫌疑人、被告人不能做出合理解释的，可以认定其明知走私、贩卖、运输、非法持有的是毒品，但有证据证明其确实不知情或者确系被蒙骗的除外：（一）执法人员在口岸、机场、车站、港口、邮局等场所检查时，要求申报为他人携带、运输、寄递的物品和其他疑似毒品物，并告知其法律责任，但未如实申报，在其携带、运输、寄递的物品中查获毒品的；（二）以伪报、藏匿、伪装等蒙蔽手段逃避海关、边防等检查，或者行程路线故意绕开检查站点，在其携带、运输的物品中查获毒品的；（三）在执法人员检查时有逃跑、藏匿、丢弃携带物品、弃车逃离或者其他逃避、抗拒检查行为，在其携带、藏匿、丢弃的物品或者遗弃的车辆中查获毒品的；（四）在体内或者贴身隐秘处藏匿毒品的；（五）采用高度隐蔽的方式携带、运输、交接物品，明显违背合法物品惯常携带、运输、交接方式，从中查获毒品的；

① 高贵君、王勇、吴光霞：《〈全国部分法院审理毒品犯罪案件工作座谈会纪要〉的理解与适用》，载《人民司法·应用》2009 年第 3 期，第 24 页。

（六）以虚假的身份、地址或者物品名称办理托运、寄递手续，从托运、寄递的物品中查获毒品的；（七）采用隐匿真实身份、支付不等值报酬等不合理方式，雇用、指使他人携带、运输或者代为接收物流寄递的物品，从中查获毒品的；（八）为获取不同寻常的高额、不等值报酬为他人携带、运输或者接收物流寄递的物品，从中查获毒品的；（九）其他可以认定犯罪嫌疑人、被告人明知的情形。”第2款规定：“具有下列情形之一，犯罪嫌疑人、被告人不能做出合理解释的，可以认定其明知制造的是毒品，但有证据证明其确实不知情或者确系被蒙骗的除外：（一）购置了用于制造毒品的工具、设备、原料、配剂或者制毒工艺的；（二）在偏远、隐蔽的场所或者采取伪装方式制造物品，经鉴定是毒品的；（三）在执法人员检查时，有逃避、抗拒检查等行为，在现场查获制造出的物品，经鉴定是毒品的；（四）为获取不同寻常的高额、不等值报酬为他人制造物品，经鉴定是毒品的；（五）其他可以认定犯罪嫌疑人、被告人明知的情形。”此外，该草案还对毒品归属的推定问题作出规定，该草案第51条第1款规定：“从犯罪嫌疑人、被告人身体、衣服、随身物品中查获毒品的，一般可以认定系犯罪嫌疑人、被告人所有或者由其实际控制，但确有相反证据的除外。”

除了会议纪要和司法解释以外，关于毒品犯罪中主观明知的推定和毒品归属的推定，我国尚未在法律中正式规定。这不利于有效打击毒品犯罪，维护社会安宁。因此，在坚持无罪推定总体原则的前提下，有必要在法律中尽快建立毒品犯罪案件中明知和毒品归属的推定规则，以进一步完善我国的禁毒法律体系，提高禁毒司法审判的公信力和权威性。

三、创设提审通知被提审人制度，防止刑讯逼供

防止刑讯逼供是贯彻无罪推定原则的要求。我国刑事诉讼的社会主义性质要求所有人的正义，即法律面前人人平等，任何人都有权平等地受到不被刑讯逼供的保护。虽然目前我国已经建立了一系

列防止刑讯逼供的规则和制度，如非法证据排除规则、反对强迫自证其罪和全程录音录像等制度，但是由于这些规则和制度设计并不完善和严密，并未能结合形成一张严密的防范刑讯逼供的网络，或者说这张网上仍旧有漏洞，以致现有的保障人权、防止刑讯逼供的制度无法得到有效的贯彻落实，各种规避这些规则和制度的做法在实践中层出不穷。譬如，一些侦查机关在讯问过程中采用有选择地录音录像的做法，先以暴力、胁迫等非法方法摧垮被讯问人的意志，然后再对接下来的讯问过程进行录音录像，形成所谓的“重复供述”，在法庭上只出示合法讯问部分的录音录像，以致全程录音录像制度成为一件摆设，不仅未能起到其应有的监督审讯人员以保证依法讯问的作用，反而成为公诉方“证明”讯问合法的工具。正如《法院院长遭遇刑讯逼供 法治呼唤换位思考》这一报道中所提到的，“……保护当事人权益的制度设计并不缺位，比如讯问职务犯罪嫌疑人，要实行全程同步录音录像。但刘德山亲身经历后认为，这一规定在实践中形同虚设：‘全是演戏’，‘先把我整服气了，让我说‘是的’，他们再开设备走一道场子。’侦查机关否认刑讯逼供。鹤壁市检察院一位副检察长向《南方周末》记者表示：事实上，办案人员对刘德山照顾有加，‘吃饭都是变着花样给他吃’；至于21天不让睡觉，他认为明显违反常识，‘常人几天不睡觉，就活不了了’”。① 可见，没有严密的防止刑讯逼供的程序设计，就无法保证保护当事人权益的制度真正落到实处。创设提审通知被提审人制度有利于解决重复供述问题，对于防止刑讯逼供，贯彻无罪推定，保障人权具有重要意义。

（一）刑事诉讼审前程序中的重复供述问题

在我国刑事诉讼的审前程序中，如果存在多次审讯，且在有些

① http://mp.weixin.qq.com/s? __biz = MzA3OTkzNDMxMA = = &mid = 205173431&idx = 1&sn = b3eb0809daa70970b09b8c7d256e5ea2&scene = 2&from = timeline&isappinstalled = 0#rd，最后访问时间：2015年5月15日。

审讯中，对犯罪嫌疑人实施了刑讯逼供等非法取证行为，而在后续的审讯时，未对犯罪嫌疑人实施非法取证行为且提取了与之前非法获取的口供内容一致的口供，那么这种情况下犯罪嫌疑人后续的口供能否排除？此即刑事诉讼中的重复供述问题。所谓重复供述（repeated statement），又称“二次供述”，是指在可能采取非法手段获取口供后，在未涉嫌采用非法手段的情况下再次审讯或多次审讯所获得的同样内容的口供。2017 年 6 月 27 日最高人民法院、最高人民检察院、公安部、国家安全部和司法部（以下简称“两高三部”）出台的《关于办理刑事案件严格排除非法证据若干问题的规定》将重复供述界定为采用刑讯逼供方法使犯罪嫌疑人、被告人作出供述，之后犯罪嫌疑人、被告人受该刑讯逼供行为影响而作出的与该供述相同的供述。[①] 重复供述问题是刑事案件侦查、提起公诉和审判过程中经常遇到的问题。对待重复供述问题的态度关系到刑讯逼供等违法行为能否得到真正禁止，关系到非法证据排除规则能否得到真正落实。在我国解决重复供述的排除问题意义重大。

（二）重复供述的可采性

1. 重复供述可采性的域外考察

重复供述是否可采，亦即重复供述能否作为定案的依据在域外是一个广受重视的问题。从域外经验来看，虽然两大法系对非法证据的排除采取了不尽相同的规定，但在重复供述是否应当排除这一问题上观点基本一致。在日本，学者将重复供述定义为根据违法获得的供述而获得的同一内容的供述。他们认为，如果第一次供述是根据违法程序获得的，犯罪嫌疑人不知道欠缺证据能力，那么第一

---

① 2017 年 6 月 27 日“两高三部”出台的《关于办理刑事案件严格排除非法证据若干问题的规定》第 5 条规定：“采用刑讯逼供方法使犯罪嫌疑人、被告人作出供述，之后犯罪嫌疑人、被告人受该刑讯逼供行为影响而作出的与该供述相同的重复性供述……”

次供述的违法性波及第二次供述，第二次供述也予以排除。[①] 在德国，德国刑事诉讼法第 136 条 a 中明确规定了针对非法讯问所得证据的排除规则，按照通常的理解，该条的前半部分确立的是“证据取得之禁止”，后半部分确立的则是“证据使用之禁止”，按照德国联邦最高法院的解释，被告人所做的陈述只要受到法律所禁止的讯问行为之影响的，即不得作为证据使用。不仅如此，该条款所确立的证据使用禁止具有继续性效力，也就是被告人即使在后来的程序中接受合法的讯问，但只要其陈述仍然受先前违法讯问行为的继续影响，则该陈述仍然不得作为证据使用。[②] 美国在 1920 年的西尔弗索恩木材公司诉美国（Silverthorne Lumber Co. v. United States）一案中首次提出了“毒树之果”理论，并确定了三项重要的例外。此后，虽然在 1985 年的俄勒冈州诉埃尔斯塔德（Orengon v. Elstad）案中，联邦最高法院就被告人第一次自白因违反告知程序予以排除后，第二次自白的证据能力如何产生了争议，但是大多数意见表示非仅是欠缺米兰达告知程序，而是在警察暴力、胁迫或者其他不当方法下作出的非任意性自白，则第二次自白在取得前进行了米兰达告知也不会消除第一次自白的瑕疵，仍应适用“毒树之果”原则予以排除。[③] 在 1943 年的麦克纳布诉美国（McNabb v. United States）一案中，美国联邦最高法院指出“本院以宪法为基础，撤销联邦和州法庭中基于对意识中警察的权力被极大地放大或者被非法单独监禁而未获得朋友或者辩护人建议的无知的和缺乏教育的人进行的拖延或者重复讯问而获得的供述的定罪……”在 2004 年的密苏里州诉塞伯特（Missouri v. Seibert）[④] 一案中，美国

① ［日］田口守一：《刑事诉讼法》，张凌等译，中国政法大学出版社 2010 年版，第 300 页。

② 陈瑞华：《比较刑事诉讼法》，中国人民大学出版社 2010 年版，第 185 页。

③ See generally Erwin Chemerinsky, Laurie L. Levenson, Criminal Procedure: Investigation 536-7 (Wolters Kluwer: Law and Business, 2nd edition).

④ Missouri v. Seibert, 542 U. S. 600 (2004).

联邦最高法院指出“此处的问题是重复供述的可采性。因为在讯问和未经警告的自白之后中途宣读米兰达警告不能有效遵守米兰达规则的宪法要求，所以，我们裁定这种情况下警告之后作出的重复供述不具有可采性”①。显然，在对于一定条件下重复讯问获得的重复供述能否作为定罪依据的问题上，美国联邦最高法院也持否定的态度，即重复供述不能作为定罪依据，不具有可采性。英国在1984年《警察与刑事证据法》实施后，通过一系列主导性判例否定了“二次供述”的证据能力，其排除的尺度归纳如下：第一次讯问的污染在第二次讯问的时候仍在发挥作用；两次讯问是紧密联系的，无论是时间上还是内容上，第二次讯问是以重复第一次讯问中已经发生的情况的方式开始的；采取第二次供述会给被告人的公正审判带来不利影响。②

2. 我国对于重复供述可采性的态度

对于重复供述可采性的态度影响着非法证据排除规则的落实，关系到犯罪嫌疑人、被告人的人权保障，直接影响着司法民主、司法文明的实现，事关重大。然而，对于重复供述的问题，2010年最高人民法院等五部门联合颁布的《关于办理死刑案件审查判断证据若干问题的规定》和《关于办理刑事案件排除非法证据若干问题的规定》，2018年刑事诉讼法及相关司法解释都没有作出规定。最高人民法院刑事审判一至五庭主办、法律出版社2017年3月出版的《刑事审判参考》（总第106集）在一个案例《郑祖文贪污、受贿、滥用职权案［第1140号］——如何处理以威胁方法收集的被告人供述及司法实践中对“重复供述”如何采信》中，对

---

① Erwin Chemerinsky, Laurie L. Levenson, Criminal Procedure: Investigation 540 (Wolters Kluwer: Law and Business, 2nd edition).

② 郑旭：《非法证据排除规则》，中国法制出版社2009年版，第143-144页。

重复供述问题进行了论述。[①] 2017 年 6 月 27 日“两高三部”出台的《关于办理刑事案件严格排除非法证据若干问题的规定》第 5 条对重复供述问题进行了回应。该条规定：“采用刑讯逼供方法使犯罪嫌疑人、被告人作出供述，之后犯罪嫌疑人、被告人受该刑讯逼供行为影响而作出的与该供述相同的重复性供述，应当一并排除，但下列情形除外：（一）侦查期间，根据控告、举报或者自己发现等，侦查机关确认或者不能排除以非法方法收集证据而更换侦查人员，其他侦查人员再次讯问时告知诉讼权利和认罪的法律后果，犯罪嫌疑人自愿供述的；（二）审查逮捕、审查起诉和审判期间，检察人员、审判人员讯问时告知诉讼权利和认罪的法律后果，犯罪嫌疑人、被告人自愿供述的。”

重复供述能否作为定案依据的问题，在我国的理论界和实务界引起了很大的争论。主要观点有三种：第一种认为重复供述不应当排除，因为犯罪嫌疑人在后续没有采取非法取证行为的审讯中进行重复供述没有直接违反刑事诉讼法等相关法律规定，为了打击犯罪，对后续的这些供述可以不排除。公检法部门普遍持这种观点。[②] 第二种观点认为重复供述不能作为定案依据，应当全部排除，一排到底，即只要查明前面的审讯中曾存在非法取证行为，则之后形成的所有有罪供述皆视为非法证据而予以排除。[③] 第三种观

① 参见《最高法院：以威胁方法收集的口供应予排除，后续的“重复供述”可视情况排除》，http：//mp. weixin. qq. com/s/SKkoar3I_ p9qAgTFj1FUEA，最后访问时间：2017 年 11 月 13 日。

② 参见陈光中：《非法证据排除规则实施问题调研报告》，载陈光中主编：《非法证据排除规则实施问题研究》，北京大学出版社 2014 年版。

③ 参见万毅：《论“反复自白”的效力》，载《四川大学学报》（哲学社会科学版）2011 年第 5 期。

点认为应当有条件的排除。[①] 在这三种观点中，主流观点认为应当完全排除或者有条件的排除。非法证据排除规则在我国刑事诉讼法中的确立经过了艰难曲折的过程。重复供述的排除对于非法证据排除规则在实践中真正得到落实具有极其重要的意义。为了使这难得的非法证据排除规则不被架空，在司法实践中落到实处，对于重复供述不应当排除的观点显然站不住脚。然而，既然要排除，是全部排除，一排到底，还是有条件地排除呢？

重复供述应否排除，或者说判断重复供述的可采性，关键是非法获取的供述与后续供述之间是否存在因果关系——如果前者效力延及后者，则应否定重复供述的证据能力，即重复供述不可采；如果因果关系阻断，或因供述重复过程中产生“稀释效应”，违法性被稀释到足以容忍，则可确认其可采性。[②] 基于此，笔者认为有条件的排除说似乎更加合理。至于具体条件的设定，应当结合域外经验和我国的国情进行综合制定。例如，取证时间和空间的变更，取证主体的变更，辩护律师的介入等。但是，由于具体案情千变万化，要想穷尽所有的具体条件是不可能的，所以除制定一些可预测的具体条件以外，设定一项一般的标准更加重要。为了使这项标准简便易行，笔者建议可将其设定为后续供述中的情形或者条件变化是否足以消除先前的非法取供对后续供述中供述人供述的自愿性产生影响的可能性。如果后续供述中的情形或者条件变化足以消除这种可能性或者使这种可能性变得极小，即先前的非法取供不可能对后续取供过程中供述人的自愿性产生任何影响或者影响极小可以忽略不计，那么重复供述就具有可采性；否则，重复供述就不具有可

① 参见龙宗智：《两个证据规定的规范与执行若干问题研究》，载《中国法学》2010 年第 6 期；龙宗智：《我国非法口供排除的“痛苦规则”及相关问题》，载《政法论坛》2013 年第 5 期；张颖：《重复自白的证据能力》，载《中国刑事法杂志》2012 年第 7 期。

② 参见龙宗智：《我国非法口供排除的“痛苦规则”及相关问题》，载《政法论坛》2013 年第 5 期，第 23 页。

采性。至于何为“先前的非法取供不可能对后续取供过程中供述人的自愿性产生任何影响或者影响极小可以忽略不计”，一方面可以通过列举的方式予以明确；另一方面其他未列举到的情形应当属于法官自由裁量权的范畴。此外，最高法院还可以通过发布案例的形式对司法实践中的具体操作提供指导和参考（如上述《刑事审判参考》（总第 106 集）中的《郑祖文贪污、受贿、滥用职权案［第 1140 号］——如何处理以威胁方法收集的被告人供述及司法实践中对“重复供述”如何采信》）。法律的生命在于经验，而不是逻辑。设想通过设立一套完善的法则体系一劳永逸地解决所有的问题是不现实的。司法不是自动售货机。在任何时候都不可能撇开法官的一切作用而使规则体系按照立法者的目的自动地运行。

《关于办理刑事案件严格排除非法证据若干问题的规定》第 5 条对重复供述的界定本身就要求后续供述受先前供述中刑讯逼供行为的影响，因此属于上述前者效力延及后者的情形，应当排除。但是对于因果关系阻断，或因供述重复过程中产生“稀释效应”，违法性被稀释到足以容忍的情况，《关于办理刑事案件严格排除非法证据若干问题的规定》仅仅列举了两种可能的情形，显然不足以准确描述不予排除的例外情形，对于重复供述似有过度排除之嫌，不利于对犯罪的依法打击。因此，建议对不予排除例外情形的规定进行改进，将《关于办理刑事案件严格排除非法证据若干问题的规定》第 5 条修改为：“采用刑讯逼供方法使犯罪嫌疑人、被告人作出供述，之后犯罪嫌疑人、被告人受该刑讯逼供行为影响而作出的与该供述相同的重复性供述，应当一并排除，但如果先前的非法取供不可能对后续取供过程中供述人的自愿性产生任何影响或者影响极小可以忽略不计，那么后续重复性供述不予排除。先前的非法取供不可能对后续取供过程中供述人的自愿性产生任何影响或者影响极小可以忽略不计的情形包括：（一）侦查期间，根据控告、举报或者自己发现等，侦查机关确认或者不能排除以非法方法收集证据而更换侦查人员，其他侦查人员再次讯问时告知诉讼权利和认罪的法律后果，犯罪嫌疑人自愿供述的；（二）审查逮捕、审查起诉和审判期间，检察人员、审判人员讯问时告知诉讼权利和认罪的法律后果，犯罪嫌疑人、被告人自愿供述的；（三）其他先前的非法取供不可能对后续取供过程中供述人的自愿性产生任何影响或者影响极小可以忽略不计的情形。”

（三）确立并完善限制人身自由及提审期间的全程监控制度，明确控方及监控责任人的举证责任——在中国国情下解决通过非法手段获取重复供述问题的建议

1. 在中国解决重复供述问题所面临的国情

当前我国刑事诉讼法已确立了与提审期间全程监控有关的制度。我国现行刑事诉讼法第 123 条规定：“侦查人员在讯问犯罪嫌疑人的时候，可以对讯问过程进行录音或者录像；对于可能判处无期徒刑、死刑的案件或者其他重大犯罪案件，应当对讯问过程进行录音或者录像。录音或者录像应当全程进行，保持完整性。”但是，并未明确规定限制人身自由期间的全程监控制度，对于限制人身自由期间的全程监控责任也没有明确的规定。这就使得作为遏制刑讯逼供措施的全程录音录像制度不能真正实现其遏制刑讯逼供的目标。这一方面与先以暴力、胁迫等非法方法摧垮被讯问人的意志，然后再对接下来的讯问过程进行录音录像的做法有关；另一方面也与我国看守所归同级公安机关领导的特殊国情有关。在我国的司法环境中，重复供述问题在很大程度上涉及看守所的管理体制问题。我国现行有效的《看守所条例》第 5 条第 1 款规定：“看守所以县级以上的行政区域为单位设置，由本级公安机关管辖。”因此，看守所实际上处于本级公安机关的领导之下，没有特殊的机制，难以作出独立于本级公安机关的决定。而本级的公安机关又同时是刑事案件的侦查机关，在刑事诉讼中，履行着侦查犯罪、获取包括口供在内的证据、追诉犯罪的职责。对于与侦查机关密切相关的重复供述问题，鉴于看守所处于公安机关的管辖之下，接受其领导，其人事权和财权也被公安机关控制，出于现实利益的考虑，看

守所难以做到独立于公安机关，难以避免会配合公安机关进行非法取证的行为，除非有其他的利益驱动机制逼迫看守所不这样做。

2. 我国创设提审通知被提审人制度的必要性

如前文所述，对于重复供述，完全不排除显然不符合现代法治精神，也是与我国司法体制改革的方向背道而驰的。对待重复供述可采性的主流观点依然是“有条件的排除”或者“完全排除”。然而，问题在于无论是“完全排除”还是“有条件的排除”，都涉及与先前是否存在非法取证行为有关的证明问题。2018 年刑事诉讼法第 58 条第 2 款规定“申请排除以非法方法收集的证据的，应当提供相关线索或者材料”，第 59 条第 1 款规定“在对证据收集的合法性进行法庭调查的过程中，人民检察院应当对证据收集的合法性加以证明”。然而，提供相关线索或者材料较容易做到，但是要想充分举证证明取证行为的合法性却十分困难，甚至对是否存在这样一次涉嫌非法取证的审讯都可能存在争议。例如，被告人可以很容易地编造一个虚假的情节，主张侦查机关曾经对其实施暴力等非法行为但未取证，后来的供述是因为受到前面的暴力等非法行为的影响才作出的，从而主张证据是非法取得的，应当予以排除。需要说明的是，侦查机关仅对犯罪嫌疑人采取暴力等非法行为但不取证，同时删除存在这一行为的相关证明材料的可能性是存在的，因为鉴于我国当前的看守所管理体制，公安机关对看守所具有管辖权，公安机关很容易通过造假的方式删除其曾经对被追诉人进行提审的相关证明材料，对于在办案场所对被追诉人实施暴力等非法行为的情况就更难以证明。如果充分认识到这一点，而由追诉方承担完全的举证证明证据收集合法性的责任，只要被追诉方提出任何种类的质疑，如果追诉方不能举证将该质疑排除，就必须承担证据被认定为违法取得的后果，那么在实践中，被追诉人的如上虚假主张就会对侦查机关的调查取证工作造成极大的阻碍，严重影响破案和社会秩序的稳定。然而，如果因此就不排除重复供述，那么侦查机关可能会大肆采取这种有些提审只对被追诉人采取暴力等非法行为但不取证，有些提审只取证不采取暴力等非法行为（即先打后取证）的做法，从而造成事实上纵容变相刑讯逼供的问题。司法实践中存在的“摄像头规律”也表明了创设这一将责任推定给看守所的提审通知制度的必要性和可行性。一篇题为《服刑犯“发生关系”视频果然丢了》的报道就深刻地反映了这一问题：“监控视频‘果然’丢了。为什么说‘果然’？因为在此前的一系列与看守所或监狱有关的事件中，一个‘摄像头规律’多次得到验证：对狱方有利的时候，摄像头们尽职尽责、监控视频一览无余；而对狱方不利的证据，它们基本上‘选择性失明’，甚至还常常在‘适当的时机’坏掉，来个‘一推六二五’。例如，云南‘躲猫猫’事件中，相关部门以监房摄像头已坏为由拒绝提供录像；武汉男子李文彦‘做噩梦’猝死，看守所称因电脑硬盘出现故障，因此事发当天的录像无法调看。现在，讷河监狱的监控视频‘找不到了’，岂非正是按规律办事、按套路出牌？”[①] 虽然《关于办理刑事案件严格排除非法证据若干问题的规定》对提讯登记等制度进行了规定，但是没有规定直接指向被提审人的通知制度，无法保证被提审人获取其曾被提审的相关证明材料的机会，无法保证其在审判阶段提供这一相关线索或者材料（证据）的能力，可谓一大漏洞。

为了解决这一问题，必须进一步明确控辩双方的举证责任，创设羁押或者限制人身自由期间提审通知被提审人制度。需要说明的是，辩方此处的举证责任并非与控方对应的证明非法取证的责任，而是将2018年刑事诉讼法第58条第2款规定的“申请排除以非法方法收集的证据的，应当提供相关线索或者材料”予以具体化和明确化，通过创设提审通知被提审人制度，提出法定的提审通知书的责任。这一点将在以下部分详述。

---

① 参见《服刑犯“发生关系”视频果然丢了》，http：//view. news. qq. com/a/20150125/007275. htm，访问时间：2015年1月24日。

3. 创设提审通知被提审人制度的立法建议

鉴于当前改变看守所受公安机关管辖的体制困难较大，所以建议创设提审通知被提审人制度（实际上，无论将看守所划归谁管理，只要具体执行时是由人来负责，则都可能被收买。只有从机制上使得实施或者配合实施刑讯逼供或暴力取证者会因其实施或者配合实施行为而危害到自己的切身利益才能彻底禁绝刑讯逼供和暴力取证）。建议在刑事诉讼法“侦查”一章增加一条：“申请人主张供述是在先前非法审讯的影响下作出，因而应作为非法证据予以排除的，应当提供先前提审时的提审通知书，对曾存在这样的审讯予以证明。人民检察院应当对相应审讯的合法性予以证明。”具体说来，这一制度要求必须书面通知被提审人，在通知书上注明提审的时间、提审的地点、提审人员、被提审人员、提审单位的印章及提审人员的签章等，[①] 同时赋予并在提审通知书上注明被提审人享有拒绝接受不依照提审通知书的规定进行提审的权利。其中，有以下几点需要注意：

第一，对被提审人的提审通知必须以书面的形式作出，不能以口头的方式代替。目的是为在以后的审判中可能提出的非法证据排除申请中要求被追诉人提供相关线索或者材料提供保障性措施。亦即制度已经赋予了被追诉人获取其曾被提审的相关证明材料的机会，在审判阶段，再要求被追诉人提供这一相关线索或者材料（证据）就显得合情、合理、合法。

第二，进一步明确决定羁押（拘留、逮捕）后的审讯应当在看守所内进行，并且如果被追诉人提出其被决定羁押后未被依法立即送往看守所并在此期间被侦查机关实施了暴力等非法行为，那么侦查机关应当对此作出合理解释并提供相关证据予以证明，对于经

① 参见“两高三部”《关于办理刑事案件严格排除非法证据若干问题的规定》第20条规定：“犯罪嫌疑人、被告人及其辩护人申请排除非法证据，应当提供涉嫌非法取证的人员、时间、地点、方式、内容等相关线索或者材料。”

查实确有相关违法行为的，应对相关责任人员依法追究相应责任，直至追究刑事法律责任。[①] 对于决定羁押后、移送看守所以前通过审讯所获取的任何口供都应当作为非法证据予以排除。这一制度与公诉方对取证合法性承担举证责任以及全程录音录像等制度一起，为避免侦查机关在将犯罪嫌疑人移送看守所之前对其实施暴力等非法行为提供了制度上的保障。同时，移送看守所的时限制度[②]也给犯罪嫌疑人捱过侦查机关有限时间内可能的暴力等非法行为提供了希望和信心。

为了保证这一措施的有效执行，还应当明确规定对于在指定居所进行提审的，指定的居所必须有 24 小时不间断无死角的监控设施，以保证被指定居所监视居住的人时时处处处于监控之下，从而适用类似看守所的建议规定。对于不具备上述条件而进行提审的，如果被提审人提出非法取证异议而公诉方无法证明取证的合法性，那么此类合法性被质疑的证据应当被排除。

第三，提审通知书必须送交被提审人本人，由被提审人本人签收，以防止侦查机关和监管机关非法变通，侵害被提审人的合法权益。同时，必须保证被提审人在被提审之前会见律师和家属的权利，以保证其提审通知书等相关证据能够得到妥善保管。

第四，这一制度必须与公诉方对取证合法性承担举证责任以及全程录音录像等制度结合在一起，才能达到预期的目的。

第五，必须建立配套措施，包括但不限于进一步明确看守场所应建立无死角的全天 24 小时监控系统，对于被追诉人主张其在看

---

① “两高三部”《关于办理刑事案件严格排除非法证据若干问题的规定》第 9 条的规定在一定程度上反映了这一立法建议。该条规定：“拘留、逮捕犯罪嫌疑人后，应当按照法律规定送看守所羁押。犯罪嫌疑人被送交看守所羁押后，讯问应当在看守所讯问室进行。因客观原因侦查机关在看守所讯问室以外的场所进行讯问的，应当作出合理解释。”

② 刑事诉讼法第 85 条第 2 款规定：“拘留后，应当立即将被拘留人送看守所羁押，至迟不得超过二十四小时……”第 93 条第 2 款规定：“逮捕后，应当立即将被逮捕人送看守所羁押……”

守所期间被采取暴力等非法措施而此间的看守所相关监控录像材料缺失的情况，看守所负有举证证明被追诉人不可能于此期间在看守所受到非法对待的责任。否则，推定看守所对于被追诉人受到的伤害负有相关责任。此举的目的是防止看守所与侦查机关串通强行对被追诉人采取暴力等非法措施。这一措施极其重要，没有此项措施，仅仅通过律师在场是解决不了问题的，因为侦查机关可能会秘密地在不通知律师到场的情况下强制性地对被追诉人采取暴力等非法措施。

（四）中国创设提审通知被提审人制度的意义

（1）有利于防止变相刑讯逼供。由于控方举证证明取证合法性的困难与刑事诉讼惩罚犯罪价值目标的矛盾，法院可能在各种因素的影响下偏向于控诉一方，对重复供述不予排除。而如果不排除重复供述，侦查机关可能会大肆采取“先打后取证”的做法，从而造成事实上纵容变相刑讯逼供的问题。这一制度的创设有利于进一步明确控辩双方在口供取证合法性证明相关问题上各自应承担的相应责任，从而避免变相刑讯逼供问题的发生。

（2）倒逼侦查机关真正完全落实讯问全程录音录像制度。控诉方为了避免所提取的口供被推定为非法证据，证明取证的合法性，必然会积极进行全程录音录像，保留相关证据，客观上倒逼侦查机关真正完全落实讯问全程录音录像制度。实际上，公安部已于2014年9月5日印发关于《公安机关讯问犯罪嫌疑人录音录像工作规定》的通知（公通字〔2014〕33号），积极推进对所有刑事案件的讯问过程进行录音录像。该通知指出：“近年来，各地公安机关大力加强执法规范化建设，执法办案场所改造基本完成，为做好讯问犯罪嫌疑人录音录像工作提供了坚实的硬件条件。各级公安机关要在严格按照修改后的刑事诉讼法要求对重大案件进行讯问录音录像的同时，根据本地实际情况，逐步扩大讯问录音录像的案件范围，并抓紧建设数量充足、功能完善、设置规范的标准化讯问室，最终实现对所有刑事案件的讯问过程进行录音录像。东部地区和执法办案场所规范化建设基础较好的地区，要力争在2015年实现对全部刑事案件讯问过程录音录像的工作目标；中西部地区要进一步加强执法办案场所的规范设置和使用管理，力争在2016年实现上述目标；个别执法办案场所规范化建设基础薄弱的地区，要积极创造条件，加快工作进度，加大资金投入，力争在2017年实现上述目标。”

（3）由于不改变现有的领导体制，改革成本较小，更具有现实可行性。如果要通过其他措施来有效解决羁押期间口供的非法取证问题，必然会涉及现有领导体制的改革以及其他一系列问题，这是一项庞大的系统工程，包括转移看守所的位置等，改革成本巨大，缺乏现实可行性。而创设提审通知被提审人制度涉及的面则要小得多，抓住了问题的核心和症结所在，能够迅速见效、成本小、可操作性强，更具有现实可行性。

（4）有利于证明证据合法性，排除刑讯逼供的怀疑，特别是在反腐等一些政治敏感的案件中，有利于证明和彰显程序的公开、透明、合法，不给恶意诽谤我国依法反腐等司法行为为政治斗争的人留下可乘之机。

（5）有利于保证诉讼效率，兼顾司法的公正和效率。提审通知被提审人制度的创设当然是为了有效遏制刑讯逼供，保障人权，保证司法的公正和文明，但同时也是出于诉讼效率的考虑，是对诉讼公正和效率的兼顾。也许有人会说“既然规定审讯只能在看守所等固定场所进行，提审场所必须有24小时不间断无死角的监控并且只要被告人在法庭上提出非法取证的时间等线索，检察院就有义务对不存在被追诉方提出质疑的非法取证行为进行证明，那么，就没有必要规定这样一种通知制度，因为没有这样一种通知制度也照样可以达到预期目的”。但是，笔者认为，这只是一种理论上的考量，缺乏现实的可操作性。理由主要有以下两点：

第一，在实际操作中，如果没有这样一种实物的通知单，那么被追诉人可能会因刑讯逼供、非法取证等而无法准确回忆起非法取证的时间、地点等线索；而如果有这样一种实物的通知单，就不会出现这种问题。对于侦查人员未依法向被追诉人发放提审通知单而强行对被追诉人采取刑讯逼供等非法行为的，被追诉人有权拒绝、反抗，并且如果事后被追诉人或其代理人举证被追诉人受到了任何可能对其提供证据的自愿性产生影响的身体或者精神上的伤害，那么公诉机关有义务提供监控资料对被追诉人受到这一伤害的情况予以证明（包括该伤害是否由侦查机关、看守所或者其他主体造成等。在必要的情况下，可以将相关期限内完整的监控资料交由被追诉方，由被追诉方承担从中找出被追诉人被采取非法手段的证据，法庭可以此为线索对证据的合法性进行调查。为此，法院可要求主张口供获取非法性的当事人及其辩护人、诉讼代理人在庭前通过查阅监控资料来提供口供获取非法性的相关证据，公诉方有义务及时提供完整的限制人身自由期间的监控资料以配合该查阅行为。为了保证当事人及其辩护人、诉讼代理人有充分的时间查阅相关的监控资料，法院应在依法受理检察院所依法提起的公诉后，立即通知当事人及其辩护人、诉讼代理人这项专门的庭前查阅监控资料的权利，并通过综合考虑当事人及其辩护人、诉讼代理人查阅监控资料的时间需求等因素合理确定开庭审理的时间。同时，为了尽量保证庭审的顺利进行和连贯性，当事人及其辩护人、诉讼代理人有义务在庭前完成查阅监控资料，对于当事人及其辩护人、诉讼代理人在庭审中提出通过查阅监控资料来提供口供获取非法性相关证据的要求的，法院可根据实际情况作出是否准许的决定）。否则，如果公诉机关不提供监控资料对被追诉人受到这一伤害的情况予以证明，那么被追诉人提供的被怀疑非自愿提供的口供将被排除。

第二，全部播放相关期限内所有的监控资料太浪费时间，违背司法效率。如果被追诉人不能准确回忆被采取非法措施的时间、地点等线索，而要求控诉方提供所有监控资料予以证明的话，将可能极大地浪费时间，严重违背司法效率。而实行这样一种确保被审讯人持有标明审讯时间、地点等信息的实物通知书的通知制度，能够通过要求被告方出示提审通知书举证相关的审讯事实来大大增强对公诉方提供相关监控资料要求的明确性，避免盲目播放大量不必要的甚至所有的监控资料。

提审通知被提审人制度的创设关系到非法证据排除规则能否在司法实践中真正得到落实，关系到防止刑讯逼供能否实现，关系到无罪推定精神的彰显，关系到尊重和保障人权的宪法原则能否在司法实践中切实得到贯彻，关系到我国能否真正做到文明司法和公正司法，意义重大。尽快建立我国的提审通知被提审人制度，以促进我国审前讯问过程中刑讯逼供等非法取证问题得以从根本上解决势在必行。

四、提高侦查能力和技术水平，增强贯彻落实无罪推定的现实可能性

惩罚犯罪，保护集体人权固然是刑法和刑事诉讼法的重要职能，也是犯罪追诉机关的重要责任。然而，实现惩罚犯罪的责任并不意味着必然要采用刑讯等“程序捷径”，并不构成刑讯逼供、侵犯人权的正当理由。刑讯逼供、侵犯人权在很大程度上是侦查公诉能力和水平落后或者侦查公诉懈怠的结果或者借口，是一种替代性的解决方案。因此，必须将打击犯罪、保护集体人权与贯彻落实无罪推定二者统一起来。其关键就是进一步提高侦查能力和技术水平，减少对口供的依赖，真正做到文明司法，贯彻落实证据裁判主义，增强贯彻落实无罪推定的现实可能性。根据法国以前的刑事诉讼经验，如果过于看重和依赖口供，对于死刑案件中辩护律师的作用不予以重视，甚至将口供视为“证据之王”，那么犯罪嫌疑人则常常会被强迫证明自己无罪，否则将导致被定罪，尽管控诉方并未

对其罪行给出具有说服力的证明。[①] 因此，要真正贯彻落实无罪推定的精神和原则，就必须改变过于依赖口供的观念，转变办案思路和模式，更加重视口供以外证据的搜集能力，积极推动科技创新并及时引进先进科学技术为侦查所用，加强侦查人员业务培训，提高其侦查能力和素质。同时，真正重视和保障刑事案件特别是死刑案件中辩护律师的作用，充分发挥辩护律师保护犯罪嫌疑人、被告人无罪推定权利的作用。

五、澄清对无罪推定相关问题的认识误区

当前，对于无罪推定相关问题的认识误区主要有以下几点：一是对于我国刑事诉讼各阶段证明标准的统一性不理解，认为“案件事实清楚，证据确实充分”的标准对于侦查机关或者公诉机关来讲太高，甚至认为如果侦查机关或者公诉机关遵循的证明标准与审判机关一样，也是“案件事实清楚，证据确实充分”的话，那么就没有必要设置后面几道程序。二是对公检法三机关之间的职能关系，特别是对每个机关在整个刑事诉讼中的职能特点认识不清。三是对公检法三机关的属性认识不清，误将三机关笼统地视为“刀把子”。

根据我国刑事诉讼法之规定，我国刑事诉讼各阶段的证明标准具有统一性：我国当前刑事诉讼法规定的侦查机关移送审查起诉，公诉机关提起公诉和法院有罪判决的证明标准都是“案件事实清楚，证据确实充分”。只要各个机关自己确实认为达到了这一标准就应当依法将案件移送至下一诉讼阶段。即便下一诉讼阶段通过审查作出了否定前一诉讼阶段的审查结论，也并不能说明前一诉讼阶段的审查结论错误，后一诉讼阶段的审查结论正确。否则，如果理

① See Jean-Marie Carbasse, Histoire du droit penal et de la justice criminelle 167-8 (2000). cited in note 159 of Francois Quintard-Morénas, *The Presumption of Innocence in the French and Anglo-American Legal Traditions*, 58Am. J. Comp. L. 107, 123 (2010).

所当然地认为后一诉讼阶段的审查结论是正确的，那就没有必要设置多道审查程序，不如直接由法院最终一次性审查作出结论即可。只有前一诉讼阶段经过审查，确实认为“案件事实清楚，证据确实充分”，应当依法定罪的条件下，才应当依法将案件移送下一诉讼阶段进行审查是否仍旧认为符合“案件事实清楚，证据确实充分”的标准，应当依法定罪。诉讼程序之所以如此一道一道关口地审查，就是因为坚守民主的理念，相信通过公检法三机关之间的相互制衡能更好地实现准确认定案件事实、惩治犯罪，目的就是防止错误追究刑事责任。如果仅由一个机关进行审查，由一个机关说了算，那便会变成专断，被追诉人在刑事诉讼过程中的诉讼主体地位将无法得到保障，将沦为诉讼客体，无法充分行使申诉权，也违反对抗原则和民主精神。刑事诉讼程序如此多重审查并不等于后一诉讼阶段审查适用的标准严于前一诉讼阶段（这在我国没有法律根据），或者说后一诉讼阶段的审查结论比前一诉讼阶段的审查结论正确（可能后一诉讼阶段经审查后认为无罪的被追诉人实际上是有罪的）。这样做的目的是保障无辜的人不被追究刑事责任，保障人权，体现的是“宁纵勿枉”的价值判断和选择。

我国刑事诉讼侦控审各阶段之间是独立判断，递进审查的关系。亦即我国刑事诉讼各阶段在统一的证明标准之下，各自独立判断，后一阶段对前一阶段进行递进审查，最终由法院作出终局结论。虽然侦查和公诉阶段并不假定被追诉人有罪，只有法院才能依法认定被追诉人有罪，但是这只是在最终的法律认定意义上讲的，对于每个诉讼阶段来讲，都应当有该诉讼阶段自身的判断。这一判断不是法律的终局判断，但也是依法作出的阶段性的判断。否则，该诉讼阶段的诉讼机关就没有必要将案件移送下一诉讼阶段继续追究被追诉人的刑事责任。如果没有依法作出的这种阶段性的判断结论，那么将案件移送下一诉讼阶段继续追究被追诉人的刑事责任就失去了根据。后一诉讼阶段的判断不受前面诉讼阶段判断结论的影响强调的是每一诉讼阶段判断的独立性。每个诉讼阶段都应当独立判断，不应受到其他诉讼阶段的影响。不能以任一诉讼阶段的判断结论否定其他诉讼阶段结论与客观真实的相符性。但是，只有法院才能依法作出对于被追诉人是否有罪的终局的正式的法律上的判断。未经法院依法认定，任何人不得被在法律上正式地认定有罪。在被依法认定为有罪之前，任何人都有权被在法律上正式地假定为无罪。这与侦查和公诉阶段的有罪认定并不矛盾，因为侦查和公诉阶段的有罪认定是内部的、阶段性的认定，不具有公开的正式认定的性质。这是理解这一系列关系的关键，也是理解整个问题的症结和关键所在。虽然有权威部门对监察机关的性质进行了定位，指出监察机关是政治机关不是司法机关也不是行政机关。① 但是，监察机关在行使职务犯罪调查权时实际上就是在行使刑事案件侦查权，理应受到刑事诉讼法的规制。监察机关在行使侦查权时，其与检察机关和审判机关的关系也是而且应当是“独立判断，递进审查”的关系。如果将来出现这样的局面，监察机关调查的案件，检察院一律都批准逮捕、提起公诉，法院一律定罪且按监察机关意见来量刑，那监察体制改革反而是失败的，“以审判为中心的诉讼制度改革”也成为一句空话了。②

总体说来，刑事诉讼中各机关的职责是对案件进行重复审查（准确地说，是三重审查），而不是重复指控。审查起诉阶段的审查构成一个以审查起诉机关为顶点的小等腰三角形，审判阶段的审查构成一个以审判机关为顶点的大等腰三角形。坚持无罪推定的法

---

① 《积极探索实践　形成宝贵经验　国家监察体制改革试点取得实效——国家监察体制改革试点工作综述》，载新华网，http：//news. xinhuanet. com/politics/2017-11/05/c_ 1121908387. htm，最后访问时间：2017 年 11 月 25 日；《使党的主张成为国家意志》，载《中国纪检监察报》，http：//csr. mos. gov. cn/content/2017-07/17/content_51847. htm，最后访问时间：2017 年 11 月 25 日。

② 谭畅、郑可书、阚纯裕：《宪法、行政法、刑诉法三角度解读监察法草案 在法治轨道上，推进监察立法》（陈瑞华语），载《南方周末》2017 年 11 月 23 日，http：//www. infzm. com/content/130895？from = groupmessage&isappinstalled = 0，最后访问时间：2017 年 11 月 25 日。

庭和行使审查起诉职能的检察机关都应当将自身职责定位为对上一诉讼阶段移送案件的审查，而不是简单地与上一阶段诉讼机关一起和犯罪进行斗争。刑事诉讼法第 7 条规定："人民法院、人民检察院和公安机关进行刑事诉讼，应当分工负责，互相配合，互相制约，以保证准确有效地执行法律。"但在司法实践中，公检法三机关过于强调"互相配合"而忽视了"互相制约"，以致法院成为与检察院和公安机关协调一致打击犯罪的工具。这是对法院制约和监督国家追诉犯罪职能的扭曲和背叛。严格地讲，行使审判职能的审判机关不能被视为行使刑事追诉职能的追诉机关，因为它并不以追诉犯罪嫌疑人为己任，而是以审查检察机关刑事追诉的准确性、合法性和正当性，对罪与非罪、此罪与彼罪以及对犯罪的具体惩罚（量刑）问题作出权威结论，力求法律得到准确适用，实现公平正义为己任。一些人将公检法三机关笼统地称为"刀把子"，实际上是对审判机关和行使审查起诉职能的检察机关职能的一种误解。诚然，侦查机关和行使公诉职能时的检察机关以及执行审判机关生效裁决的机关①是"刀把子"，具有惩罚犯罪、保护人民的职能。但是，将行使审判职能时的法院以及行使审查起诉职能时的检察院也称为"刀把子"，就属于对这些机关的职能和属性认识不清。行使审判职能时的法院以及行使审查起诉职能时的检察院更主要的属性是公平正义，如果此时也将其称为"刀把子"，甚至要求其负有像"刀把子"一样专门打击犯罪的职能，则会使其存在失去意义，不如直接由其前一阶段决定结果。② 因此，笼统地将政法机关及其职

① 如监狱等，在我国目前的法院职能设置的情况下还包括法院中的执行局。

② 根据列宁在《国家与革命》一书中的阐释，马克思主义者认为，军队、警察和监狱是国家的暴力强制机关，是"刀把子"，但并没有讲审判机关（法庭）也是暴力强制机关（"刀把子"）（参见列宁:《国家与革命》第一章第 2 节"特殊的武装队伍，监狱等"，人民出版社 1960 年版，第 6-8 页）。在笔者看来，只有以执行为主要内容的权力（如执行权）以及行使这一权力的机关才是"刀把子"，而以判断为主要内容的权力（如审判权）以及行使这一权力的机关不能被称为"刀把子"。

能称为“刀把子”是对各个政法机关的职能和属性认识不清，不利于法院和检察院依法独立行使职权，特别是公正客观地行使具有“审查”性质的职权，不利于刑事诉讼各有关机关职能的有效运行。对此必须予以澄清，以改进我们的认识，促进我国法治科学、可持续发展。当然，澄清对政法机关“刀把子论”的认识误区，并不等于不重视我国政法机关的人民性。为保证我国政法机关的人民性，必须加强党对政法事业思想和组织上的领导（而不是具体业务上的指导），加强对政法干警的思想政治教育，加强政法机关的思想政治建设，保证我们的政法队伍既有过硬的法律知识和技能，又能保持为人民服务的本色。

结 论

作为一种思想，无罪推定广泛存在于世界上大多数法律制度中，可以讲无罪推定思想萌芽具有“多地起源”的特征。然而，“被证明有罪之前即无罪”的无罪推定格言则起源于13世纪晚期和14世纪早期的欧洲大陆，由罗马教会的红衣主教，一位法国人，教会法学家，约翰内斯·莫纳克斯（Johannes Monachus）首先提出。后经贝卡利亚等法学家的努力和法国《人权宣言》及美国《权利法案》等立法的影响，无罪推定思想广泛传播于全世界，无罪推定原则也成为现代刑事司法的一项基本准则。

从“推定”和“假定”的内涵来看，“无罪推定”准确地讲其实应当叫“无罪假定”。其不需要基础事实，直接以被追诉人无罪的假定作为认识的起点，其原因主要不在于被追诉人实际无罪的可能性有多大，而在于正义、自由、民主、人权等的价值判断和价值选择。无罪推定的适用范围不应仅限于刑事庭审之上，还应扩展适用于庭审之外的审前诉讼阶段，甚至是诉讼程序之外。无罪推定的核心和基本精神就是“任何人在未被依法证明并宣告有罪之前应被视为无罪”。然而，从不同的层次看，无罪推定又呈现出不同的内涵。无罪推定是一个具有多层次内涵的概念。它不仅是一种理念，也是一种制度，一项原则，还是一项权利。作为一种理念，无罪推定是一种思想观念，反映着人们对于刑事诉讼活动应具有某种价值的判断和选择。作为一种制度，无罪推定是一种体系的存在。它不仅包含了基本的原则，而且包含了一系列与之配套的原则、规则和权利，是由一系列原则、规则和权利构成的体系。作为一项原则，无罪推定是刑事诉讼活动普遍遵守的一项准则，是处理刑事诉讼活动中诸多问题的依据。作为一项权利，无罪推定是被追诉人一系列合法权益的保障，维护着当事人的尊严，不仅自身是人权的一部分，而且保障着人权的其他部分。

无罪推定在法学、伦理学、政治学、哲学、心理学和决策理论上都有确实的根据。在法律上，无罪推定有利于促使人们守法；在伦理上，无罪推定有利于促使人们向善；在政治上，无罪推定有利于社会稳定、政治廉洁；在哲学上，无罪推定有坚实的认识论基础和价值论基础；在心理学和决策理论上，无罪推定具有扎实的形而下学基础。如果一个人一旦被指控就将被假定为有罪，而作为个体来讲，证明自己无罪通常并不容易，有时会十分困难，甚至不可能，那么人们更多关心的便不再是能否证明自己无罪，而是自己是否被“抓捕”、被指控。如此一来，是否犯罪、是否遵纪守法便不再是最关键的问题，而是否被抓、被指控便成了关键的问题。这样，人们便不再有动力去遵纪守法，而是将主要精力放在如何去逃避法律的制裁上。刑法规范人们行为和引导人们守法的功能也将受到极大削弱。法律是最低的道德。法律引导人们守法的功能也在一定程度上是在道德上引导和促使人们向善。法律引导人们守法的功能被削弱，其促使人们向善的功能也将会消逝。无罪推定促使人向善的这一功能不仅适用于仅有少部分适格犯罪主体实际犯罪的情况，也适用于大部分适格犯罪主体实际犯罪的情况。例如，假使社会上有资格犯贪污贿赂罪的主体中大部分都触犯了贪污贿赂罪，并且在追诉贪污贿赂犯罪的刑事诉讼中实行有罪推定，任何适格犯罪主体一旦被指控就将被假定有罪，那么适格的贪污贿赂犯罪主体所关心的将主要不再是能否证明自己有罪或者无罪，而是自己是否会被抓到。由此导致的结果就是，这些适格的贪污贿赂犯罪主体将不再对自己是否从事了贪污贿赂犯罪行为特别在意，因为即便自己实际没有从事贪污贿赂犯罪行为，一旦被抓捕、被指控，由于其难以保证能证明自己无罪，因此也可能最终被认定为有罪而被惩罚。这样，潜在的贪污贿赂犯罪主体在从事贪污贿赂犯罪行为时将不再有所顾忌，其所关心和防范的是自己的罪行不被发现，自己不被抓捕、被指控。这导致刑法本来引导人们守法向善的功能消失至少是被大大削弱了。结果是越反越腐，越反，腐败的手段越隐蔽，对腐败犯罪的侦查和证明越困难。因此，无罪推定的确立和贯彻落实不仅对于有效反腐、政治清明具有重要意义，对于社会风尚的向善也具有重要的意义。无罪推定不仅有哲学、政治学上的基础，也有法学、伦理学、心理学以及决策理论上的基础；不仅有社会科学上的基础，也有自然科学上的基础；不仅有形而上学的基础，也有形而下学的基础。因此，无罪推定具有充分的根据与正当性，我们应当明确确立和加强无罪推定的理念、制度、原则和权利，促进司法文明的进步。

无罪推定是沉默权存在的原因，而沉默权具有反对强迫自证其罪、禁止酷刑和可在一定程度上防止冤假错案的重要意义。因此，无罪推定是沉默权的存在及实现其意义的源头：只有实行无罪推定，才能实现这一切。

在正当法律程序的语境下，无罪推定是正当法律程序的一部分，并且是部分其他正当法律程序的根据。正如无罪推定权利是人权的一部分，并且是部分其他人权的根据一样。正当法律程序和无罪推定既包含了权利的内容，也包含了义务的内容，在一定程度上都可以归属于制度的范畴；而无罪推定权利和人权属于权利的范畴，是在权利的层面上探讨问题。

无罪推定与证据裁判原则的联系点主要在于无罪推定的证据规则维度与证据裁判原则的密切关联。二者的相同点在于都需要运用证据进行证明，即无罪推定在证据规则维度上遵循证据裁判原则。二者的区别则在于无罪推定在证据规则维度上规定了明确的证明内容，即要证明有罪，而证据裁判原则却没有这样的明确内容，仅是强调认定案件事实的依据（证据）。二者的另一个区别在于虽然无罪推定在证据规则维度上遵循证据裁判原则的要求，但又允许存在特定的例外。坚持证据裁判原则有利于减少对口供的依赖，进而有利于减少刑讯逼供等强迫自证其罪的现象，有利于保障被追诉人的沉默权，有利于贯彻无罪推定。

虽然目前我国在无罪推定精神的彰显方面取得了一定的成就，但是还面临着许多问题。中国还未在法律上正式规定无罪推定原则，也未明确规定适用联合国国际刑事司法准则中的无罪推定。为了促进无罪推定精神在中国的进一步彰显，有必要尽快在宪法和刑事诉讼法中明确确立无罪推定原则，在监察法中体现无罪推定精神，甚至在民法典中设立无罪推定权，至少应当明确允许适用联合国国际刑事司法准则中的无罪推定；同时，处理好无罪推定与反恐、反腐、禁毒等例外之间的关系；积极创设提审通知被提审人制度以促进从根本上解决我国审前讯问过程中刑讯逼供等非法取证问题；提高侦查能力和技术水平，增强贯彻落实无罪推定的现实可能性；阐明我国刑事诉讼各阶段证明标准的统一性，刑事诉讼侦控审各阶段“独立判断，递进审查”的理论，并对政法机关“刀把子论”的认识误区进行澄清。

参考文献

（按拼音字母排序）

一、中文文献

（一）著作

1. ［爱尔兰］J. M. 凯利：《西方法律思想简史》，王笑红译，法律出版社 2002 年版。

2. 班固：《汉书·刑法志》。

3. 班固：《汉书·于定国传》。

4. 陈光中：《刑事诉讼法学五十年》，警官教育出版社 1999 年版。

5. 陈光中主编：《刑事诉讼法》（第五版），北京大学出版社、高等教育出版社 2014 年版。

6. 陈光中主编：《中华人民共和国刑事诉讼法——再修改专家建议稿与论证》，中国法制出版社 2006 年版。

7. 陈瑞华：《比较刑事诉讼法》，中国人民大学出版社 2010 年版。

8. 陈瑞华：《刑事审判原理论》，北京大学出版社 1997 年版。

9. 陈瑞华、田文昌：《〈中华人民共和国刑事诉讼法〉再修改律师建议稿与论证》，法律出版社 2007 年版。

10. 陈卫东主编：《模范刑事诉讼法典》（第二版），中国人民大学出版社 2011 年版。

11. 《法国刑事诉讼法典》，罗结珍译，中国法制出版社 2006

年版。

12.《德国刑事诉讼法典》，李昌珂译，中国政法大学出版社1995年版。

13.［德］黑格尔：《法哲学原理》，柏林，1821年。

14.［德］黑格尔：《美学》（第一卷），朱光潜译，商务印书馆1979年版。

15.［德］卡尔·拉伦茨：《法学方法论》，陈爱娥译，商务印书馆2003年版。

16.［德］康德：《道德形而上学原理》，苗力田译，上海人民出版社1986年版。

17.［德］莱奥·罗森贝克：《证明责任论》，庄敬华译，中国法制出版社2002年版。

18. 樊崇义：《沉默权与我国的刑事政策》，中国人民公安大学出版社2002年版。

19. 樊崇义、王建明主编：《〈联合国反腐败公约〉与我国职务犯罪侦查研究》，中国方正出版社2011年版。

20. 房玄龄等：《晋书·王湛传附王坦之传》。

21. 高鸿钧：《伊斯兰法：传统与现代化》，清华大学出版社2004年版。

22. 胡康生、李福成主编：《中华人民共和国刑事诉讼法释义》，全国人大常委会法制工作委员会刑法室编著，法律出版社1996年版。

23. 贾谊：《新书》卷四，文渊阁四库全书本，卷695，上海古籍出版社2003年版。

24. 江伟主编：《证据法学》，中国人民大学出版社2000年版。

25. 姜田龙：《无罪推定论》，中国检察出版社2014年版。

26. 李学灯：《证据法比较研究》，台北五南图书出版公司1992年版。

27. 刘向：《新序·杂事第四》，湖北人民出版社1986年版。

28.《马克思主义哲学》编写组：《马克思主义哲学》，高等教育出版社 2009 年版。

29. ［美］爱伦·豪切斯泰勒·斯黛丽、南希·弗兰克：《美国刑事法院诉讼程序》，陈卫东、徐美君译，中国人民大学出版社 2002 年版。

30. ［美］E. 博登海默：《法理学——法律哲学与法律方法》，邓正来译，中国政法大学出版社 1999 年版。

31. ［美］卡尔维因、帕尔德森：《美国宪法释义》，徐卫东、吴新平译，华夏出版社 1989 年版。

32. ［美］摩根：《证据法之基本问题》，李学灯译，台湾世界书局 1960 年版。

33. ［美］乔恩·R. 华尔兹：《刑事证据大全》（第二版），何家弘等译，中国人民公安大学出版社 2004 年版。

34. ［美］约翰·罗尔斯：《正义论》（修订版），何怀宏等译，中国社会科学出版社 2009 年版。

35. ［美］约翰·V. 奥尔特：《正当法律程序简史》，杨明成、陈霜玲译，商务印书馆 2006 年版。

36. ［美］约书亚·德雷斯勒：《美国刑事诉讼法精解》（第 2 卷），魏晓娜译，北京大学出版社 2009 年版。

37. 彭伶：《不得强迫自证其罪原则研究》，中国政法大学出版社 2007 年版。

38. ［日］松尾浩也：《日本刑事诉讼法》（下卷），宋英辉译，中国人民大学出版社 2005 年版。

39. ［日］田口守一：《刑事诉讼法》，张凌等译，中国政法大学出版社 2010 年版。

40. ［日］土本武司：《日本刑事诉讼法要义》，董璠舆、宋英辉译，台北五南图书出版公司 1994 年版。

41. 宋英辉主编：《刑事诉讼原理》，法律出版社 2003 年版。

42. 宋英辉主编：《刑事诉讼原则》，法律出版社 2010 年版。

43. ［苏］列宁：《国家与革命》，人民出版社1960年版。

44. 孙长永：《探索正当程序——比较刑事诉讼法专论》，中国法制出版社2005年版。

45. 伍廷芳著，丁贤俊、喻作凤编：《伍廷芳集》，中华书局1993年版。

46. 武延平等编：《刑事诉讼法学参考资料汇编》，北京大学出版社2005年版。

47. 巫宇甦主编：《证据学》，群众出版社1983年版。

48. 熊元襄：《刑事诉讼法》，安徽法学社1911年刊印。

49. 薛波：《元照英美法词典》，法律出版社2003年版。

50. 《学说汇纂》（第48卷·罗马刑事法），薛军译，中国政法大学出版社2005年版。

51. 杨寅：《中国行政程序法治化》，中国政法大学出版社2001年版。

52. 易延友：《沉默的自由》，中国政法大学出版社2001年版。

53. ［英］戴维·M.沃克编：《牛津法律大词典》，北京社会与科技发展研究所组织翻译，光明日报出版社1988年版。

54. ［英］丹宁勋爵：《法律的正当程序》，李克强、杨百揆、刘庸安译，法律出版社1999年版。

55. ［英］亨利·萨姆奈·梅因：《古代法》，高敏、瞿慧虹译，中国社会科学出版社2009年版。

56. 尤志安：《清末司法改革研究》，中国人民公安大学出版社2004年版。

57. 张礼恒：《从西方到东方——伍廷芳与中国近代社会的演进》，商务印书馆2002年版。

58. 张千帆：《西方宪政体系》（上册·美国宪法），中国政法大学出版社2000年版。

59. 张小海：《无罪推定权利论》，中国民主法制出版社2015年版。

60. 郑旭:《非法证据排除规则》, 中国法制出版社 2009 年版。

61. 周辅成:《从文艺复兴到 19 世纪资产阶级哲学家、政治思想家有关人道主义人性论言论选辑》, 商务印书馆 1996 年版

62. 左丘明:《左传》, 蒋冀骋点校, 岳麓书社 2006 年版。

(二) 论文期刊

1. 白冬:《如实回答与沉默权的功能主义分析与文化解释》, 载《法学杂志》2012 年第 2 期。

2. 陈光中:《苏联的辩护制度》, 载《政法研究》1955 年第 2 期。

3. 陈光中:《应当批判地继承无罪推定原则》, 载《法学研究》1980 年第 4 期。

4. 陈光中:《中国刑事诉讼法学 40 年(下)》, 载《政法论坛》1989 年第 5 期。

5. 陈光中等:《诉讼真实与证明标准改革》, 载《政法论坛》2009 年第 2 期。

6. 陈光中、邵俊:《我国监察体制改革若干问题思考》, 载《中国法学》2017 年第 4 期。

7. 陈光中、张佳华、肖沛权:《论无罪推定原则及其在中国的适用》, 载《法学杂志》2013 年第 10 期。

8. 陈光中、张建伟:《联合国〈公民权利和政治权利国际公约〉与我国刑事诉讼》, 载《中国法学》1998 年第 6 期。

9. 陈光中、郑曦:《论刑事诉讼中的证据裁判原则——兼谈〈刑事诉讼法〉修改中的若干问题》, 载《法学》2011 年第 9 期。

10. 傅达林:《反恐中的秩序与自由》, 载《检察日报》2014 年 7 月 2 日第 7 版。

11. 高贵君、王勇、吴光霞:《〈全国部分法院审理毒品犯罪案件工作座谈会纪要〉的理解与适用》, 载《人民司法·应用》2009 年第 3 期。

12. 何家弘:《论推定概念的界定标准》, 载《法学》2008 年

第10期。

13. 贺平凡：《论刑事推定规则》，载《政治与法律》2003年第2期。

14. 胡治洪：《〈尚书〉真伪问题之由来与重辨》，载《江苏师范大学学报》（哲学社会科学版）2014年第1期。

15. 黄道：《略论刑事诉讼中的无罪推定原则》，载《法学》1957年第2期。

16. 黄道、铁犁：《无罪推定在新中国的命运》，载《法学》1997年第7期。

17. 黄维智：《刑事证明责任分配的三项基本原则》，载《社会科学》2007年第3期。

18. 《加强社会主义法制的有力措施——刘复之同志答（法律与生活）记者问》，载《中国法制报》1984年1月20日。

19. 蒋铁初：《中国古代的罪疑惟轻》，载《法学研究》2010年第2期。

20. 蓝全普：《无罪推定原则有利于正确执行刑事诉讼法》，载《民主与法制》1979年第4期。

21. 李奋飞：《庭审布局：于细微处见法治》，载《检察日报》2014年7月2日第7版。

22. 李光灿、李剑飞：《肃清反人民的旧法观点》，载《人民日报》1952年8月22日第3版。

23. 李玉华：《刑事诉讼证明中事实推定之运用》，载《现代法学》2005年第3期。

24. 林欣：《"无罪推定"还是"无罪假定"?》，载《中国社会科学》1983年第3期。

25. 刘东亮：《什么是正当法律程序》，载《中国法学》2010年第4期。

26. 刘根菊：《在我国确定沉默权原则几个问题之研讨（上）》，载《中国法学》2000年第2期。

27. 刘欢、梁竹苑、李纾：《行为经济学中的损失规避》，载《心理科学进展》2009 年第 4 期。

28. 刘庆林：《怎样对待刑事案件的被告人》，载《法学研究》1956 年第 3 期。

29. 龙宗智：《两个证据规定的规范与执行若干问题研究》，载《中国法学》2010 年第 6 期。

30. 龙宗智：《推定的界限及适用》，载《法学研究》2008 年第 1 期。

31. 龙宗智：《我国非法口供排除的“痛苦规则”及相关问题》，载《政法论坛》2013 年第 5 期。

32. 罗荣：《试论刑事诉讼中的被告人》，载《法学》1957 年第 2 期。

33. 梅芳、尚进：《论刑事沉默权的诉讼价值及缺陷》，载《当代法学》1999 年第 5 期。

34. 宁汉林：《论无罪推定》，载《中国社会科学》1982 年第 4 期。

35. 裴苍龄：《论无罪推定》，载《河北法学》2015 年第 1 期。

36. 裴苍龄：《再论推定》，载《法学研究》2006 年第 3 期。

37. 曲夫：《略谈刑事诉讼中被告人的诉讼地位》，载《法学研究》1957 年第 3 期。

38. 沈德咏：《论疑罪从无》，载《中国法学》2013 年第 5 期。

39. 田采：《一个值得研究的问题》，载《人民日报》1979 年 2 月 17 日。

40. 万选才、肖秀敏：《论推定规则在刑事审判中的运用——兼论我国刑事立法确立推定规则的必要性》，载《法学家》2001 年第 5 期。

41. 万毅：《论“反复自白”的效力》，载《四川大学学报》（哲学社会科学版）2011 年第 5 期。

42. 王秉新、赵虹：《论无罪推定中的几个问题》，载《未定稿》1983 年第 21 期。

43.《王汉斌答新华社记者问——就有关审判林江反革命集团案的几个法律问题》，载《人民日报》1980 年 12 月 12 日。

44. 王明高、曾志雄：《论贿赂推定》，载《湖湘论坛》2008 年第 2 期。

45. 王学棉：《论推定的逻辑学基础——兼论推定与拟制的关系》，载《政法论坛》2004 年第 1 期。

46. 文玮：《论无罪推定原则》，载《南华大学学报》（社会科学版）2003 年第 4 期。

47. 吴磊：《关于我国刑事诉讼中辩护人诉讼地位的研究》，载《法学研究》1957 年第 4 期。

48. 晓华：《"无罪推定"原则与我国刑事诉讼实践格格不入》，载《法学研究》1980 年第 1 期。

49. 肖中华、张少林：《刑事推定与犯罪认定刍议》，载《法学家》2002 年第 3 期。

50. 徐灿：《论腐败案件中明知的推定规则在中国的确立》，载《澳门法学》2015 年第 14 期。

51. 杨宇冠：《论不强迫自证其罪原则》，载《中国法学》2003 年第 1 期。

52. 杨宇冠：《论构建我国刑事诉讼的正当法律程序体系》，载《杭州师范学院学报》（社会科学版）2004 年第 5 期。

53. 杨兆龙：《法律的阶级性和继承性》，载《法学》1956 年第 3 期。

54. 易延友：《沉默的自由（一）》，载《中国律师》2000 年第 1 期。

55. 易延友：《论无罪推定的涵义与刑事诉讼法的完善》，载《政法论坛》2012 年第 1 期。

56. 于志：《无罪推定不能作刑事诉讼的指导思想》，载《民主与法制》1980 年第 3 期。

57. 曾辉林：《简论沉默权对完善我国刑事诉讼制度的意义》，载《人民司法》1999 年第 6 期。

58. 张成敏：《20 世纪 50 年代的无罪推定学术观点》，载《政法论丛》2010 年第 1 期。

59. 张颖：《重复自白的证据能力》，载《中国刑事法杂志》2012 年第 7 期。

60. 张子培：《“无罪推定”原则剖析》，载《法学研究》1980 年第 3 期。

61. 张子培：《评“无罪推定”》，载《中国政法大学学报》1983 年第 4 期。

62. 赵秉志：《中国反腐败刑事法治的若干重大现实问题研究》，载《法学评论》（双月刊）2014 年第 3 期。

63. 赵钢、刘海峰：《试论证据法上的推定》，载《法律科学》1998 年第 1 期。

64. 赵虹、窦继梓：《对“无罪推定”原则的理解》，载《法学研究》1979 年第 3 期。

65. 周国均：《拒绝强迫自证其罪与沉默权》，载《法制日报》1999 年 1 月 2 日第 7 版。

66. 庄惠辰：《刑事诉讼中审判与侦查起诉的关系问题》，载《法学研究》1957 年第 3 期。

（三）论文集

1. 陈光中：《非法证据排除规则实施问题调研报告》，载陈光中主编：《非法证据排除规则实施问题研究》，北京大学出版社 2014 年版。

2. 陆锦碧、铁犁：《建国初期司法改革的得失》，载郭道晖等主编：《中国当代法学争鸣实录》，湖南人民出版社 1998 年版。

3. ［美］巴巴拉·J. 夏皮罗：《对英美“排除合理怀疑”之历史透视》，熊秋红译，载王敏远主编：《公法》（第 4 卷），法律出版社 2003 年版。

4. 叶自强：《论推定法则》，载陈光中、江伟主编：《诉讼法论丛》（第2卷），法律出版社1998年版。

5. 中国政法大学刑事法律研究中心：《英国刑事诉讼制度的新发展》，载陈光中、江伟主编：《诉讼法论丛》（第2卷），法律出版社1998年版。

（四）学位论文

1. 程远：《无罪推定原则在我国的命运》，南京师范大学2007年硕士学位论文。

2. 贺志军：《论明知的推定》，湖南师范大学2003年硕士学位论文。

3. 李振林：《刑法中法律拟制论》，华东政法大学2013年博士学位论文。

4. 隋钰南：《拟制问题研究》，苏州大学2012年硕士学位论文。

5. 奚丹霓：《论无罪推定》，中国政法大学2013年博士学位论文。

6. 张华：《无罪推定原则的历史演进》，中国人民大学2008年博士学位论文。

7. 张云鹏：《刑事推定论》，吉林大学2007年博士学位论文。

8. 赵俊甫：《刑事推定研究》，吉林大学2008年博士学位论文。

（五）网址及其他

1. 《2017年末我国农村贫困人口减少到3046万人》，载新华网，http://www.xinhuanet.com/politics/2018-02/01/c_1122353906.htm.

2. 《2019年国务院政府工作报告》，http://news.sina.com.cn/c/xl/2019-03-05/doc-ihsxncvf9915493.shtml.

3. 百度百科“汉谟拉比法典”词条，http://baike.baidu.com/link? url=bozlpinrrryksnr58kvdo6-saex5vwycqwic6zqptoqjq9s8azl5psjqwizbu12swrjpuzgdmlnm2mbqdlszjk.

4. 百度百科“加拿大宪法”词条，http：//baike. baidu. com/link？url=cqv_ woujxpfbdsu5o3ulhznrvkgukex4h7ezqn-d-yjbimkh5iotjgqptczfmy7zxnbcbufqvraotclrhj4gq.

5. 百度百科“印度法系”词条，http://baike.baidu.com/view/801311.htm.

6. 百度文库“世界主要法律体系 第七讲印度法系”，http://wenku.baidu.com/link？url=dr03qvomakmds29q_hzxljdzsyonqmrmiblpv-ijrbu9inmew_d11pm4nugpzlcinjnv5r5wtym6e73ksemthmihrvdx8q0wvnja72ggzss.

7. 陈光中：《〈监察法〉的立法工作不能急于求成》，http://mp.weixin.qq.com/s/vbas9z5mnqv3irpqvicc8a.

8. 《办理毒品犯罪案件适用法律若干问题的意见》。

9. 陈光中：《制定〈监察法〉应贯彻人权保障原则》，http://china. caixin. com/2017-08-17/101131939. html.

10. 陈瑞华：《当监察法与刑诉法关系遭遇困境》，http://www. sohu. com/a/206189302_650721.

11. Dieter Grimm：《如何建成实质的法治国》，http://news.ifeng.com/exclusive/lecture/special/grimm/#_www_dt2.

12. 非洲人权和人民权利委员会：http://www. achpr. org/.

13. 《服刑犯“发生关系”视频果然丢了》，http://view.news.qq.com/a/20150125/007275.htm.

14. 《改变庭审布局有利于维护辩护权利》，http://sichuan.hexun.com/2015-05-07/175588672.html.

15. 古埃及国王托勒密八世于公元前118年4月28日颁布的法令，http://www. app. cc. columbia. edu/ldpd/app/apis/item？mode=item&key=berkeley. apis. 263.

16. 国际刑事法院英文网站：http://www. icc-cpi. int/Menus/ICC？lan=en-GB.

17. 《积极探索实践　形成宝贵经验　国家监察体制改革试点

取得实效——国家监察体制改革试点工作综述》，载新华网，http://news.xinhuanet.com/politics/2017-11/05/c_1121908387.htm.

18. 李蒙：《为什么这么多冤案能够平反？——〈平反冤案这三年〉系列报道之二》，http://blog.sina.com.cn/s/blog_5ff29ca40102w0rr.html.

19. 联合国：http://www.un.org.

20. 联合国人权事务高级专员办事处（人权高专办）：http://www.ohchr.org.

21. 联合国条约汇总：http://www.un.org/chinese/documents/decl-con/chroncon.htm.

22. 联合国文件中心：http://www.un.org/zh/documents.

23. 联合国正式文件系统中文版（ODS）：http://www.ods.un.org/ods/.

24. 美国法律、判例发布网站：http://law.justia.com/.

25. 美洲人权委员会：http://www.cidh.org/DefaultE.htm.

26. 《〈民主与法制〉杂志社记者李蒙的〈平反冤案这三年〉专题系列报道》，http://blog.sina.com.cn/s/blog_5ff29ca40102w0pd.html，http://blog.sina.com.cn/s/blog_5ff29ca40102w0rr.html 等。

27. 欧洲理事会：http://www.coe.int.

28. 欧洲人权法院英文网站：http://www.echr.coe.int/ECHR/Homepage_En/.

29. 《全国部分法院审理毒品犯罪案件工作座谈会纪要》（大连会议纪要）。

30. 《全国人大常委会法律草案征求意见》，载中国人大网，http://www.npc.gov.cn/npc/flcazqyj/node_8176.htm.

31. 《人大代表呼吁批准实施〈公民权利和政治权利国际公约〉》，http://www.mala.cn/thread-13378056-1-8.html.

32. 《尚书·虞书·大禹谟》，http://so.gushiwen.org/guwen/bookv_3083.aspx.

33.《深改丨两高三部：关于推进以审判为中心的刑事诉讼制度改革的意见》，http://dy.163.com/v2/article/t1397720048954/btg4ae580521007n.

34.《十八大后纠正23起冤假错案　疑罪从无不再停留纸面》，http://www.chinanews.com/gn/2014/12-17/6883197.shtml.

35.《使党的主张成为国家意志》，http://csr.mos.gov.cn/content/2017-07/17/content_51847.htm.

36. 斯坦福哲学百科全书（Stanford Encyclopedia of Philosophy）：http://plato.stanford.edu/entries/civil-rights/.

37. 搜狗百科“不可知论”词条，http://baike.sogou.com/v1168190.htm?ch=ch.bk.innerlink.

38.《苏维埃社会主义共和国联盟宪法》，http://www.cccpism.com/book/lilun/1977fa.htm.

39.《孙善武：希望在秦城监狱问周永康 为何把我打成贪官》，http://finance.ifeng.com/a/20150313/13551917_0.shtml.

40. 吴尧：《陈光中：监察制度改革不能忽视程序法治》，http://news.caijingmobile.com/article/detail/327138?source_id=40.

41. 英国法律发布网站：http://www.legislation.gov.uk.

42. 赵红旗：《河南高院推进庭审布局改革》，http://www.law-lib.com/fzdt/newshtml/yjdt/20131211161819.htm.

43. 赵晓阳：《传教士与中国国学的翻译——以〈四书〉〈五经〉为中心》，载《近代中国研究》，2005年，http://jds.cass.cn/Item/433.aspx.

44.《浙江法院改变刑案庭审格局　被告人将与律师同桌》，http://news.xinhuanet.com/legal/2015-05/07/c_127772690.htm.

45. 中国人大网：http://www.npc.gov.cn/.

46.《中华人民共和国监察法（草案）面向社会征求意见（2017年6月第十二届全国人大常委会第二十八次会议审议稿）》，http://www.ccdi.gov.cn/xwtt/201711/t20171107_111288.html.

47.《中华人民共和国监察法》，载中国人大网，http://www.npc.gov.cn/npc/xinwen/2018-03/21/content_2052362.htm? from=timeline&isappinstalled=0.

48.《最高法院发布司法改革白皮书：十八大以来纠正重大刑事冤假错案34起》，http://www.legaldaily.com.cn/zfzz/content/2017-02/28/content_7031724.htm? node=81122.

49.《最高法院：以威胁方法收集的口供应予排除，后续的“重复供述”可视情况排除》，http://mp.weixin.qq.com/s/skkoar3i_p9qagtfj1fuea.

50.《最高人民法院关于全面推进以审判为中心的刑事诉讼制度改革的实施意见》，http://www.court.gov.cn/zixun-xiangqing-36422.html.

51.《最高人民法院决定依法再审聂树斌故意杀人、强奸妇女一案》，http://www.court.gov.cn/fabu-xiangqing-21751.html.

52.《法国民法典》。

53. 中共中央马克思恩格斯列宁斯大林著作编译局：《马克思恩格斯全集》(第6卷)。

54. 中共中央马克思恩格斯列宁斯大林著作编译局：《马克思恩格斯全集》(第8卷)。

55. 中共中央马克思恩格斯列宁斯大林著作编译局：《马克思恩格斯全集》(第1卷·上册)(第二版)。

56.《牛津高阶英汉双解词典》(缩印本)，商务印书馆、牛津大学出版社2014年版。

57.《申命记》。

58.《世界各国宪法》，中国检察出版社2012年版。

59.《中华人民共和国刑事诉讼法》。

60.《最高人民法院关于民事诉讼证据的若干规定》。

61.《最高人民法院关于行政诉讼证据若干问题的规定》。

二、外文文献

(一) 著作

1. Abraham Fraunce, The Lawiers Logike, Exemplifying The Praecepts of Logike by the Practise of the Common Lawe (London, 1588).

2. Adhemar Esmein, A History of Continental Criminal Procedure With Special Reference to France (John Simpson trans., Augustus M. Kelley Publ. 1968) (1913).

3. Albert Desjardins, Les cahiers des Etats Generaux en 1789 et la legislation criminelle XXIX (Paris, 1883).

4. Antoine Astaing, Droits et garanties de l´accuse dans le proces criminel d´Ancien Regime XVIe et XVIIIe siecles: Audace et pusillanimite de la doctrine penale francaise (1999).

5. Antoine Bruneau, Observations Et Maxims Sur Les Matieres Criminelles (Paris, 1715).

6. Augustin Nicolas, Si la Torture est un moyen seur a verifier les crimes secrets (Amsterdam, 1682).

7. 2Bracton, on the Laws and Customs of England (Cambridge, Harvard University Press 1968).

8. 1Capitularia regum Francorum (Paris, 1780).

9. Charles Eleonor Dufriche de Valaze, Loix penales, dediees a Monsieur, frere du Roi (Alencon, 1784).

10. Charles H. Whitebread & Christopher Slobogin, Criminal Procedure: An Analysis of Cases and Concepts (5th Edition, Foundation Press, 75th Anniversary, University Textbook Series).

11. Chen Jianfu, Chinese Law: Context and Transformation (Martinus Nihoff Publishers, 2008).

12. Christopher Osakwe, "The Bill of Rights for the Criminal Defendant in American Law" in Human Rights in Criminal Procedure

(Martinus Nihoff Publishers, 1982).

13. Clyde Pharr, The Theodosian Code and novels, and the Sirmondian Constitutions: A Translation with Commentary, Glossary, And Bibliography (Princeton: Princeton University Press 1952).

14. Daines Barrington, Observations on the Statutes Chiefly The More Ancient, from Magna Charta to the Twenty-First of James The First (London, 1766).

15. 1 Daniel Jousse, Traite de la justice criminelle en France (Paris, 1771).

16. 3 Daniel Jousse, Traite de la justice criminelle en France (Paris, 1771).

17. 3 David Houard, Dictionnaire analytique, historique, etymologique, critique et interpretatif de la Coutume de Normandie (Rouen, 1781).

18. De Laudibuslegume Angliae (1st edn 1545-6).

19. Decretales D. Gregoriipapae IX: Suae Integritati Und Cum Glossis Restituae: Ad Exemplar Romanum Diligenter Recognitae (Lyon, 1584).

20. Demosthenes, Against Meidias, Androtion, Aristocrates, Timocrates, Aristogeiton (J. H. Vince trans., Harvard University Press 1935).

21. 2Dictionnaire de Jurisprudence et des Arrets, ou Nouvelle Edition du Dictionnaire de Brillon (Lyon, 1772).

22. Edmund M. Morgan, Basic Problems Of Evidence (September, 1962) (Philadelphia: Joint Committee on Continuing Legal Education of the American Law Institute and the American Bar Association, 1963).

23. Erwin Chemerinsky, Laurie L. Levenson, Criminal Procedure: Investigation (2nd Edition).

24. Eugene Blum, La declaration des droits de l´homme et du ci-

toyen: texte avec commentaires (1902).

25. Eyal Zamir & Barak Medina, Law, Economics, and Morality (2010).

26. Eyal Zamir, Law, Psychology, and Morality: The Role of Loss Aversion (Oxford: Oxford University Press, 2015).

27. F. Liebermann, Die Gesetze der Angelsachsen (Berlin 1903).

28. Fortescue, De Laudibus (circa 1468-71).

29. Geoffrey Gilbert, The Law of Evidence (London, 1756).

30. George Herbert, Outlandish Proverbs (London, 1640).

31. Glanville Williams, The Proof of Guilt (London: Stevens, 3rd edn. 1963).

32. Hegel, Philosophy of Right.

33. Hyacinthe de Boniface, 1Arrests notables de la Courde Parlementde Provence, Cour des Comptes, Aydes & Finances du mesme Pays (Paris, 1670).

34. Immanuel Kant, Critique of Practical Reason, translated and edited by Mary Gregor (Cambridge University Press, Revised Edition, 2015).

35. Immanuel Kant, The Metaphysical Elements of Justice, translated by John Ladd (The Bobbs-Merrill Company, Inc., 1965).

36. J. H. Wigmore, A Treatise on the Anglo-American System of Evidence in Trials at Common Law, Vol. 8 (Boston: Little, Brown, 3rd edn, 1940).

37. James A. Brundage, Medieval Canon Law (London - New York: 1995).

38. James Bradley Thayer, A Preliminary Treatise on Evidence at the Common Law (Little Brown, 1898).

39. Jean-Baptiste Janety, Journal du Palais de Provence, ou Recueil des Arrets rendus depuis les derniers Journalistes, par le Parlement

& la Cour des Aides de cette Province. Annees 1775, 1776, 1777 & 1778, at 161 (Aix, 1785).

40. Jean Boutiller, Somme rural, ou, Le grand coustumier general de practique civil et canon (Paris, 1603).

41. Jean-Marie Carbasse, Histoire du droit penal et de la justice criminelle (2000).

42. Jean Papon, Recveil d' arrestz notables des covrs sovveraines de France (Lyon, 3d ed. 1559).

43. Johannes Monachus, Gloss on Pope Boniface VIII's Decretal Rem non novam (1303) (ca. 1310).

44. John Almon, A Letter to the Right Hon. George Grenville (London, 1763).

45. John Bigelow, II The Works of Benjamin Franklin (ed., fed. Ed., 1904).

46. John D. Jackson and Sarah J. Summers, The Internationalisation of Criminal Evidence: Beyond the Common Law and Civil Law Traditions (Cambridge University Press, 2012).

47. John H. Langbein, Torture and the Law of Proof: Europe and England in the Ancient Regime (1977).

48. John Kaplan, Robert Weisberg & Guyora Binder, Criminal Law: Cases and Materials (Wolters Kluwer Law & Business, 7th Edition, 2012).

49. Jourdan, Decrusy, Isambert, 7 Recueil general des anciennes lois francaises depuis l' an 420 jusqu' a la revolution de 1789 par MM (Paris, 1822).

50. Kant's Groundwork of the Metaphysic of Morals, translated by H. J. Paton as The Moral Law (Hutchinson University Library, London, 1966).

51. Karl R. Popper, The Open Society and Its Enemies, Volume I

(Princeton: Princeton University Press, 5th rev. ed. 1966).

52. Kenneth Pennington, The Prince and the Law, 1200-1600: Sovereignty and Rights in the Western Legal Tradition (1993).

53. Kenneth S. Broun, 2 McCormick on Evidence ([St. Paul, Minn.]: Thomson Reuters, 2013, Seventh Edition).

54. Larry Laudan, Truth, Error and Criminal Law: An Essay in Legal Epistemology (Cambridge, CUP, 2006).

55. Laurent Jovet, La bibliotheque des arrests de tous les parlemens de France.

56. Leonard MacNally, The Rules of Evidence on Pleas of the Crown (London-Dublin: 1802).

57. Louis Charondas le Caron, Memorables, ov observations dv droict Francois rapporte av romain civil et canonic (Paris, 1601).

58. Louis Lassere, L' art de proceder en Justice, ou La science des regles judiciaires, pour decouvrir la Verite, tant en matiere Civile, que Criminelle (Paris, 2d ed. 1680).

59. Ludovic Kennedy, 10Rillington Place (Grafton, 1971 [1961]).

60. Matthew Hale, Pleas of the Crown, or A Brief but Full Account of Whatsoever Can Be Found Relating to that Subject (1678).

61. Michael H. Graham, Federal Rules of Evidence in a Nutshell (2nd ed. 1987).

62. Mohammed - Jalal Essaid, La presomption d' innocence (1971).

63. Moore, Placing Blame (OUP, 1997).

64. Nigel Walker, Why Punish? (Oxford University Press, 1991).

65. P. Levy, The Origins of the Fifth Amendment: The Right against Self-Incrimination (Oxford University Press, 1968).

66. Paul Roberts & Adrian Zuckerman, Criminal Evidence (OUP, 2nd edn. 2010).

67. Pierre Brillon, Dictionnaire Des Arrests; Ou, Jurisprudence Universelle Des Parlemens De France, Et Autres Tribunaux (Paris, 1727).

68. Pierre-Francois Muyart de Vouglans, Lettre de l' auteur des loix criminelles (1785).

69. 2 Pierre-Francois Muyart de Vouglans, Les loix criminelles de France, dans leur ordre naturel (Paris, 1781).

70. Plucknett, Common Law.

71. Principia Legis & Aequitatis, Being an Alphabetical Collection of Maxims, Principles or Rules, Definitions and Memorable Sayings in Law and Equity (London, 1753).

72. Richard Card, Card Cross and Jones Criminal Law (Butterworths, London, Dublin, Edinburgh, 12th ed. 1992).

73. Richard Helmholz, The Spirit of Classical Canon Law (Athens, Georgia-London: 1996).

74. Robert Nozick, Anarchy, State, and Utopia (1974).

75. Robertson A. J., The Laws of the Kings of England (Cambridge 1925).

76. Samuel P. Scott, The Civil Law, including the Twelve Tables, the Institutes of Gaius, the Rules of Ulpian, the Opinions of Paulus, the Enactments of Justinian, and the Constitutions of Leo: Translated from the Original Latin, Edited, and Compared with All Accessible Systems of Jurisprudence Ancient and Modern (Cincinnati, Vol. 13, 1932).

77. Shelly Kagan, Normative Ethics (1998).

78. Sir Edward Coke, The Second Part of the Institutes of the Laws of England (London, 1669).

79. Sir Samuel Romilly, Observations on the Criminal Law of England (T. Cadell and W. Davies, 1810).

80. Stenton F. M., Anglo-Saxon England (Oxford 1947).

81. 1 The Earliest English Law Reports (Paul A. Brand ed., Selden Society 1996).

82. The Mirror of Justices Edited for the Selden Society By William Joseph Whittaker (London, Bernard Quaritch 1895).

83. Theodore F. T. Plucknett, A Concise History of the Common Law (4th Ed. London 1948).

84. Vinogradoff, Roman Law.

85. W. Twining, Theories of Evidence: Bentham & Wigmore (London: Weidenfeld, 1985).

86. Weeramantry C. G., Islamic Jurisprudence: An International Perspective (Macmillan Press, 1988).

87. William Barlow, an Answer to a Catholike English-Man (London, 1609).

88. William Blackstone, IVCommentaries Book (1765).

89. William L. Burdick, The Principles of Roman Law and Their Relation to Modern Law (1938).

90. William of Ockham (1285-1349), Dialogus (Paris, 1476) (on file with the Northwestern University Library).

91. William S. Holdsworth, IIIHistory of English Law (1925).

92. Yann Riviere, Detention preventive, in Carcer: Prison et Privation de Libertg dans l'Antiquitg Classique (1999).

93. 2Year Books of the Reign of King Edward the First: Years XXI and XXII (Alfred J. Horwood ed., Longman & Co. 1873).

(二) 论文期刊

1. A. R. N. Cross, *The Right to Silence and the Presumption of Innocence-Sacred Cows or Safeguards of Liberty*?, 11 Society of Public Teachers of Law 66 (1970-1971).

2. Allen H. Godbey, *The Place of the Code of Hammurabi*, 15 the Monist 199 (1905).

3. Barton L. Ingraham, *The Right of Silence, the Presumption of Innocence, the Burden of Proof, and a Modest Proposal: A Reply to O'Reilly*, Journal of Criminal Law and Criminology, Vol. 86, Issue 2 Winter (1996), Article 10.

4. Charles V. Laughlin, *In Support of the Thayer Theory of Presumptions*, 52 Mich. L. Rev. (1953).

5. D. S. Kris, *Law Enforcement as a Counterterrorism Tool*, Journal of National Security Law and Policy, Vol. 5: 1, 2011.

6. Daniel Kahneman, Amos Tversky, *Prospect Theory: An Analysis of Decision under Risk*, Econometrica, Vol. 47, No. 2 (Mar., 1979).

7. Edna Ullman-Margalit, *On Presumption*, The Journal of Philosophy, Vol. 80, No. 3 (1983).

8. Fleta, 73 Eng. Hist. Rev. 672 (1958).

9. Francois Quintard-Morénas, *The Presumption of Innocence in the French and Anglo-American Legal Traditions*, 58Am. J. Comp. L. 107 (2010).

10. Gaines Post, *A Romano - Canonical Maxim*, "*Quod Omnes Tangit*," *in Bracton*, 4 Traditio 197 (1946).

11. Gregory W. O′reily, *England Limits the Right to Silence and Moves towards an Inquisitorial System of Justice*, 85 J. Crim. L. & Criminology 402 (1994-1995).

12. James Bradley Thayer, *The Presumption of Innocence in Criminal Cases*, 6 Yale L. J. 185 (1897).

13. Jeffrie G. Murphy, *Marxism and Retribution*, *Philosophy & Public Affairs*, Vol. 2, No. 3 (Spring, 1973).

14. John H. Langbein, *The Historical Origins of the Privilege against Self-Incrimination at Common Law*, Michigan Law Review, Vol. 92, No. 5 (Mar., 1994).

15. Joseph N. Sorrentino, *Demystifying the Presumption of Innocence*,

Glendale Law Review, 1996, Vol. 15.

16. Kahneman, D., Knetsch, J. L., & Thaler, R. H. (1991). *The endowment effect, loss aversion, and status quo bias*. Journal of Economic Perspectives.

17. Kenneth Pennington, *Innocent until Proven Guilty: The Origins of a Legal Maxim*, 63 Jurist 106 (2003).

18. M. Cherif Bassiouni, *Human Rights in the Context of Criminal Justice: Identifying International Procedural Protections and Equivalent Protections in National Constitutions*, 3 Duke Journal of Comparative and International Law 235 (1993).

19. Michael S. Moore, *Torture and the Balance of Evils*, 23 Israel LR 280 (1989).

20. Paul Roberts, *Double Jeopardy Law Reform: A Criminal Justice Commentary*, 65 Mod. L. Rev. 393 (2002).

21. R. A. Duff, *In Defence of One Type of Retributivism: A Reply to Bagaric and Amarasekara*, 24 Melbourne University LR 411 (2000).

22. Rao L-L, Zhou Y, Xu L, Liang Z-Y, Jiang T, et al. (2011) *Are Risky Choices Actually Guided by a Compensatory Process? New Insights from fMRI*. PLoS ONE 6 (3): e14756. doi: 10. 1371/journal. pone. 0014756.

23. Richard Helmholz, *The Bible in the Service of Canon Law*, 70 Chicago Kent Law Review 1557 (1995).

24. Robert S. Gerstein, *The Self-Incrimination Debate in Great Britain*, The American Journal of Comparative Law, Vol. 27, No. 1 (Winter, 1979).

25. Tom P. Conom, *Bulwarks of Liberty: Presumption of Innocence and Reasonable Doubt*, 45 Wash. St. B. News (1991).

26. Tom, S. M., Fox, C. R., Trepel, C., & Poldrack, R. A. (2007). *The neural basis of loss aversion in decision-making under risk*, Science.

27. Walter Ullmann, *The Defence of the Accused in the Medieval Inquisition*, 63 The Irish Ecclesiastical Rec. 481 (1950).

(三) 论文集

1. D. Clementi, *The Anglo - Saxon Origins of the Principle "Innocent until Proven Guilty"*, Herrschaftsvertrge, Wahlkapitulationen, Fundamentalgesetze (Gottingen: 1977).

2. Gaines Post, *Ancient Roman Ideas of Law*, in 2 Dictionary of the History of Ideas: Studies of Selected Pivotal Ideas (Philip P. Wiener ed., 1973).

3. Hock Lai Ho, *The Presumption of Innocence as a Human Right* in Paul Roberts and Jill Hunter (eds), Criminal Evidence and Human Rights - Reimagining Common Law Procedural Traditions (Oxford: Hart Publishing, 2012).

4. Howell, 7State Trials, 32 Charles II.

5. R. H. Helmolz, *The Privilege and the Ius Commune: The Middle Ages to the Seventeenth Century*, in R. H. Helmolz, C. M. Gray, J. J. Langbein, E. Moglen, H. E. Smith and A. W. Alschuler (eds.), The Privilege against Self-Incrimination: Its Origins and Development (University of Chicago Press, 1997).

6. Richard M. Fraher, *'Ut nullus describatur reus prius quam convincatur': Presumption of innocence in medieval Canon law?*, Proceedings of the Sixth International Congress of Medieval Canon Law, Berkeley, California, 28 July-2 August 1980 (1985).

(四) 学位论文

1. Jerome E. Janssen, *The Legal Procedure of the 13th Century French Inquisition*, Ph. D. dissertation, University of Wisconsin (1954).

2. Randy Martin Johannessen, *Cardinal Jean Lemoine: Curial Politics and Papal Power*, Ph. D. dissertation, University of California, Los Angeles (1990).

（五）网址及其他

1. ［1935］AC 462，481-2，HL. Available at http://www.bailii.org/uk/cases/UKHL/1935/1.html.

2. Article 1，Section 9，Clause 3 - Alexander Hamilton，A Second Letter from Phocion，http://press-pubs.uchicago.edu/founders/print_documents/a1_9_3s6.html.

3. CAL. PENAL CODE § 1096，http://www.leginfo.ca.gov/cgi-bin/displaycode? section=pen&group=01001-02000&file=1093-1130.

4. Code Just. available at http://www.constitution.org/sps/sps12.htm.

5. "Code of Hammurabi"，available at http：//en. wikipedia.org/wiki/Code_ of_ Hammurabi.

6. Corpus Juris Canonici-Wikipedia，http：//en. wikipedia. org/wiki/corpus Juris Canonici，last visited on March 2. 2019.

7. Dick Cavett，An Innocent Misunderstanding，N.Y. TIMES，Mar. 28，2007，available at http://cavett.blogs.nytimes.com/2007/03/28/an-innocent-misunderstanding.

8. DIG. Available at http://www.constitution.org/sps/sps05.htm.

9. 3 Edw. I，c. 15（1275）（Eng.），available at http://en.wikisource.org/wiki/Prisoners_and_Bail_Act.

10. Evan Andrews，"8 Things You May Not Know About Hammurabi's Code"，December 17，2013，available at http://www.history.com/news/history-lists/8-things-you-may-not-know-about-hammurabis-code.

11. George Herbert，http://en.wikipedia.org/wiki/George_Herbert.

12. "Infer verb - Definition，pictures，pronunciation and usage notes | Oxford Advanced Learner's Diction"，available at http://www.oxfordlearnersdictionaries.com/definition/english/infer? q=infer.

13. "Inference noun-Definition，pictures，pronunciation and usage notes | Oxford Advanced Learner's Dic"，available at http://www.oxfordlear nersdictionaries. com/definition/english/inference? q = infer-

ence.

14. "Indirectly adverb - Definition, pictures, pronunciation and usage notes | Oxford Advanced Learner's", available at http: //www. oxfordlearnersdictionaries. com/definition/english/indirectly? q=indirectly.

15. Karl Marx, "Capital Punishment", New York Daily Tribune (18 February 1853), available at http://www. marxists. org/archive/marx/works/1853/02/18.htm.

16. Kenneth Pennington: Due Process, Community, and the Prince in the Evolution of the Ordo iudiciarius, http://faculty. cua. edu/pennington/Law508/procedure.htm#Establishment%20of%20Ordo.

17. Mohammed Abdellaoui, Han Bleichrodt, Corina Paraschiv, (2007) Loss Aversion Under Prospect Theory: A Parameter-Free Measurement. Management Science 53 (10): 1659-1674, 1659. http://dx.doi.org/10.1287/mnsc.1070.0711.

18. "The Code of Hammurabi", available at http://www.sacred-texts.com/ane/ham/ham05.htm.

19. The Presumption of Innocence Belongs Only in the Courtroom. Discuss, available at http://blogs. wsj. com/law/2009/02/27/the-presumption-of-innocence-belongs-only-in-the-courtroom-discuss.

20. Turner, Ralph (2003b). Magna Carta: Through the Ages. Routledge. ISBN 978-0582438262. P123. Cited at http: //en. wikipedia. org/wiki/Magna_ Carta.

21. Http://dy.163.com/v2/article/T1397720048954/BTG4AE580521007N.

22. Http://www.court.gov.cn/zixun-xiangqing-36422.html.

23. Http://www. nytimes. com/2011/03/25/us/25miranda - text. html? _r=0.

24. Http://news. xinhuanet. com/politics/2005 - 11/08/content _3750946.htm.

25. Http://mp.weixin.qq.com/s? __biz = MzA3OTkzNDMxMA = = &mid=205173431&idx=1&sn=b3eb0809daa70970b09b8c7d256e5ea2&scene=2&from=timeline&isappinstalled=0#rd.

26. Allenet de Ribemont v. France, 308 Eur. Ct. H. R. (ser. A) (1995).

27. Arret de la Cour de Parlement qui ordonne un plus amplement informe pendant trois mois, contre Jean Magre, Claude Marechal et Marie Louise Thibault pendant lequel temps, lesdits Magre et Marechal tiendront prison et ladite Thibault mise en liberte (Paris, 1722).

28. Bell v. Wolfish, 441 U. S. 520 (1979).

29. Black's Law Dictionary (8th ed. 2004).

30. Bracton.

31. Coffin v. United States, 156 U. S. 432.

32. Comte de Mirabeau, Des Lettres de cachet et des prisons d´Etat. Ouvrage posthume, compose en 1778, at 344 (Hambourg, 1782).

33. constitutionum regni siciliarum libri iii (Naples, Vol. 1, 1773) (1231).

34. Cool v. United States, 409 U. S. 100 (1972).

35. criminal procedure code of the french republic.

36. Dan Abrams, Presumed Innocent? Bernie Madoff?, WALL ST. J., Feb. 27, 2009.

37. declaration du roi, relative a l´ordonnance criminelle 5 (Versailles, 1788).

38. declaration des droits de l´homme et du citoyen.

39. Du Roy and Malaurie v. France, 2000-X Eur. Ct. H. R. 34.

40. Flores v. State, 1995 OK CR 9 [Okla. Crim. App., 1995].

41. 2 Oeuvres de M. Duplessis 17-18 (Paris, 1728).

42. 5 Recueil general des anciennes lois francaises depuis l' an 420 jusqu´a la revolution de 1789 par MM. Jourdan, Decrusy, Isambert

(Paris, 1822).

43. Arrest de la Cour de Parlement, Portant Reglement pour l' execution des Decrets de Prise de corps (Metz, 1697).

44. 156 U. S. 432, 455.

45. 25 Edw. I, c. 29 (1297) (1215).

46. Innocence and Guilt, WALL ST. J. EUR., May 26, 2000.

47. In re Winship, 397 US 358, 364 (1970).

48. 4 Jac. I (1606) (Eng.).

49. Missouri v. Seibert, 542 U. S. 600 (2004).

50. New York v. Quarles, 467 U. S. 649 (1984).

51. Oeuvres de M. Le Chancelier d'Aguesseau contenant les plaidoyers prononces au Parlement en qualite d'Avocat General, depuis le mois d'avril 1696, & dans les annees 1697, 1698 & 1699 (Paris, 1764).

52. Oregon Constitution of 2000.

53. Proces verbal des conferences tenues par ordre du Roi, pour l'examen des articles de l'ordonnance civile du mois d'avril, 1667 et de l'ordonnance criminelle, du mois d'aout, 1670 (Paris, 1709).

54. People v. Molineux, 168 N. Y. 264, 291 (1901).

55. R v Derek William Bentley (Deceased) (2001) 1 Cr App R 307, CA.

56. R. v. Oakes (1986), 24 C. C. C. (3d) 321 (S. C. C.).

57. Records of Massachusetts, iii.

58. Rerum Gestarum.

59. 1 Rich. III (1483) (Eng.).

60. Rhode Island Constitution of 1842.

61. Sir John Scott on Criminal Procedure, TIMES (London), May 25, 1900.

62. The Criminal Ordinance of 1670.

63. The Director of Public Prosecutions v. Broderick [2006] I. E.

S. C. 34 (Ir.).

64. The Public Laws of the State of Rhode-Island and Providence Plantations, As Revised by a Committee, and Finally Enacted By the Honourable General Assembly, at Their Session in January, 1798, at 79-81 (Providence, 1798).

65. Webster's New World Dictionary of the American Language (2nd College Edition; 1978).